Criminal Justice in America

Criminal Justice in America

Advisory Editor
ROBERT M. FOGELSON

CRIMINAL

COURTS

IN

NEW YORK

STATE

ARNO PRESS
A New York Times Company
New York • 1974

Reprint Edition 1974 by Arno Press Inc.

Reprinted from copies in The State
   Historical Society of Wisconsin Library

Criminal Justice in America
ISBN for complete set: 0-405-06135-8
See last pages of this volume for titles.

Publisher's Note: This volume includes
selections from Documents of the Senate
of the State of New York, 132nd Session, 1909,
Proceedings of the Commission to Inquire into
the Courts of Inferior Criminal Jurisdiction
in Cities of the First Class, Selections from
Volumes 3, 4 and 5, 1909 and Documents of the
Assembly of the State of New York, 133rd Session,
1910, Final Report of the Commission to Inquire
into Courts of Inferior Criminal Jurisdiction
in Cities of the First Class.

Manufactured in the United States of America

Library of Congress Cataloging in Publication Data

New York (State). Commission to Inquire Into Courts
     of Inferior Criminal Jurisdiction in Cities of the
     First Class.
        Criminal courts in New York State.
        (Criminal justice in America)
        Reprint of selections from vols. 3-5 of the Proceed-
   ings of the Commission to Inquire Into Courts of Inferior
   Criminal Jurisdiction in Cities of the First Class, issued in 1909 as no. 30 of Documents of the Senate of
   the State of New York; and of Final report of the commission, which was issued in 1910 as no. 54 of Documents of
   the Assembly of the State of New York.
        1. Municipal courts--New York (State) 2. Criminal
   justice, Administration of--New York (State)
   I. New York (State). Commission to Inquire Into Courts
   of Inferior Criminal Jurisdiction in Cities of the First
   Class. Final report. 1974. II. Title. III. Series.
   IV. Series: New York (State). Legislature. Senate.
   Documents of the Senate of the State of New York, 30.
   V. Series: New York (State). Legislature. Assembly.
   Documents of the Assembly of the State of New York, 54.
   KFN5970.A83   345'.747'01   74-3841
   ISBN 0-405-06141-2

Proceedings

of the

Commission to Inquire Into the Courts of

Inferior Criminal Jurisdiction in

Cities of the First Class

Volumes III and IV

BUFFALO, N. Y., Thursday, Feb. 4, 1909,
10 A. M.

The Commission met pursuant to adjournment.

CHAIRMAN PAGE:

It might be well to state for the information of the citizens of Buffalo that this Commission is appointed pursuant to Chapter 211 of the Laws of 1908, which requires the Commission to make careful inquiry into the manner in which justice is administered in courts of inferior criminal jurisdiction in cities of the first class and their methods of procedure, systems of records, the conduct and duties of clerks, attendants and other employees, the arrangement and condition of court houses, and all other matters connected with the administration of justice in said courts, and, so far as in the discretion of the Commission may seem necessary, the methods employed in other cities.

The Commission has already investigated somewhat the conditions in the greater city, in Manhattan and Brooklyn, and has arranged for Judge Olson, of Chicago, to appear before the Commission here. He will be with us to-morrow morning.

The scope of the Commission is very broad as far as relates to the courts of lower jurisdiction—criminal courts —and co-ordinate subjects, such as probation and the proper handling of juvenile criminals.

Mr. Mayer, are you ready to proceed?

MR. MAYER: Yes. If the Commission please, for the information of the Commission, I offer in evidence Title 17 of the Revised City Charter, and running from Section 382 to Section 390, inclusive; and as this is not very long and as doubtless most of the Commission are not familiar with the system prevailing in the City of Buffalo, I will read the Title referred to:

TITLE SEVENTEEN.

POLICE JUSTICE AND JUSTICES.

Par. 382. There shall be elected a Police Justice who shall hold his office for the term of four years and who shall have and execute in the city all powers conferred by law upon justices of the peace of towns in proceedings in criminal cases and in the execution of the laws relating to the internal police of this State, and shall also have jurisdiction of the offenses designated by Chapter 409 of the Laws of 1886. He shall take the usual oath of office and file the same with the clerk of the County of Erie. He shall hold in the city a court and shall have, in respect to offenses committed in the city, all the powers and jurisdiction conferred by law upon Courts of Special Sessions held out of the City and County of New York. It shall also have jurisdiction of the misdemeanors mentioned in this act.

All fines imposed by the Police Justice or by the Police Court shall be paid by the officer who shall receive them into the city treasury. The Police Justice shall make a monthly report to the Common Council of his doings and of the fines received by him. Warrants issued in criminal cases and in the execution of the laws relating to the internal police of this State shall be returnable before the Police Justice, who shall proceed with the hearing. No person issuing such warrants shall receive any fee therefor. During the sickness, temporary absence or other inability of the Police Justice to discharge his duties, the Mayor may perform his duties or may appoint an elector of the city to perform them. Said Police Justice may be removed from office by the Supreme Court at a general term as precribed by the Code of Criminal Procedure.

Par. 383. The Police Justice shall be paid in monthly payments an annual salary to be fixed by ordinance by the Common Council and shall not receive any other fees or compensation for services as Police Justice.

Par. 384. The Police Justice shall appoint a clerk and a deposition clerk, which appointments shall be in writing and filed with the clerk of the County of Erie. The clerk appointed under this act shall take the usual oath of office and file same with the County Clerk, and shall hold office during the pleasure of the Police Justice. The clerk shall keep a complete and accurate record of all the proceedings in said court and of all moneys received, or fines imposed. He shall daily file with the Clerk of the County of Erie all convictions in said court, which records shall specifically state the crime and pleas of each person convicted in said court. He shall prepare the monthly report to the Common Council prescribed in Section 382 of this act and shall perform such other clerical duties in connection with the proceedings of said court as shall be prescribed by the Police Justice.

Par. 384a. The Police Justice shall appoint a stenographer, which appointment shall be in writing, and filed with the Clerk of Erie County. The stenographer appointed under this act shall take the usual oath of office and file the same with the County Clerk, and shall be the official stenographer of the Police Court during the pleasure of the Police Justice. He shall also act as private clerk to the Police Justice. In an examination held in any criminal proceedings by the Police Justice the testimony of each witness may, in discretion of the said Police Justice, be taken as a deposition by the official stenographer of his court. Such minutes of the testimony when so taken and when certified by the stenographer and Police Justice shall both with reference to such examination and all procedure in connection with such examination provided for by any section of the Code of Criminal Procedure not inconsistent herewith, be regarded as actually taken down in writing by such Magistrate and subscribed by the witness or witnesses at such examination. The salary of such stenographer shall be fixed by the Common Council and shall not exceed twelve hundred dollars per year.

Par. 384b. PROBATION OFFICERS.—The Police Justice shall have authority to appoint or designate not more than ten discreet persons of good character to serve as probation officers to receive no compensation from the public treasury. Whenever any child under or apparently under the age of sixteen years shall have been arrested, it shall be the duty of the said probation officers to make such investigations as may be required by the court, to be present in court in order to represent the interests of the child; when the case is heard, to furnish to the Police Justice such information and assistance as he may require and to take charge of any child before and after trial as may be directed by court.

Par. 384c. Whenever any such child is found guilty or pleads guilty to the commission of any crime or misdemeanor before the Police Justice, the said Police Justice may in his discretion suspend sentence during the good behavior of the child so convicted. The child so convicted may be placed in charge of the probation officer for such time not to exceed three months and upon such conditions as may seem proper. Such time may be extended one or more additional terms not exceeding three months each by the Police Justice in his discretion. Said probation officers shall have the power to bring the child so convicted before the Police Justice at any time during the probation for such disposition as may be just. When practicable, said child shall be placed with a probation officer of the same religious faith as that of the child's parents.

Par. 384d. The Police Justice shall appoint an interpreter of the Italian and Polish languages, which appointment shall be in writing and filed with the Clerk of the County of Erie. The interpreter under this act shall take the usual oath of office and file the same with the County Clerk. He shall be the official interpreter for the said Italian and Polish languages in proceedings before said Police Court and Justice during the pleasure of the Police Justice, and shall perform such other duties as shall be prescribed by said Police Justice. The salary of such interpreter shall be fixed by the Common Council of the City of Buffalo.

Par. 385. There shall be three Justices of the Peace elected by the electors of the City of Buffalo on the general city ticket as hereinafter provided. The terms of office of each shall be four years, commencing on the first day of January next succeeding the election of each. The present Justices of the Peace in said city, together with the Justice of the Peace elected in and for the Twenty-fifth ward shall be the three Justices herein provided for, and shall constitute a board of Justices to the Police. This board shall on or before the first day of the month next following the passage of this act, and thereafter on the first day of each year, or oftener, if necessary, apportion the station houses of the city into three districts. As nearly as practicable such division shall be made in such manner that the amount of business shall be transacted in the several districts shall be equal. Said Board shall assign from its members a Justice of Police to each one of said districts for the remainder of said month, and for each month thereafter, whose duty it shall be to attend the Police Station Houses in their respective districts at the hour prescribed by the Police Department and examine into the case of every person confined therein and make delivery. Such assignments shall be so arranged that each Justice shall attend a different district, and an equal number of times at each of the districts during the year. A Justice of the Peace shall be elected hereafter on the general city ticket at the municipal election preceding the first Monday in January in each year, when the term of any Justice of the Peace herein provided for shall expire. Said Justices shall have power to try cases of drunkenness, vagrancy, and all other offenses against any of the laws of the States or the ordinances of the City of Buffalo, which may be tried summarily and without a jury by a Justice of the Peace or a Court of Special Sessions, committed by any person confined in the Station House, and to sentence every person found guilty of any such offense pursuant to the statute or ordinance creating such offense. In all other cases such Justices shall have and possess such powers and jurisdiction as are prescribed in this act. Each of said Justices shall execute a bond to the City of Buffalo with sufficient securities to be approved by the Mayor for the faithful performance of his duty, and for the accounting for and paying over all fines and penalties received by him as such Justice, in such sums as the Common Council shall require. All suits or actions brought on said bonds shall be in the name of the City of Buffalo. The salaries of the said Justices and of the Justice elected in and for the Twenty-fifth ward shall be fixed by the Common Council in joint session of the boards thereof immediatley after the passage of this act and the same shall be uniform; such salaries shall be not less than fifteen hundred dollars nor exceed the sum of two thousand dollars per annum, to be paid from the police fund as other salaries are now paid therefrom.

Said Justices may be removed or suspended from office for misconduct in office or neglect of duty, by the Supreme Court at any special term thereof held in Erie County. The grounds for such suspension or removal shall be stated in the order therefor, and no removal shall be made without reasonable notice to the Justice complained of and an opportunity given him to be heard in his defense as prescribed by the Code of Criminal Procedure. In case of the sickness, absence or inability of any Justice of the Peace another Justice of the Peace may perform his duties during such sickness, absence or inability, or the Mayor may temporarily appoint any elector of said city for that purpose, and the Justice of the Peace so temporarily appointed shall have all the powers and perform all the duties of Justices. All fines and penalties imposed by any or either of said Justices, collected by them or the keeper of the Erie County Penitentiary shall be paid over every week by the person receiving the same to the treasurer of the City of Buffalo, and be by said treasurer credited to the police fund of said city and for the use and benefit thereof.

The Police Board shall designate a suitable room at every station house, in which said Justices of the Police shall hold court. While court is in session said room shall be deemed a court room for all purposes thereof. Such rooms shall be properly furnished, ventilated and heated. The Police Board shall provide said court room with all necessary legal blanks, stationery and writing material as required by said Justices. The Police Commissioners shall detail a competent member of the police force on duty at such station houses, whose duty it shall be to act as clerk of the court when a session thereof is being held, and keep such record of the proceedings as shall be required by said Justices. All the provisions of this section shall be made applicable to the Justices of the Police and Justices of the Peace in office at the time of the passage of this act.

Par. 386. If any person confined in a station house is charged with criminal offense, the Justice shall enter the charges in a book kept for that purpose, and send such prisoner to the Police Justice for examination.

Par. 386a. The Justices to the Police shall have jurisdiction, the first instance, to hear and determine charges of intoxication in a public place, in violation of Section 40, Chapter 112 of the laws of 1896 and the laws amendatory thereof, and to sentence every person found guilty of this misdemeanor pursuant to the liquor tax law of this State.

Par. 387. If any person therein is charged with a violation of any ordinance of the city, the Justice shall enter the charge in his book, and read it to the person charged, and enter in his book the plea of such person thereto. If such person denies the charge, the Justice, if he deems it expedient, or if the person charged requires it, shall:

1. If the violation charged is punishable by fine only, issue a warrant at the suit of the city against such person, returnable before the Municipal Court of Buffalo.

2. If the violation charged is punishable by imprisonment, issue his warrtnt and cause such person to be taken before the Police Justice. The Justice shall cause notice to be given to the Corporation Counsel.

Par. 388. If the Justice shall not issue a warrant as above provided, he shall proceed summarily to hear, try, and determine the charge, and if he shall find such person to be guilty, he shall sentence him pursuant to ordinance.

Par. 389. If the Justice shall sentence such a person to pay a fine, and if it is not paid immediately, he shall, by warrant, commit such person to the penitentiary, there to be confined for the term of one day for each and every dollar of such fine, not exceeding six months, unless it shall be sooner paid. If the Justice shall sentence such person to imprisonment, he shall, by a warrant, commit such person accordingly.

Par. 390. When the Justice shall commit any person, he shall, on the same day, make and file with the Clerk of Erie County a record of the conviction, in which it shall be sufficient to state the charge so specifically as to show a violation of the ordinance, the plea of the person charged, the fact of conviction, and the judgment.

MR. MAYER: Now, if the Commission please, Judge Nash, the Police Justice, has been on a vacation for some time, and for that reason is not here. We shall communicate with him on his return, if the Commission deems it desirable for him to appear before it in New York.

———

THOMAS H. NOONAN, called as a witness, having been first duly sworn, testified as follows:

BY MR. MAYER:

Q. You are a member of the bar? A. I am, fourteen years and over.

Q. Yes? Now, have you acted, in the absence of the Justice, as a Police Justice? A. I have, on one occasion for a week when Mr. Knight was away, some—oh, I suppose four years ago, four or five, and then during the year 1907, through the courtesy of Judge Murphy, I acted in all about a month. I served on at least four and perhaps five different occasions.

Q. Yes; well, Judge Murphy was the predecessor of the present Police Justice? A. He was.

Q. Now, having thus acted, I assume you have had some actual experience in the work of the Police Court in this city? A. I have, yes.

Q. As I understand, the Police Justice acts as an examining magistrate? A. He does, and virtually as Coroner also.

Q. Virtually as Cononer, and as a committing magistrate? A. Yes, sir.

Q. And also as a Court of Special Sessions? A. Yes.

Q. In a word, in his capacity as Court of Special Sessions, he tries misdemeanors? A. Yes, so—I so understand.

Q. And he has the authority to make a finding of guilt or acquittal? A. Yes.

BY CHAIRMAN PAGE:

Q. For what term can he imprison? A. As I understand —I don't want to be taken as accurate on those matters, some of them, because I only served over there intermittently and have not made a complete study. But, I take it, the usual misdemeanor period of six months.

BY MR. MAYER:

Q. Before I ask you any specific questions, as the result of your experience, did any suggestions occur to you in re-

spect of any improvement of method or procedure? A.
Yes, a good many.

Q. Now, will you state them to the Commission? A.
Why, my idea on the question of courts and limited jurisdiction here in Buffalo is this, that we would get the best
results, in the long run, by having a city court of general—
limited civil and criminal jurisdiction. I think that all the
limited courts, of limited jurisdiction, in the city at the
present time, that includes the Municipal Court for the trial
of civil cases, the Police Court for the trial of the majority
of criminal matters, and the matters in which the counsel
is referred—or the disposition of them and the so-called
morning courts, should be combined into one court and
called perhaps the City Court of Buffalo, with, as I said,
this civil and criminal jurisdiction. Then I think the Police
Court ought to be divided into two parts. I think there
ought to be one Police Court out on the East Side with a
magistrate sitting there all the time; the location to be
determined by the geographical conditions, and perhaps in
the vicinity of William and Fillmore Streets, is in the most
central place.

Q. Let me interrupt you to ask: On the East Side of
Buffalo, as you call it, there is a large population of foreign
birth, is there not? A. Yes, very large. A great many
of the Polish nation, practically all the Polish people live
on the so-called East Side and generally in the one locality,
out in the vicinity of Fillmore Avenue, Lovejoy Street and
Broadway, out in there, and on Sycamore Street. There
is a——

Q. Now, for the information of the Commission, will you state about how far a person residing on the East Side of Buffalo must go, to where the Police Court is now situated? A. Well, anywhere from—up to five and a half to six miles, and as I understand it, that is, if a man is in the extreme northeasterly part of the city, it is something like five or five and a half miles, by the nearest street car line, to the City Hall here.

Q. Yes, continue Judge? A. And then, as I say, I think this court should be situated out there, with a clerk, a stenographer and with such an official force as is necessary to dispose of the business. At that court there should be an interpreter who is familiar, if possible, with the German and Polish languages, because they are the two foreign languages that are talked out there, and that it is necessary for the magistrate to have interpreted in order to properly dispose of his business. There are scattering colonies of Poles in other sections of the city, but not enough to make any great difference. The people out there, I think, would be greatly benefited by a magistrate who would sort of be a "Little Father" to the community; a man who would give them friendly advice and to whom they could go in their trouble. A lot of the things, in my judgment, in my observation, that came before the court were petty things that could have been obviated by a little wise counsel given to these people in advance, showing them the uselessness of a lot of things that they bring into the Police Court.

Q. That is, troubles between neighbors and in the family and the like? A. Yes, sir.

Q. Your idea is that it would be a matter of much value if these people could get an idea of what courts deal with? A. Yes, I do.

Q. And should be advised before getting to the point of issuance of a warrant and subsequent arrest? A. Yes, and that a sympathetic Judge and likewise a level-headed, sympathetic clerk of the court could do a great deal to make things run smoothly in a locality where the rights of the people as related to their personal liberty are somewhat hazy oftentimes. Then, I think a similar court should be maintained in this general section where the court has always been maintained.

Q. By that you mean the business section of Buffalo? A. Yes, the business section proper, and to that should be brought practically all the cases west of a dividing line, perhaps not Main Street, Michigan street perhaps would be a more natural dividing line. In that court there should be an Italian interpreter, and such a clerical force as is necessary to keep the records complete.

Q. Now, in the Police Court in the business section there come not infrequently cases of great importance? A. Yes, a great many of them.

Q. Am I correct in saying that that court has to do with cases involving alleged crimes in regard to large institutions, financial institutions and the like? A. Yes, it has everything that comes before a committing magistrate, everything that comes before the Police Court of Buffalo in the first instance, unless it comes before the grand jury.

Q. And not infrequently cases where capital crime is

charged? A. All the cases where capital crime is charged, where there is a preliminary investigation, where there is a hearing before a magistrate, and also, as I said before, the old Coroner's system has been done away with here, and we have in lieu thereof a county medical examiner and a deputy, and if they deem the case—or if there is anything suspicious about it, and they deem that a regular inquest should be held, such as the Coroners were supposed to hold in days gone by, that comes before the magistrate, and cases where capital crimes are involved. For instance, when I was sitting down there, the man who murdered Forrestel was brought before me and a hearing was held, and we held the man for the grand jury. Now, one of my reasons for—one of my reasons for advocating a court of the kind I have mentioned: I have found that it was very exacting, the business of the court, that a man naturally felt tired sitting there, and had an inclination to be peevish no matter how much he tried to get along smoothly, and I know that Judge Nash feels the same way on that proposition. He has told me personally that it was the hardest thing that he had to contend with, to sit in that court day after day and keep on—in other words, it gets on a man's nerves, the disposition of that business. Now, my idea is that if this court was constituted as I have stated, there should be a rotation of judges, that a man would—if there were six judges he would hold criminal term four months in the year, two months in the West Side Court, two months on the East Side Court, and the other, say seven months, he would be in the Municipal Court, and the other month he would have for a vacation.

Q. Do you regard one month as sufficient vacation in this jurisdiction? A. Well, we could get along with it—I don't know—I suppose we would be happier if we had more. A man at least needs that. Now, under the system as it is administered here, a Police Court Justice is allowed two weeks' vacation with pay, and if he is away longer than that, the man who serves as acting Police Judge has to do it as a friendly matter, or the Justice has to pay him out of his own pocket. Two weeks is not long enough, and, further, a man acting as Police Justice of the City of Buffalo, if he does his full duty, is on call fifty weeks in the year, twenty-four hours a day, and seven days in the week, because he has to hold court six days, taking him up until, I take it—I don't know—two o'clock, and then two or three days in the week there is the Juvenile Court, two afternoons in a week, and then he is likely to be called up at all times of the night to admit people to bail.

Q. I will ask you there, when a Police Justice is away and another person is designated to act, such as you have been, has the substitute power to take bail? A. Yes, so I understand it, that he possesses all the powers of the regular magistrate—that is my understanding.

BY CHAIRMAN PAGE:

Q. How many Municipal Courts are there in Buffalo? A. There is just one Municipal Court, with two Judges, at the present time, and there has been a provision made for the election of a third Municipal Court Judge at the next election, at which time there is a vacancy also, so that there will be two elected next fall. Mr. Weimert, I believe, has taken steps to amend the law so that one of these Judges would be elected for four years and the other for six years, so if the court is continued with three Judges, there will be one Judge elected every three years.

BY MR. MAYER:

Q. You refer to Member of the Assembly, Mr. Weimert? A. Yes.

Q. Are there any suggestions that have come to you as a result of your experience in this court that you would like to make to the Commission? A. Yes, I think—as I understand it now, if a warrant is issued by the Police Court of Buffalo and sent outside of the city, it has to be endorsed in the locality where it is served, just the same as a Justice of the Peace's warrant has to be endorsed. Now, I understand that the Police Court in Rochester, for instance, if a warrant in that city is issued, it is good all over the State without endorsement, the same as a bench warrant of the Supreme Court. I think that could be well applied to the court here. Then, I think it might be well to give the Judge here power to dispose of certain felonies. There are any quantity of cases that come before a magistrate here that are technically felonies, and, as I understand the law, a sitting magistrate has no power to dispose of them other than to hold the man for the grand jury.

Q. That is correct. A. Now, a lot of these—I think I can safely say, a majority of these cases are not of crimes involving large amounts, they are simply technically felonies.

Q. Like what, for instance? A. The criminal receiving

of stolen property, for instance, where the amount is five or ten dollars, and where a prison sentence, or sentence to the Penitentiary for five or six months, would be sufficient punishment. Now, if the magistrate had power to dispose of these cases—I don't mean the absolute power—but the power to dispose of them unless the man elected to go before the grand jury, why it would relieve the work of the higher criminal courts to a large extent. I don't know to what extent, because I do not think it would be possible to determine that without careful statistics.

Q. Don't you think it is dangerous to give a single Judge —not now referring to any Judge, but as a matter of principle—any power greater than to deal with misdemeanors? A. I would not think it unwise if the man has the right to elect to be held by the grand jury rather than be tried before this magistrate.

Q. Now, of course, a Police Justice, who is really in one capacity a Court of Special Sessions, can adjudicate the guilt and sentence in petit larceny cases, can he not? A. Oh, yes, all misdemeanors. I understand that the court has jurisdiction to dispose of them by trial or by dismissal as the facts warrant.

Q. What you are talking about, as I understand, is that where the amount involved might be no greater than in a petit larceny, but the character of the crime is technically a felony and not a misdemeanor, you would extend the jurisdiction of the court, if there were power so to do, giving the defendant, however, the right to elect whether he desired to be tried before the Police Justice or to submit himslf to a trial under indictment? A. Yes, I think that is a phase of the proposition that might well be given serious consideration—I think it would work out all right.

BY CHAIRMAN PAGE:

Q. You would not suggest, would you, making the receiving of stolen goods under $25.00 a misdemeanor? A. No, I don't know that the thing is practicable, it might be that you are running up against some provision that I am not familiar with, about the power of a magistrate to sentence for a felony. There may be some general law, or there may be some constitutional provision—no, I would keep the definition of the crime just the same, but give the magistrate the power to dispose of these cases if feasible.

Q. The Constitution provides that the Legislature may give the Court of Special Sessions such jurisdiction over misdemeanors, but it does not give them any power—— A. If it runs up against that proposition, I take it that there is nothing that can be done. I suggested that as a means of relieving the county of a lot of grand jury investigations of small offenses that could be disposed of more advantageously by a magistrate if it is possible to give him that power constitutionally.

BY MR. MAYER:

Q. In the absence of that power, could not the situation always be met by a thorough examination of the charge of felony, so that the District Attorney could determine, even if the magistrate may have held, whether there is a crime? A. Well, I suppose the District Attorney can determine whether or not on a thorough examination he ought to present the case to the grand jury, and if he cannot hold, he can let the man go.

Q. Your idea is to relieve the higher courts, if power existed, of the time taken in trying this character of cases? A. Yes, and the grand jury of the time, and the county of the expense, of making an investigation of a lot of these matters that I say are trivial. Sometimes we get around the matter by reducing the charge to petit larceny and disposing of them in that way.

Q. Have you any further suggestions? A. Why, I think —now, what I say here and what I am to say and what I have said, is entirely impersonal. I think that the theory of the morning court has gone—is not good any longer. It was originally established here in order that the people that had committed some trivial offense, such as trying to carry home a bigger load than they could stagger under, or who had violated some ordinance, might have a trial early in the morning and get away to work. The courts used to be held in time for the people to do that, that is, about 5 o'clock in the morning. At one time the magistrates were a very unsatisfactory lot here—that does not prevail any more. We have three very reputable, and I guess, as far as I know, competent men who are so-called Morning Court Justices, but I think the theory of the court is wrong. There is no provision made for the perpetuation of the testimony—as I understand it there is no stenographer present, and the court officer who acts, not being a shorthand report, cannot make——

BY COMMISSIONER MURPHY:

Q. What time do they hold that court in the morning?
A. Eight o'clock, as I understand it.

BY MR. MAYER:

Q. The court officer you refer to is a police sergeant?
A. A desk sergeant, as I understand it. I think if we had
two Criminal Courts, two parts of the Criminal Court, the
two Judges could do the criminal work, and, as I said before, they could get relief from this exacting grind that the
present Police Justice is up against at the present time.

Q. Do you think that under any modern administration
of justice in these cases a police station is a proper place
to hold court? A. I should imagine not. I think it affects
the impressions of the people—many of whom are somewhat ignorant and have loose ideas as to the administration of justice, I think it makes a good deal of difference if
we have a properly appointed court room, and conduct the
court with such solemnity as is possible, with as much
dignity as is possible consistent with getting this work
through. Of course, you all appreciate that we have to
move somewhat rapidly or we would never get through.

Q. Do you regard the impression of the courts created
upon the persons coming to them as a very important matter for the welfare of the community? A. Yes, I do.

Q. Is it a fact that great numbers of these persons are so
situated in life that they do not get into other courts, and
get their impressions solely from these courts? A. Yes, I
suppose a large majority of the people.

Q. What time does the Police Court open? A. I think Judge Nash is there at 9:30 for the issuing of warrants.

Q. So that these three Morning Courts simply, in practical operation, fill in from eight to nine or 9:30 o'clock, as the case may be? A. Yes, and they dispose of these little ordinance violations and vagrancy cases, and intoxication cases, unless the man asks for a trial in the Municipal Court, and then the law gives him the right to that.

Q. Right on that point, have you any experience in that regard, as to the rather anomalous system of dividing up the criminal jurisdiction whereby some of these cases are tried in the Municipal Court? A. No, I suppose the idea was to give a man who feels that he has run up against a Judge who has some prejudice against him, to get his case into another court; but I don't think that the right is exercised very often, and at the present time I don't think it could be exercised with any reason, because I don't believe that the present Morning Justices are the kind of fellows that would let their personal feelings have anything to do with their administration of the cases before them.

Q. Have you now stated to the Commission all the suggestions that you had in mind? A. I think I have, Mr. Mayer, particularly those in regard to the Police Court. I am inclined to think that if one court was established here that the civil jurisdiction should be limited to $500.00. I don't know whether you want me to go into that or not.

BY CHAIRMAN PAGE:

Q. What is it now? A. It is $1,000. It used to be $500,

and a lot of us thought it would expedite matters if it was increased to $1,000. I, for one, was in favor of that proposition, but I notice that with the increase of jurisdiction it has simply swamped that court, and I take it the first purpose of a court of limited jurisdiction of the character of our Municipal Court, taking the place of a Justice's Court, is to provide a place where litigation can be disposed of in small matters speedily. At the present time there are enough cases on the "ready calendar" over there to keep the court going, I guess, for two months.

BY COMMISSIONER MURPHY:

Q. Have you a County Court here? A. Yes, sir, the County Court has jurisdiction in civil matters up to $2,000, and in foreclosure and partition matters it has concurrent jurisdiction with the Supreme Court. I think there ought to be another County Court established here, where these small matters, from $500 up to $2,000, could be disposed of, and a lot of the criminal matters disposed of also.

Q. Is the calendar of the County Court pretty well congested? A. Not unusually so at the present time, but if there were another Judge there, one of them could devote his time to the disposition of these felonies other than capital cases, and leave the Supreme Court Judge free to deal with civil cases. The Supreme Court calendar is the one that is congested here. The County Court in its disposition of cases has always been a very satisfactory court. I think on that account its calendar is tending to be filled up and there is a tendency towards crowding that calendar that could be obviated by another Judge. The County

Judge at the present time has to hold all his civil terms and two or three criminal terms and practically a special term, because nine-tenths of the foreclosure and partition cases are brought in the County Court here as a matter of practice. That is my opinion. I know it is the general practice here to bring those cases in that court.

Q. How many Supreme Judges are there in this Department? A. Twelve, I think. You fellows have got a lot of them in New York, and the rest are here. I think there are enough Judges here in the Supreme Court since Judge Hooker has returned, and the man who took Judge Hatch's place sits here, to dispatch their business all right. They have recently adopted some new rules, and have established an extra civil trial term, so that there are three civil trial terms here running all the time, that is, for jury cases, and one term of court that alternates one month with equity cases—or two months—and the other time with criminal cases.

BY CHAIRMAN PAGE:

Q. Does the County Court now handle any criminal cases? A. Yes, they have either two or three criminal terms a year of about a month each, and a lot of the minor cases are disposed of in that court.

BY COMMISSIONER MURPHY:

Q. Which does the District Attorney use, the Supreme Court criminal part, or the County Court criminal part? A. Both. They are so framed up that when the County Court criminal term goes out, the Supreme Court terms comes in, and indictments are transferred from one court to another as the convenience of the District Attorney requires. I might say here that Judge Kenefick once expressed the opinion that the Supreme Court was a far more satisfactory place for the District Attorney to try cases, and he used to be District Attorney before he became Judge. Judge Murphy informs me that I am mistaken as to the extent of the jurisdiction. He says there are some misdemeanors that the court has not jurisdiction of, and that the jurisdiction is prescribed by Section 56 of the Code of Criminal Procedure. There are one or two other things that I have forgotten. I would suggest that it would be wise, and I think it is feasible, that the clerk have power, the clerk of the Police Court have power to issue warrants, taking the depositions and issuing the warrants. The men who have been the clerks here have always been competent to do that. That leaves the Judge freer to dispose of the cases that are before him on trial. I was impressed with a late experience I had through the fact that there is no right kind of place to send a child to. As an instance of the point, there was a young Polish fellow brought in one day by one of the good humane officers on the police force for stealing coal. The boy, I don't think, was inclined to be criminal, but he was mentally and physically defective. He had an injured hip, and the mother told the police officer that when he got work he was not strong enough and big enough to hold his job, and it was a case of sort of steal or starve with him. The boy was capable of earning a living, and I think had a tendency or willingness to work, but he could not go out in the world and compete. Now, perhaps, Judge

Murphy knows of a place where he could have been sent, where he could have earned his own living or earned enough to pay for the expense of his keeping. I didn't. It was such a trivial matter that we took some time, with the aid of the clerk, who was pretty well posted on those things, to devise some place we could send him to, but the offense was small, and we let him go finally. That phase of the matter impresses me very forcibly.

MR. MAYER: Section 384-B of the Revised City Charter of Buffalo, relating to the appointment by the Police Justices of probation officers, was amended by Chapter 50 of the Laws of 1908, so that a Police Justice has now the authority to appoint as many persons as probation officers as he may deem proper.

———

THOMAS MURPHY, called at witness and being duly sworn, testified as follows:

BY MR. MAYER:

Q. You were a Police Justice of the City of Buffalo? A. Yes, sir.

Q. For how many years? A. Eight years, and about three years in the Morning Court.

Q. Prior to that time? A. Prior to that time.

Q. Now, will you briefly state for the convenience of the Commission the jurisdiction of the Special Sessions of the City of Buffalo? A. It has all the powers of Justices of the Peace of the towns and also of the Court of Special Session, who have the right to try all cases, have exclusive jurisdiction, in the first instance, to try all cases enumerated in Section 56 of the Code of Criminal Procedure; also has such jurisdiction to try such misdemeanors as the statute creating the crime permits him to try. And there are some other chapters in the Laws of 1886 in relation to offenses in employing children in factories, and disturbing the peace on religious grounds, two different chapters; but there are many misdemeanors that a Police Justice has not now jurisdiction to try or dispose of in his court.

Q. Will you tell us some of these? A. Well, all of the excise provisions, all the excise violations, now must be tried by indictment. A Police Justice has no power to try those misdemeanors. There are several others that I have not thought of.

Q. I want to inquire first as to the Juvenile Court. As I understand it, you organized or prepared a part for the trial of children's cases? A. Yes, sir.

Q. And beginning with what year? A. Well, in the Morning Court—to get that Juvenile Court history correct, Massachusetts, it seems, several years before 1891 had passed a law permitting magistrates, I believe, to separate the trial of children from those of adults.

Q. You mean in 1901? A. No, 1891. That law never went into effect. The State of New York passed a law in 1892 permitting magistrates to separate the trials. In 1896 they passed an amendment to that Act. It seems that the law never was taken advantage of by any of the Judges, except that there was an unsuccessful attempt, I believe, by one of the Judges in New York City. In the Morning Court I tried so far as I could to separate the trials of the children from those of the adults. That was twelve years ago. In 1889 I was elected Police Justice. I assumed the bench in 1900, and immediately announced that I would hold the Children's Court separate from that of the adults, and they have never been tried with any sessions of the Police Courts since, since which time we have established the Juvenile Court separate and apart from the Police Court entirely.

Q. The Juvenile Court has been held in a building separate and apart? A. Separate and apart from the Police Court.

Q. And at times separate and apart from the trial of adult cases? A. Yes, twice a week.

Q. What are the days? A. Tuesdays and Fridays were those that I used, and I understand that my successor is using the same days.

Q. In the afternoon? A. Yes, sir.

Q. Now, begin, if you will, with the arrest of the child; what is the process, my question being directed, among other things, to calling the attention of the Commission to the fact as to whether or not there is a place of detention for children in the City of Buffalo? A. That is a question I was going to bring up if you had not. I am very glad that you have brought it up.

Q. Describe the process from the time that a policeman arrests a child until the child is brought into court, and when you have reached that point I will ask further questions? A. The child is apprehended, taken to a police station, its record taken, and there is an understanding—there was in my time, and I understand it is so today—with the

Superintendent of Police, who at the time that our understanding first went into effect was a police captain, that no child should be locked up if he had a home, even if the parents did not have the requisite property to bail him. The purpose was to let the child go home at first whenever arrested, and that obtains to-day. Notwithstanding that a great many of the children were locked up, and must be locked up now, particularly those who have no home.

Q. Locked up in a police station? A. In a police station, if they have no home—those are dependent children, but delinquent children also if they have no home, nobody to take care of them, must be locked up in a police station or a jail. There is no other place.

Q. So, if I may interrupt you, as you very properly call attention to two classes of children, if a child is deserted by its parents and has done no wrong, it must, nevertheless, under your present situation be detained in the station house or jail? A. Yes, sir.

Q. Where adult persons are detained? A. Yes, sir.

BY COMMISSIONER FRANCIS:

Q. And in a cell? A. There is no other place that I know of unless they allow them to remain in the reserve room.

Q. No matter what the age may be? A. No matter what the age may be. There was one period, however, when that condition did not obtain here. We organized the Juvenile Improvement Association, and leased a home, the expenses of which were paid and maintained by this Association for a period of two years or more, up until, I think, last July we had a detention home for children, so that where it be-

came necessary to lock a child up, the child was taken to
that home. The expenses of that were all paid by private
subscription by the members of the Association, who paid
so much to become members. The Association as constituted at that time did not feel, as I understand it, that they
could continue.

BY MR. MAYER:

Q. That was a voluntary Association? A. Yes, I organized it myself. Judge Nash is President of it now. I re-
signed the office when I went out of office. They did not
feel as though they could meet the expenses thereafter, and,
as a consequence, the Juvenile Detention Home went down.
We made several efforts, a committee of the Bar Association was appointed, of which I was chairman, to try and
have an appropriation made for that purpose; and if there
is any one thing that I want to suggest here and urge
upon this committee, it is that in your recommendations
you make it mandatory upon cities of the first and second
class—and I don't know but all plaes where it is necessary
to lock children up—that some place other than station
houses or jails be provided to detain children in. I think
that is most important. Another thing——

Q. Let me just call attention to the fact that in the matter of bail, by an amendment to the Code of Criminal Procedure, Section 554, subdivision 4, if a child is arrested
charged with any offense except a felony, or a crime which
if committed by an adult would be a felony, the police captain or sergeant may now take bail? A. Yes, that was
passed subsequent to our agreement. Another thing, the

detention home, as Judge Lindsey says, is the right arm of the Juvenile Court. There are many times when a child on probation must be disciplined. He may become careless, and may not report, and yet his offense may have been so trivial that you would not want to send him away. Now, with a detention home you could place him in this institution for a few days—it is a discipline.

Q. So it would be valuable both before and after conviction? A. Before and after conviction, yes.

Q. Have you any idea how many children come before the Children's Court? A. Over one thousand every year.

Q. Have any statistics been kept of the number of children? A. We always sent in a report to the Common Council, yes, sir.

Q. Can you recollect how many of those were delinquent and how many dependent children? A. No, but the most of them were delinquent children.

Q. To what institution, if any, do you commit delinquent children? A. It depends upon the age and sometimes upon the religion. If it is a Catholic child between seven and fourteen years of age, we commit to Father Baker, a splendid institution; the State Industrial School of Rochester, the George Junior Republic, and the Berkshire Farm.

Q. Under what circumstances does the George Junior Republic take a commitment? A. Well, I believe they wish them over fourteen years of age. The boys there have to work, and they get along better, I believe, at that age than the younger children.

Q. Is the Juvenile Court held now in the same place as it was when you were Police Justice? A. Yes, sir.

Q. I understand it is held in the building where the Morgue is—is that correct? A. Well, it is the County Building, and the Morgue is in the rear, but, however, there is never anything there that a child could see in any way at all. That was the only place we could go to ,or could have for the Juvenile Court. I don't know but you may have received the same report from Philadelphia that I have received. I see a quotation from you, as well as from myself. There is a picture of the building that they have there now. It is one of the latest Juvenile Courts that they have. I intended to have brought the picture of the building with me. They have a splendid building there for the Juvenile Court, and it is a detention home as well.

Q. Do you regard the present quarters of the Juvenile Court as a suitable place—I am not talking of the present necessities, but whether the place itself is the proper kind of a place wherein to arraign children under the age of 16? A. No, it is not.

Q. Is it physically arranged so that the children in any manner come into contact with the Morgue of the building? A. They do not come into contact with the Morgue part of the building. I don't know of any instance where they have ever had any unpleasant sight or experience; but the fact that it is held in that building, and the room itself is not arranged as a Juvenile Court room should be arranged, but we had to make a virtue of necessity.

Q. Did you put into operation any probation plans when you were on the bench in connection with children? A. Oh, yes, the probation system was instituted under my jurisdiction.

Q. What is your view as to the employment of probation officers; do you favor the employment of probation officers? A. Yell, yes, but I would not do away with volunteers entirely. I believe that the court, in order to be efficient, must have paid probation officers, because a man cannot afford to give the time that it requires unless he is paid.

Q. Is the system in vogue under Judge Nash in the Juvenile Court on the same principle as your system? A. Yes, but he has a paid probation officer, which I did not have.

Q. With that exception, it is the same? A. Yes, with that exception, it is the same.

Q. Briefly, what is that system? A. Well, we have several people who are interested in the work—I was particularly fortunate in that regard, I had some of the very best probation officers, I think, that could be found, people who really loved the work. They acted as volunteers, and when a child is placed on probation he has to report to these probation officers as directed, usually once a week. The probation officers are supposed to visit the court and its sessions if they can.

Q. Just a moment; did you, however, appoint these volunteers as probation officers? A. Yes, I did.

Q. So that you invested them with the powers of probation officers? A. I did.

Q. And by the word "volunteer" you mean that they received no compensation? A. They received no compensation. For a time I received a little support in the way of providing street car tickets for them to go back and forward to the homes of the children, as it was very important that the probation officers become familiar with the environments of the children. If attending school, the child brings a report from its teacher showing what its attendance is, and its decorum, and all that. If it is old enough to be employed, they try and have some report brought, not from the employer, because sometimes the child would not want his employer to know that he was on probation, but in some way to know just what the child is doing, and he is made to feel that if he lived up to the duties that are imposed upon him on his probation or term of probation, in the end he will be discharged, and, of course, he is working all the time with that object in view. They usually report once a week to the probation officers, and the probation period is usually three months, which may be extended or abrogated by the Judge. Sometimes the child is kept on probation for six months or nine months. Sometimes they are allowed to go earlier than the three months. At the end of that time—I assume that Judge Nash has the same rule, I required the child to come into court at the time the probation was up, and if the probation officer recommended that he be discharged he was discharged.

Q. When a child was discharged, you always required his appearance in court? A. I did not always, but before I got through I did. At first I allowed the probation officers to discharge the child without bringing him back, and then I thought it would be more impressive if the child appeared in court.

Q. Is it your opinion that the ultimate disposition of

the child should be made in the presence of the Judge? A. It is.

Q. And in that manner the child will receive better impressions than it receives if it thinks it gets its freedom from the probation officer. A. Yes, I think so and right along that line, the thought occurs to me now, something that has always been in my mind. When I send these children to these institutions, I think when they are liberated if they are given to understand in some way that they must report to the Judge or that he has something to do with their liberty, that it gives him an influence over the child that is beneficial to the child.

Q. And after the return from the institution? A. After the return from the institution.

Q. And during minority. A. During minority.

Q. Or at any rate prior to majority? A. Exactly.

Q. Is there any suggestion that occurs to you in regard to the Juvenile Court? A. I think that is about all. I want to say again that I would make it mandatory in cities of the first and second class that some places be provided other than the station houses and jails to detain children.

BY CHAIRMAN PAGE:

Q. Have you any branch of the Society for the Prevention of Cruelty to Children in this city? A. Yes, sir.

Q. Don't they have any provision of that sort? A. Well, they have a room up there, but they have no such accommodations as they have in New York city. In New York city it is not necessary to have any place other than they have. They have a splendid building there, but the branch of the society here has not any such buildings or place that would be adequate.

BY COMMISSIONER MURPHY:

Q. How would you have a juvenile courtroom arranged? A. Well, I would have it arranged in two departments. I would not have any other child in the room with the Judge except a child whose case is to be disposed of. I would have no one there except the parents or guardians, and witnesses, and officers—those people who are interested in the case.

Q. In other words, you would not have any of the paraphernalia of a court? A. No, sir, I would remove that atmosphere as far as possible. It is not necessary to have those benches that are usual in courts—something more in the way of a class room.

Q. Would you have the judge in a gown? A. No, I don't think I would.

BY CHAIRMAN PAGE:

Q. Reverting to this question of the Society for Prevention of Cruelty to Children, is there any provision made for paying the Society for taking care of children and feeding them? A. I don't think they have ever done anything of that kind here, though I presume that could be done. Some society, either the Juvenile Improvement Association, which we already have and which has been engaged in the work, or the Society for the Prevention of Cruelty to Children, could have control of it, or they might establish it in connection with the Police Department—have them rent some place, the city rent it—though I don't think that is feasible; I would rather have the Police Justice have full control of the institution if possible, which he would have if the Juvenile Association had charge of it. The Police Justice is president of that association.

Q. If an additional court was established as has been suggested, would you give that court jurisdiction of all misdemeanors within the city? A. The Juvenile Court?

Q. No, I am going back to the adult court, the Police Court itself. You say there are certain misdemeanors that are not now triable by the Police Court. Would you give them the jurisdiction which is now given to the Special Sessions in New York to try all misdemeanors? A. I think that would simplify matters.

Q. Do you think it would be wise? A. I do.

BY MR. MAYER:

Q. Before we go to the questions relating to the Police Court as distinguished from the Juvenile Court, is there anything else that occurs to you in regard to the Juvenile Court? A. I don't think of anything now, Judge.

Q. (Previous question read to the witness.)

A. I cannot recall anything just no. Mr. Noonan's statement suggested something.

Q. That is, his statement in regard to a place to commit children to? A. Yes. It isn't right in line with that, but suggested a thought as to some of the things we had down there. Sometimes we find a child that seems to be delinquent through some mental disturbance. We have sent in a few cases of those kind of children to the hospital and had them treated and they have gone all right afterwards. That was suggested to me by what Mr. Noonan said. As to a place to send a child that is defective, I don't know whether the George Junior Republic would want to take a child that couldn't work. I believe the most of the boys there have to work. They may take a child, however, at the Berkshire Farm; they take them.

BY COMMISSIONER MURPHY:

Q. Where is the Berkshire Farm situated? A. That is in the Berkshire Hills, Canaan's Four Corners.

Q. Is that in the State. A. Yes. I don't know what the county is. It's Canaan's Four Corners.

BY CHAIRMAN PAGE:

Q. Is it in the Berkshire Hills? A. It is in the Berkshire Hills.

BY COMMISSIONER MURPHY:

Q. Is the George Junior Republic a State institution or supported by State funds in any way? A. Well, they receive pay for boys that are committed there, of course, but it is not maintained; it is not supported originally by the State as I understand it.

BY COMMISSIONER HAMILTON:

Q. Judge, don't you think every delinquent child ought to be examined by a physician for mental or physical defects? A. It would be a good idea; it would be a good idea.

Q. Have you any opinion as to what proportion of them would be found to be mentally or physically defective in a way that a physician could help. A. No, I couldn't say the percentage, but undoubtedly a great many cases would be benefited by it.

BY MR. MAYER:

Q. Now, referring to the Police Court dealing with adults, I want to ask you about the matter of the Police Justice acting as Coroner; did that occur in your time? A. Yes.

Q. Do you know whether the elimination of the Coroners gave general satisfaction, whether the new system was regarded as a better system? A. Oh, yes; I think there isn't any doubt about it.

Q. How many Coroners had you prior to that time? A. I believe we had two Coroners and then a Coroner for the south town and the north town. I am not certain about that.

Q. And now the Police Justice deals with that whole subject, does he? A. Yes, whenever there is reason to believe—now the medical examiners perform the autopsy and where there is any reason to believe that a crime may have been committed then they make a report to the Police Justice and he holds the inquest.

Q. And he performs all the offices heretofore performed in such regard by the Coroner? A. Performed by the Coroner and that can be done by the County Court and either upon the motion of the Medical Examiner or the District Attorney.

Q. Have you any idea of how many cases, how many excise violations, are presented to the Grand Jury in this County, that is covering the city of Buffalo, I mean, more particularly? A. I haven't thought of the number, but there are a great many hundreds, I believe, every year.

Q. Elaborating a little the question asked by the chairman, is there any reason why those cases could not be considered by the Police Justice sitting as a Court of Special Session? A. None whatever, and could originally as well, some of them could have been, but that was amended so none can be now by the Court of Special Sessions.

Q. Do you think that would relieve the business of the higher courts in such regard? A. Yes, I do.

Q. Are there any misdemeanors not now triable by the Police Justice that occur to you, any important class of misdemeanors. A. Well, there are so many, where the punishment is a year or a fine of $500 in the Code and on the statutes, I could not enumerate them.

Q. Is the jurisdiction of the Police Justice in the matter of commitment limited to six months? A. Six months and $50 fine. I may say that in Section 211 of the Code of Criminal Procedure, a misdemeanor that is not enumerated in Section 56, may be tried by the Police Magistrate at the election of the defendant.

Q. Yes? A. (Continuing.) But it says no such jurisdiction can be conferred where the penalty is more than six months or more than a $50 fine or both.

Q. Well, to put it in popular, as distinguished from technical, language, about all the misdemeanors of which—all the misdemeanors usually committed of which the Police Justice has jurisdiction—are petit larceny and assault in the third degree? A. And assault in the third degree. Those that are enumerated in Section 56.

Q. Did you hear Mr. Noonan's testimony in regard to the necessity of two justices for the city of Buffalo? A.

No, I did not hear what he said at the start; I think he just about finished on that point when I came in.

Q. Well, what is your view as to that, do you think it would be desirable to have more than one police justice?

A. Well, that I think would depend on whether the Police Justice feels that he can do the work or not, whether he feels that he is able to do the work and the people who have business with the court feel that they can have their matters attended to.

Q. Well, is the total amount of this business increasing to such an extent that there must come a time shortly when more than one justice will be required? A. There will undoubtedly be a time when more than one justice will be required.

Q. How would you divide the city, then, as to judicial districts, if you had two justices; I don't mean exactly, but generally. A. Well, I haven't thought of that. I would, if that were going to be a law, I would divide up—taking the station houses, station house districts, as my cue. I would say so many station houses in one district, so many station houses in the other; the boundaries of those station houses to comprise the judicial district. Similar to that in the Morning Court at the present time.

Q. Now, have you any suggestions to make, in addition to those you have already made, in regard to a police court for the trial of adults? A. Why, if there is much work there for the Police Justice—and I know that a police justice has a whole lot of work to do—is a very busy man, I myself think there is more work than he ought to be compelled to do; but I would suggest a remedy that I think we could get along with very well, with one police court for a time.

Q. What is that, Judge? A. It was partly brought out by what Mr. Noonan stated before he went away. He said that his clerk should have the power to issue warrants. I would say have the Judge appoint a warrant clerk. He has now a clerk and a deposition clerk who have all the work they can attend to. I would appoint a warrant clerk, a good man, and give him the power to issue warrants and sign the Judge's name and his own and make it returnable, of course, before the Judge, and also give that clerk the power to take bail. The life of the Police Justice of Buffalo—before he gets out of bed mornings there are people at his house, who have some troubles they want to talk to him about. When he comes into court there are sometimes thirty or forty in line waiting to consult him, some for warrants, all kinds of trouble; some people that really haven't anything in the criminal line, but they have got troubles and have to tell them to somebody. And at night when he gets home the people are there waiting to see him, and then he is called up sometimes all hours of the night to take bail. Now, if that part of the work of hearing everybody's troubles and issuing warrants in bailing cases was—if he was relieved of that—why, I think he could get along with the work of trying and disposing of cases, at the present time.

Q. Do you think it would be a dangerous power to give a clerk the power of issuing warrants? A. No. He is subject to the control of the judge, of course, and an appeal could always be allowed—would always be had—to the Judge, in case he refused to give a warrant; the person could go to the Judge; a good man who would make it a specialty.

BY CHAIRMAN PAGE:

Q. Where would the appeal lie, if he should improperly issue a warrant and arrest an innocent man? A. The Judge may do the same thing.

Q. Oh, yes, I know; but the Judge is a judicial officer. A. He is a part—he would be a part of the Court, and I don't think that there is much danger of that happening any more than it would with the judges issuing the warrants themselves, and not as much so, because he would have the time to—all the time he could wish to give to the case before he issued the warrant.

BY COMMISSIONER MURPHY:

Q. Wouldn't it be better to have another judge instead of giving the power to the clerk? A. Well, you could have another judge if you wanted one. It would save expense and I think you could get along very well with the warrant clerk, and that would separate, also, that crowd of people who are there looking for warrants, from the court-room. Now, after the Judge has gone through the line, sent them over to his clerk to get the warrants, they fill up the room and they are talking to his deposition clerks and he is trying to dispose of his cases with all the noise and with all that crowd, which would be absent if there were such a clerk.

BY CHAIRMAN PAGE:

Q. What do you call a deposition clerk; does he draw the complaints? A. He draws the information.

Q. The information? A. Yes, and also I think I heard somebody say something about having an attorney at the Police Court. Was anything——

BY MR. MAYER:

Q. No, I think that possibly has been discussed outside. A. Well, I did not know, whether Mr. Noonan referred to that or not.

Q. You mean an attorney for the people? A. Yes. Now, the deposition clerk could take the part of an attorney, not to prosecute, but in the way of preparing the cases for the officers, if they feel as though they need anybody to prepare their cases for them; the deposition or this warrant clerk could perform that duty too.

Q. That is, advise them as to whether the facts constituted a crime and what evidence is and so on. A. Yes, and if necessary prepare the information for them.

BY COMMISSIONER WINTHROP:

Q. Well, at present, how much time is taken up with these warrants; the complaints, I presume, are presented to the Judge already made out. A. Yes.

Q. And all he does is to swear the complainant? A. Well, I always examined every one in line and went into the case and after I had examined as to the facts——

Q. Examined the complaint? A. No, examined the persons orally, and after going through the facts then I sent them to the deposition clerk, if I concluded to give him a warrant; I would send him over to the deposition clerk and he would state the facts as he stated them to me. It takes up a great deal of time sometimes.

BY COMMISSIONER HAMILTON:

Q. That is usually done—the first part of the morning is devoted to that? A. The first part of the morning.

Q. You would not have anything going on in the Police Court room, practically, except the hearings or the summary trials? A. A summary trial or an examination.

BY MR. MAYER:

Q. That is, your procedure was—that the person seeking the warrant must first present the facts to you as Judge. A. Yes.

Q. And if you should then decide a warrant should issue, you ordered the deposition clerk to prepare the complaint or information. A. The information, yes.

Q. In practice were there many cases which went to the municipal court for violation of ordinances? A. Not from the police court; from the morning court. The police court has no jurisdiction of ordinances cases. The morning court has. Once in a while a person would prefer to be tried in the municipal court.

Q. Well, in your experience as a judge of the morning court, did you find that many cases had to go to the municipal court? A. Well, there were some, but I cannot say a great many.

Q. Well, do you think that is a good system or do you think those cases should be tried by a person invested with criminal jurisdiction where the case is a criminal case? A. Well, for disorderly conduct, there may be elements of crime involved in it and yet they may be charged with disorderly conduct, creating a noise and disturbance. Now it is all right to try that in the morning court.

Q. Well, perhaps I don't make myself clear. I was referring entirely to those cases under the charter of Buffalo of violation of ordinances? A. Yes.

Q. Which are sent to the municipal courts? A. Well, where the men ask to be tried in the municipal court?

Q. Yes, I mean in your experience is that a good practice; is it a practical thing, or does it unnecessarily divide jurisdiction? A. No, you can get a jury trial in the municipal court and you cannot in the morning court. Usually if a person wishes a trial outside of the morning court they ask for a jury trial and they could not get it there, and we would send them to the Municipal Court.

Q. Yes, but is it your experience that there is any necessity of sending these violations of ordinances to the Municipal Court. A. Well, some men prefer to be tried in a municipal court. There may be some reason why they may not want to be tried before a judge; may be some reason why the judge would not feel as though he would want to try the person.

Q. You think it is a good plan to leave that latitude, do you? A. Why, I think so; yes.

Q. I ask you as a matter of experience? A. Yes, I think so.

BY CHAIRMAN PAGE:

Q. What do you think of the suggestion that has been

made of combining the jurisdiction of the police and municipal courts and making them different parts, practically, of the same court? A. Well, that isn't a bad system. But it is a return, it seems to me, to the old system of justices of the peace, that had civil and criminal jurisdiction and where they held court of special sessions in the towns; it doesn't seem to be anything new, but that—the municipal court took the place of the justices of the peace, took their civil jurisdiction, and they could also take the criminal jurisdiction. But, whether it is the best plan or not, I wouldn't want to say it was, because I think that question must have been up when the police court was established. Originally we had justices of the peace, prior to the municipal court, who had civil jurisdiction and criminal jurisdiction. The justices of the peace in those days performed the duties that the morning justices do now. The morning justices, by the way, are justices of the peace at the present time. Well, the fact that they created the police court suggests some reason for it; where a man was specially employed to dispose of criminal cases, it seems to me—of course, I don't know what their reasons were at that time, but a man may make a very good municipal court judge or supreme court judge and he may not be the kind of a man the people want as police justice.

BY COMMISSIONER SMITH:

Q. Judge, did I understand you to say a man brought to the morning court for violation of a city ordinance, could have a trial in the municipal court by jury if he requested. A. Yes.

CHAIRMAN PAGE: The charter provides, as I remember the reading, that in any case where the punishment was not imprisonment, where it was merely a fine, he could have it transferred.

MR. MAYER: Yes.

BY COMMISSIONER MURPHY:

Q. Isn't that a reason, then, the old system was a good one and it might be a good thing to have these two combined. A. As I say, it isn't a bad system at all. I wouldn't be afraid of that system, but I believe you could—the people are more interested in the police justice than they are in a supreme court judge, or a municipal court judge. They all want to know who the police justice is, and to have a police justice with no other duties than that of police justice, you can or ought to get a man, the kind of a man the people want for that place.

BY COMMISSIONER HAMILTON:

Q. What about the effect on the police justice himself, Judge, of the continuous—— A. Looking at the "lowbrows?"

Q. (Continuing.) Lack of variety. The continuous criminal terms. A. Well, I wouldn't want to plead.

Q. Do you think he feels the lack of variety, the lack of variation in his work? A. Well, I think it would be better for himself, perhaps; it would be better for his— if he is a lawyer, to keep up on the civil branch of his profession. But as to the effect upon himself, I don t know.

BY MR. MAYER:

Q. Well, what is your own experience; I mean, did you feel that you went to your work fresh every day? A. Oh, yes, the only—the troubles were those that I have suggested. People are at your house in the morning and there at night and you are called up at night and they even stop you on the street to tell you their troubles. But the real work of the police court itself, I don't think a man of ordinary nerves can do it and feel all right. There is another point to this consolidation theory. The police justice must finish his case, if there were cases that were unfinished. Oftentimes we have to adjourn a hearing.

Q. Cases where examinations are being had? A. Well, I wouldn't say an examination; I don't know but that a new judge might go on with an examination, because that really isn't a trial; but in the trials, cases which he disposes of, no other judge can dispose of that case after he enters on it, so that if the time came for him to leave why he would have to come back and hold court anyway in order to dispose of those cases.

Q. Yes, really, he is sitting as a judge of special sessions? A. Yes, really sitting as a judge of special sessions.

Q. Or court, rather, of special sessions? A. He would have to finish up the cases that were undisposed of. So, as I said before, it is not a system that would be very bad at all; it is not a bad system, but I think the people can get the man they want for police justice and it requires some different qualification from that of municipal court judge.

Q. In the morning courts no stenographer's minutes are taken, are there? A. No.

Q. And there is not any perpetuation of testimony? A. No, they have no stenographer at the present time.

Q. Do you, without, of course, referring to the personnel of the gentlemen who have been so highly spoken of by Mr. Noonan, but referring only to the system, do you think it is desirable to continue the system of the morning courts; and I ask you as you have been both a justice of the morning court and a justice of police? A. Yes, I do; I think the system is all right. I think if they want to do anything, they can get a stenographer. Of course, on an appeal, if minutes are not taken, I understand that is good ground for reversal, though the court can order a new trial. We had that question up and the county court simply ordered a new trial.

Q. Suppose, instead of morning justices, you had two police justices with full equipment? A. Well, if you are going to change the system, I would suggest that, if you are going to change the morning court, then I would say two police justices.

Q. Having the police justices open their courts at nine in the morning? A. Yes, but I don't know whether any of you gentlemen have ever been in a morning court.

Q. We may be before we leave Buffalo. A. I hope not. But the atmosphere there is anything but that which you would want to mix up with the people that come at a later part of the day. Sometimes the air there is so thick that you can almost cut it. There are all kinds of drunks and all kinds of conditions that are brought before the people in that court, or brought before the magistrate in that court. Now, I believe it is a good thing to keep them separated from the people in the police court. And this law, the morning court system now, I think is a very good one. It was drawn under my direction. I don't say it for that reason, however, but prior to that time the police commissioners, assigned the station houses to the different justices, which gave them an influence over the morning justices. We had a law framed putting all the justices on the same salary.

Q. Well, as I understand you, it is a desirable separation for purposes of early jail delivery. Of men arraigned over night for drunkenness, disorder and vagrancy? A. Well, not on that ground particularly, because as a rule that—yes, that is one of the grounds, but not so much so. But the condition that the people are in that are brought before the court, the morning court, is entirely different from the people that are brought into the police court. You see them there in all kinds of shapes—sick, filthy and dirty, and everything else. Now, I would not want to mix those people up, they wouldn't want to be mixed themselves, if you could dispose of them in this court.

BY COMMISSIONER FRANCIS:

Q. Does the convenience of the morning court encourage repeaters? A. Repeaters?

Q. Yes. A. No, that is as far as I know.

BY MR. MAYER:

Q. Is there any suggestion that occurs to you in regard to the adult court? A. Nothing further than what I have stated. There is one thing that may be a little out of the line of your examination here that I would suggest, and that is to make it the duty of somebody other than the judge to enforce Section 118 of the Penal Code.

Q. What is that? A. That makes it a misdemeanor for anyone who wilfully and wrongfully fails to bring a prisoner before a magistrate without delay. Now, at present there is no one to enforce it. The judge does not feel inclined to do it, even though it has been stated to him. The prosecuting officer of the county does not feel disposed because it is embarrassing for him; he is the attorney for the policemen. And I think in all parts of the State, in fact, all places where they have a police department, that a great many abuses grow out of the non-enforcement of that law.

Q. You evidently are speaking from experience? A. Yes, I don't know of anything that will do more to create respect for the courts and for the law than to make the defendant feel that all his rights have been protected.

Q. What abuses specifically do you refer to? A. Well, a man taken into a station house and locked up for six or seven days and no one being allowed to see him; put through the third degree, where they figure or suspect him of having committed some crime.

Q. And not arraigned before the magistrate? A. And not arraigned before the magistrate.

Q. Has that occurred often in Buffalo? A. Such cases have been brought to my attention. I don't say particularly under this administration, but all through. This is as good an administration as any we have had, but I don't find any difference anywhere in the State in regard to that section, in regard to its enforcement.

Q. Does the police department here take photographs before conviction? A. Well, I don't think they do now. I think there was a law passed prohibiting that.

Q. Do they take Bertillon measurements? A. I think, yes, I think they take Bertillon measurements; I am not sure about that. But whether they—whether they do before or after, they undoubtedly comply with the law in that respect.

Q. Do I understand you to say cases have been called to your attention where a police official has made an arrest, taken a man to the station house and kept him there for several days? A. Yes.

Q. Without arraigning him before the police justice? A. Yes.

Q. Or a proper magistrate? A. Yes.

BY COMMISSIONER WINTHROP:

Q. And not allowing him to communicate with the outside world? A. Not allowing him, yes.

Q. Or his friends? A. Yes.

Q. Not even allowing counsel? A. Not allowing counsel.

BY MR. MAYER:

Q. How many cases of that kind would you say had come to your attention in your experience as a police justice? A. Well, I couldn't say.

Q. I mean many? A. Not a great many, no. but there were a few.

BY CHAIRMAN PAGE:

Q. That is a practice that is growing not alone here, but in other large cities, isn't it? A. Yes.

Q. Introducing the Continental method of dealing with criminals instead of our method that has come down through the English jurisdiction? A. That is right.

BY COMMISSIONER WINTHROP:

Q. What is your suggestion to prevent that? A. Well, you could make it the duty of a representative of the Attorney General to investigate these cases, or make it a special duty of the grand jury. But, as I say, it would always be embarrassing for the District Attorney, as he is really the attorney for the Police Department.

BY MR. MAYER:

Q. As it stands now, as I gather from what you say, the various officials who act in connection with police administration find it difficult, embarrassing in order to—— A. Sure. I don't know of an instance where there has been any effort made to enforce that law or prosecute anybody for its violation.

BY CHAIRMAN PAGE:

Q. Well, the district attorneys are not altogether free from that same system, are they? A. No, no; it is natural for a man preparing his case to try and perfect it he can. But it is important, I believe more important than anything else, to make the defendants feel that every right which they have has been protected, if you want to have the law respected and the courts respected.

BY MR. MAYER:

Q. Let me ask you this before you leave the stand: You did not employ for misdemeanors the paper known in New York as a summons, did you? A. No, a subpoena I used instead. Used the subpoena for the same office.

Q. But you instituted something in the nature of a John Doe proceeding? A. Yes.

Q. And used subpoenas? A. Yes.

Q. Now, was that for the purpose of inquiring whether a crime had been committed? A. Yes, and in cases of children, instead of issuing a warrant whenever it was possible, I issued a subpoena instead.

Q. In the statistics of the court, did you keep a record of the number of suboenas of that character issued? A. Well, we, or my clerk, had a book—no, I don't think there was a record kept, unless an investigation, like the bank investigation which you are interested in, got on the docket, and of course that appears on the docket.

Q. Well, now, from your experience, what do you think of a paper, call it summons, if you please, which could be served upon a person in a case where the police justice desired to be satisfied prior to the issuance of a warrant? A. I think it is his duty and I think he can already.

Q. Well, he can in the method you say, by subpoena? A. Yes.

Q. But are you at all familiar with the system prevailing in the city of New York? A. Well, I don't know whether it was you or some other judge down there told me, explained it one time, but I have forgotten.

Q. Well, the system in brief is to issue a paper called a

summons which notifies the defendant to appear before a magistrate. It is not an arrest. The magistrate issues the summons in cases where he is not satisfied that a crime has been committed and yet the subject matter is one which he believes should be inquired into? A. Exactly.

Q. And in that way an arrest is obviated until the magistrate satisfies himself. Now do you think such a system would be practicable here? A. Very practicable and very good.

Q. And if it had clear authority in law, you believe it would be useful to the police justice? A. I do.

Q. And might obviate this John Doe proceeding in many instances? A. Yes; well, it would do away with the John Doe proceedings, but many times an innocent man is arrested under the old system where a man comes in and files an information, and there is something about that that the judge does not feel satisfied to issue his warrant, justified in doing it, by the information which he has received; perhaps the defendant, an innocent man, may be arrested and there is always that stigma of arrest. If possible, it is the judge's duty to avoid that.

Q. Well, you employ a John Doe proceeding, I assume, as a sort of a way around that? A. Yes.

BY CHAIRMAN PAGE:

Q. Would you extend that summons to some of the minor offences? A. Yes, oh yes.

Q. Violation of corporation ordinances, sanitary and building code? A. Yes.

Q. I don't know whether you have a system of traffic regulations here? A. Of what?

Q. Traffic regulations for the regulation of traffic in your streets. The driver of a truck has to go down to a certain corner and turn around in a certain direction, etc. If you have those, would you also use the summons in cases of violation of those traffic regulations instead of arresting the driver of the truck? A. Yes, I think the summons would be—in fact, in all ordinances that are not really crimes, it seems as though the summons would be all that is necessary.

BY MR. MAYER:

Q. Following up the Chairman's question, what would you think of this system, stating it generally; instead of the police officers arresting citizens for these minor violations, such as of corporation ordinances, hackmen driving the wrong way, or perhaps automobiles exceeding the speed limit, what would you think of a system whereby, instead of a police officer arresting the person, he were to give him a notice or mandate to appear before the police court the next morning, in cases where, by virtue of the person having a license or by some other method, the defendant could be readily identified and followed up if he did not appear? A. I think that would be a very good plan, unless the arrest be made to prevent an assault of something of that kind. Sometimes, where there is a violation of the ordinance of disorderly conduct, an arrest may be necessary to prevent an assault taking place. But for these other violations, wherever possible I would say that assuredly that is a good plan.

Q. I am referring now to cases where there is nothing to suggest an intended breach of the peace? A. I would favor it; and I want to say now, as you have asked that question, that the charter of Buffalo ought certainly to be amended on that point, as the ruling of one of the justices of the municipal court, in a case which I had not many months ago, was the officer not only had the right to arrest the person who was violating the ordinance at the time, but that he had the right to arrest him on that day, which would give a policeman more of a right to arrest for violation of an ordinance than for a felony.

———

DANIEL McCUE called as a witness, having first been duly sworn, testified as follows:

Q. Mr. McCue, are you clerk of the police court in the City of Buffalo? A. I am.

Q. How long have you been such? A. A year ago last January.

Q. Are you a member of the bar? A. I am.

Q. How long have you been a member of the bar. A. Going on four years.

Q. Now, is the paper which I show you a copy of the report made January 18th, 1909, to the Common Council of the City of Buffalo? A. Yes.

MR. MAYER: That is offered in evidence as Exhibit 67. (Said paper was marked Exhibit 67.)

I read this for the information of the commission (Reads said exhibit.)

BY MR. MAYER:

Q. Now, Mr. McCue, some of the defendants who are fined pay their fine at the court? A. Yes, sir.

Q. Now, others pay them at the Erie County Penitentiary? A. Yes, they can.

Q. To what body are the authorities of the Erie County Penitentiary required to report the collection of fines? A. Why, they make some kind of a report to the City Treasurer or the County Treasurer, I don't know which. It does not go through us at all. We just get a receipt from the penitentiary showing they have been put in there; afterwards they deal direct with the county.

Q. So you have no record of those fines? A. We cannot tell anything about what they receive.

Q. Therefore, there is no one place where the statistics as to the fines imposed, fines paid by defendants as the result of conviction in the police court, may be found? A. No.

Q. The police court make that—— A. That would be the penitentiary and police court together, and then you would find the right report regarding fines.

Q. Will you describe for the benefit of the commission what is called the courtroom now of the police court? A. The room which we have there?

Q. Yes. A. Why, the building was formerly—they started to build it, at least, with the intention of building a theatre, and it is more like a store front . Just got plaster inside, about one hundred and forty feet deep and maybe thirty feet wide. We are on the ground floor. Just above us, one floor, is a bowling alley, a big bowling hall, where they are bowling all day, during the trials and at other times, and half of the time they are bowling there so much that you cannot hardly hear. Above, I imagine, they have got a bar where the water, when they are cleaning up or some other way, it comes over about two or three times a week; there is a flood, and it may be eight or ten gallons that falls upon the spectators below from above. The courtroom is too small and it is a very dirty courtroom.

Q. It is long and narrow, is it not? A. Very long and very narrow.

BY COMMISSIONER HAMILTON:

Q. How about the ventilation? A. The ventilation is bad.

BY COMMISSIONER MAYER:

Q. Is there any at all? A. When the door is open.

Q. Well, now back, the space where the judge sits is very confined, is it not? A. It is; very, yes.

Q. And in that space, behind the bench, he must keep his stenographer? A. His stenographer.

Q. And the interpreter usually sits there, does he not? A. Why, sometimes, he is sometimes, again he is right in front of the Judge.

Q. Yes, now what have you in the way of a private room where you can do your clerk work and keep your records? A. Why, there is really not—there is a private room of the judge's. That is a real small room. He has got a desk there and some law books.

Q. What would you say were the dimensions of that room? A. Why, I would imagine about maybe 12 by 15, something around that measurement.

BY CHAIRMAN PAGE:

Q. Twelve by fifteen? A. Feet, yes.

BY MR. MAYER:

Q. Well, it is not as large as that.

BY CHAIRMAN PAGE:

That's a pretty good sized room.

BY MR. MAYER:

Q. It isn't as large as that, it is a very small room? A. It is a very small room. I never measured it.

Q. Would you say the place was absolutely unfit for the purpose for which it is intended? A. I would say it is, entirely.

Q. And it is dark, is it not? A. It is very dark.

Q. Now, will you tell the commission the composition of the force of the court; that is, you have your police justice, now that is correct, is it not? A. Yes.

Q. Now, go on with the clerks. A. Then there is the deposition clerk, a warrant clerk, a stenographer, a German interpreter, a Polish interpreter and a court officer.

Q. Well, now, what are you, the warrant clerk? A. Why yes, I am the clerk of the court, I get out the warrants. Usually the warrants——

Q. Well, what is Judge Nash—the system of Judge Nash,

the present police justice; does a person go to him first and tell his story before he gets a warrant? A. Yes, he goes to the police justice first.

Q. Yes? A. And tells his story.

Q. Yes? A. Then if he is entitled to the warrant he is sworn and then he comes to me for the warrant.

Q. Well, doesn't the deposition clerk first make out the deposition? A. Well, I make out the deposition—no, he first of all applies to the judge, then, after the judge swears him and says he is entitled to a warrant, he comes to me and alleges the facts that he told the judge, then the warrant is issued.

Q. Who prepares the deposition? A. I do.

Q. Is your title then warrant clerk or just clerk? A. Why, I think it is just clerk.

Q. Then you prepare the warrant and the judge signs it? A. Yes.

Q. The judge does not issue the warrant then, unless the person has first told him all about the matter? A. And been sworn, yes.

Q. Now, what is your salary, Mr. McCue? A. $1200.

Q. And what is the salary of the deposition clerk? A. $1000.

Q. And the stenographer? A. I think the stenographer's is $900.

Q. The German interpreter is not appointed by the police justice, is he? A. No.

Q. He is attached to the Police Department? A. To the Police Department.

Q. And the Polish interpreter is appointed by whom?
A. By the judge.

Q. And what is his salary? A. $900, I believe.

Q. And the court attendant, what is his salary? A. $900,
I think, the same.

Q. What are the duties generally of the deposition clerk?
A. Why, his duties are to index the dockets, the judge's
dockets, and when the police come in in the morning, he
gets out the deposition and gives that to the judge and
sees it is a correct deposition; makes out bail bonds of
cases for further examination, or in cases held for the grand
jury.

Q. Now, are there any police officers who are assigned
by the Police Department as attendants in the court?
A. No, sir.

Q. You have now stated all the court attendants and
clerks and other attaches? A. All, and then there is a
woman that is the janitor.

Q. Is she appointed by the court? A. I think; well,
yes, she is under civil service, taken from the list, I believe.

Q. Appointed by the Police Justice. Mr. McCue, in addition to the report to which reference was made before
as Exhibit 67, have you brought here the report of the
present Police Justice, Judge Nash, to the Comptroller
of the City of Buffalo? A. I believe I have, yes.

Q. Or a copy of the report? A. Yes.

Q. If this is a copy, that is all I care about. A. This
is the book (indicating).

Q. You may bring those up, Mr. McCue. I just want
to get it in evidence, that is all, the report, also of the
business of the Juvenile Court. A. Well, I tell you, I

would not be able to give you a definite report on that, as I just do the clerical work at the Juvenile Court, where the probation officers have made out their report, and they are both here.

MR. MAYER: Is Mr. Fifer here, is that the report?

MR. FIFER: I believe it is, yes.

BY MR. MAYER:

Q. Isn't that a true copy of the report of the Judge, and also the report of the Judge as to recommendations in regard to the conduct of the court (handing paper to witness)? A. Yes, this is the same as was filed.

Q. With the Common Council? A. With the Common Council.

MR. MAYER: Well, now that is—those are all offered as a continuation, part, of Exhibit 67.

Q. Are you familiar with Judge Nash's report as to the court room at the Juvenile Court? A. Why, yes.

Q. You have heard it read just now? A. I have heard it read, yes.

Q. As a part of Exhibit 67? A. Yes.

Q. From your experience as clerk, is that a very undesirable place? A. I think it is very undesirable, yes.

BY COMMISSIONER WINTHROP:

Q. In your court room for the trial of adults, where are the persons kept that are brought in? A. They are kept right on the side of the judge, right in front of the judge, in some kind of a cage or screen.

Q. All kept there? A. All kept there, and called in turn.

BY COMMISSIONER HAMILTON:

Q. What is the largest number you have seen placed in that screen enclosure? A. Why sometimes it has been so large I think they had to keep them outside and have the officers sit right next to them.

BY CHAIRMAN PAGE:

Q. Keep them in the body of the court room? A. Yes, because the crowd varies quite a little at different times.

BY COMMISSIONER WINTHROP:

Q. Does that interfere with the quiet? A. It would have quite a good deal to do with it.

CHAIRMAN PAGE: The Commission will stand in recess until two o'clock.

AFTERNOON SESSION.

February 4th, 1909.

DANIEL McCUE recalled:

Q. Mr. McCue, I now direct your attention to the records kept by your court—do you have charge of those records? A. I do.

Q. Now, take up each book in order, and briefly explain to the Commission what the record is. For instance, first we have a book called "Statement Book concerning persons convicted"? A. Yes, sir.

Q. Generally speaking, what does that contain? A. that contains the names of the persons convicted that are either fined or imprisoned.

Q. It does not contain the names of the persons discharged? A. No.

Q. There is no record of the person discharged? A. The judge's docket contains that.

Q. Just describe this book (referring to the book last mentioned)? A. This book is called "Statement concerning persons convicted by the Police Court of the City of Buffalo" and the book contains the following columns: "Date of Conviction," "Name of Convict," "Crime of Which Convicted," "Occupation," "Age," "Social Relations," "Place of Birth," "Degree of Instruction," "Parents," "Sentence," "Former Offense."

Q. Now, "Social Relations" means what? A. Married or single.

Q. "Degree of Instruction" means what? A. Whether they can read or write.

Q. Under the heading "Parents," what is entered? A. Both the parents, mother and father, whether both are living, or either one living.

Q. And under the head "Former Offense"? A. That states whether the fine has been paid or not. We don't use that column for showing whether there was a former offense or not.

Q. Is any inquiry made as to whether the prisoner convicted has been guilty of a former offense? A. Yes, that record is shown to the Judge during the trial, but we don't make a record of it in this book.

Q. Do you make a record of it in any book? A. None.

BY CHAIRMAN PAGE:

Q. Is it endorsed on the papers? A. Generally when an arrest is made, the policeman that makes the arrest, looks up the record at the police station to see whether he was ever convicted of a crime before, or how many crimes. Then when the case is called, the policeman puts that in evidence to show that he was convicted of so many crimes, but we don't take any record of the crimes.

Q. That is after conviction? A. During the taking of evidence.

Q. Not before conviction is it? A. Yes, during the trial. They might ask him if a man was ever convicted before, and if he says yes, they would ask him what the crime was.

BY MR. MAYER:

Q. Then there is nothing in the records of the Police Court which show previous convictions? A. Well, no more than say, for instance, this book showing that the man was convicted; that goes back for five or ten years, and if you will go through it, it would show whether he was convicted, but otherwise there would be no record.

Q. But there is no convenient record that would show the name of John Brown under the heading "Former Offense," there would be no entry to show whether John Brown had ever been convicted before? A. No.

Q. That would depend in your court practically entirely on police information? A. Yes.

Q. Are any methods of identification used here at all? A. The police use—they have the Bertillon system, and of course, photographs. The police generally come with the Bertillon clerk here, and any photographs or any other information they can get, and present it to our court.

Q. Do the police here use the finger print system? A. I believe they do.

Q. Do you know whether they do or not? A. I don't know positively.

Q. Have they used it in the court at all? A. I don't believe they have, not to my knowledge.

Q. Where are vagrants sent? A. To the penitentiary.

Q. Have you any—what is your law as to vagrants? A. they are generally tried in the morning courts.

Q. So very few of them come into your court? A. Very few, yes.

BY CHAIRMAN PAGE:

Q. Before passing from this, is there any index to that book? A. Yes, sir, there is an index.

BY MR. MAYER:

Q. Now, it would be perfectly easy for you to enter under the heading "Former Sentence" whether there was a former conviction or not, would it not? A. Yes.

Q. So that you could without difficulty make such a record? A. Well, we could to this extent: we would have to look up maybe for five or ten years, except the police have better information than we have.

Q. What I am getting at is this: suppose a man was convicted and the police adduced evidence before the Police Justice that he had been previously convicted, and give the nature of the conviction, the date and the court, you could make some such entry in your record books, could you not? A. Yes.

Q. Do you know whether that has ever been called to the attention of Judge Nash? A. Not to my knowledge.

Q. As you are both an attorney and clerk of the court, do you not think it would be a very valuable thing? A. I do.

Q. Now, what other book is kept? A. That book shows——

Q. Another book which shows "Fines Imposed"? A. Fines imposed and collected.

Q. How often do you remit fines to the City Treasurer? A. Every month.

Q. And you receive his receipt? A. Yes, sir.

Q. Who, if any one, audits the accounts of the Police Court? A. I think that is done by special audit committee appointed by the Mayor. The first year we were in there our books were examined—at least our predecessors' books were examined—but none has been there since.

Q. Well, this "Fines Imposed" Book is practically a blotter with the date of the imposition of the fine, the name of the person, and whether the fine was paid or not? A. Yes.

Q. What is this book that I now show you? A. That is the Probation Book.

Q. Who keeps that book? A. Why, I do.

Q. State the headings in this book. A. "Name,' "Age," "Charge," "Probation," "Probation to," "Date placed on Probation," "Date Discharged from Probation."

Q. Well, now there seem to be practically no entries under the heading "Date Discharged from Probation." Why is that—are all these people on probation? A. I will tell you. In our court there is no paid probation officer, and the keeping of this book was originated when Judge Nash went in there. The most of the people whom the people were placed on probation to were police captains.

Q. The words "Probation to" indicate the person with whom the prisoner is placed on probation? A. Yes, sir.

Q. Now George H. Prince is your deputy Supt. of the Poor? A. Yes.

Q. And many others of those are police captains? A. Yes, sir, the majority of them are police captains.

Q. How much probation work do they do? A. The police captains?

Q. Yes? A. Well, we have two cards when people are placed on probation. One is sent to the probation officer and the person that is placed on probation gets the other card.

BY CHAIRMAN PAGE:

Q. Are those the cards furnished by the State Probation Commission? A. I believe they are.

Q. Proceed? A. The captain is sent one of the cards stating that so and so has been placed on probation with him, and that he is supposed to report to that person once a week. generally for three months. Now in these cases, a number of times the police will send in a letter stating that so and so called, but we don't keep any special entry of them any more than that they were placed on probation to a certain party.

BY MR. MAYER:

Q. Now what happens with a prisoner who is placed on probation in regard to the final disposition—does the term run out with the police officer, or does the judge know about it or what? A. In some cases we do know about it, but in other cases we do not. Now in a great many cases, if the person does not report within a reasonable time we would receive word from these different persons to come into court and then when they came we would find out why they did not report.

Q. You really have no supervision? A. None.

Q. You have no paid probation officer? A. None.

Q. Has this gentleman, Mr. James Kane, acted as a probation officer? A. Yes.

Q. Does the judge require the police captains to report in writing? A. I don't know just what the judge has done on that. Since we came in we have tried to make this probation work as good as we could to start in from the first of January this year. We have a method where at the end of the time for which they are placed on probation we are to receive word that they are discharged, and they will be discharged by the judge at the court and we will state that in the right place.

Q. So that up to this time, the probationer when discharged did not necessarily appear before the Judge? A. No.

Q. So that the police really manage the probation as to adult offenders? A. Yes.

Q. And you have had no record of a consistent or systematic character in that regard? A. No.

Q. Is that right? A. That is right.

Q. And many times men have been discharged without ever going to court again? A. Yes.

Q. And without necessarily knowing that they were getting their discharge from the judge—isn't that so? A. Yes.

Q. So that it is not unlikely, you would say from your experience, that they think they are actually discharged by the police captains? A. Well, it might appear that way, but that is a case when a man would be placed on probation with a police captain and if he reported as he should do and as I feel he did, he was simply discharged because he has reported, and it would be the same whether it was the police captain or the judge.

Q. But you have had no reports from the police captains to the court as to what has actually taken place? A. No.

Q. The police captains have not been expected in any manner to positively dispose of these probationers in any way? A. Not that I know of.

Q. You don't know, I suppose, how many of these men have finally escaped? A. What do you mean?

Q. Well suppose a man was ordered to report to a police captain and then took the next train out of Buffalo? A. In that case I would say we would hear from the police captain, because the same day that the man is placed on probation we send a notice to the captain that so and so will report to him once a week.

Q. Suppose he reports for two or three weeks and then disappears? A. I would say that the captain would notify us.

Q. Are you sure? A. I am not sure, I cannot say I am sure.

BY CHAIRMAN PAGE:

Q. Do you know of any case where a captain has notified you where a probationer has disappeared? A. I don't know that, but I know of a number of instances where the police captains have written a letter stating that so and so who was on probation with them had reported regularly and should be discharged.

BY MR. MAYER:

Q. The probation system to police captains has really amounted to a reporting system? A. That is all as I understand it.

Q. There has been nothing brought to the attention of the judge as to the surroundings of the probationer, has there? A. I don't believe so.

Q. And, so far as you know, there has been no effort made beyond imposing a sort of penalty on the man to report to the police captain—is that about it? A. I think that is about it.

Q. Do you know whether Judge Nash has asked the Common Council for a paid officer for the Police Court? A. I can't just say. He might have, but I can't say positively.

BY COMMISSIONER WINTHROP:

Q. Does the police captain report in every case where the probationer is discharged? A. No.

Q. He does not? When he does report, is that report in writing or oral? A. Oral; that is, a number that I have seen have been in writing.

Q. Is that filed in court or is it attached to the papers in any way? A. No.

Q. It is not filed in the court? A. No.

BY MR. MAYER:

Q. Do you know whether the judge has entered upon some new system since the first of this year? A. Yes.

Q. What is it? A. The new system is about the discharge on that probation book; that is, after a man has reported for that length of time, that we are to receive word or we are to write to the different probation officers regarding how he has been there, and so on, and then we put here under "Date Discharged from Probation" such a date.

Q. When did you begin keeping this probation book? A. Why, shortly, before the first of this year.

Q. The first of this year? A. Yes.

Q. So that the entries beginning January fourth, 1908, were only recently made? A. Yes.

Q. And where did you make those entries from? A. We had little books we had used in the juvenile court—the probation officers have them. We used them. We took them from the other book and placed them in this.

Q. Are you at all sure that this probation book which you have produced here is complete as to the number of names? A. I don't believe it is.

Q. Then you have made up this book as best you can from hunting around among the papers in the court? A. Yes.

Q. And this book does not, in your opinion, correctly set forth the number of persons on probation? A. I don't believe it does—quite correctly.

Q. And therefore, of course, not the names or other data —is that correct? A. Yes.

Q. Have you observed the working of Judge Nash sufficiently to know what kind of people he places on probation in the adult court? A. Yes.

Q. What sort of people? By which I mean convicted of what crime or offense? A. Generally it might be petty larcenies, or may be a slight assault case—where it don't amount to much—disorderly persons—but still there was evidence enough to arrest him, and then from the evidence he felt that he should put him on probation—and non-support cases.

Q. What do you call disorderly persons? A. Those are under Section 899 of the Code—that beat their wives.

Q. Section 889; isn't it? A. 889 or 899; I am not sure which.

Q. Those persons who fail to support their wives? A. Yes.

Q. Does he put those on probation? A. Yes.

Q. Have you any record of how those worked out? A. No more than they are put on probation to one man, and that is Mr. Prince, who is one of the men in the office of the Poor Department.

Q. And that class of cases are placed on probation to Mr. Prince, and one of the things in that probation is, I assume, to collect the money which he is ordered to pay to the wife?

A. Yes; and to see that he supports his family in the regular way and goes around on good conduct.

BY COMMISSIONER WINTHROP:

Q. Would the commitment papers show, whether or not, the person convicted was placed on probation? A. Yes.

Q. That would be stamped or marked on the commitment papers? A. You mean a commitment? Well, for probation there is no commitment made out, but the judge's docket would show whether the man was placed on probation or not—that is, the book that he tries his cases from, where the entries are all made.

BY CHAIRMAN PAGE:

Q. Is there any probation order entered? A. No; it just states that he has placed on probation So and So.

Q. He enters that on the papers? A. Yes.

BY COMMISSIONER WINTHROP:

Q. On the papers? A. In the docket—in the judge's docket—the police court docket. Whatever becomes of each case is marked by him, whether the man has been fined or whatever becomes of him.

BY CHAIRMAN PAGE:

Q. There must be a complaint or something on which a man is arraigned in court? A. Yes.

Q. There is no endorsement placed upon those papers which are filed away, I suppose? A. No.

BY COMMISSIONER WINTHROP:

Q. Is this judge's docket that you refer to one of the records of the court? A. Yes.

BY MR. MAYER:

Q. Have you that with you? A. I did not bring it.

Q. You can get that, of course? A. Yes.

Q. Now, in your book "Fines Imposed" I note you have the following entries: "General Fund," so much; "Police Pension Fund," so much; "Forest, Fish and Game," so much, and "Cruelty to Animals," so much? A. Yes.

Q. What is the "General Fund?" A. The "General Fund" is the full amount received, except the "Police Pension Fund" and the "Cruelty to Animals" fund, which are taken from the total amounts received.

Q. What goes to the "Police Pension Fund"? A. Carrying a gun without a permit—and then, under "Cruelty to Animals," just cruelty to animals. There are two special funds and we divide them up and send them up to the Comptroller.

Q. Do you do the dividing? A. Yes.

Q. And "Forest, Fish and Game" is where the penalty goes to the State for that class of cases? A. Yes; we send that through the Comptroller in the same way.

Q. Have you stated all the different funds into which these fines go? A. Yes.

Q. Have you any medical society transactions· in that court? A. Yes.

Q. Where do those fines go? A. Well, in those cases they are out of our jurisdiction. We hold them for the Grand Jury, where they waive the examination and, of course, they go before the Grand Jury.

Q. The judge has not power to try those cases? A. No.

Q. Is that so, with regards to transactions for violations of the Dental law? A. I believe that goes in the same way.

We see from the complaint that it is a violation of a certain law, and when we look up that law we can see whether it is a felony, and what the punishment is.

Q. How about cases of cruelty to children? A. I believe that comes under Section 56 of the Code of Criminal Procedure. In those cases we have exclusive jurisdiction; there are thirty-seven subdivisions.

Q. Are those cases tried by Judge Nash? A. Yes.

Q. Have you seen any of those cases tried? A. Yes.

Q. What becomes of the fines imposed in those cases? A. They go in that book—they go into those three funds. If they don't come under "cruelty to animals" or "carrying guns without a permit" they go into the general fund.

Q. Do you know whether the Society for the Prevention of Cruelty to Children gets any part of the fine. A. I can't answer that.

Q. You report that to the State Treasurer as a part of your general fund? A. Yes.

Q. Let me ask you this question, if you know: Has the police justice any power to order the release of a person after he is committed to the penitentiary—have you a workhouse here? A. I don't believe here; except, may be, in a disorderly case. I want to make a statement about this book. The report that I sent to the council that you see in this list was taken from the Judge's docket. That is exact, making the total amount of $140; but this book—the probation book—has not been fully written up to date.

Q. Have you received any instruction or advice from the State Probation Commission? A. I have not.

Q. Do you know whether the judge has? A. I cannot say.

THOMAS H. BOORMAN, called as a witness, being duly sworn, testified as follows:

BY MR. MAYER:

Q. What is your position in the Police Court? A. The title of my position is Deposition Clerk, but I have been acting in the capacity of general clerk of the court—as clerk in general of the records, and the like of that.

Q. When did you enter on your work as a clerk of this court? A. January, 1908.

Q. When you entered the court was there any alphabetical index? A. No, sir.

Q. Have you established such an index? A. Yes, sir.

Q. Have you it with you? A. Yes, sir.

Q. Will you let use see it please? A. (producing book) This is an index—not alone an index, but it shows the names of every person who is arraigned in the police court and shows the disposition of the case in the front part of the book; shows the fines, both paid and unpaid, and it is indexed from the front of the book over on to the back by letters; that is, we have all the names indexed under letters.

Q. That is, the names of the defendants? A. And every person brought into the police court, no matter what disposition has been made of the case.

Q. You mean every person who has been brought in as being charged with something? A. Yes, sir.

Q. Now, under the heading of this book, will you state the headings in the book? A. The "Name of the Person Arraigned in the Police Court" and the "Charge" made against them by the police officer; the "Disposition of the Case" after being arraigned before the magistrate, and the "Fine;" that means if the fine was not paid the man was committed to the penitentiary, and the "Fine Paid" and a "Docket Number" for each alleged defendant.

Q. And then it has an alphabetical index in the back part of the book—the name of the defendant. A. Yes, sir; with the docket number after the man's name.

Q. The docket number? What is that? A. The police justice's docket.

Q. Now, for instance, the first entry in this book appears to be January 4th—"Henry Zimmerman, assault, third degree, discharged, 6—D." What does the number "6" and the letter "D" mean? A. That means the page of the Judge's docket. We run the index A, B, C, D, E, and the like of that, and, of course, each page number begins with the head.

Q. Have you charge of this probation book? A. Mr. McCue has handled this.

Q. Now, in preparing the annual report for the council, do you classify the character of the offences—that is to say, so many assaults, so many petit larcenies, and so on? A. No, sir.

Q. Would that be perfectly feasible to do? A. It would be on the convictions; yes, sir.

Q. Do you think that would be a desirable thing in the way of obtaining correct statistics? A. I think it would be a very good idea.

Q. Now, do you think, with the addition of that classification and the proper keeping of the probation book that any other books would be necessary than those you have, in order to furnish full information at any time to those who were entitled to know? A. I think that as the conditions are now in police court, with reference to the probation system, it is not what Judge Nash intended; it is not as he intended it. As to the probation work in police court, Judge Nash has stated that he wants to have that, and his intention is to have it run along the same as he has it in the juvenile court, but he has given a great deal of time to probation matters in the juvenile court—more than he has in police court; but he intended to do so at the commencement of this year, and that is in the way of keeping of a record of a detailed character and on the line of the card system, or envelope system, and that is the system that he intends installed in the police court.

Q. That he is in entire sympathy with the probation system? A. Entirely, sir; yes, sir.

Q. Do you know whether he asked the Common Council for a probation officer—a paid probation officer? A. He has asked the Common Council for a paid probation officer, and the court has a paid adult probation officer; but Judge Nash when he took office, of course, that had not passed the Common Council; but later on in the year he was allowed by the Common Council, and Mr. Kane was appointed, with the title of "adult probation officer," and Judge Nash has used Mr. Kane as a court attendant in addition to the work of probation officer—Mr. Kane has been acting in the capacity of a court attendant and as a messenger to the judge, and in fact as a general utility man around the court, and he has not had time to devote to probation matters. In that way it seems that he has depended a great deal upon volunteers.

Q. Most of the probation cases have been to police captains; haven't they? A. Well, we have had a man from the Y. M. C. A. He has had some of the adults, and Miss Smith has taken care of them.

Q. Who is she? A. She is a probation officer. She has been a probation officer for the past fifteen years in the city of Buffalo, but I don't believe she received any salary; that I am not sure of.

Q. She does not receive any salary from the city? A. I don't think she does.

Q. Does she represent any particular faith? A. I believe she represents the Catholic faith; but I don't know as the lines are drawn entirely too fine.

Q. I merely meant whether she represented some association that was interested in prisoners of a particular faith? A. That I don't know; I can't explain that.

Q. Mr. McCue, as I understood him, draws the deposition? A. Yes, sir.

Q. Do you draw any depositions? A. Occasionally.

Q. What books do you keep besides the one just referred to with the alphabetical index? A. There is a book that we call "the warrant book," which is a record of the warrants issued, and after the deposition has been made and the warrant made out, at the adjournment of court the warrants are sent to the Police Department, and the depositions are recorded by me in the warrant book and filed, and undoubtedly the warrants are sent to the various precincts by Police Headquarters, and when returned they come to me. When the officer brings the prisoner to police court he comes with the warrant to me, which he has signed, and I get the deposition from the package where we have them filed in the court and turn to the record book showing the precinct in which the warrant has been served. The warrant, with the deposition, is turned over to the stenographer, and the particulars contained in the warrant are entered in the Judge's docket, and then, after disposition is made of the case, the warrant is returned to me with whatever disposition in the case shown, and it is filed by me as a record of the court.

Q. You, I suppose, agree with Mr. McCue's description of that court room? A. Yes, sir, and I think I can make it stronger than he did, and he made it strong enough. I think the ventilation is simply awful. He stated that we have a door; we have three windows. They would come just near where the witnesses stand; where the audience is there is no window, and there is absolutely no ventilation whatever.

Q. Is your court room large enough for the business? A. No, sir; it should be twice as large to make it convenient for the people in there.

Q. What time does Judge Nash open court? A. Nine-thirty.

Q. What is his custom as to sitting there? A. Well, the judge has been holding court until every case on the calendar was cleaned up.

Q. You mean, without intermission? A. Without intermission; there may have been one or two exceptions.

Q. I mean his general custom? A. His general custom is that.

Q. That carries him to what time? A. There are times when it is one o'clock, or two o'clock; we have been there as late as two-thirty or three o'clock.

Q. Now, you have the juvenile court on what days? A. Tuesday and Friday afternoons.

Q. And that is in that other building connected with the morgue? A. Yes, sir.

Q. What do you think of that building for the juvenile court? A. I think it is no fit place to hold a juvenile court.

In fact, we feel over there as if we were intruders; we are simply being allowed accommodation from the medical examiner.

Q. Is it a proper place for children to be in proximity to?
A. I don't think it is.

Q. How does giving the warrants to the police work out? Do they promptly execute the warrants? A. Yes, sir; if not they are held for a length of time, and, of course, in the case of a misdemeanor, they investigate to find out as to where the defendant or the complainant is to be found, and then the officer brings the warrant to me. In fact, they make that notification on the warrant, signed by themselves.

Q. Do you send those warrants to one headquarters or to various precincts? A. To headquarters.

Q. To Police Headquarters? A. Yes, sir.

Q. And the police officials there distribute them? A. Yes, sir.

Q. Do they distribute them to the different station houses or to officers at headquarters for execution? A. To the different stations.

Q. Depending on where you suppose the defendant lives? A. Yes, sir.

Q. And there is no difficulty in promptly executing the warrants? A. No, sir. There is one thing that I would like to state in regard to our criminal record in the police court. While we have not a record that shows "John Brown, second offence or third offence," if a prisoner is brought before the judge—say "John Brown"—and he is charged with petit larceny, or assault, or grand larceny, and the officer states that this man has a record, since Judge Nash has been in office he will turn to me or to Mr. McCue and give us the name of the defendant and ask us to look up and see whether or not this man has been in police court on a previous occasion. And I find in this index that we have started we can look it up inside of two or three minutes, by using the docket page for each man. I turn to the judge's docket, if it be an old one, and put the case immediately before the judge, showing what disposition was made of the defendant when arraigned in the police court on the previous charge, and, of course, the stenographer has the minutes in every case.

Q. But the question that I asked was directed to this—I will state it so you will understand it—that for proper statistical information for some use somewhere, for a commission of this character or otherwise, that an entry as to whether it was more than the first offence might be of great value in determining the character of the crimes that were committed in any jurisdiction? A. That is entirely kept by the Police Department, that criminal record.

Q. But the Police Department does not always keep an exact record of convictions in any one year, classified by years; does it? A. We have had prisoners charged with petit larceny, second offense, and the like of that; that would be the charge against them.

Q. Do you know whether you have any law here such as prevails in New York city, whereby persons convicted of vagrancy or disorderly conduct, or disorderly person—I have forgotten which—disorderly person, I think—whereby certain penalties attach automatically for the first offense. A. In non-support?

Q. No; in vagrancy. A. We have not had much experience with that—vagrancy.

Q. The morning justices would know about that? A. Yes,
sir.

BY COMMISSIONER HAMILTON:

Q. The judge's docket shows the nationality of the person arrested; does it not? A. No, sir.

Q. Do you keep any record of the nationality? A. When
a conviction is had we do.

Q. That is entered in what? A. In the ''statement of convictions.'' If a man is convicted we docket that in our statement of persons convicted.

Q. Then you have these statistics as to all convictions?
A. No, sir; not in every one of them.

Q. You have the nationality of all persons convicted?
A. Yes, sir.

Q. Do those figures show in the annual report of the
court? A. Not from police court; it does not.

Q. This index here is entered up to the 12th. What is
your custom with regard to posting this index? A. The
custom is to post it every day, but the bookbinder was a little late in getting it out for nineteen hundred and eight.
We just used the one book for the year, and that was ordered before the first of January, but he was a little late
in turning it over to us.

Q. And these figures in the book here showing under the
prisoners' names entries for the 28th and 29th of January
are simply cases where you have posted to the back of the
book and have not posted to the front part. A. That is
where we have posted only the back; that is on account of being a little bit behind in the work.

LAWRENCE J. COLLINS, being called as witness and duly sworn, testified as follows:

BY MR. MAHER:

Q. Are you an attorney at law? A. Yes, sir.

Q. And how long have you been such? A. In 1902 I was admitted to the Bar.

Q. In the absence of Judge Nash have you been acting as police justice? A. I have been appointed by the Mayor to act in the absence of the Judge.

Q. How much have you acted all together? A. I have been appointed on three occasions. The first occasion I served two days, during an illness; the second occasion I served during the month of July, when he was on his summer vacation, and this is the third appointment. I have now served—this is the commencement of my third week.

Q. Is it the custom in the police court to have a special day set aside for hearing bastardy cases, alleged seduction under promise of marriage, and other cases in regard to the sexual relations; is that correct? A. It is the custom to hold those cases on Wednesday afternoons.

Q. What is the theory for setting aside a special day for that purpose? A. So as to exclude the public from the hearing of this vile testimony.

Q. I assume that you agree with the testimony already given as to the unfitness of the police court room? A. Yes, sir.

Q. Have you ever sat in the juvenile court? A. Yes, sir.

Q. What is your opinion of that sort of place to try children? A. I think it is a most unfit place to bring those little children to. It is right up against the morgue—the waiting room is rather like an icebox. The waiting room is a very small place, I should say about 8 by 8, and there is a door to the morgue leading into the dead house, and that is very bad accommodation for the children. In the summer time they wait on the streets, but in the winter time they have to pile into that little waiting room.

Q. From your experience, which you have just stated, have any suggestions occurred to you for improvement or change in the practise and procedure of the police court? A. Yes, sir.

Q. Will you be good enough to state them, in your own way to the Commission? A. I notice that in application for bail in cases of a felony the Police Department, the Desk Sergeant or the Captain has power to bail in cases of misdemeanor, but they have not power to take bail in cases of felony. No one has that power but the judges of the Court of, the Supreme Court Judges and a Police Magistrate. The people all over the city seldom think of the Supreme Court Judges when the opportunity offers. If some business man is taken in on a felony he has heard of the right of the Supreme Court Judges to take bail and he gets his law and applies to them; but the vast number of people charged with a felony will wake up a police magistrate at all hours of the night; they will come to his home and ring and ring at four o'clock in the morning. I would suggest that the jailor be given power to take bail, and that the clerk of the police court be given power to take bail, to admit to bail. The clerk of the court is a lawyer usually and is so at the present time, and a competent man, and as a usual thing we have intelligent, educated, clever men, holding the position of jailor. In fact, the men are placed in their custody.

Q. What is the jailor—is it one man? A. Yes; he serves as an assistant to the Sheriff.

Q. Is he practically like a warden? A. Yes, sir.

Q. You are now referring to one particular person? A. One person who stands at the head of our county jail.

Q. And he is an assistant to the Sheriff? A. An assistant to the Sheriff.

Q. And in the Sheriff's department? A. Yes, sir; the Sheriff appoints him.

Q. Is he at the jail at night? A. All the time; he lives there; his living apartments are there.

Q. Your idea would be that, in that way, there would be an additional person whose specific place of abode at night was known? A. Yes, sir. Now one has to depend on the courtesy of the jailor or the police captain and desk sergeant to telephone to one's relatives or friends that they are locked up, charged with felony. Nobody can get them out; they can't be gotten out, except on an order from a police judge. They are told they will have to get an order from a police judge. They start around to find a police judge—usually that information is given out at the police station. They go around and inquire until they find where he lives, and they will stick at the door until they get him up.

Q. You have had some recent experience, I assume? A. Yes, sir; unpleasant ones.

Q. What chance has a man who is arrested of communicating with his relatives or friends? A. During my last sitting in the police court I came across two cases where that privilege was denied the accused. The first case was the case of a boy. It is true, he was a worthless fellow; a vagrant known as a bum, a hanger-on in the Tenderloin district.

Q. You have such a district here? A. Yes, as in all cities. When he was arraigned before me he stated to me that he had been held seven days, and this was his first arraignment. Of course, as a lawyer, that shocked me.

Q. Did you investigate it? A. I asked the officer if it was true, and he said yes. I said, "Why did you hold him? Don't you know he has a right to immediate arraignment? Don't you know you must bring him in the next morning after his arrest?" He said that a job had been pulled off over in the Tenderloin—by "job" he meant a burglary— and they couldn't get any clue to it, and figured that this fellow hung around there and would know about it; that they had tried to fasten the thing on him, but had been unable to do it. Another case: An intelligent, clever man was arrested and he was arraigned the very next morning. He had asked them to telephone to his people or his friends, and that privilege was denied him. That man also had on his person a large sum of money that he wanted to deposit as cash bail, and the police denied him that privilege.

Q. Was he arrested for a felony? A. Yes.

Q. I guess they could not take bail in a felony? A. No; the only thing they could do for him was to telephone for some friend to go to a police magistrate; that privilege was denied him.

Q. At the station houses are there any messengers? A. The police reserves act as messengers. Of course, they don't have to do that. I believe they do under the code. I think they do have to act.

Q. In certain instances? A. Yes.

CHAIRMAN PAGE—That is, only to send for counsel.

Q. After a person has been committed by a police justice

where is he taken? A. To the jail. You mean committed for further hearing?

Q. No; finally committed? A. To the work house, called the penitentiary.

Q. You have no place of detention in connection with the police court? A. Just that little room that you saw. You mean, waiting for the afternoon to come to take the prisoner away?

Q. Yes. A. We have a very small room which is wholly inadequate. That is a purely temporary purpose—for half an hour or so.

Q. And there is no prison attached to the police court? A. No.

Q. Now, suppose that you or Judge Nash fined a defendant five dollars, and in default five days—where does the defendant go? A. To the work house.

Q. Is the work house in the city of Buffalo? A. Yes, sir.

Q. How far is that from the court house? A. I should say a mile or mile and a half.

Q. And the defendant is taken there at once? A. No; at the adjournment of the court the van driver comes with the van—the Black Maria—and takes all the prisoners that are to go.

Q. When you say "The adjournment of the court" do you mean once a day or twice a day? A. Once a day.

Q. At the end of the day? A. At the close of the calendar.

Q. You telephone to the work house authorities? A. He comes as a matter of custom.

Q. Suppose you have committed him there, say, at ten

o'clock in the morning, because he has no money to pay the fine; what means has that man of communicating with his relatives or friends before the van comes? A. The clerks in the court are always very courteous in that respect and invariably help the man out. The van driver will drive to the man's home. I had a case the other day where a man said to me that he had a room three blocks from there. I had fined him fifty dollars, and he said if I would send somebody with him, that he had the fifty dollars in his trunk. I asked the van driver if he would take him there, and he said "Sure."

Q. So you don't charge anything in the city of Buffalo for sending such messages? A. We receive no compensation from the prisoner.

Q. And you have no messengers who make their living out of them? A. No, no; that is unknown here.

BY CHAIRMAN PAGE:

Q. When a man is convicted is he put back among those that are still awaiting trial? A. No; the men awaiting trial are alone in one place, enclosed by a wire cage, and as their case is called they come up, the officer in charge goes over, opens the cage, takes the prisoner and brings him before the court. After the examination, if he is convicted or if he is held for the Grand Jury, the officer in charge takes him back of where the judge sits to this small room that I say is so inadequate. Back there there is another cage, somewhat stronger than the one outside, where he is locked up and kept there awaiting the adjournment of the court, when he will be taken away by the van driver. If he is held for the Grand Jury he is taken away immediately by the officer who has charge of the case. In cases of misdemeanor, where the police magistrate has jurisdiction to determine, those convicted persons must wait back in that small room until the adjournment of court, when they are taken to the penitentiary or work house to serve out their sentence.

BY MR. MAYER:

Q. Now, I think I had asked you for any suggestions which occurred to you from your experience, and you were relating some of them, and I interrupted you. Will you be good enough to continue? A. Another suggestion that I would make is that a police magistrate should be given power ultimately to determine cases of burglary in the third degree; not necessarily car burglary. The great majority of the cases arraigned in the police court are from the railroad section—boys taken in as car burglars. A great many of them are attempts at car burglary, where they just get the seal broken, do not succeed in getting the door open; do not get at the bulk of the freight. Now, in the police courts they get a thorough hearing. Usually they have counsel and the whole case is threshed out, and all the police magistrates can do at the end is to hold them for the Grand Jury. They are taken over to the Grand Jury, and in due time the Grand Jury sits. The whole thing is threshed out again on the part of the complainant before the Grand Jury, and indictment is returned, and a week or two afterwards the District Attorney is ready to go on, and the whole thing is threshed out again and then ultimately determined. I believe in these small cases the police magistrate should have that power. It would relieve the county of a great expense; it would give the District Attorney time to get down to the more important business of his office and not take it up with these small cases. In this county the greater part of the

District Attorney's time is taken up prosecuting these car burglars.

Q. This is a great railroad center? A. Yes, sir.

Q. And you have many such cases? A. A great number; a great many.

Q. In order to determine just such a question, would not statistics be of great importance to show how many you have got? A. I presume they would.

Q. There has been no method of classifying crimes in annual reports or for statistical purposes; has there? A. I cannot answer that.

Q. What other suggestion have you? A. To relieve the burden of work on the police court I would suggest that such small cases as disorderlies, failure to support a wife, that the lower court be given jurisdiction of these cases.

Q. You mean the morning justices? A. The morning justices.

Q. Do you believe in the morning justice system? A. I think it works well here. We have three very competent men.

Q. I mean the system, irrespective of the men? A. I think it is good.

Q. You think that is better than having an increased number of police courts? A. Well, it might be better to have two police courts or have an additional police magistrate, with the powers that the morning justice has, and that, of course, would relieve the present situation and throw the burden over partly on the additional justice.

Q. Have you ever acted as a morning justice? A. No; I have never acted as a morning justice. I have never been in the morning court.

Q. What is the salary paid here to a Police Justice? A. $5,000.

Q. Has anything else occurred to you? A. That is all that occurs to be at present except to reiterate and repeat that suggestion on the bail. Speaking as an attorney outside of my experience as a Police Magistrate I do that. Some decent fellow, wrongfully accused of a felony may be arrested and locked up on Saturday afternoon and held until his arraignment on Monday, although he may have people in position to give bail for him. He cannot find a Supreme Court Justice—they often go to the country over Sunday, and the Police Magistrate may have gone visiting somewhere, and I say for that reason there should be somebody in a big city like this to whom a lawyer or a prisoner can go and get bail.

Q. So it practically works out that in the great mass of cases the Police Magistrate is the only person to whom the lawyers look to make an application for bail? A. Yes, sir; the great bulk of the people do not know that they have a right to apply to the Supreme Court.

Q. Have you had any opportunity to observe these cases of non-support of wives by husbands? A. Yes.

Q. Have you had any chance to observe the working of the probation system? A. Well, no, on account of my small experience; but in the cases arraigned before me when I am satisfied that the defendant is guilty and ought to be committed, before I pronounce a commitment, I ask the woman if she has any means of support, any revenues, moneys, if her brothers live in the city, or her parents, and will give her money, if this man is sent to the workhouse. In a great majority of the cases the answer is no, that there would be no need of money if he would only stop drinking. I give the man the pledge and make him promise that he will stop drinking, and instead of committing him, which would work an injustice, I put him on probation with his wife, and adjourn the case for two weeks, and ask her to come and notify the Police Magistrate if he does not keep his word. I think that is a good system.

Q. Do you find they make good probation officers? A. I think they are the best.

Q. They promptly report to the Court I suppose failure of the probationer to report to the probation officer? A. Of the production of the coin.

Q. Do you make an order then? A. No, I leave the case open.

Q. Do you tell the man what he shall pay to his wife? A. I am glad you mention that.\ The custom has arisen in this city, and it has been a custom of long standing, for a police court magistrate to allow in cases where he finds the defendant guilty $3.00 a week. Now, I think that is absolutely ridiculous. A man will come in there who is earning $100.00 a month, and to say that woman I can only tell your husband to give you $3.00 a week to my mind is ridiculous.

Q. There is no warrant in law for it. A. I don't believe there is. I have examined the law, and the law says that he shall be directed to give according to his means.

Q. Has that been a long established custom? A. Ever since I have been at the bar.

Q. That amount being fixed quite irrespective of the inquiry into the means of the man? A. Yes.

Q. You don't follow that yourself I assume? A. Oh, no.

Q. Then, as I understand you, you see and strongly favor a plan for keeping a man out of the workhouse and make him support his family. A. Yes, sir.

Q. Are those cases increasing in the city of Buffalo? A. Well, I don't know, I am not in a position to say that. Of course in the poor times a great many cases arise. You will size a man up to be a good-meaning fellow who would work if he could get work to do.

Q. Do you have many cases of boys between 16 and 21? A. Many.

Q. In comparison with your total. A. Not a great many —they are younger than that. The juvenile offenders are 14 or 15.

Q. Let me for the information of the Commission take up the various institutions to which commitments are made and ask you what character of cases or persons are sent there? A. The Asylum of Our Lady of Refuge, The Ingleside Home, Western House of Refuge, Albion, Training School for Girls at Hudson, St. Agnes Training School for Girls.

BY MR. MAYER:

Q. Where is the Asylum of Our Lady of Refuge? A. Here in the City of Buffalo.

Q. What kind of cases are sent there? A. Wayward girls, usually Catholic girls.

Q. Under or over 16 years of age? A. Any age.

Q. And the Ingleside Home? A. The Ingleside Home is an institution similar to the Good Shepherd, as we call Our Lady of Refuge, where Protestant wayward girls are sent.

Q. Of any age? A. Of any age.

Q. Western House of Refuge, Albion, that is a State institution, is it not? A. That is a State institution.

Q. What does that take? A. I am not familiar with that.

Q. Training School for Girls, at Hudson, is a State institution? A. Yes; I am not familiar with that either.

Q. St. Agnes Training School for Girls? A. A place where wayward children are sent who have no homes; little children who are brought in as vagrants, found down in the Tenderloin district, are brought in and committed to St. Agnes; it is a branch of Our Lady of Refuge, I am informed, and is in the City of Buffalo.

Q. Is there a permanent Salvation Army home in this city? A. There is some kind of a home here, I don't know whether it is permanent. Do you know, Mr. Wade?

MR. WADE: I don't know whether it is permanent or not.

BY MR. MAYER:

Q. What cases are sent to the Erie County Penitentiary by the Police Court as distinguished from the Erie County Jail? A. Convictions, persons convicted.

Q. Go to the penitentiary? A. In the great majority of cases where the Police Magistrate has the power to ultimately determine, as in misdemeanors, the convicted person goes to the workhouse of the city of Buffalo. The jail is merely a place of detention. It is not a place for convicted persons.

Q. I see, commitments are there made by the Police Justice? A. Awaiting trial.

Q. In his capacity as an examining or committing magistrate? A. Yes.

Q. Did you hear what was said before the Commission in regard to the necessity of a detention place for children under 16? A. No, sir; I did not. I know there is.

Q. In a word, it was urged that such a place should be established? A. Yes.

Q. What is your view as to that? A. Most assuredly such a place should be established. Some of these little chaps are so wayward that they won't come to the session of the juvenile court when they are directed. Those cases I will say are exceptional, but they ought not to be at all.

Q. How about the original arrest of the child; as the Commission understands there is no place where that child can be kept pending arraignment? A. There is no place to keep that child, no. He is brought into the police station and the mother or parent is sent for and notified the child is under arrest and that he is to appear the following Tuesday or Friday, as the case may be, at three o'clock at the Juvenile Court. Now, the parent is expected to produce the child there; the police officer does not go after it, the parent is expected to produce it.

BY CHAIRMAN PAGE:

Q. Suppose the child has no parents, or the parent cannot be found? A. Well, in the great majority of cases they have a parent, but in a case where there is nobody looking after the child, why I presume the police would detain that child.

BY MR. MAYER:

Q. Even if there is a parent, it is some period of time, some hours pass by and the child, as I understand, is detained in the police station? A. I think so.

Q. From your experience then you join in the——A. Need of a detention hall.

Q. In the recommendation of a detention place? A. Oh, yes.

Q. Now, would you give to the Police Justices any greater jurisdiction than you have stated? A. The only things that occur to me from my limited experience there, is this vast number of burglaries.

Q. Would you give the same jurisdiction that is given to

the Court of Special Sessions in the City of New York of trying all misdemeanors, except libel, and—— A. Yes, I would suggest that, too. I did not think of that.

Q. Would you authorize the police justice to try violations of the liquor tax law? A. Where they are declared misdemeanors?

Q. Yes. A. Yes, I would give the police justice jurisdiction over all misdemeanors.

Q. Would that include cases of disorderly houses, Section 322 of the Penal Code? A. Yes.

Q. You have not that jurisdiction now as to disorderly houses? A. No, I think wherever the penalty is over six months, or fifty dollars fine we have no jurisdiction to ultimately determine. We simply have jurisdiction to discharge or hold for the Grand Jury.

Q. Well, do you think it would be extending the power of the police justice too much to give him disorderly house cases and excise cases? A. I don't think so, if you take away some of the petty matter; of course the suggestion then would come up for additional help, an additional justice, giving him the additional work. Before I get through, I must not forget that, I want to recommend that, in the matter of these warrants, it would be a great saving of time if some arrangement could be made whereby the clerk could hear the complaints and issue the warrants, the magistrate knows nothing about it, because he hears the statement of the complainant and when the case comes on before him he is rather biased, he had heard one side of the case already. Not only that feature of it, which is a bad feature, but it would be the means of saving of time if the complainant could go direct to the clerk, because he will go there ultimately.

Q. Why should you not adopt a system such as prevails in New York, of the complainant going to the clerk, stating fully his story to the clerk, and the clerk drawing a complaint or information, and then the man swearing to it before the magistrate and the magistrate issuing the warrant; could you not adopt that system without any further legislation? A. That would take up a lot of time, too.

Q. It would only take up the clerk's time, wouldn't it? A. No, the clerk would go over, when he had finished his deposition with the complainant, and say, "This is the fellow who swore to this, this is his signature," and you are trying a case there, you are hearing something; you have got to stop and swear that fellow to that information.

Q. Well, then, that condition is created to some extent because you try cases where you have final jurisdiction to—— A. Yes.

Q. To find guilty or not guilty? A. Yes.

Q. In your practice do you examine all the cases before an order is made to the clerk to issue a warrant? A. Yes; the custom is, at 9:30 the court opens, and when the magistrate takes his seat he announces that he will hear all applications for warrants, and most every day about twenty persons will line up, and the magistrate will listen to each tale and out of that total he will reject about one-half. About half of them have a *prima facie* complaint enough to issue a warrant on, and he will hear their story and tell them to step over to the clerk and get a warrant—assault third, larceny second; he will tell the applicant what to tell the clerk; and the clerk hears, he will hear it out more in detail, and if he disagrees with the magistrate he will come back and suggest something that perhaps the complainant did not tell the magistrate.

Q. Where you are not satisfied that a warrant should issue, but you feel that an inquiry should be made, you conduct a John Doe proceeding? A. Yes, we usually get the name and address of the complainant and the person complained against and we issue what we call a summons.

Q. Do you call it a summons or a subpœna. A. A subpœna. We send it to the police station, near which that person resides, the police go over and serve it gratis, and if the service is made, the police will notify the complainant that he has made the service, and directs them both to appear. The complainant knows he is to appear at nine-thirty in the morning. After the applications for warrants and after the call for adjournment cases, we then take up those cases.

Q. Well, now, do you think that if a summons were issued, provided it were legal, that that would simplify that procedure? A. Well, it would have the same effect, there would be no difference between the issuance, to my mind, that I can see between the issuance of the summons and of the subpœna.

Q. Then the purpose of your John Doe proceeding is to inquire whether a crime has been committed? A. To inquire as to whether a warrant should issue.

Q. Are there many arrests made in the city of Buffalo for minor offenses? A. Yes.

Q. I mean are there many arrests for violation of corporation ordinances? A. Well, that would not come before the Police Justice.

Q. You would not know? A. No.

Q. What minor matters come before you every day? A. Assault third, a great many of them, fights, and petit larcenies, a great many petit larcenies, and assault third degree.

Q. But all this other business, of corporation ordinances and drunkards—intoxication, and the like, comes before the morning justices? A. The morning justice.

Q. And do the women who are charged with some offense in connection with the social evil, come before the morning justice? A. The morning justice.

Q. In the matter of taking minutes, does a stenographer take minutes in every case? A. Full and complete minutes, the same as in the Supreme Court.

Q. In every case of every kind and description? A. Everything.

Q. Whether it be an examination where the justice sits in his capacity as a magistrate, or whether it be a trial where he sits as a court of special sessions? A. He takes full and complete minutes.

BY MR. WINTHROP:

Q. Of complaints, too? A. Oh, no, not these preliminary complaints to see whether a warrant may issue, but after the warrant issues and the accused is arraigned before the magistrate, the stenographer takes full minutes of everything that transpires.

BY MR. MAYER:

Q. Now, take a case where examination is had and the police justice holds, does the stenographer forward a copy of the minutes to the District Attorney or are those minutes only furnished on request? A. I believe on request, we furnish a report immediately that same day to the District Attorney of every one held, the name, just as the Code requires, I believe, the name of every witness, residence, charge and whether or not the defendant waived or made a statement.

Q. Do you keep a record of the attorneys who appear in a case? A. I do and I believe Judge Nash does.

Q. Where is that record kept? A. Especially in felonies. It is kept right in the docket.

Q. Right in the judge's docket? A. Right in the judge's docket; not both attorneys, but my custom is merely to show that the defendant was protected. Of course, I advise them of their rights and then, to show that they were fully protected, I note the counsel who appeared for them.

Q. Do you think it would be advisable or assist in the proper administration of the work of this court if a representative of the District Attorney's office was in attendance each day? A. Yes, it would save the police justice a lot of work. The police justice in very, very many cases has to act as lawyer.

Q. As prosecutor practically? A. As prosecutor.

Q. He must bring out the people's case? A. Bring out the case; frequently when I am there, I act for both parties if they have no counsel, and bring out the facts I think should be brought out from both parties.

Q. Do you believe it would get better results if the people were represented by an assistant of the District Attorney? A. Yes.

Q. Is there anything else you think of, Judge Collins? A. I guess that is about all.

BY COMMISSIONER FRANCIS:

Q. What is the average penalty inflicted in these burglary cases when they are finally disposed of? A. Well, they are mostly all young men and they are sent to Elmira on an indeterminate sentence from the Supreme Court. In a great many of the cases sentence is suspended after all this work;

after the time of the Police Magistrate has been taken up, the time of the Grand Jury taken up and the time of the District Attorney taken up, sentence is suspended.

Q. Would you say in fifty per cent. of the cases sentence was suspended? A. I would not say fifty per cent., but I would say in twenty-five per cent. anyway.

BY COMMISSIONER WINTHROP:

Q. Do you keep a record of the subpœnas issued in these John Doe proceedings? A. No, not that I—I am quite certain, no.

Q. Do you keep a record of the proceedings instituted? A. No, in the subpœna that I issue, while I am there, I do it for my own information rather than issue a warrant against a man, where I think it should not be issued. For my own information I issue the subpœna and get the defendant in and let him listen to the complainant. In a great many of the cases, after the warrant is served and after persons have spent the night in the jail or the police station, the complainant fails to show up. In many cases they are taken for spite; absolutely no foundation.

Q. Well, then you don't know whether the subpœna has been served or not? A. Oh, yes; the police will notify us if they do not serve it.

Q. If it has been served and the person does not appear, you don't keep a record of that? A. No, then I immediately issue the warrant.

Q. I mean, if you don't keep any record of the subpœna issued, how can you tell whether it is obeyed or not? A. Well, the complainant keeps pretty close after you.

Q. It depends upon whether the complainant reminds you or not? A. Yes.

BY COMMISSIONER HAMILTON:

Q. If you would increase the jurisdiction of the Police Court, as you suggested, would you correspondingly increase the jurisdiction of the Morning Justices? A. The morning court.

Q. In order to relieve the Police Court? A. Relieve the Police Justice, take away some of the petty matters from the Police Magistrate?

Q. What cases would you place under the jurisdiction of the Morning Justices that do not now come under their jurisdiction? A. I think disorderly persons, especially persons who fail to provide for their wives and family; that I would take away from the Police Justice and give to the Morning Justice. Petit larcenies they might take, a great many of the cases where some person has stolen two dollars or one dollar from another.

Q. In that case you would have practically the same organization as they have in New York City; that is, a Court of Special Sessions and the several magistrates' courts, would you not, they would cease to be morning justices as they are now? A. They have co-ordinate jurisdiction with the Police Magistrate?

Q. No. A. I am not familiar with the New York system.

Q. If you increase their jurisdiction, they would cease to be morning justices, as they are now, simply having a jail delivery, so to speak. A. Yes.

Q. And would have to sit practically all morning? A. Yes, I see what you mean; they would have this increased matter being given them, they would have to sit probably all the full morning, the same as the police magistrate does.

BY MR. MAYER:

Q. Have you given any thought to the question of having one set of justices for courts of inferior jurisdiction, assigning various parts, each justice doing a certain amount of civil and criminal work each year? A. Rotating in office?

Q. Yes. A. The only objection I can see to that is a great many of the offenders that are brought in are habitual offenders. The Police Magistrate sitting there day after day during his four-year term comes to know those fellows, and he will know how to deal with them. Under the system of rotation in office, in holding the Police Court, these judges would not know them.

Q. Do you think if you had competent and faithful men in subordinate capacities, such as the clerks and attendants, that that same result could be accomplished? A. Well, the clerks, their duties are rather onerous, they have very little time to come over and talk to the Judge.

Q. Well, suppose you had a thorough system, installed a thorough system of identification? A. Well, that would do away with that objection.

Q. Well, if that objection were removed, do you think it would be a good plan to combine civil and criminal jurisdiction? A. I know of no other objection to it.

Q. Now, from your own experience, limited as it is, and in acting as police justice, do you find that the work is wearing work? A. Yes, it makes one very nervous, listening there to every complaint that humankind is subject to.

Q. Well, being as you are now an active practicing lawyer, and therefore not too much removed from the Bar, do you think that a man could do better work if he had a variety of civil and criminal procedure? A. Yes, there is something to that.

Q. You think that such a system would develop better justices, more patient justices—not that any of the judges now are not patient, but I mean as a general proposition— would the constant dealing day after day with criminal cases be likely to develop nervousness in the judge, irritation and impatience, would it have a tendency—dismiss from your mind that we are talking about any judge, we are not, we are talking about a system? A. Yes, I appreciate that. Well, I don't know, of course, from my limited experience there, I know that the annoyances that I suffer there make one nervous, and irritable, but I think after one would get accustomed to it, he would not notice it.

BY COMMISSIONER FRANCIS:

Q. Why was the old system abolished; was it because of a desire to specialize, for some abuse, or because of the incompetence of the justices to deal with both civil and criminal cases? A. I am not familiar with that. You see, that was before my time at the Bar, and I was not familiar with that.

———

DANIEL McCUE, recalled, testified as follows:

BY MR. MAYER:

Q. Is the book which I now show you the Judge's docket of the Police Court? A. Yes.

Q. Will you give a typical entry? A. People, plaintiff, against John Blank; offense, assault third degree; officer, Blank; defendant charged, on complaint under oath of Blank, to wit, that on or about the first day of September, 1908, at the city of Buffalo, the defendant did, against the form of the statute in such case made and provided, unlawfully beat, wound and ill-treat the complainant without just cause or provocation; September 11, arraigned and plea of not guilty; attorney Blank for defendant.

Q. Then follow the names of witnesses? A. Yes.

Q. And then the notation in this case the defendant was discharged? A. Discharged.

Q. Now, are the entries in this docket made by the Judge himself or the clerk? A. Yes, they are made by the Judge. The name is first written in by the clerk, but the entry, the original entries are all made by the Judge that has the jurisdiction, and so on.

Q. I think that is all. A. Now, I would like to say, every case where a person is arrested and brought into the Police Court, their name is put in that docket and then they are tried, and then it shows just what has become of each case.

———

WILLIAM P. BRENNAN, called as a witness, having been first duly sworn, testified as follows:

BY MR. MAYER:

Q. You are a practicing attorney? A. Yes.

Q. And how long have you been a member of the bar? A. I was admitted in 1900, I think.

Q. You are what is familiarly called a morning justice? A. Yes.

Q. And the technical title is what? A. Well, it is variously described, it is Justice to Police and Justice of Peace.

Q. You are permitted also to practice your profession? A. There is no prohibition; however, I assume that imposes some restriction upon me, which I have carefully observed.

Q. No legal prohibition? A. No legal prohibition, no.

Q. I assume you refer to not appearing in the police court? A. And to abstaining from police court work and more or less activity, perhaps too much so for my own interests.

Q. I can't hear. A. Perhaps too much so for my own interest.

Q. Well, your action in that regard is your own notion of the proprieties of the case? A. Entirely.

Q. What is the salary of the justice? A. Eighteen hundred dollars a year.

Q. There are how many in the city? A. There are three.

Q. Do they rotate? A. We hold court in three separate districts, for a period of one month, and move from that district into another district where we stay for a month.

Q. Now, what time do these courts open? A. Eight o'clock in the morning.

Q. Does the number of prisoners vary with the location? A. It varies with the district, more or less, varies with the season and varies with a number of other conditions.

Q. Where are the courts held? A. There is court now held at No. 3 Station for stations in that district, and one at No. 2, which was formerly held at No. 1 until the fire at police headquarters, and one at No. 8 in East Buffalo; the idea being to locate them convenient to the police in the various sections of the city.

Q. Are these courts now located conveniently for that purpose? A. They are, they are reasonably convenient.

Q. How many prisoners are brought before you daily; of course, I realize that varies, but from what to what? A. Well, it varies at the present time, I should say, from 20 to 100, and I believe they have been as high as 125.

Q. Who acts as clerk of the court? A. Well, we have no clerk. There is a desk sergeant who happens to be serving at that particular time and aids us at that hour. He is designated by the Police Department to serve as clerk, but he serves there only during the court session.

Q. What part of the police station do you hold the court in? A. At present we hold it in the reserve room, until— when we entered that office the courts were held in the general assembly room of the station house, and after continual protest we finally obtained leave to use their reserve room.

Q. By that you mean the room in which the police officers on reserve are situated? A. Yes.

Q. Seated around? A. Well, they have that privilege, and where they play checkers and amuse themselves during the few moments they are there.

Q. Well, are these police officers in the reserve room when court is being held? A. Well, they may enter there just as any spectator during that hour, it is a court room during our possession of it.

Q. Are these prisoners brought from the various station houses to the particular station house where the justice is sitting? A. Yes.

Q. What class of cases do you deal with each day covering all offenses? A. Violation of city ordinances, vagrancy and intoxication.

Q. Well, take up violation of city ordinances, what right of motion for removal has a defendant under your system? A. Why, in case of violation of a city ordinance, the Municipal Court has co-ordinate jurisdiction and either upon our motion or upon the demand of the defendant, a case may be sent there.

Q. Well, now, what classes of violation of ordinances come before you, generally speaking? A. Mostly all of the —of course, we have jurisdiction of all violations.

Q. Yes? A. But they are usually for disturbances in the street, common prostitutes and residence in houses of prostitution, general disorderly behavior on a public street.

Q. Well, are those complaints taken under the ordinances here? A. Yes.

Q. And, therefore, violation of a city ordinance would mean, as I understand you, generally speaking, public—— A. Offenses committed in the presence of the officer, not crimes.

Q. Disorder of some kind on the street? A. Yes.

Q. Is the punishment for these matters fine, or imprisonment, or both? A. There is a fine prescribed with the alternative of service in the penitentiary for one day for every dollar of fine imposed.

Q. What is the outside limit of the fine jurisdiction? A. Well, there is some conflict between the ordinances and the decision of the Appellate Division. The Code of Criminal Procedure, I think the fine is fifty dollars, although there are some ordinances which authorize the imposition of a greater fine, two hundred, two hundred and fifty; but being in conflict with the decision of the Appellate Division, we impose no larger fines than $50.

Q. Can you cite us the Appellate Division decisions which you have in mind? A. The case of Cronin, I haven't the citation here.

Q. Well, now, do you have ordinances of this kind which are brought before the morning justices, violations of smoke nuisance ordinances or matters of that kind? A. No, those are always presented in the Municipal Court. I believe they impose a penalty and there is some distinction between fine and penalty which deprives us of jurisdiction.

BY CHAIRMAN PAGE:

Q. You don't have any ordinance here against the use of soft coal, do you? A. The use of what?

Q. The use of soft coal? A. I believe there is one—anti-smoke nuisance at least, whether it specifically forbids soft coal or not.

BY MR. MAYER:

Q. That doesn't come before your court? A. No.

Q. Then the classes of violations of city ordinances are generally of the character you stated? A. Rather those that impose a fine or prescribe a fine as a penalty.

Q. Or the alternative of imprisonment? A. Yes.

Q. But I mean, do you have violation, for instance, relating to incumbering the streets by goods, or traffic violations, or anything of that kind? A. I believe there is a specific penalty provided for that in the Municipal Court.

Q. You have nothing of that kind? A. No.

Q. Well, now, are there many cases which you have referred to the Municipal Court of your own motion? A. Very seldom we refer them, I know of no reason why we would. It is only a defendant who is distrustful of the court and who fears it that asks to have it sent to the Municipal Court.

Q. Do you have many requests? A. Not many, no, sir.

Q. Well, now, you have been in office since January 19th, 1908, or prior to that time? A. Since 1906.

Q. 1906. Now, during your experience of three years, how many such motions have been made before you? A. I could not state precisely; I suppose twenty-five or thirty, probably.

Q. What classes of cases? A. Usually women charged with residing in houses of prostitution or keeping them. Usually offenders who are known to us, habitual offenders and who are recognized by the magistrate and perhaps fear the imposition of a——

Q. Severe penalty? A. A severer penalty than if they were unknown.

Q. I see. Well, can you see any reason why that jurisdiction should be divided? A. I know of no reason.

Q. Or rather, should be co-ordinate, to be more accurate? A. I know of no reason. I recently made some suggestions to the Bar Association, in which I proposed that this court be given exclusive jurisdiction of all violations of city ordinances, as it is complained in the Municipal Court that their calendar is congested constantly by these cases of violation of city ordinences.

Q. Was that what your suggestion was to the Bar Association? A. That was one of my suggestions offered to them.

Q. Will you state the others in that connection? A. Well, they are almost identical with those made here by Acting Judge Collins. I also proposed that they be given exclusive jurisdiction of the offenses of vagrancy and intoxication. At present the Police Court has co-ordinate jurisdiction with them. We meet with that situation there occasionally, in fact very frequently the habitual offender, who is apprehensive that a severe penalty will be imposed, will ask for a trial elsewhere than the Police Court.

Q. Does the same system exist in regard to vagrancy and

intoxication as in the Police Court? A. In those cases the Police Court has co-ordinate jurisdiction.

Q. Co-ordinate jurisdiction, either by request of the defendant or upon motion of the Morning Justice, is that correct? A. Yes.

Q. Well, are there many applications in the cases of vagrancy? A. Well, there are more in the cases of intoxication and vagrancy than in cases of violation of city ordinances.

Q. And is the motion made in your opinion because the defendant wishes to escape the penalty? A. Almost entirely, sir. Occasionally, however, I—the counsel appears and I believe he desires witnesses or something like that, or thinks it is more convenient to try the case at a later hour, I presume those reasons impel him.

Q. Now, cases of intoxication, are those cases of persons intoxicated in public places? A. Yes.

Q. What is the penalty here for them? A. Why, it is a violation of the liquor tax law. The penalty is a fine not to exceed ten dollars or six months' imprisonment.

Q. Or six months' imprisonment? A. Yes.

Q. When they imprison, where is the prisoner sent? A. Erie County Penitentiary, or, in the case of females, habitual offenders, we commit them either to the Asylum of Our Lady of Refuge or Ingleside Home, where their age does not exceed thirty years, with their consent. That is another thing I would change. It requires their consent. Frequently we prefer to commit a woman to a home rather than the penitentiary, and I guess there is more or less— they get more labor there and they object to that, and the discipline is severer than it is in the penitentiary, and they object to that, and some of them prefer to go to the Erie County Penitentiary, and others assert that they can get out of there easier.

Q. Out of the Erie County Penitentiary? A. Than they can out of one of these homes.

Q. Well, is there any authority which can release them before the end of the term? A. Yes, the County Judge has that power, under the law, either to modify or—he hears the appeals but he has the right to modify the sentence to the time served.

Q. Well, is that a matter that is entrusted entirely to his discretion? A. Entirely so.

Q. Has he, then, a sort of pardoning power? A. He possesses that power virtually.

Q. Then that, if he has the right to cut down the term of imprisonment, is not dependent upon any errors in the hearing? A. He can modify the sentence to the time served for any reason that he deems sufficient. I wish to say in behalf of Justice Taylor that his work has been excellent in that respect. He has co-operated with the Morning Justices and I think he has prevented a great deal of injustice. He has been quite rigid in that practice, that they must produce the very best reasons or he will not exercise his discretion in those cases.

Q. Have the Morning Justices any power of lessening the imprisonment after commitment? A. He has not.

Q. None whatever? A. Virtually by agreement with the County Judge, if there are sufficient reasons presented to us why the sentence should be modified, we recommend it to him. However, the petitions are addressed to him and he determines.

Q. Now, under the head of vagrancy, what classes of cases come before you? A. Well, there are several specifications, principally the person is without visible means to maintain himself; they are habitual drunkards or persons who live off the proceeds or earnings of prostitution.

Q. Of prostitution? A. And those who have contracted diseases in the practice of debauchery.

Q. In such cases, what is the outside limit of the commitment? A. Six months.

Q. And is the release of such persons accomplished in the same manner as you have stated in regard to intoxication? A. Yes.

Q. You have no power? A. No power whatever.

Q. That power resides with the County Judges? A. Entirely.

Q. From your observation are these cases of vagrancy increasing? A. Well, the arrests have increased during the last year. There are a great many accusations of vagrancy that are not very satisfactorily established, especially during this period of commercial depression, there are so many wanderers and idlers and the police have good reasons, I assume, for apprehending a great many of them and arraigning them before us. A great many of them are discharged; most of them are discharged.

BY CHAIRMAN PAGE:

Q. Are there any reports made by the justices or any sources from which we could get the statistics? A. The Police Department, I guess, has all the information you desire in that particular.

BY MR. MAYER:

Q. Wherein was the police evidence lacking or the evidence adduced by the police? A. Well, I—they arrest a man on sight, technically perhaps he is a vagrant; I assume he is, but if he is a man of good appearance and satisfactorily explains his idleness, I would feel very loath to commit him to the penitentiary as vagrant, especially during a period of commercial depression when there are so many worthy men out of employment.

Q. Do you depend on your memory and on the police reports as to whether a defendant is a second or habitual offender? A. Well, we are required to depend largely upon memory and the veracity of the defendant.

Q. Have you a system of identification? A. We have not any at all.

Q. Do the police use the Bertillon system at all in such cases? A. I don't believe so.

Q. Or the finger print system? A. I don't believe so.

Q. Then whether or not a defendant is a habitual offender is largely a matter of haphazard? A. No, sir; depends upon our personal recollection almost entirely, and of course, we know, that is we know most of the habitual offenders of the city of Buffalo. We come in contact with them so frequently, especially with common prostitutes or women who solicit on the public street, that sort of thing.

Q. Is there much of that? A. Well, no; I should say the police conditions in the City of Buffalo were very satisfactory in that regard.

Q. Well, you keep no record of any kind, do you? A. We have no records aside from the judgment docket, no records whatever. We have no clerk. I believe the police have a record, of course, of all depositions.

Q. Well, your record is only a blotter, is it not, practically? A. That's all.

Q. You have no clerk? A. We have no clerk. I also, if you will permit me to interrupt you, in my suggestions to the Bar Association, recommended that we be provided with adequate clerical assistance so that they could furnish satisfactory records, especially on that point as to whether the defendant is a habitual offender or not—that we could— something that is readily accessible, and also with a stenographer to preserve the evidence.

Q. Do you regard a police station as a proper place to hold these courts? A. I do not.

Q. Will you give us your reasons for the conclusion? A. There is more or less confusion there; noise, and it never really ceases to be a police station. I cannot entirely describe my feelings on the subject, but——

Q. Well, it lacks order? A. You are there by their leave, mostly. I cannot exactly explain my objection. There is an air to it that is offensive to it.

Q. It is a sort of police atmosphere? A. There is a police atmosphere there.

Q. An atmosphere for conviction, I assume. A. Well, of course, that prevails. However, most policemen that I come in contact with are fair-minded men and reliable. Of course we come in contact with the other class of officer who is quite eager to obtain convictions.

Q. Do you think the present system of giving a certain jurisdiction to the morning justices and other jurisdiction to the Police Justice is a good system? A. I proposed that in my suggestions to this Committee, too, that the jurisdiction of the Morning Court be enlarged, that is that it be invested with the jurisdiction of these petty offenses, petit larceny and disorderly persons.

Q. A little louder? A. Petit larceny, disorderly persons, assault in the third degree, virtually the powers now possessed by the present Police Court, and I would enlarge the jurisdiction of the present Police Court, giving it jurisdiction of all misdemeanors. Now that jurisdiction is conferred on all police courts in cities of the second class by this Uniform Charter Act, applying entirely to cities of the second class.

Q. What would you think of giving the Morning Justices all necessary authority in summary cases and the powers of a commiting magistrate, leaving the trial of all misdemeanors to the Police Justice? A. What is your suggestion?

(Question read.) A. What rights would you reserve, what powers would you reserve to the Morning Court?

Q. Well, the Morning Court to have power in all cases of summary jurisdiction—— A. Yes.

Q. (Continuing.) Such as vagrancy, disorderly person, intoxication and the like? A. Yes.

Q. Also to have the power of holding in misdemeanors for trial by the Police Justice? A. That would be—I would prefer the other system, but that would be some improvement over the prevailing system.

Q. You mean you would like to see the morning justices have power to finally dispose of certain misdemeanors? A. Particularly those misdemeanors that are enumerated in Section 56 of the Code of Criminal Procedure. Usually they are petty matters and when finally disposed of only a slight penalty is imposed, and at present they take up a lot of time in the other courts.

Q. Well, in Section 56 are petit larceny and assault in the third degree, are they not? A. I believe they are, yes.

Q. Well, now, do you not have a great many of those cases here, out of the total I mean? A. Well, I couldn't give you just the figures on that, we don't try those cases.

Q. Would you deprive the Police Justice of jurisdiction in those cases? A. No, would give co-ordinate jurisdiction in such cases, but not in these other cases, cases of disorderly persons, vagrancy and intoxication.

Q. In those cases you would only resort to the morning justices? A. I would.

Q. Have you given any consideration to the idea of combining civil and criminal jurisdiction in one court of justices, an inferior criminal jurisdiction? A. Well, I know it has been proposed. I haven't thought of it, examined it carefully. I don't know what particular benefits could follow from it, unlesss in increasing the jurisdiction you render the duties more difficult of performance and perhaps atttract a higher grade of men. Take for instance in the Morning Court to-day, the jurisdiction is very simple and any man of sound sense and good morals can make a good morning justice. But on account of the fact the jurisdiction is so simple there is—there are a great many men aspire to it who are unfit for the place. I suppose if you conferred this added jurisdiction upon the police courts that——

Q. Upon the morning courts? A. (Continued) Only lawyers would be eligible. That suggests an objection to me, because the present lay justices here are rendering such satisfactory service that I think any scheme that contemplates either their removal or exclusion from office would be unpopular and perhaps be defeated, and you would get no relief at all.

Q. Well then, an increase of jurisdiction to an extent which might require a legal training might really be an impracticable thing? A. I think it would imperil the whole project of reform here. The time is not opportune. The present lay justices are very able men and render very satisfactory service, and I do not think the public would countenance any legislation that would exclude them from office.

Q. What do you think of the suggestion of having two police courts? A. I would suggest that in the alternative we have two police courts and two of these courts of lesser jurisdiction.

Q. And as I understand you then, your plan would contemplate a certain amount of co-ordinate jurisdiction? A. Yes, at least of the graver misdemeanors.

Q. Now is there any other suggestion that has occurred to you? A. I believe that is all I care to offer now.

Q. Do you have any cases in the morning justice courts which you place on probation? A. Yes.

Q. What is your system in that respect? A. The system was just recently installed. It is simply in a formative state now. If we observe a person that we think is not a habitual offender, or who has commenced a criminal career, why we place him on probation.

Q. Who is not a criminal offender? A. Who is not a confirmed, habitual offender, but I would use that term simply distinguishing from the occassional offender. We have for instance, a person charged with intoxication and perhaps never arrested before in his life, and probably never will be again. I don't believe in placing such a person on probation, but some girl who seems to have started astray, or some young man who has commenced a course of debauchery, why we place them on probation.

Q. Well, what officers have you for that purpose? A. We have a probation officer, recently appointed.

Q. What is his name? A. Kelley, Edward F. Kelley.

Q. Is he a police officer? A. No, sir, he was appointed from the competitive list. He was first on the list.

Q. He covers the three courts? A. He covers the three courts. I would suggest in that connection that there be two additional probation officers, one for each court, if this present system is continued.

Q. How many people do you suppose you have come before these three courts in the course of a year? A. Twenty-five thousand.

Q. Twenty-five thousand? A. That is, I won't attempt to be precise, but I think that is it approximately, twenty to twenty-five thousand.

Q. In round numbers. You issue no warrants? A. No, sir.

Q. You are merely judges here and determine the cases before you? A. Yes, all these cases, committed in the presence of the officer.

Q. As it is now, you as justices have no system of records? A. No, sir; it is very unsatisfactory in that respect, too.

Q. And that, I assume, is due in great measure, to lack of help in an appropriation for that purpose? A. There is no appropriation whatever other than the salaries for the three justices.

Q. Since when has Mr. Kelley been appointed? A. He was appointed I guess about August, July; late in July or August.

Q. Have you observed his work? A. I have.

Q. And is the system working out well, in you opinion? A. I think it will be very satisfactory when it is fully developed.

Q. It is still in the initial stages? A. Yes.

Q. What is the extreme limit of the commitment or sentence which can be imposed upon a street walker or a person—— A. Well, the offense that is charged, it depends upon the charge preferred against them; vagrancy, of course, a common prostitute is a vagrant under the law; six months' imprisonment, or, if the charge is violating a city ordinance, soliciting on the public street, the maximum penalty is a $50 fine.

Q. Or an equal number of days' imprisonment? A. Or an equal number of days' imprisonment.

Q. Now, have you many cases of soliciting on the public streets? A. A great many.

Q. A great many? A. A great many.

Q. How many would you say? A. Well, I wouldn't attempt to give you the figures, but——

Q. I mean five thousand in a year? A. No.

Q. A thousand? A. I should say three thousand, perhaps.

Q. I am speaking of the three courts? A. Three thousand perhaps.

Q. Is any effort made to keep track of repeated offenders in that regard? A. Only our personal acquaintance with them, if——

Q. Only your memory? A. Contracted there. Our memory we rely on. Of course the police volunteer information in that particular.

Q. Is the punishment usually a fine? A. Well, when they are charged with violating a city ordinance it must be a fine. We simply impose such a fine as to discourage the practice of the street walker. There is a certain zone here where vice is tolerated and we endeavor to confine it to that particular locality, which I think is a good idea.

Q. Well, then there is a practical although not a statutory segregation? A. Yes, there is.

Q. That is about the size of it? A. A recognition, they are not molested I guess as long as they conduct their houses in an orderly way.

Q. And the justices and the police co-operate in that direction? A. Why we never expressly.

Q. No? A. But I should be inclined to ask why if a particular place was entered and the occupants arrested. I should be inclined to ask why they were arrested.

Q. If in the zone to which you referred? A. Yes, and why their neighbor was not disturbed.

BY COMMISSIONER MURPHY:

Q. Just for my own information, Judge, I want to ask what is your method when these persons are arraigned in the morning, does a police officer make the complaint and furnish the evidence, as a general thing? A. Yes, swears to the evidence of his own, and then he has other witnesses if he thinks his case needs bolstering up a little; and I would say in that connection the court room facilities are very inadequate, that there is no provision made for separation of offenders. We have no benches there. The court rooms are a disgrace to the City of Buffalo.

BY COMMISSIONER HAMILTON:

Q. I am going to ask you to describe the court rooms, Judge? A. Well, it is a bare room, meanly furnished, used as a desk sergeant—used as a reserve room. There is no furniture there at all aside from the desk, which was given to us after about a year of asking. Until that time we held court in the outer room over the police station desk.

BY COMMISSIONER SMITH:

Q. You have no power to take bail, have you, Judge? A. No, sir.

Q. A man is arrainged before you, say, this morning and you desire to postpone the hearing in his case, for any reason, for a couple of days; if he has not been bailed out, so that you cannot continue the station house bail, what do you have to do, send him to the police station? A. Why, if it is seen that he cannot procure bail we send him over to the jail, which is a more suitable place to keep him; that is, the jail is a much better place than the police station.

Q. Suppose he is a stranger in the city and he wouldn't know anybody to bail him out, he would have to go to jail? A. That would be pretty tough on him.

Q. What? A. That would be pretty tough on the stranger, I should think.

Q. Well, that is not altogether what I am getting at. Who would you send for to take the bail, suppose it was offered? A. Oh, bail for any offense triable by our court can be accepted there in the station house, by the desk sergeant.

Q. But not by you? A. No, sir; we accept no bail at all. But there is always someone in attendance at the police station, there would never be any difficulty on that point.

BY COMMISSIONER MURPHY:

Q. Well, do you—how do you deal, for instance, with a common drunk, fine him a dollar or five dollars, or something like that? A. Well, if he is a man of family or if it is his first offense, we let him go, and are apt to let him go for a second offense if not an habitual offender, if it seems there is some interval separating the offenses. Most of the men arraigned in our court are first offenders, I am satisfied.

Q. Do you think it is punishment enough to have them in the court room? A. Plenty enough punishment to be detained in the station house all night.

Q. In case of a man arrested after you adjourn court on Saturday on the charge of intoxication, who is unable to precure bail, doesn't he have to wait there until Monday morning? A. Sunday morning, we hold court every day in the week.

BY MR. MAYER:

Q. What arrangements do you make for vacation? A. Why, during that time the prisoners of that particular district are sent to the other districts for trial. Two courts are held in place of one.

Q. What proof do you require that a woman is a common prostitute? A. Why, they usually get some sort of a case on the place. Send some one in the place, and an officer testifies to what he observes of her habits and where she resides.

Q. Do you require proof of previous conviction? A. Well, I think before we impose a penalty there would have to be some evidence, unless some one locates in a section of the city where disorderly houses are not tolerated. We do our best to get those circumstances, whatever they are, whether it is the first offense or second. The disposition depends a great deal upon the circumstances in each particular case.

Q. So that in practice the judges are familiar with the conditions in the city? A. Yes, sir.

Q. And they apply their knowledge of those conditions in the punishment that they administer? A. Yes, sir.

Q. In regard to this class of offenses? A. Yes, sir.

BY COMMISSIONER MURPHY:

Q. And is that disposition pretty well sanctioned by the people? A. It seems very satisfactory.

BY MR. MAYER:

Q. Is there co-operation between the Police Department and the justices? A. In what respect?

Q. I mean to say—— A. There is no dissension.

Q. There is no friction, is there? A. No, now and then we might displease an individual.

Q. Well, you are the Judge. I mean to say there is no condition of being at odds? A. No, sir; there is harmony so far as that is concerned.

BY COMMISSIONER WINTHROP:

Q. Is no record kept of the disposition of the cases that come before you? A. Only the record of conviction, that is filed and preserved by the Police Department. They keep a record of all offenses.

Q. In all of the offenses? A. All of the offenses and all of the dispositions.

Q. That is to say, when they arrest somebody that appears on their books? A. They have a complete record, a history of that case, including the disposition.

Q. The records of your court are really the record of the police station houses? A. That is right. This was always a police court, a police bench, and under the control of the Police Commissioner.

Q. Do you issue warrants? A. No, sir.

BY COMMISSIONER HAMILTON:

Q. What would you say about the necessity for new quarters if any added jurisdiction were to be given these courts or any rearranged jurisdiction, would you say that there should be new quarters for the morning justices? A. I should say there should be whether there is any added jurisdiction or not.

Q. Where would you say this should be, in connection with the police stations or not? A. I should locate them in sections of the City conveniently accessible to the people. I believe in the District Police Courts.

Q. Do you think it is a good plan to have them in the same building with the police station? A. No, sir—I replied to that question to Mr. Mayer.

BY MR. MAYER:

Q. If the Morning Court system were to be continued, whether as at present or changed in some way, is there any reason why power should not be given to the morning justices to take bail? A. Not the least, I cannot imagine any.

Q. Might that be a solution of the difficulty to which some other witnesses have referred? A. I have always thought that since I have been there—in fact, it has been a source of annoyance for us that we have not the right. Frequently application is made to us.

Q. You are elected by the whole city are you not? A. Elected by the City of Buffalo.

BY COMMISSIONER MURPHY:

Q. Would you let the police still have the right to take bail? A. Yes, sir.

BY MR. MAYER:

Q. In misdemeanors? A. Yes, sir.

Q. Have you any information at all as to arrests in the City of Buffalo for violations of ordinances not connected with public disorder? A. No, sir.

Q. Do you know the class of ordinances that I refer to? A. Those in the nature of a civil suit in the Municipal Court for the recovery of a penalty.

Q. Those are not treated as criminal cases here? A. No.

DR. ARCHIBALD D. CARPENTER, called as a witness and being duly sworn, testified as follows:

BY MR. MAYER:

Q. Doctor, are you one of the Civil Service Commission? A. I am.

Q. Are you familiar with the kind of examination that has been prepared for probation officers? A. We have only given one, and I was a member of the Committee that gave it, with Mr. Davidson, who was the other member of the Committee.

Q. You are familiar with that examination? A. Yes, sir.

Q. Have you brought with you any of the papers? A. I have.

Q. Now, was the examination both written and oral? A. Yes, sir.

Q. Was part of the examination the ascertainment of the experience of the competitor? A. Yes, sir.

Q. Do you recollect what percentage was given for experience, or what value? A. I don't recollect the exact value—I think it was twenty-five, but I am not sure.

Q. Would you ascertain and let us know? A. Now?

Q. No, I mean later on. Did you have a part of the examination as "technical"? A. Yes, one part we called technical, and the other "experience."

Q. And what was the oral examination? A. The oral examination consisted in questions by which we tried to ascertain the mental alertness of the man as much as possible, and his general mental sympathetic qualities for the position.

Q. Did you have any person connected with probation who was present at the oral examination? A. Mr. Weed was present at the oral examination.

Q. Mr. Weed is a member of the State Probation Commission? A. I think so.

Q. Do the papers I now show you set forth the examination questions for experience and for technical equipment? A. They do.

MR. MAYER: I will offer this in evidence and mark it Exhibit 68.

(Paper offered and marked Exhibit 68.)

Q. Do you recollect some of the questions that were asked by you or Mr. Davidson of these applicants? A. I cannot remember the exact questions.

Q. Well, the substance of them? A. One question, of course, was as to the amount of time the man would expect to spend on his duty as probation officer. That was to ascertain whether he was willing to give up his whole time to it. Another one, he was given the case of a boy who had broken his parole—I think they call it—and was seen by the probation officer on the street, what he would do in such a case, as near as I remember, to ascertain what the candidate understood were his powers as an officer, or as probation officer; then we referred in some cases to their answers to the other questions. For instance, a man would answer that question in regard to the organization of a corps of volunteer workers—there was a great difference in their answers; some of them would say four or five, and some of them wanted three or four hundred, and we tried to find out why they answered the way they did.

Q. Did you mark the papers? A. Mr. Davidson and I together marked these papers.

Q. Do you recollect what you gave as a result of your oral examination of these men? A. I cannot recollect that now.

Q. You provided certain values or percentages, I assume, for the three branches, that is "experience," "technical qualification" and "the oral examinations?" A. If this is an answer to that question we first gave a percentage to experience. We first marked the experience papers, and then we decided, previous to marking the papers, that a man who did not obtain 60 per cent. of the amount required, of the total allowance on experience, was thrown out and we would not examine his so-called technical paper.

Q. Is Mr. Davidson the attorney of the Civil Service Commission? A. He is a member of the Commission and an attorney.

Q. Who is the other member? A. Of the Committee? I

was the other member of the Committee. There are seven members of the whole Commission.

Q. This was a sub-committee of two? A. Yes, sir.

Q. Which conducted personally this examination? A. Yes, sir.

Q. Had you ever attended at the police courts? A. No, sir.

Q. Have you ever been there? A. No.

Q. You have not followed up personally cases brought to your attention where men were placed on probation? A. No, I think not.

Q. Had Mr. Davidson? A. I presume he has.

Q. Do you think as Civil Service Commissioners you are qualified to ascertain the qualifications of these men as well as the men who deal daily in police court with the subject? A. Well, I cannot say that, I can say that we obtained all the literature we could on the matter, and made ourselves as qualified as possible.

Q. Did you obtain the human equasion? A. As much as we could, yes. We could not get that out of literature, I suppose.

Q. Let me ask you this, Doctor, not in any unpleasant way, but you will appreciate exactly what I am getting at because the Commission is very anxious to be informed on this point: what would you do if a six-foot longshoresman were placed—put it this way. Suppose a six-foot longshoreman, with a record of having been drunk twice, came to you, the testimony showed that he had beaten his wife on one of these occasions, the testimony was that he was a good worker and a good earner, and he had a wife and

three children, what disposition would you make of him?
A. After reading all of the books, pamphlets and everything that we read, I would be personally anxious to give the man a chance.

Q. Would you place him on probation? A. Yes, sir; certainly.

Q. Would you require that man to put in proof of his relations with the probation officer, or of the probation officer with him? A. What would I require, or what is required?

Q. How would you judge whether a man had a proper sense of the duties of a probation officer? Suppose one probation officer said that he would require that man to report to him, and suppose another probation officer said that he would visit that man's home, what would be your impression of the better way to treat the case? A. I believe that both of them could be used. Certainly if the man at the end of his probation was living up to what was required of him by the Court he might be allowed to go to the probation officer and make report, but before this I believe it would be much better for the probation officer to go to the home, go to the place where the man works and to find out definitely, not directly from the man, but by any one who was around him how he was behaving.

Q. In your determination of this oral examination did you take into consideration the appearance of the man? A. We tried to.

Q. Did you take into consideration or allow, for instance, the correctness of their speech to play any part in the marking that you gave them? A. Yes, sir; that is I would not say that we said so many points out of say a possible 40 were allowed for correct language; but the man who could talk properly and would appear properly, was clean and neat in his appearance, we would say was the man who got the better marking on those points.

Q. Were some points accorded to these men in accordance with the impressions they made upon you and Mr. Davidson? A. Why, I can say safely that there were the impressions conveyed to both of us. I don't believe either of us marked one man because we thought he looked particularly one way or the other.

Q. But you say some of the points which these men received in the marking, whatever your system was, was so received as a result of your impressions of the men, as to whether you thought they were capable or good men? A. After hearing their conversation and asking these questions, yes.

Q. So that that was one of the elements of qualification? A. Yes, sir.

Q. Now, where did you get the information on which these questions were based—I mean to say from anybody like the State Probation Commission or from the judges that are dealing with this question? A. We ascertained from the judges, as near as possible, after talking with three of them I think at one time, the duties of the office, and then it being, as far as we could ascertain, a reasonably new development, we read magazines and pamphlets showing the result of the work in the different juvenile courts and the different courts where probation was allowed, and then worked our questions up from that.

Q. You are a physician by practice? A. Yes, sir.

Q. You are a practising physician. A. Yes, sir.

BY COMMISSIONER FRANCIS:

Q. This examination was local to this particular place, Buffalo—there is no uniformity of examination throughout the State? A. Not to my knowledge.

BY MR. MAYER:

Q. Was Mr. Pfeifer appointed on this examination? A. Yes, sir.

Q. For the children? A. Yes, sir.

Q. And Mr. Kelley for the adults? A. Yes, sir.

Q. Was Judge Nash consulted as to the character of the examination, do you remember? A. I think we had a talk with Judge Nash, and with—I don't remember the name of this judge that was here.

Q. Judge Brennan, who preceded you on the stand? A. Yes, sir; that is it. We talked with them simply in regard to the duties and requirements of the position, what they would expect the men to do.

Q. Did you give a large value, if you remember, to experience? A. As I remember it, they were about equal. The experience, the technical and the oral, although I would not make that as a definite statement.

Q. Can you let me have that by Saturday? A. Yes, sir.

Q. As to the exact percentage of marks, or the system on which you developed the order of the eligible men? A. What you want is just simply the percentage of the total 100 that we allowed for experience, technical and the oral examination?

Q. Yes? A. Yes, sir.

JAMES KANE, called as a witness, being duly sworn, testified as follows:

BY MR. MAYER:

Q. Mr. Kane, you are employed in the Police Court? A. Yes, sir.

Q. In what capacity? A. Well, my title is, Adult Probation Officer. I assume to do court duty.

Q. Did you pass the civil service examination? A. No, sir.

Q. How did you get through without a civil service examination? A. There were no lists then. I believe Judge Nash asked power of the Common Council to appoint a probation officer in his court.

Q. What salary do you get? A. Nine hundred dollars.

Q. What was your occupation before? A. I was deputy sheriff.

Q. How many cases of probation have you had? A. I have got four now.

Q. You have four cases now? A. Yes, sir; since the new year.

Q. Since the first of January, 1909? A. Yes, sir.

Q. When were you appointed? A. I was appointed in January, 1908, but I did not take the office until March, 1908.

Q. How many probation cases have you had? A. Four.

Q. Four altogether? A. Yes, that was my duty as court officer.

Q. You mean you have been spending most of your time as a court officer? A. All of my time, I may say.

Q. So that you have really done no probation work to speak of? A. No, sir.

Q. And all the cases you have had from the time you were assigned to the court have been four? A. Yes, sir.

Q. What are those four cases, I mean what kind of cases are they? A. Boys—petit larceny.

Q. All four of them? A. Yes, sir.

Q. What are their names, don't give the last names, just give the initials? A. John B., Edward F., Sereno H., William O.

Q. What is the oldest case among those? A. Nineteen.

Q. I mean what is the longest case among them?

BY CHAIRMAN PAGE:

Q. The first one that was put on probation with you? A. Sereno H.

BY MR. MAYER:

Q. When was he put on probation? A. January 15th,

Q. 1909? A. Yes, sir.

Q. Then, these are all very recent, are they? A. Yes, sir.

Q. Were they given to you by Judge Nash or by Judge Collins? A. Two of them by Judge Nash and two of them by Judge Collins.

Q. Are they all petit larceny, the four of them? A. Yes, sir.

Q. What do you do? A. Why the boys are just simply told to report to me once a week for three months.

Q. Where do they report? A. Two at the Police Court and two at **my home.**

Q. The two at home are boys working in the day time? A. They live in that locality.

Q. Have you visited their homes at all? A. No.

Q. What do they say to you when they report? A. I ask them if they are working, how they are getting along.

Q. After they tell you that, do you try to find out if they are telling the truth? A. Yes, sir.

Q. What do you do? A. Find out from the neighbors in the locality.

Q. Do you go to the neighbors? A. Yes, sir.

Q. Is any effort made to communicate with their local religious authorities? A. No, sir.

Q. Well, it is all pretty new to you, isn't it? A. Yes, sir.

Q. And it has really only been started since the 15th of January? A. Yes, sir.

Q. The next case, that of William O., was on January 18th? A. Yes, sir.

Q. And that of Edward F. and John B. on January 22d? A. Yes sir.

Q. So thus far you don't know very much about probation? A. No, sir.

Q. Did each of these boys receive a card telling him to report? A. Yes, sir. This is the card.

Q. Is the card you now show me a card of the character that these young men received? A. The same as the white card.

Q. You speak of a white card, meaning the cards that you keep? A. Yes, sir.

Q. And this yellow card? A. They keep.

Q. The probationers keep? A. Yes, sir.

MR. MAYER: I offer this card in evidence.

Card marked in evidence as Exhibit 69.

Q. Have you had anybody instruct you as to what to do

in these probation cases? A. Only what Judge Nash told me.

Q. What did he say? A. To look out for them boys.

Q. Did he tell you how to look out for them? A. Yes, sir.

Q. What did he say? A. Told me to give them a visit once in awhile.

Q. Did he give you any further details? A. No, sir.

Q. What I am trying to get at is have you had any advice from people experienced in probation work. A. Only what I seen. I have got to attend the Juvenile Court Tuesday and Friday.

Q. And you see Mr. Pfeifer's work there, do you? A. Yes, sir.

BY COMMISSIONER FRANCIS:

Q. What led up to this new system—what is the cause of the new system of probation? A. What led up to it?

Q. Yes? A. I suppose—all I know is that they asked for it. I don't know much about it.

Q. You don't know what the custom has been heretofore, do you? A. No, sir.

BY COMMISSIONER WINTHROP:

Q. Are you a probation officer in the adult court or the Juvenile Court? A. The adult court.

Q. In what capacity do you attend the Juvenile Court? A. As court officer, to keep order in the Juvenile Court as well as the Police Court.

BY COMMISSIONER HAMILTON:

Q. You have one juvenile probationer, haven't you? A.

Why, I guess there is one there, but he was in the Police Court.

Q. He was not arraigned in the children's part? A. No, sir.

Q. That was just the other day, January 18th? A. Yes, sir.

BY COMMISSIONER SMITH:

Q. Was there any reason for bringing him to the Police Court? A. I don't know what the reason was.

CHAIRMAN PAIGE: The Commission will stand adjourned until to-morrow, Friday, February 5th, 1909, at 10:00 A. M.

BUFFALO, N. Y., Friday, February 5, 1909, 10 A. M.

CHAIRMAN PAGE: Judge Mayer, the counsel for the Commission, having been called to New York on business, Mr. George S. Buck of the Buffalo Bar has kindly consented to assist the Commission today in the capacity of counsel.

HARRY OLSON, called as a witness, having been first duly sworn, testified as follows:

BY MR. BUCK:

Q. You are the Chief Judge of the Municipal Court of Chicago? A. I am.

Q. And you have been so since the court was started? A. For two years.

Q. How long experience did you have in the administration of criminal law prior to becoming the Judge of the Municipal Court of Chicago? A. I was admitted to the bar in 1891 and in 1896 I became an assistant State's attorney, District Attorney, I think you call it in New York, in Chicago, and remained in that office in the trial of criminal cases for ten years.

Q. Well, will you outline the conditions that existed in Chicago which led up to the creation of the present Chicago Municipal Court? A. The minor criminal cases and the minor civil cases were tried before justices of the peace. We had in Illinois, the justice of the peace system and the constable system. The justices had jurisdiction in civil suits up to $200 and the jurisdiction in criminal cases for such offenses as were punishable by fine not exceeding $200 and for violations of city ordinances. Some of these justices were selected by the Mayor as police magistrates. There were fifty justices altogether in the City of Chicago and about one hundred constables. The constables served the writs in civil cases and sometimes in criminal cases when they were brought before justices who were not magistrates, or police magistrates.

The organization of the Municipal Court was brought about by two conditions, the action of the justices and constables in civil and criminal cases. Perhaps more because of the action of some of the justices and some of the constables in civil suits. Having jurisdiction throughout the county and there being fifty of them and the county being a large county—I think Cook County is the first in the value of its agricultural products besides containing the City of Chicago, and there are long distances from one part of the county to the other. Many lawyers began suits against citizens of the city in remote courts far from their homes, from thirty to forty miles. Many suits were begun out in the country and they were set occasionally at ten minutes before the early morning train arrived. If the train arrived at 9 o'clock, the case was heard at 8:45; so that the defendant was obliged to go there the night before with his witnesses if he wanted to be on hand. There were no hotel accommodations and generally the defendants did not go but appealed the case to the Circuit Court, which corresponds with your Supreme Court, that court had jurisdiction to try the case *de novo,* not on the record. That was one of the abuses.

Other abuses were common and general throughout the city, one complaint being, and the principal one, that judgments were rendered for the plaintiff in many cases notwithstanding the evidence. In some cases no doubt that was almost invariably the rule and in other cases the bar suspected it to be the case when it was not perhaps. Some of the justices in the Loop District or the center of the city were honorable men and tried their cases fairly. It was the act mostly of a few of the justices that brought the whole system into contempt. The constables were men of no particular character. Many of them were "plug uglies." Some of them were common criminals. Citizens were shot during the making of levies. Money was extorted from people. False returns were made. In many cases the defendant never knew that he had been sued at all until the constable arrived with an execution to make a levy. The latter had made a false return that he had served the defendant when he had not. And abuses of that kind were quite common among the constables. One in particular by the name of Greenberg became so notorious that public attention was focused upon the whole constabulary system and the justice of the peace system.

I think the action of the justices and constables in civil suits was the one first to attract public attention, but I think their action in criminal cases was more serious than their action in civil suits. The justices were often selected by the Mayor at the instigation of the aldermen of a particular district where the large police force were located.

The bailiff of the court was selected in the same manner and usually through the influence of the aldermen of a particular ward. So was the Clerk of the Court. The machinery therefore for the administration of criminal justice in the court of first instance was an adjunct of the political machine that happened to control the administration of the city. The jurors in the justice courts were picked up from the body of the county. The bailiff had the duty and the right to go and pick any citizen he saw fit. The result was that in these cases plaintiffs frequently engaged the counsel or the bailiff to select a particular class of jurymen to sit in the court. He might take those any place he pleased. Abuses of various sorts were engaged in by the bailiff of these courts. Among others they acted as agents for the aldermen and his chief henchmen in seeing to it that bail was furnished defendants. They became very active agents in notifying the chief bailor as to what defendants were arrested the night before and what sureties they had and what the prospects were as to what they could pay for bonds in these cases. The clerk was a part of the system occasionally also in some of these courts. The chief bondsman at the principal courts had a list with the same numbers as the Judge had upon his sheet, so that he would know when a case was called what it was by number. These clerks occasionally failed to endorse the name of witnesses, the correct name of witnesses, on the back of the paper that went to the grand jury when defendants were bound over in criminal cases. Sometimes they gave the proper name of the witness but gave his wrong address so there would be difficulty in apprehending the witnesses before the grand jury. Many of such cases came to my notice during the ten years I was in the State Attorney's office.

In short, the whole system for the administration of justice in the minor cases had become such as to have lost the confidence of the bar and public in many of the men charged with its administration. As I said before we had many men who were honest and honorable and against whom there could be no charges made of any sort, and yet the public I think lost confidence in the whole system. So that when nominations for municipal court judges were being considered by the political parties, it was considered dangerous to name any man who had sat on that bench, as a candidate; one of the parties named quite a number of the better men and the other party named only one, who was a very reputable man and a very good lawyer and he is now serving as municipal court judge, having been elected a second time. So there were many good men among these justices. These in brief are some of the conditions that brought about the change.

Q. Who were the men who drew the Municipal Court Act? A. The Chicago Charter Commission had the matter in charge. They appointed a committee consisting of John P. Wilson, a very eminent lawyer of the Chicago bar; Mr. John S. Millor, another very eminent member of the Chicago bar; and Judge Murray F. Tuley, one of the distinguished judges of the Chicago Circuit Court; and two business men, Mr. Bernard E. Sunney and Mr. Bernard E. Eckhardt. Mr. Sunney was president of the Commonwealth Edison Company and Mr. Eckhardt was a promi-

nent miller. This committee selected **Mr. Hiram T. Gil-**
bert, a well-known lawyer and ex-judge of the Circuit
Court of Lascelle County, who has been practicing law in
Chicago, as their representative to do the work, the legal
work, in drafting the Municipal Court Act. That committee labored for several months in preparing this act
and it was then submitted to the Legislature, after a constitutional amendment had been carried through permitting the City of Chicago to create municipal courts within
the city limits for the administration of the law, criminal
and civil, within the city limits.

Q. Well, will you describe the constitution of the court,
that is, the personnel? A. The law provides that the judge
must be thirty years of age, and must have practiced law
for five years in the City of Chicago prior to his election.

Q. How many judges are there? A. There are 28
judges. One of these is elected chief justice by the people
and the others are called associate justices.

Q. What are the salaries? A. The salary of the associate judges is $6,000 a year and of the chief justice
$7,500. The Legislature at the last session amended the act
so that the City Council may at any time it sees fit make
the salary of all the judges $10,000 a year.

Q. What are the other officers of the court? A. The
court has a chief bailiff who has 115 deputy bailiffs; a
chief clerk who has about 120 deputy clerks; then the entire
police department of the City of Chicago are ex-officio
deputy bailiffs of the municipal court and serve all process
practically in criminal cases. The sheriff of Cook County
also serves papers in criminal cases and executes process

that runs outside of the City of Chicago. The court, however, has jurisdiction only over defendants whose offenses may be committed in the city or may be served in civil cases in the City of Chicago, and in cases where one defendant lives outside of the city limits and one defendant inside, the court has jurisdiction to try the case and send his process outside of the city limits for the other defendant. But in case the suit against the defendant living in the city is dismissed, so must the suit against the defendant living outside of the city be dismissed.

BY CHAIRMAN PAGE:

Q. How are the associate judges chosen? A. They are all elected by the people.

Q. You said the chief justice was elected by the people and the associate judges. I didn't know but they were in some way distinguished? A. Yes, I see, I want to draw this distinction. He is not selected by the associate judges but is elected by the people for a definite term.

BY COMMISSIONER MURPHY:

Q. Are the associate judges elected over the entire city or a district? A. Throughout the entire city. For the first election nine were elected for two years, nine for four years and nine for six years and thereafter for six years.

BY MR. BUCK:

Q. The court has both civil and criminal jurisdiction? A. Yes, its jurisdiction is divided into six classes. The court was instituted not only to do the work formerly done by the justice of the peace but the court was created for the purpose of aiding the circuit and superior courts of

Cook County. These courts are courts of general jurisdiction differing practically only in name, and they were
behind in their calendars from three to five years in the
trial of civil cases. Misdemeanor cases were often delayed
from six months to three years without trial because the
criminal court, which is composed of judges of the circuit
and superior courts who were assigned there for the trial
of criminal cases, were engaged in trying felony cases and
cases of men who were incarcerated in jail and who were
entitled to their liberty in case they had been in jail four
months without trial.

Q. As this Commission is dealing with the inferior criminal courts I will ask you to outline the criminal jurisdiction of the court? A. The jurisdiction of the municipal
court is direct and indirect. Its direct jurisdiction in criminal cases covers all cases known as misdemeanors, that
is, cases punishable by fine and imprisonments otherwise
than in the penintentiary, and also in the cases for the
violations of city ordinances. Its indirect criminal jurisdiction is over such cases as may be transferred to the
municipal court by the criminal court of Cook County,
which may be a homicide or any felony case. This jurisdiction, however, is doubted and the court does not try cases
transferred from the criminal court, for the reason that
it is regarded as special legislation; that is to say, if the
circuit court of Cook County may transfer a criminal case
to the municipal court, it may dispose of a criminal case
in a different way from the circuit court of Sangamon
County; to-wit, it can transfer its criminal case, hence
that is not general legislation; and the court is now seek-

ing or will seek at this session of the legislature other legislation to cover this defect. It will be sought in one of two ways, either by the institution of a grand jury for the City of Chicago and within the court, or by the abolition of the grand jury and the trial of cases on information. If the grand jury is abolished, which is likely, the municipal court now, by reason of the jurisdiction which it has, will be able to try felony cases on information.

Q. How are bastardy cases tried? A. Bastardy cases at the time of the institution of the municipal court were tried in the criminal court of Cook County. At the last session of the legislature a year ago the municipal court was given jurisdiction of bastardy cases and the court now has jurisdiction of that class of cases.

Q. Are the cases tried by the judges alone? A. Yes.

Q. Isn't a jury used in determining the question of fact in bastardy cases? A. Jury trials may be had upon demand in criminal cases. During the past year there have been tried seventy-four thousand and more—seventy-four thousand I think—this is an important matter and I will give you the exact figures. (Consults book.) There was disposed of in the municipal court of Chicago during the past year in criminal and quasi-criminal cases seventy-four thousand nine hundred and thirty, out of seventy-five thousand one hundred and thirty-four filed in the court; that is to say, all but two hundred and four cases filed during the year were disposed of—that is in number. Of these cases three hundred and twelve were tried by jury. That is, I think less than one-quarter of one per cent., and in all these cases the defendant had the right to a jury trial upon demand without cost.

BY COMMISSIONER MURPHY:

Q. Is there any one particular court to try bastardy cases or are they placed on the regular calendar? A. They are placed on the regular calendar unless a jury is demanded, when they are transferred to the jury judges—part of the time two judges have sat in the trial of jury cases. When a jury trial is demanded in any of the criminal branches, and there are ten criminal branches of the criminal court located in different parts of the city—if a jury trial is demanded the case is immediately transferred to the Criminal Court Building where a judge sits with a jury, and if these demands are numerous another judge is assigned to try the cases with a jury.

BY MR. BUCK:

Q. Ordinarily do you have more than one judge trying jury cases? A. Ordinarily one judge can do the work, but once in a while there is an accumulation and then two or more judges are assigned.

BY COMMISSIONER WINTHROP:

Q. If no jury trial is demanded is the case disposed of by one judge? A. By one judge. The court, while it is one court, has as many branches as there are judges, and each judge exercises all the powers of the court in his branch.

BY MR. BUCK:

Q. In speaking of one judge disposing of jury trials are you referring to the criminal side of the court? A. I was referring to the criminal side. On the civil side we have an average of ten judges trying jury cases. Out of forty-six thousand eight hundred and forty-five civil cases disposed of during the year there were two thousand three hundred and sixty jury trials or about five per cent. of the civil cases were tried by jury. In civil cases a jury may be had upon demand and the payment at the time of entering the suit, or at the time of entering the appearance, of six dollars. It seems that this small sum for a jury trial has discouraged the trial of civil causes by juries to such an extent that as I say only five per cent. of the civil cases are tried by jury. These civil cases include cases that involve any sum from one dollar to any sum.

Q. Are the juries composed of twelve men? A. Twelve men.

BY CHAIRMAN PAGE:

Q. Is not your jurisdiction limited in amount? A. In some classes of cases, for example, since the court was organized to aid the other courts in disposing of their business the jurisdiction was divided leaving the tort cases, the negligence cases in sums over one thousand dollars with the other courts, circuit and superior courts, and the chancery jurisdiction. Our court was given jurisdiction in suits for money and property in any sum, so that the commercial cases are brought in the municipal court of Chicago. Our court enters in money judgments nearly every month double the amount of that entered in the circuit and superior court. For instance in the month of November last our court entered nineteen thousand dollars more than twice that of all the other courts combined.

BY COMMISSIONER MURPHY:

Q. You have an equity jurisdiction? A. By transfer. Equity cases are transferred to us, but that is the jurisdiction of which I have expressed doubt, so that we have tried but few equity cases.

BY MR. BUCK:

Q. Who has authority to take bail?A. The police officers of the city may take bail under rules and regulations prescribed by the court in all cases when the court is not in session; they may not take bail in misdemeanor cases, criminal cases, when the court is in session.

Q. What are the hours of the sessions of the court? A. The criminal courts convene at 9 o'clock, sometimes they have an afternoon session where they have a good deal of business; the civil courts convene at 9:30.

Q. Take the case of a person who wishes to make a complaint that some crime has been committed, what are the steps that that person will go through? A. The plaintiff or the complainant will go to one of the branch courts nearest to his residence, and the State's Attorney now maintains an assistant in the court, and the City Law Department has an assistant in the courts for the prosecution of violations of city ordinances. Occasionally one man does the work for both officials, and looks after both classes of cases. Under those circumstances the State's Attorney or the Assistant City Prosecuting Attorney is there, he examines the witnesses and presents the matter to the court. If he is not there, if it occurs in the night time, the complaint may be made to a police officer who prepares a complaint, and in the morning at 9 o'clock it is submitted to the Judge. He examines the complaining witness when the case is called or when the matter is called before him and orders a warrant to issue if he thinks a warrant should issue. That warrant is then given to a police officer for service.

Q. Do you have in connection with this court a Bureau of Information? A. Yes, the court contains a department in the clerk's office for furnishing information to lawyers and the public generally regarding any matter that they may inquire about in the court. I want to speak of the constitution of the court on its administrative side, which I regard as very important in the disposition of the criminal and civil business. The judges of the court have larger powers than those granted generally in this country to courts. The judges may prescribe rules of practice and procedure in the court, not such rules as are ordinarily prescribed, but those affecting the procedure and the practice. They may do that at a meeting of the judges of the court, and one is required by law to be held each month except in the month of August. The judges may discharge the deputy bailiffs or the deputy clerks with or without cause by entering a proper order in the records of the court. The judges fix the number of deputy bailiffs and deputy clerks required in the court, and the judges fix the salary of the deputy clerks and the deputy bailiffs in the court, except the Chief Deputy Clerk and the Chief Deputy Bailiff. The Chief Justice of the court is General Superintendent of the business of the court. He is Superintendent of the clerk's office, he is Superintendent of the bailiff's office, and he has charge of the calendars. He may assign judges to different parts of the city, to different branch courts, as he sees fit. He may create within a district any number of branch courts that he desires, by entering a proper order. The machinery therefore is elastic, and can meet the conditions of business. For example there is laid on my desk, usually on the first day after the end of the month, a complete report of the business of the court for the prior month. I know therefore the number of cases of the different classes brought in the court, how many were disposed of, what judge disposed of them, and therefore can for the next month assign additional judges for the trial of any particular class of cases that seem to be behind. For example, there are more contract cases brought than there are torts, and if those cases are not being rapidly disposed of an additional judge can be assigned from another branch court to try that class of cases for the next month, and keep the calendar up to date all along. The Chief Justice has an auditor who audits the business of the court each month, and makes his report to the Chief Justice of such conditions as he finds, with such recommendations as he thinks ought to be made. The books are closed each month ending with this report to the Chief Justice. The judges meet for the discussion of any matter that seems to them important in the court. Different rulings of the different judges are discussed, and if the judges differ on some matter that is brought to the attention of the entire body, brought up for discussion at the monthly meetings. One of the important features of the law is the fact that the Police Department is connected with the court, that is to say, each police officer is a deputy bailiff of the court. I may illustrate the importance of that by one circumstance. Prior to the establishment of the Municipal Court warrants were frequently served in criminal cases and quasi-criminal cases by police officers. The return of those warrants was often a perfunctory matter, the officer wrote "Not found" or "Not in the city" on the back of the warrant. Sometimes it was returned to the files, sometimes he forgot it at home or left it in another coat pocket, and it did not become part of the files. After the institution of the Municipal Court I instituted inquiries in various branch municipal courts as to the number of warrants not served, or where the defendant was not found. On one occasion I found as many as one hundred and twenty-seven that were not served. The court therefore instituted a warrant record by general order of the court, and made it a public record, which it is a criminal offense to alter or falsify. This warrant record is kept in each criminal branch of the Municipal Court and the name of the officer who received the warrant, his number, the date upon which he received it, is recorded by the Clerk of the Court in this book. The officer makes his return to the court, and the character of that return is kept in the warrant record. The return is required to be made just as a sheriff would make a return and instead of writing on the back of the warrant "Not found" or "Not in the city," the officer now makes a complete return. "The above-named defendant John Jones, not found in the City of Chicago—John Smith, police officer, 44th precinct.'' The responsibility for the handling of the criminal process therefore is placed upon the individual officer. Some two or three years ago, in 1905, the Police Department had rules, Section 137 of which read as follows: "Warrants not to execute. Patrolmen except those detailed at the Detective Bureau shall not execute a warrant of arrest or a search warrant which may be sent to their commanding officers unless such warrant is endorsed by the General Superintendent or the commanding officer of the Detective Bureau." Manifestly of course the Chief of Police or the head of the Detective Bureau had no right to intercept the processes of the court, and the attention of the officers was called to that. In other words, the fact that the officers are deputy bailiffs of the court protects the citizen in his dealings with officers. Complaints may be made to the branch court where an officer has brought a defendant regarding mistreatment. On the other hand the officer is before the court as its bailiff and the court can inquire into charges that are unfounded against the officer and adjust those matters. There has been no friction between the Police Department of the City of Chicago and the court during the past two years of any serious consequence.

BY COMMISSIONER WINTHROP:

Q. In addition to the bailffs or deputy bailiffs that are directly appointed by the court as I understand it you have these police officers that are detailed to the court and become bailiffs of the court? A. Not only detailed to the court but every police officer of the city is ex-officio a bailiff of the court, and is a bailiff of the court when he does anything for the court in the matter of executing its processes.

Q. Does the court ask a certain number of these police officers to be detailed for duty with the court or is its business naturally taken care of by its own deputy bailiffs? A. The civil business in the Municipal Court is taken care of by the bailiffs of the court, the criminal business is generally taken care of by the police officers of the city.

Q. Who become deputy bailiffs of the court? A. They are deputy bailiffs of the court, and each commanding officer has a number of officers connected with every branch court who carries out his orders. For example, if we had to serve two thousand processes they would be sent out through the Police Department to the various stations nearest where the defendants live, and the officers of that station, the commanding officers, would assign them to his officers, his patrolmen.

BY COMMISSIONER MURPHY:

Q. That is, in practice when you have a number of warrants you send them at a certain hour of the day to the police and the commanding officer distributes them among his men to be served? A. Yes, sir.

BY COMMISSIONER WINTHROP:

Q. Then in addition to serving your warrants in this way you have a certain number of these police officers detailed to service with the court to keep order in the court? A. No. The order in the court is kept by the Court's own bailiffs, but occasionally a police officer does that work. Generally, however, they serve the processes in the criminal cases.

Q. The Court uses the Police Force principally in the service of processes, and in little else? A. Little else.

BY COMMISSIONER HAMILTON:

Q. What control does the Court exercise over the police officers acting as deputy bailiffs? A. What it does and what it might do are two different things. At the present time it prescribes the rules for taking bail, and regulates that matter. Its only interference, if you might call it such, was in the case of the establishment of the warrant record. That was done because some warrants found their way into the Detective Bureau and were not served promptly. The Court felt that it was the result of this rule of the Police Department, and hence established the warrant record, and established that control over the action of the officers in the handling of the processes, placing the responsibility upon the individual officers.

Q. Suppose a citizen complained to the Court of abuse by a police officer in acting as deputy bailiff what would be the Court's procedure? A. The Court might investigate that matter since the officer was a bailiff of the Court.

Q. And has it power to discipline the officer? A. It has not exercised such power, it would have power, yes.

BY COMMISSIONER MURPHY:

Q. Effective power? A. Just such power as a court has over its officers.

Q. Could you remove the man or bring him up on charges? A. No. We have not the power to remove a police officer as we have the regular bailiffs of the Court. but we would have power to hold him, for example, in contempt, for any act which he may have committed in carrying out the Court's orders that was improper or illegal.

BY CHAIRMAN PAGE:

Q. Do I understand that the municipal courts having civil jurisdiction sit in one place, or are they scattered around the city? A. It was contemplated when the law was passed that the city should be divided, and it was divided into five districts. That was impracticable for several reasons. In the first place the court having such wide jurisdiction it required the attendance of members of the bar in remote portions of the city, for example, in South Chicago, which is twenty-five miles away from the northwest side. Counsel may have one case in one place and one case in another on the same day, and he cannot attend to that matter. Besides that we found it unwise to have a number of courts scattered around the city, little local courts. They became contaminated with the local influences. The bar desired that the courts should be brought together, and we thought it was best in the administration of justice, not only in its administration but also to keep it pure, that the courts be consolidated; and therefore all the civil branches are now in one building, a temporary building now, but they will be established in the court house when it is completed, twenty-four court rooms being reserved in that building for the several branches of the Municipal Court, and the main criminal branches will be consolidated in the Loop District. A new building is being contemplated, in fact the ground has been bought for the erection of a criminal court building for the Municipal

Court and for the Police Department, for its headquarters, and for a modern city jail. This building is to contain these three branches of administration, and we will have from four to six court rooms in this building, so that about 65% of the criminal business, such as comes from the levee districts of the city, will be tried in this one building. We will require then perhaps four or five courts in the outlying districts, criminal courts.

BY COMMISSIONER WINTHROP:

Q. Is this distribution of courts made by you as Chief Justice? A. Yes, sir. Wherever one seems to be necessary in a district it may be created by a general order. The Chief Justice has not the power to create districts— the judges as a body and the City Council together may create the districts.

Q. What do you mean by a district? A. The City of Chicago was originally divided into five districts.

Q. Having civil and criminal jurisdiction? A. Both. We eliminated all but two of those districts, and now a large part of the city conforms to the first district. South Chicago, which is remote at the foot of Lake Michigan, is made the Second District, by reason of the long distance from the other part of the city.

BY MR. BUCK:

Q. You have more than two criminal courts in one district then? A. We have only one in the Second District, and the other nine are in the First District.

Q. You possess the absolute power to assign the judges to the different districts? A. Yes, and to the trial of different classes of cases.

Q. If a judge is giving satisfaction in the way he is handling criminal work in one district, do you leave him there? A. No, the trial of criminal cases and cases for the violation of city ordinances is a difficult task, it is trying upon the nerves, and the Judge is changed usually every six months, although sometimes a judge is left in a criminal branch as long as a year, but not longer.

Q. So you would agree with the opinion expressed here yesterday that it is extremely trying on a man to continuously try criminal cases? A. I think it is. I think it is best for him and best for the community or those he may come in contact with, that he be shifted occasionally, and it is a good idea, too, because some judges are not as careful about some matters as other judges are, and if one who is careless about the way his court is run in many ways is succeeded by one who is punctilious and careful, the bailiffs, clerks and police officers get different ideas of how the court should be run. Ruts which the court gets into are removed in that way.

BY CHAIRMAN PAGE:

Q. Your criminal courts, the criminal branches, are scattered around the districts throughout the city? A. Yes, sir.

Q. Are they largely in connection with the police station houses? A. They are at the present time.

Q. Do you think that is a good plan? A. No, I do not. I think that the court should be near enough to the police station so that prisoners can be readily transferred, but I think it would be better if it was in a separate building, for the reason that the court is too apt to seem to be a part of the Police Department, and whether the Court is partial to police officers or not many of the public will suspect that it is, and that is nearly as bad as if it were.

Q. Is the Municipal Court the court in which a defendant who is arrested is first arraigned? A. Yes, the defendant is arraigned in the branch court where the warrant is returnable.

Q. Can a defendant charged with felony, in a case which the Municipal Court would not have jurisdiction to try be arraigned by one of the judges of that court? A. A preliminary examination is held and if there is probable cause he is bound over to the grand jury.

Q. This number of cases that you have given of seventy-four thousand nine hundred and thirty are only those that were actually tried in that court? A. They include preliminary examinations in felony cases, criminal cases, misdemeanors, and cases for the violation of city ordinances.

Q. It includes all of those? A. Yes, sir.

Q. And not merely trials? A. No, sir.

BY MR. BUCK:

Q. What do you say to the proposition that it is necessary that the same Judge should sit in the trial of criminal cases in order that he may know the old offenders? A. That is not necessary for the reason that the Police Department has a bureau of identification, called the Bertillon System, by which they furnish the Court every morning with the records of the defendants who are habitual criminals.

Q. Each district court possesses a complete record? A. 'No. The City Police Department has one central bureau, but the officers are furnished the record of defendants.

Q. That is as soon as the prisoner is brought before the Court—— A. As soon as a prisoner is arrested, if he is an offender, that is determined by the Bertillon System, if he is an habitual offender, and the Court therefore knows about that before sentence.

Q. Have you a probation system in Chicago? A. The State of Illinois has no law for adult probation, except the law called the indeterminate sentence, which applies to offenders incarcerated in the State Penitentiary and in the State Reformatory.

BY CHAIRMAN PAGE:

Q. That is more a system of parole, isn't it? A. Yes, a parole system.

Q. At the expiration of the early term the prisoner is released and required to report during the continuance, or at the end of his term? A. Prior to 1903 the courts of Cook County sometimes suspended sentence, and let the defendant go on his own recognizance, but in that year in the 202d Illinois, page 300, the Court decided in the case of the People against Barrett that a judge in Illinois had not the right to enlarge a defendant on a suspended sentence or on his own recognizance; that it was his duty to pass upon the case; that the only system of parole known to Illinois law was the Indeterminate Sentence Act. It said in effect that if the defendant was allowed to go on probation indefinitely after having made promises to the Judge, that those promises might be as varied as the different judges might make them, and that hence a citizen might be oppressed, and that the liberty of the citizen did not rest upon any such insecure foundation. We have had an experience illustrating how clearly the Judge who wrote that opinion foresaw what might happen. We have had an experience in the case of a judge who extracted promises from defendants that they would or would not do a certain thing. He entered maximum sentences against defendants for disorderly conduct, for example, $100 and costs, and that meant at 50 cents a day 200 days in the House of Correction. Then he allowed a motion to vacate and continued the motion sometimes indefinitely, extracting promises from the defendant that he would or would not do certain things. In some cases, and generally that was, not to take another glass of liquor or not to go into a certain saloon. If the Court found that the defendant had violated that pledge and had taken a glass of liquor or had gone into the saloon, the motion to vacate was overruled, and the sentence fell upon the defendant, and I regarded that he was punished, not for what he had done originally but for breaking his promise to the Judge for doing what he had under the law a perfect right to do, and that it was not a punishment for the violation of a criminal law, but for violating a promise that he had made to the Judge, and I removed that Judge from the trial of criminal cases at that time, and afterwards reinstated him in the trial of criminal cases with a full explanation of this situation, and with the admonition that he would be again removed if he resorted to that practice.

BY COMMISSIONER MURPHY:

Q. Do you think that any probation system is unconstitutional? A. Well, I think that no probation system which makes the liberty of the citizen dependent upon promises which he may make to the judge according to the whim of the judge can be constitutional. In 1896 Judge Barnes, of the Superior Court, who was associated with me in the Criminal Court for eight years, suggested that we ought to do something in regard to a first offender to permit him to escape punishment in such cases as the Court thought in his discretion he might be restored to society, because of the fact that so many of the first offenders are adolescent; that is, between the ages of 15 and 21. Judge Barnes prepared an adult probation law which I sent to the Legislature with the endorsement of the Municipal Court judges. This bill failed to pass, but another bill drawn up by Judge Gibbons, of the Superior Court, which provided for parole officers, was passed. It was vetoed by the Governor on the ground that it was not constitutional; and then Judge Stephen A. Foster, of our court, prepared an adult probation bill, after examing the ten laws of the ten different states. That is now pending in the Illinois Legislature, together with a number of miscellaneous bills. The Foster bill provides that the judges by rule may regulate the limits of discretion of a particular judge.

BY MR. BUCK:

Q. Have you any juvenile probation system? A. We have a separate court known as the Juvenile Court. The judges of the Circuit Court select one of their number, who presides in the Juvenile Court; and while juveniles have been brought into our court, at least one thousand of them have been transferred by our judges to the Juvenile Court.

The Judge of the Juvenile Court is now contemplating drafting a law which will enable the Municipal Court to assist the Juvenile Court in the handling of the juvenile cases.

Q. Can you tell us, does the Circuit Court correspond to our Supreme Court here? A. The Circuit Court and the Superior Court are courts of general jurisdiction, and I think they correspond to your Supreme Court.

Q. How are the probation officers selected? A. That is, how do these bills that are pending before the Legislature provide for that selection?

Q. Yes. A. They provide that the judges of the court may select the probation officers.

Q. But in connection with the Juvenile Court you have a probation system? A. Yes, there is a probation system in connection with the Juvenile Court.

Q. How are those officers selected? A. I am not sure how they are selected; I believe they are selected by the Judge, but I am not certain about that. On reflection I believe the judges of the circuit fix the number and the County board appoint.

Q. Are you familiar with the system that is followed in your probation cases? A. In the Juvenile Court?

Q. Yes, in the Juvenile Court? A. Only generally.

Q. Tell us what you can about it? A. The Juvenile Court has a number of probation officers——

Q. Are they paid officers? A. Yes. They received notices from the police officers when juveniles are apprehended, which of the stations they are at, and they immediately investigate the case. If it is a serious case, it is presented to the Juvenile Court, and the Judge takes the matter in hand. If it is not so serious, it is sometimes adjusted without being brought into the court.

Q. Do you know whether volunteer probation officers are also employed in the Juvenile Court? A. I assume there are some volunteer officers to help out—I don't think that is a good idea, however.

Q. Did I understand you to say that the same Judge continuously holds the Juvenile Court? A. Yes, for such period as the Circuit Court judges select them. Judge Tuthill, Judge Mack and Judge Pinckney have held the Juvenile Court most of the time in the last few years.

Q. Have they alternated or has one judge held continuously? A. One judge holds continuously until another judge is selected by his associates to preside in that court.

BY COMMISSIONER WINTHROP:

Q. How long do they usually sit? A. Usually more than a year.

BY CHAIRMAN PAGE:

Q. Judge Mack sat for some time, didn't he, continuously? A. I think he sat for two years or more.

BY COMMISSIONER MURPHY:

Q. Do you think the judges of the Circuit Court recognize the fact that juveniles need special attention, a special character of judge? A. It is so regarded, the fundamental idea is that juveniles shall not be arraigned in court as offenders before the law, but that it shall be a hearing without the formalities of a court. That is the objection to bringing them into the Municipal Court, because they come in contact with other offenders, and it looks as if they had been charged with crime.

BY COMMISSIONER WINTHROP:

Q. This Juvenile Court of the Circuit Court has not criminal jurisdiction, or does not exercise in dealing with juvenile offenders its criminal jurisdiction? A. They permit the Criminal Court to exercise it if they see fit. The Circuit Court judges have criminal jurisdiction over juvenile offenders.

Q. But when it sits as a Juvenile Court it sits in what capacity? A. As a Juvenile Court, under the statutes applicable to that class of cases.

Q. Is that a court of civil or criminal jurisdiction or both—I mean sitting in its civil side or chancery side or its criminal side? A. It sits—let me see if I understand your meaning. It exercises, I should say, its power under a special statute. It may detain a juvenile, as a delinquent. If the defendant is to be tried and sent to a reformatory, for example, he may be bound over to the Criminal Court— that court has criminal jurisdiction, the Circuit Judge sitting as a Criminal Court.

BY CHAIRMAN PAGE:

Q. That is, a judge of the Juvenile Court cannot sentence a child to the reformatory? A. No, he does not do it as a Juvenile Court Judge.

BY COMMISSIONER WINTHROP:

Q. But would send it to the criminal docket? A. To the criminal court for trial.

Q. Then the Juvenile Court Judge exercises practically only the parental powers of the Court? A. Yes, and he determines whether or not the defendant should be incarcerated in a Juvenile Court detention home—they have a home for those boys, but only the bad cases are put in this place.

Q. Does your court have jurisdiction of misdemeanors committed by juvenile offenders? A. Up to the time that we find that they are of juvenile age, in which case the Court discharges the defendant, because it has not jurisdiction. The Juvenile Court has jurisdiction. A justice of the peace had the right to transfer a juvenile upon discovering that he was of juvenile age to the Juvenile Court. That jurisdiction was intended to be given to the Municipal Court, but it was not given to us. We were given the same jurisdiction that a justice of the peace had in civil cases, and then certain criminal jurisdiction was left out, that right to transfer. Our judges have dismissed the cases, and told the officer to take him to the Juvenile Court, but we have not the legal power to transfer him to the Juvenile Court. I think the juvenile jurisdiction ought to be the jurisdiction of the Municipal Court rather than of the Circuit Court. It has better facilities to handle that class of cases, and ultimately that may be the disposition of that class of cases in Chicago.

BY MR. BUCK:

Q. In order to get your opinion on our local proposition, let me ask you this question: Suppose that court should have jurisdiction of all the juvenile cases, would you deem it advisable to assign one judge to sit continuously in the Juvenile Court? A. For a long period, yes, for a period of at least one year and perhaps more.

Q. Would you think it inadvisable that the Judge should sit longer than a year? A. For his own sake, he may get tired of it, the handling of juveniles requires a man of peculiar temperament, and some judges may be better fitted for that class of work than others.

Q. If you found a judge peculiarly adapted for that work, would you keep him right at it? A. I would likely keep him in that court a reasonable length of time. Of course, if he desired to get into some other class of work, he would be accommodated—no hard and fast rule about that. In fact, the assignment of judges in the past two years in the Municipal Court has seldom been by letter, it is sometimes at the request of the Judge to sit at such and such a place, and by inquiry as to where he would like to sit. The judges prefer to sit in places sometimes near their homes, at other times they prefer to go about the city.

BY COMMISSIONER FRANCIS:

Q. There is no fixed system of rotation? A. Except such as may be determined by the Chief Justice.

BY COMMISSIONER WINTHROP:

Q. In that connection, do you assign judges to sit in criminal cases near their homes? A. When the Court was first instituted the judges who sat in criminal cases were taken from remote parts of the city, so that they were strangers to the neighborhood. I don't regard that as so important now as I did when the Court was first organized. We were anxious to cut all relations with aldermen, police officers and neighborhood influences at the beginning, and since the interference with the administration of justice on the part of those who frequently came in because it was their custom was discouraged, there is very little or none of it now, so it makes less difference than it did when the Court was organized.

BY MR. BUCK:

Q. Would you describe to the Commission what you consider the best arrangement for a police court, I mean the best arrangement of the judge's bench, and the clerks, and the witness stand, and the prisoners' box? A. My idea is that a court of first instance for the trial of minor cases should be as dignified a court as there is in the community. The poor citizen, the citizen of foreign extraction, the citizen of foreign birth, gets his ideas of our entire government generally and mostly from the judges sitting in the minor courts, and if these men be men of character, ability and integrity the large body of the citizens get a better idea of their government than they do where the Court is one of less dignity and less character, less ability. The idea has been general throughout this country that anybody may sit to try the cases of the minor offender, or the minor civil action, but the poor man is as much entitled to a just and able decision of his case as is the rich man, and that is the idea back of the organization of this court. The idea was to pay the judges as well as any other judges were paid in nisi prius courts. The fact that they are paid less now has led to the effect that a great many incompetent men become candidates for judges of the Municipal Court; it leads to the effect that we are not able to induce leading members of the bar to become candidates for the position, because they would prefer to run as judges of the

Circuit Court or Superior Court, where they would be paid $4,000 a year more, and unless the salaries of the Municipal Court judges are made equal to those of Circuit Court judges or those of Superior Court judges we will have an inferior bench in the Municipal Court. I think that is appreciated by the public, because the last Legislature provided that the City Council might raise those salaries to $10,000. My judgment is that they will be raised, or that the Court will deteriorate in its personnel, because the judges cannot afford to sit on the bench of that court when their work is more ardurous and they are able, politically and otherwise, to sit in the Circuit Corut or the Superior Court.

BY COMMISSIONER MURPHY:

Q. Have any of the judges of this Municipal Court, because of the record they have made, been elected to the Superior Court or the Circuit Court? A. No, for several reasons: First, the court is only two years old, but I may say that at the last gathering of the party leaders of the Republican party I understand a resolution or a suggestion was made that no Municipal judge would be considered for the Circuit bench. That was due to the fact that there were three or four men on the Municipal Court bench with considerable political influence, and men of capacity and experience who were anxious to become candidates for the Circuit Court bench, in view of the larger salary. I don't think it was done to discriminate against the Municipal Court or against its judges, but rather to fix up the political slate and eliminate the complication that would arise by placing in nomination a number of Municipal Court judges, and then have to have another Municipal Court election. I think that was the occasion of it. Most of the judges of the Municipal Court are lawyers of experience at the bar, and many of them are university graduates.

BY MR. BUCK:

Q. Would you not at all subscribe to the proposition that a layman at a moderate salary is good enough to try cases of drunkenness and disorderly conduct? A. Many times laymen make very good magistrates in the minor cases, but generally when a layman sits in a minor case, the case is a very minor one; if the court is to have any extended jurisdiction, of course, it is necessary that the Judge sitting there should be a trained lawyer and generally I think that no layman should sit as a judge in the administration of justice.

BY COMMISSIONER MURPHY:

Q. Do the judges wear gowns? A. They do not. It has been agitated, however, and is under consideration by the Bar Association and the judges of the courts.

BY CHAIRMAN PAGE:

Q. Now, in regard to the physical surroundings of the court room, do you arraign each prisoner separately, and have the others outside of the room? A. They are arraigned as they are brought in, generally one at a time.

Q. Well, take in Manhattan, for instance, in the Borough of Manhattan, it is the custom of many of the magistrates, most of them, in fact, to have a long line of prisoners in the morning, each prisoner accompanied by the officer who makes the complaint, and this line stretches from the court room out into the corridor that leads to the detention pen, and they are brought up, one at a time, of course, before the Magistrate, and his case is disposed of, and then the next one is put on, the line moving up. Do you have any such practice as that? A. In some of the courts that is done, but in most of the courts the defendant is brought in and he is arraigned, and it is then determined whether or not he wants a jury. If he does not want a jury trial, and he is ready for trial, he can have that trial immediately. Most criminal cases are disposed of, I should say 90 per cent of the criminal cases are disposed of the day following the arrest.

Q. Of course, in New York our magistrates have very limited jurisdiction to dispose of cases; they are generally committing magistrates, either to hold for the Court of Special Sessions or for the Grand Jury? A. That leads to the discommoding of witnesses, the case is put off, and they are told to come another day, and when the case—it was so with us—when the case was turned over to the criminal court the grand jury sessions had to be attended by the witnesses, then they had to come back at the trial, and the witnesses were dragged from pillar to post so that many times they sought to avoid the prosecution of the case because of the amount of time they would lose. There is no reason why the first Judge should not have full jurisdiction to deal with the defendant on the spot, and our experience is that if the case is tried within five days of the time the offense was committed the defendant himself, if guilty, accuses himself; he realizes that he is guilty, and he believes it the first few days, but his opinion changes as time goes by, and very son he is convinced that he is really innocent and abused.

BY COMMISSIONER MURPHY:

Q. In this criminal branch you have a witness' chair, and an attorney's railing, just as it is in the civil court? A. Just about as it is in the civil court. Of course, we may not have it in some of the police stations, and we have only two new Criminal Court buildings in the outlying districts. Most of the criminal branches are old stations, new ones are being built continuously.

Q. Is the Shakespeare Avenue criminal branch a new court? A. The Shakespeare Avenue branch is a new court, and it is in the rear of the police station, connected with the police station, but far enough away so that it cannot be said to be a part of it. The officers do not attend unless they are in court for business.

BY MR. BUCK:

Q. I wish you would describe a little more in detail what you consider the ideal arrangement for a police court? A. Well, it would be the ideal arrangement for your Supreme Court room, it would be just the same as the room I saw in the hallway here; the bench, the jury box, etc. If the Grand Jury is abolished we shall try jury cases in some of these criminal branches, and a jury box will be required. I think the bench should be elevated above the floor, and the place for clerks and bailiffs elevated above the floor, the witness' chair, and the jury box; in other words, the ideal court room.

Q. Every court has a stenographer, I suppose? A. Only stenographers that are brought by the parties, though our

Act provides that the Court may appoint stenographers in each branch. We are now in a rented building, and the court pays its own rent; we pay $100,000 a year rent until the new Court House is completed, and it is our intention as soon as we get rid of this item of rent to appoint stenographers in each court. Perhaps we will have them within a year.

Q. That is, you will have a stenographer in both the civil and criminal parts? A. In every court.

BY CHAIRMAN PAGE:

Q. When a prisoner is brought in, who prepares the complaint or information or whatever you call it? A. The State's Attorney generally. It is our idea that a State's Attorney should be on hand in these branch courts, and examine the witnesses and prepare these papers, though our law provides that any citizen may file a complaint in court. When the State's attorney files a complaint, it is not sworn to, but when a citizen files it, he is obliged to swear to it and is examined by the Judge to determine whether or not there is probable cause.

Q. The State's Attorney corresponds to our District Attorney? A. Yes.

Q. Does he have a deputy in each of these branch courts? A. Yes, in each of the branch courts. There is one court where he has not, but the city prosecutor has acted for the State's Attorney, so I may say yes.

Q. You find that very desirable, don't you? A. Yes, sir, and it is desirable also that the citizens may file complaints over the head of the District Attorney, in case he finds that the District Attorney will not do it he may apply to the Court.

Q. Have you any clerk that is designated as a complaint clerk to receive these complaints and put them in proper legal form? A. Yes, we have two and sometimes three clerks at the large courts. At the Harrison Street Court we have two branch courts. Each judge has two clerks, sometimes three, and the Police Department has a very competent man who prepares these papers.

Q. The Police Department man prepares the papers for the police officers when they bring in a prisoner? A. They may do so. Those papers, however, are prescribed by the Court. All the court papers, complaints, informations, mittimi, are prepared by the Chief Justice of the court.

Q. On blanks? A. On blanks, and those blanks are furnished by the city not only in criminal cases but in civil cases. For example, after the institution of this court we had run about six months, when I found that an execution issued by the Court in the hands of a bailiff brought no results as a rule. Many times the defendant said simply, "I haven't anything," and the bailiff knew nothing about it. We thereupon adopted your New York proceeding subsequent to judgment, supplementary proceedings I believe you call them. We took your statute and the Wisconsin statute and combined the two and made it a part of our law, and it thereupon became my duty to prepare orders for that class of cases. This will illustrate how that work is done (referring to book). Here is one book devoted solely to that subject, regarding entries and abbreviated forms in supplementary proceedings. These are prepared under the law, under your New York decisions, which, of course, will be adopted by our Supreme Court if a case goes there. In this way the Court is enabled to do its work effectively. The Judge does not have to stop to see whether the papers are in legal form or not, as he would have to do if these forms were not provided. There will be less chance of error, or all would be error, depending on how carefully this work is done. The Court prescribed therefore all orders in criminal and in civil cases, and abbreviates those orders. The Court enters on its record the abbreviated form order. In view of the large volume of business, it would be expensive and impracticable to write full orders in the records of the court, hence we write the abbreviated form, and in case of a transcript being called for, or in case of a writ of error or appeal, the full form record is written up. Since so few of the cases are appealed, very little work has to be done in writing up the full form orders and the books are condensed. In addition to that, the court records are in form such as this paper that you may mark as an exhibit. In each envelope there is a copy of the half sheet, and the record is in the files. That contains a complete list of all orders entered by the Court, it contains a complete list of the papers filed in the court, so that the Court, when the envelope containing all this is laid on his desk, may open it and have before him all the orders entered in the case, all the papers filed in the case, and all the postponements, and knows how many times a case has been before the different judges of the court.

Q. Do you find that they have left sufficient blanks for postponements there? A. No, I was going to say that this is not the particular size. In the original we put the postponements here with the general orders. They are not orders of the Court, and it cluttered up the record so that we have recently devised the scheme of putting that here. That could be put on the outside of the envelope. It is only for the convenience of the Judge to know how many times the case has been before the Court.

Q. Is that small space an intimation to the Judge that few postponements should be granted? A. Well, it prevents disputes of counsel as to how many times the case has been before the Court.

Q. What I mean if the leaving of so small a space for postponements is a quiet hint from the Chief Justice that few postponements should be granted? A. Not necessarily, but that is the disposition of the Judge when he sees a large number of postponements, he feels that the case ought to be disposed of. It is always a reminder that it has been hanging a long time.

BY COMMISSIONER MURPHY:

Q. This is a copy of the original? The original is similar to this.

BY COMMISSIONER FRANCIS:

Q. Do you keep a record of counsel in all cases? A. Yes.

BY COMMISSIONER WINTHROP:

Q. You use this in criminal courts, too? A. Yes, sir.

BY CHAIRMAN PAGE:

Q. Are the clerks who take complaints in the same room with the Judge who tries the cases, or are they in a separate room? A. Occasionally they may be in the same room, but in the new stations that are being built a prosecuting attorney's room is provided where the prosecuting attorney examines these witnesses and prepares complaints. The complaints are generally prepared outside of the court room.

Q. I mean where a citizen comes in? A. He does not come into court except after the complaint has been prepared. It is then brought in and he is sworn by the clerk and the Judge then interrogates the witness.

BY COMMISSIONER HAMILTON:

Q. Is a separate time set apart for the interrogation of witnesses on complaints, or is that allowed to interrupt the judges in their business? A. Generally it is done before 9 o'clock in the morning, before the Judge comes in these complaints are prepared and brought before him the first thing. He runs over the complaints that are there, and in cases that are not filed by the State's Attorney he examines the witness. In cases where they are filed by the State's Attorney, the Judge does not examine the witness.

BY COMMISSIONER MURPHY:

Q. Then the State's Attorney is more in the character of an examining judge, and he takes all that work away from the Court? A. It relieves the Court to a large extent, yes, just as the District Attorney would in the Supreme Court where he presents matters to the Grand Jury, he makes the investigation and presents it.

BY CHAIRMAN PAGE:

Q. Do you have processes which are more restricted than warrants, like a summons, that you use? A. Yes, warrants in the Municipal Court may be issued for violation of city ordinances where the offense is also a violation of a state statute. It may issue also in cases where the complainant charges in the complaint that there is danger of the escape of the defendant. In most cases of violations of city ordinances summons are issued.

Q. What is the character of them? A. The city ordinances are very numerous. General warrants are issued for disorderly conduct, many cases are brought in by arrests on view for violation of city ordinances, by a city department, such as the Health Department, which prosecutes for violations of the milk ordinance, by summons, for violations of the smoke ordinance, by summons, for violations of various other health ordinances. The State Board of Pharmacy and other state boards may prosecute, and generally they prosecute by summons.

Q. In case of inquiry to find if crime has been committed, is that started by summons also? A. No, those cases are started by warrant, that is, those for crime, such violations of city ordinances are regarded as civil suits.

Q. I was just going to ask whether they were fines or penalites? A. They are penalties.

Q. Then in any criminal case, do you issue a summons, or do you always issue a warrant? A. We always issue a warrant in a criminal case.

BY MR. BUCK:

Q. Suppose a policeman sees a man speeding, does he give him a summons, or does he arrest him? A. If that is prosecuted as a violation of the State statutes, he files an information and the defendant is arrested on a warrant. If the officer can arrest him on view, he has a right to do that and bring him in and the complaint is filed when the defendant is brought to the station.

Q. But in case of a violation of a city ordinance, does the officer give him a summons or arrest on view? A. The officer prosecutes by summons for violation of a city ordinance, but if that same offense is also a state offense we may prosecute by warrant.

BY CHAIRMAN PAGE:

Q. Well, do you have ordinances the violation of which is a misdemeanor? A. No—that is—yes, we have ordinances the violation of which may be a misdemeanor. Take, for example, speeding through the streets. We have a city ordinance against that and we have a state statute against it. It is both a state misdemeanor and a violation of a city ordinance. Disorderly conduct is a state offense, and it is also a violation of a city ordinance. Generally those cases are prosecuted as violations of city ordinances.

BY COMMISSIONER WINTHROP:

Q. And, therefore, civilly prosecuted? A. Yes, civilly prosecuted.

BY MR. BUCK:

Q. You stated that in this Municipal Court Act were

embodied many of the recommendations that Judge Taft had made for the improvement of the administration of criminal law? A. Yes, the provision in the law that the judges of the court may prescribe the practice and procedure of the court is an important one, and the upper courts, the courts of appeal, may not reverse a municipal court cause as readily as they could a circuit court or superior court cause. There they might reverse for error of practice or procedure. Not so in the Municipal Court. The Court of Appeals may not presume that harm resulted to the defendant because of error of the trial court. The upper court, before it may reverse, must be of the opinion that substantial injustice was done on the merits of the case before it may reverse, and in that regard it meets the suggestions of Judge Taft, Judge Amidon and President Roosevelt in his message.

BY COMMISSIONER MURPHY:

Q. How is that brought about, by the difference between the Municipal Court and the Circuit Court and Superior Court? A. Because the Circuit and Superior Courts have gradually been interfered with by the Legislature. Originally, practice and procedure was a matter in the hands of the Court, but lawyers frequently went to the Legislature. They had been defeated sometimes in cases in court by the Judge, and to get even they surrounded themselves with other lawyers in the Legislature and passed some act of practice and procedure to limit the action of the Court. And in that way the Legislatures, not only of our state but other states, have gradually taken from the Court the right to control its practice and procedure and prescribed it as a legislative matter. They have done that to a considerable extent in Illinois, and the Court therefore is not elastic, it cannot meet conditions, especially as presented in a large city. And those who drafted the Municipal Court Act thought that a judge who was capable of passing upon the question of subjective law might be trusted with the details of objective law.

Q. So that your practice is practically absolutely controlled by the Court instead of prescribed bf your Municipal Court Act? A. Well, certain features are prescribed by the Municipal Court Act, but the judges may by passing proper rules control the procedure in the court. Now, to illustrate, I think less than one-tenth of one per cent of the total number of cases filed in the Municipal Court in the first year were reversed in the higher courts. Not over 275 or 280 of them were appealed to the upper courts, the Appellate Division or the Supreme Court of our state, which corresponds to your Court of Appeals. The result is finality of litigation in the court of first instance to a large degree. Of course, everybody can go to the upper courts, but the idea is to have the case tried upon its substantial merits. Frequently cases are reversed for errors in practice or procedure that do not affect the merits of the cause at all. That is not generally true in our court.

BY COMMISSIONER HAMILTON:

Q. Judge, what you say with regard to the different rulings being discussed at your monthly meeting and differences in rulings be largely avoided is very interesting, inasmuch as we have not found that same condition to obtain in some places in this state. How do you find that the discussions at your monthly meetings operate to bring about uniformity of rulings on the part of judges? A. They bring about uniformity of rulings, or the matter is subject to debate and if not clear some judge is assigned to brief that particular subject and sometimes more than one, and the matter is discussed at a subsequent meeting of the judges and action taken. I regard the assembly of the judges in monthly meetings as highly important. In courts where the judges are not bound together with responsibility for the court as a whole, one judge may not take as much interest in what the other judge does as he should. Sometimes I have known the case to be that it was regarded as a joke what some particular judge did when another judge discussed some matter that he had heard about, as, for example, the issuance of a writ or the unwarranted granting of a writ of habaes corpus, which was an evil in our state. Any action that seems subject to criticism is freely criticised at the judges' meeting. For example, I think at our last meeting, or the next to our last meeting, one judge arose and said: "I understand that one of our judges has continued a case from November," I think it was, "until the next March over the protest of the plaintiff." There was a heated discussion as to why that was done, and the Judge was criticised for having done that, putting it off so far. The action of one judge who had refused bail in minor cases and who had fixed excessive bail in minor cases was severely condemned at a judges' meeting, and the judge who had resorted to that was—it was called to his attention and the matter debated freely.

I think that is a very important provision of the act. It also brings about uniformity of action in the court, and if a decision is rendered by the Supreme Court it is at once called to the attention of all the judges and debated in the court; and any matter affecting the administration of justice is brought to the attention of all the judges of the court simultaneously. You get uniform and immediate action in the whole court and all branches thereof. Then, too, it is an important matter for this reason; I think it was Emerson who said that one wise man in a company of 25 will make the whole company wise, and so in a body of 28 judges there are always some men stronger than others, and such men take leadership.

Q. How about cases where different judges differ widely in the sentences that they impose for the same offense and each takes the action that he does on what he regards as sound ground? A. Well, that is debated, of course, and discussed so as to bring about some uniformity. Of course, each case rests upon its own bottom, and there can be no hard and fast rule as to what the Judge should assess as a fine or fix as imprisonment. That is difficult to determine, and yet in case of wide limits it would be discussed and debated. It also affords the members of the bar, this idea of the judges being one body and meeting as one body, it affords the members of the bar an opportunity to get redress when they feel that they have been unjustly treated. I have in mind one case where a lawyer complained bitterly about his treatment in the presence of his client on a motion for a new trial in a civil cause. He submitted to me a transcript of what had occurred and what the Judge had said. He felt greatly aggrieved. I thought it was a matter about which he had some cause for complaint, and I wrote on the stenographic transcript that he gave me, "My dear Judge," naming the judge, "I enclose the indictment in your case," and signed my initials, and sent it to him. In a little while it came back endorsed, "Nine-tenths justified." The lawyer came back to find what I had done, and I said, "What can I do? I have no authority over this judge." "Well," he said, "I though your body of judges could hear complaints." "Well," I said, "I don't think this is serious enough." "Well, did you do anything about it?" "Yes," and I showed him what the judge had written. He said, "What, does he admit it?" I said, "Yes." "Well," he said, "that is some satisfaction." And lawyers frequently complain to associate justices, not only to me but to the associate justices of their treatment by some other justice. Sometimes there is some occasion for it, sometimes there is none, but if there is occasion the whole body takes notice of what the bar thinks, also what their brethren think of what the bar thinks.

BY COMMISSIONER WINTHROP:

Q. These abuses, when there be any abuses, are they corrected merely by the force of the public opinion of the judges, or is there any way provided? A. There is no way provided in the law for any discipline of the Judge. The only power the Chief Justice has is to take a judge out of one class of cases if he thinks he is not trying those cases properly; he may remove him from such trials and substitute another judge. But the judges have no authority over each other except to discuss it and debáte it, and the force of the opinion of the other judges generally has weight with the individual whose action is criticised.

BY MR. BUCK:

Q. What method have you so that the decisions of one judge are brought to the attention of the other judges, so that if there is any difference of opinion between the judges on the rulings they will find it out? A. Well, that is debated, and if it cannot be settled on that occasion, as I say, a brief is prepared after the question has been looked up carefully and a report made by a committee to the judges.

BY COMMISSIONER MURPHY:

Q. Do you find that a good thing? A. I assume your question contemplates that there is frequently occasion to review another judge. There is not. Very seldom, if ever, is the action of any particular judge in a case brought up for review in the nature of having the body of the judges pass on whether his action is right or wrong. That is seldom done, but occasionally some judge may do things that require the action of the whole body, and it ought to be freely discussed, as, for example: One judge fixed bail at $10,000 for the violation of a city ordinance, the penalty for which was $200. That was excessive bail and amounted to a denial of the man's right in the court. That matter came before the body of the judges and they expressed their opinion of it in no uncertain language.

BY CHAIRMAN PAGE:

Q. And what was the effect? A. The effect was that the Judge realized that that was improper. He had been betrayed into doing that by carrying out a so-called adult probation system outside of the law, one of his own invention which he called "his system," which was condemned by the other judges.

BY MR. BUCK:

Q. What effect has the methods of your court had upon the commission of crime in Chicago? A. The number of arrests in the city of Chicago has fallen, in 1904 and 1905, the total arrests in the city were 78,000. That was the next to the last year of the justices of the peace. The last year of the justices of the peace, there were 92,761, arrests in criminal and quasi-criminal cases. During the regime of the Municipal Court, the first year the arrests were 57,490. Last year there were 63,993, or about 28,000 less than before; nearly 33 per cent. reduction in the number of arrests.

Q. How do you explain the increase? A. The increase over the——

Q. From 57,000 to 62,000? A. From 57 to 62?

Q. Yes? A. Why, the city of Chicago grows rapidly. We add a city the size of Peoria, Illinois, 100,000, every year. We have 200,000 more people than we had the first year of the court. The activity of the Health Bureau, presided over by Dr. Evans, in prosecuting those who violated the milk ordinances, the smoke ordinances and other health ordinances, have added a large number of those cases. It has not been an increase of criminal charges, but an increase of violations of city ordinances.

BY COMMISSIONER WINTHROP:

Q. How do you account for the enormous decrease from 92,000 to 57,000 when the court was established? A. Unwarranted arrests were made before the justices of the peace, raids were made on some suspected for the purpose of enabling a bail bond concessionary to collect fees from the unfortunates who were dragged in by patrol wagon loads. I put that as suspected.

Q. Is it a decrease in arrests or a decrease in crime? A. Both. It is a decrease in arrests, but there has been an increase in those who were punished for violation of the law. Ten per cent. of those arrested were punished under the justices of the peace. In the first year of our court 18 per cent were punished by imprisonment, and this last year 20 per cent. of those arrested were punished by imprisonment. In other words, the right man is getting in the right place. Now, for instance, under the justices of the peace there were 16,000—19,000, I think there were 19,000 arrests before the justices of the peace in felony and misdemeanor cases, and the Grand Jury indicted about 3,000 of those. The other 16,000 were discharged either because they were not guilty or they escaped punishment. And that isn't true now.

Q. Is the punishment swifter in your court than before? A. It is swifter than in any other city in the world, I think. Criminal cases are tried the day following or a few days following the arrest. If a jury trial is demanded, it is generally tried within two weeks. Of course, there are exceptions. If the defendant desires delay to consult counsel, or if he desires delay to get witnesses, or for any other reason, the Court is not arbitrary about that, but delays are readily granted; but not delays for weeks or months; it is a question of days or weeks. The idea is to clear the docket.

BY COMMISSIONER FRANCIS:

Q. If you postpone a case today at the request of counsel for the plaintiff, then two weeks from to-day do you postpone it at the request of counsel for defendant? A. Well, that might be done for a good reason, but the idea is to dispose of the cases, and there would have to be some special reason why he wanted that delay. He could get it if he had a good reason.

Q. Do you have many cases of that nature of, say a month or more? A. Not many, not many.

BY CHAIRMAN PAGE:

Q. You have no judges that believe that every man arraigned has the right to an adjournment of at least a week? A. Well, the Court is not arbitrary about that. We find the defendants are generally ready to go to trial either that day or within a few days. There is not much trouble about it.

Q. Well, isn't that largely because of the fact that the Court does hold them down pretty well? A. Well, partly that. They have become accustomed to a speedy trial.

MR. PAGE: We found in one case that we investigated,

in certain class of cases would be carried along for several months of adjournments of from two weeks to a month at a time.

BY COMMISSIONER MURPHY:

Q. Do you have many excise cases? A. What is the character of those?

BY CHAIRMAN PAGE:

Q. Selling liquors at prohibited hours or on Sunday? A. Oh, yes, we have a great many of those. There was some consternation the other day; I understood some citizen brought a complaint into the court on the ground that certain houses of ill fame were not provided with liquor licenses as required by law. A citizen could prosecute those if the Police Department failed.

BY MR. BUCK:

Q. Do you separate disorderly conduct cases from other cases? A. No, the cases come in their order on the sheet.

Q. You don't make any separation of criminal cases, then? A. No; that is, the civil suits are never brought in the criminal courts.

Q. Yes? A. But there is no distinction in the cases. Of course, sometimes a case that requires longer to try is put over to the afternoon, and when a jury trial is demanded a case is immediately transferred to the branch court having a jury. That Court sits over next to the County Jail, and, psychologically, I suppose that has had something to do with the few demands for jury trial.

BY COMMISSIONER HAMILTON:

Q. What special classes of criminal cases do you have tried in your special parts—— A. What?

Q. What special classes of criminal cases do you assign to special parts? A. To special courts?

Q. To special parts of your court? You spoke of assigning judges to special parts? A. Yes, the Judge sitting in the branch court tries all classes of cases that are brought in that police district. The police chief and the inspectors divide the city into districts for their management, and the court districts are outlined, and all cases within that district are brought to that branch court, of all classes. But on the civil side some judges are assigned to try contract cases—or what you would call assumpsit cases, I suppose—other judges are assigned to try tort cases, others to try forcible detainer, others to try attachment or replevin, and others to try the regular jury docket.

Q. Is there any such classification in the criminal side? A. No such division of the class of cases.

Q. Do you try bastardy cases along with other cases? A. Yes. There have been a great many more bastardy cases brought since our court had jurisdiction of bastardy than were ever brought before, and I account for that on the ground that it was not given the attention by the criminal court that it is given to-day by our court.

BY COMMISSIONER FRANCIS:

Q. Two years ago, when your court was organized, were the dockets of the Circuit Court and the Superior Court and the County Courts clogged to any extent? A. Yes, they were. I think the Superior Court was between two and three years behind in its docket and the Circuit Court between three and five years behind.

Q. You have no idea of the number of cases? A. Yes, I have. In our annual report we published a table showing the effect our court has had upon those other courts. That table indicates about what they had; that is, I am not advised as to how many were pending; that is the total number pending, but they had about 18,000 cases per year, the year before our court was instituted, the Circuit Court, Superior and County Courts, the two, Circuit and Superior, having about 8,000 and a little over, and the County Court about 759. They dropped in the first year of our court to 12,273, and this last year it dropped to 11,613. In other words, our court has disposed of 36 per cent. of the business of the Circuit Court, civil business, 31 per cent of the Superior Court business and 79 per cent. of the business of the County Court, or 35 7-10 per cent. of all the civil cases brought in the other three courts. Their receipts from civil cases in the courts fell from $259,885 to $199,988 this year. As against that figure, $199,988, our court's receipts were $722,000, to give you an idea of the magnitude of the business of the court.

Q. So the institution of your court has aided the higher courts to a great extent? A. Yes, to the extent indicated by those percentages, and besides that it has relieved the criminal court of misdemeanor cases. About 35 per cent. of the business of the criminal court has been disposed of in our court. The court is nearly self-sustaining. The first year it turned over a balance to the city, after paying for rent, paying the salaries of the justices, clerks, bailiffs, and for furniture, fixtures, law books, carpets and all equipment, $8,000. This last year our expenses were $743,000 that is the rough figure; and our total receipts were $722,-000. Of those total receipts $604,000 went back to the taxpayer. And when the court is given quarters rent free, the court will not cost the taxpayers of Chicago a cent, if criminal conditions keep up. If criminal conditions get better, the court will earn less on its criminal side.

BY COMMISSIONER WINTHROP:

Q. Your receipts are from fines exclusively? A. Our receipts are from fines for violation of city ordinances, fines for violation of the State Law, misdemeanor cases; many of those are punishable by fine or imprisonment or both, on the criminal side. And the receipts on the civil side are from the regular fees in the court in filing suits and appearances, from jury demands, $6.00 per jury; that does not begin to pay for the jury, however. A jury costs about $32.00 more than we get from each side when they both contribute for the jury.

Q. Does the court itself get the fees, or are they transferred? A. No, those are turned over to the city.

Q. Then, is an appropriation made for the court, or does the court run its own business? A. The City Council provides so much annually for the court on estimates provided by the Court, and the fees are then turned over to the city, those that belong to the city. Those that belong to the State's Attorney, to him, and to the different state boards as the law provides to them; and the park boards to them.

BY COMMISSIONER SMITH:

Q. What is the procedure, Judge, in a case of failure to support, when a woman comes to court and claims her husband is not supporting her? A. The non-support cases are —the County Court has jurisdiction of that class of cases. We are thinking of taking that jurisdiction over because that business belongs in our court. It is now being attended to in the County Court.

Q. Have you any societies in Chicago for the Prevention of Cruelty to Animals? A. Yes, the Humane Society.

Q. Do you have jurisdiction over the cases that they bring in? A. Yes.

Q. Do they get the fines? A. I don't remember whether they do or not. I think they do, but that depends upon the statute, the general statute of the State. If the general statute of the State provides that they shall receive the fines, they get them from our court; if it does not, why we turn it over to the city.

Q. Do the Municipal Court judges dispose of those cases at once—do they? A. Yes.

Q. Let's suppose a case of an arrest for some assault made at 2 o'clock in the afternoon: Follow that case along for us until it is disposed of? A. The defendant is brought to the police station nearest where he was arrested. If there is a branch Municipal Court there, he is brought to the desk sergeant. The Court, by its rules, fixes the amount of bail in that class of case, which the police officer has notice of, and the police officer may take bail in such sum as provided by the rules. The complaint may be made out by the desk sergeant, or in the larger courts by a clerk who sits at the court or by the State's Attorney; and that is filed in the court on the next morning, or filed then, and the defendant allowed to go on bail if he can give bail. If he doesn't give bail, he is incarcerated until the next morning, when he is brought up and arraigned and generally tried.

Q. Well, his case is disposed of—— A. The next day.

BY MR. BUCK:

Q. You have no night court, then, I take it? A. The act originally provided for a night court and the judges sat taking turns, one each night. We found that with the provision of the rules that permitted the police officers to take bail, under the sanction of the Court, that we seldom needed the services of the night judge; though the time may come when we will have to reinstitute that court.

BY COMMISSIONER SMITH:

Q. Supposing that man to have been admitted to bail in the station house on the afternoon of his arrest; would his case come up the next morning, any way? A. Yes.

Q. About what would be the average adjournment that he would be allowed? A. That depends upon what his request was. If he has a witness that is out of town and wants time to get him he is permitted to get that witness. If he wants counsel he is given time to get counsel. No hard and fast rule.

Q. Well, you would not say he would get more than two months' time. A. No; he would not get any two months' time unless for some extraordinary reason. He would get two months' time if it took two months to get a witness from England. But generally he would not have an excuse requiring more than a week, and seldom that.

Q. So that a case of that kind that would not be tried inside of a month would have to have some extraordinary circumstance? A. Very extraordinary, not to be tried that week.

BY MR. BUCK:

Q. Are counsel assigned to the defense? A. Yes.

Q. Who sees to it that criminals are promptly brought before the Magistrate? A. The Police Department bring most of the charges in the court.

BY COMMISSIONER SMITH:

Q. Well, Judge, while we are there now, it is kind of interesting, supposing the assault to be of a nature that would constitute a felony—say felonious assault—what happens? A. The defendant is given a preliminary hearing either then or at such time as he is ready for trial and bound over to the Criminal Court or discharged. With the abolishment of the Grand Jury we will be able to dispose of them in the court of first instance. Now he is bound over to the Grand Jury.

Q. At the present time he is held for the Grand Jury? A. Yes.

BY MR. BUCK:

Q. I don't think I made my other question quite clear. Yesterday one of the witnesses—a former police judge— said that cases had been brought to his attention of persons who had been held for a week without being brought before a magistrate. Under your system who sees to it that such a thing does not occur? A. The judge sitting at the Branch Court would know about that, because every morning the arrest sheet is subject to his inspection, and the arrest of the night before and the complaints that are brought, and that would be immediately called to the attention of the Judge sitting in the Criminal Branch.

BY COMMISSIONER MURPHY:

Q. Have you an elastic system of electing judges—that is, if your population should increase a hundred thousand this year, could you take cart of it by additional judges? A. Our act provides that upon the judges of the court certifying to the City Council that more judges are needed, by a joint resolution of the Court and the City Council an election may be called at the nearest pending election for nine more judges, or any number such as the judges and Council may agree upon not exceeding nine. So, provision is made for an increase of nine more judges, and I think the Court will be increased within two or three years, because we are now calling in county judges from other counties in the State of Illinois to help us out. Three or four are sitting now.

BY COMMISSIONER FRANCIS:

Q. No advantage has been taken of that provision as yet? A. Partly for this reason. The judges think they are not sufficiently paid, and they don't care to increase the Bench, until they are.

BY MR. BUCK:

Q. Do you have a physician connected with the Juvenile Court to examine the defective children? A. Connected with our court?

Q. No; with the Circuit Court? A. With the Juvenile Court?

Q. Yes? A. I am not familiar with the details of that, but I think the City Physician is called upon. I know he is called upon in all cases whenever it seems necessary, and in large cities where so many defectives are brought into the courts I think there should be connected with the courts alienists and medical men who can advise the Court as to what ought to be done with some defendants—what their condition is.

BY COMMISSIONER SMITH:

Q. Have you a house of detention for witnesses? A. For witnesses?

Q. The State's witnesses? A. No house of detention. When the Court needs to do so it may require that the witness shall give bond for his appearance, and on failure to give the bond he may be committed to the County Jail.

BY MR. BUCK:

Q. Is there any detention place for—— A. Debtors' department, I suppose.

Q. Is there any place for detention of juvenile offenders? A. Yes; they are detained in the Juvenile Court building, recently completed, or at the John Worthy School.

MR. BUCK: I think I will offer this form in evidence. (Said form was marked Exhibit 70.)

THE WITNESS: I have brought some books with me to illustrate the methods of keeping records, which I will leave with the Commission. The Court keeps complete judicial statistics such as the Commission will notice by the Second Annual Report. So that the status of all the business of the Court is quickly ascertained at any time.

BY COMMISSIONER MURPHY:

Q. Is there a good deal of co-operation between the Police Department, the District Attorney's office or the State's Attorney's office and the Court? A. Yes; along right lines.

Q. That is, the Police Department are very glad to furnish any information for identification of habitual criminals? A. Oh, yes; complete harmony, so far as all officials charged with administration of justice are concerned.

BY CHAIRMAN PAGE:

Q. You do not find any disposition on the part of police officers, in colloquial phrase, to put it up to the magistrates to discharge and take the responsibility from the police? A. Well, of course, that occurs occasionally.

Q. That is, an officer will make a number of arrests in a particular kind of crime, having really no evidence, and the case is presented to the Court, and, of ocurse, is dismissed, and the Chief of Police, the Superintendent of Police, immediately publishes in the newspapers that it is useless for his officers to make arrests, because the courts won't hold them. Have you any conditions such as that existing between your local courts and the police force? A. One of our judges reported such a condition. We are having one that is developing. In one of our criminal courts a judge has attempted to carry on a system of adult probation. And it is my judgment that the officers in that district are beginning to think that they can dispense adult probation as well as a judge, as long as there is no law for it. And I think a condition is developing of that sort in one court which can be removed, of course, in our elastic system.

BY COMMISSIONER FRANCIS:

Q. Also by the proposed law? A. Yes; warrants were not speedily served on one occasion by the officers, and that led to the creation of the warrant record. But there was no question about it, because it was only carrying out the law, and the Chief of Police understood why the Court created the warrant record. The police rule wasn't created by him or during his administration. So there has been no friction between the Police Department and the Court. There has been some friction in the court between the judges and the clerk and the bailiff of the court. When the court was first instituted the chief bailiff appointed a number of ex-constables—nine out of ten. It was my duty to approve the bonds, and I refused to approve them until they could be investigated as to their previous record, it being assumed by the Court prima facie that a constable needed to be investigated before he was appointed. That led to some friction because it happened on the first day when the Court was instituted in the Public Council Chamber. The City Council had provided for 120 clerks and about 120 bailiffs to be given the chiefs, and those officers assumed that they were going to have 120 clerks and 120 bailiffs, they having the power of appointment—that is, to name the individuals. And the Court began by giving the bailiff 67 bailiffs, and the clerk about 85 clerks. There has been pressure from below to get more men and more salaries, the number and the salary being in the hands of the judges. There has been political pressure to help the good cause along, and the judges must hold that situation down, of course. That has led to some friction. Then the Court found that the Chief Deputy Clerk sought to raise a jury voucher from $2.50 to $22.50. He was apprehended before he cashed the voucher for the money and he was discharged by a general order of the Court. There was a time when—because the salaries were not raised by the judges as rapidly as some of the clerks thought they should be—some of the insurgents in the Clerk's office thought they would organize a "clerks' Republican club." All but one of the judges of the court were Republicans at that time.

BY COMMISSIONER FRANCIS:

Q. No Democrats among the clerks? A. Only one—well, yes, there were some Democrats among the clerks, and there was one Democratic judge. They had one meeting, and the object of it became known to the judges. I sent for the Chief Deputy Clerk and I asked him for the names of those who belonged to the organization. He wanted to know what was the trouble, and I said the Court was going to discharge them all at four o'clock. I was going to call a special meeting. "Oh," he said, "what's the matter?" I said: "I understand you are organized to discipline the various judges as they come up for office, because you don't get enough men and money. I understand that is the object of the organization." He said: "No; that is not the purpose of it." I said: "I want the list. I want it before four o'clock." He said: "There is an easier way than that—to disband." "Can you disband before four o'clock?" "Yes." Before four they had disbanded, and they haven't organized since. It illustrates the necessity of the Court having control. It would be better if the Justice had the power to name a chief clerk and a chief bailiff, because there is this friction. No doubt if the clerks and bailiffs were selected by some system of civil service it would be better, because there is constant frictions. Some of the judges, of course—candidates for office—are more or less annoyed by the activity of some of the clerks and bailiffs in these offices.

BY COMMISSIONER WINTHROP:

Q. Who names the Chief Clerk and the Bailiff? A. They are now elected by law, and they have the power to appoint their own deputies.

Q. Elected from the city at large? A. Yes; in the city, the same as the judges.

Q. Yes, and they name the individuals who are to be deputy clerks? A. They name the individuals who are to be deputies. The number that they shall have is fixed by the judges. The judges increased the salaries of the clerks

at the big criminal courts and immediately the clerks trans-
fered favorites into those courts to get the larger salary.
The judges had fixed the salary of so many clerks at
so much per annum. This year they fixed it: "John
Jones, clerk at Harrison street, so many dollars," the
judges have fixed the salary coupled with the name of the
individual, so there cannot be transfers for political reasons. And the preference and the pay, it is the intention of the judges, shall be given to the men who do the
greatest amount of work and render the greatest service to
the Court, regardless of how active they are in their precincts.

BY CHAIRMAN PAGE:

Q. Do you think it would be wise for the justice to have
the appointment of all the clerks? A. It would be an annoyance to the justices to have the appointment of all the
clerks, because then political pressure would be on them
for places. It would be better for them to appoint the
Chief Clerk and the Chief Bailiff, and then some system,
either created by law or some board created by the judges
to have charge of examinations for clerkships and the position of bailiff. At the same time, I wish to say this: that
the bailiffs and clerks of the court are men of mature years,
honest and capable. You will see their pictures in this volume. We print their pictures—of the bailiffs and the clerks
also—to get them interested in the court and let them feel
they are personally responsible for the administration of
justice. Because they come in contact with the public, it is
necessary that they be courteous always to the public, and

our bailiffs and clerks have been exceedingly courteous to members of the bar and to the public generally. As a whole we have very good men—very capable men—in those offices. The standard has been set high by both the Chief Clerk and the Chief Bailiff, as a general rule.

BY CHAIRMAN PAGE:

Q. Well, if the names were taken from a civil service list, as they would have to be in this State, where would you place the power of appointment then—with the judges or with the Chief Clerk, allowing the judges to appoint the Chief Clerk? A. Well, I fear that will be regulated by politics as a rule, but it would be better if the judges were not bothered. I consider it an annoyance to have to deal with committeemen from all the wards as to whether John Smith or John Jones shall have place. The Judge is too busy, has too many other interests, and he ought not to be called upon to listen to these petitions for places in the court. That, I think, would be an interference with his time, and it is an influence that he ought not to come in contact with, I think. It is perhaps better to have the Chief Clerk and Chief Bailiff appoint their deputies when they themselves are appointed by the Court.

Q. By civil service? A. Either by civil service or by a board appointed by the judges. I think the Chief Bailiff and Chief Clerk ought to be appointed by the judges. They are then responsive to the judges and try to carry out their wishes fully. Any other way there is apt to be some friction. We have had some friction about some matters—the Clerk and Bailiff and myself. By reason of the large number of political appointees they had, there was a feeling that the judges didn't amount to anything and that they were the court rather than the judges of the court. It has taken a little time to settle the equities as to who's who.

BY COMMISSIONER WINTHROP:

Q. The Chief Clerk and Chief Bailiff—are they removable by the Court? A. No; not the elected officers; the deputies.

Q. They are removable by the Court? A. By the Court.

Q. Without cause? A. Yes; we have removed two clerks and two bailiffs for cause by a general order of the Court. That had a great disciplinary effect.

Q. Judge, do you consider yourself responsible for the general conduct of this court—its good name or its general administration of justice? A. Well, yes, and so are the judges of the court, they are chargeable with the management of the court and its administration, and I think that the success of the court has been due to two things—to the law under which it operates, the system, and also to the general management of the court by the judges of the court. The clerks and bailiffs, too, have helped.

Q. Does the community—the people of Chicago—consider you to be the person responsible? A. Well, of course, I might hope they did, but it would not be true.

BY COMMISSIONER WINTHROP:

Q. You as Chief Justice? A. Well, I have certain responsibility. The business men who created this court were anxious to place in connection with this court an administrative department, because in that place more than any other the courts were deficient, and these business men created the office of Chief Justice, just as the chief executive officer of a corporation, a chairman of a board of directors. In other words, if anything goes wrong with the administration of justice the law is framed in such a way that the Chief Justice can be blamed. As to whether he gets credit, I don't know. He will get blame.

Q. If anything goes wrong the Chief Justice would be the one who would get the blame? A. I think it is his business. It is made his business by law. If a bailiff is uncivil to a lawyer, if a police officer maltreats a citizen, if anything goes wrong in the court itself it is his business to look after it.

Q. Now, the limit of the Chief Justice's authority over his judges is assigning the judges to different parts? A. To different courts; controlling the calendar.

Q. What do you mean by controlling the calendar? A. He can assign different causes to different judges. He examines the jurors in the court and assigns them to the different judges. That is done by assigning them to different courts the first morning, and after that by rotation through a box provided. He has the duty of examining the jurors in the court, but over the judges his only power is to assign them to different branch courts.

Q. Now, where is the power of removing the judges lodged? A. Removing the judge?

Q. Yes? A. In the Legislature.

Q. By impeachment? A. We have a provision that he can be removed on a two-thirds vote of the General Assembly, as well as by impeachment, which I suppose amounts to an impeachment.

CHAIRMAN PAGE: We have the same here; we have the two forms of procedure in our constitution.

BY COMMISSIONER WINTHROP:

Q. And that duty, I suppose, would be in the Chief Justice to set that procedure in motion if, in his opinion, the case required it? A. Well, I couldn't say as to that; whether that is his duty or not; but perhaps so. The idea that he is general superintendent has more reference to the management of the court's financial business, the movement of its calendars, the handling of jurors and clerks and bailiffs. The Chief Justice presides at the meeting of the judges, but the court as a body—all the judges, acting as a board of directors—manage the court's business, and when a bailiff was removed he would be removed by a majority vote of the Court, spread on the record.

Q. And when the Court passes rules of procedure and practise, that is really passed by a majority of the Court? A. By a majority of the Court.

BY COMMISSIONER HAMILTON:

Q. Those rules when passed are binding upon the several judges, are they? A. Yes. The Supreme Court has passed upon that particular feature of the act to this extent: In the case of Morton vs. Pusey, decided December 15th, 1908—"The provisions of the Municipal Court law making the practise in the Municipal Court different from the practise in other courts of record in the State and providing special rules of practice, are constitutional. The right to instruct juries orally or in writing, as the Court may in its discretion see fit, is upheld.'' So that particular feature has been passed upon.

Q. Do your administrative duties leave you any time for judicial duties? A. My administrative duties are very great indeed. The law provides that I must first attend to administrative duties. I have a chief clerk, I have an attorney, I have a stenographer and a bailiff in my department, also an auditor, who audits the court every month and presents to me his report. The organization of a new court is not completed with the passage of the law. That is only the beginning. The court orders, the court papers and writs and mittimi and all that must be prepared. Besides amendments to the law must be prepared from time to time. Of course, the first two years have thrown upon the administration of the court unusual and exceptional burdens, though I have held court about one-third of the time and expect to open court next Monday morning and hold court until vacation. I think I will be able to do that, but complaints are made to me by citizens, by lawyers, by police officers; and these complaints are numerous, some ill-founded and some well-founded, all, however, demanding attention, and my door is always open for any one to come in.

BY COMMISSIONER WINTHROP:

Q. Do you think your powers as Chief Justice of that court are sufficient? A. They are very great, and they are so great that I handle some of those powers in a special way. As, for example: I have the power to assign a particular judge to a particular case and to select particular jurors for him. That is an enormous power in the hands of any man, and that power is exercised by me in this way:

I do not know what juror will try a particular case, because the jurors are assigned to each court room. When they have served in that court they return to a jury assignment room. Their names go in a box in a particular order —in the order of their numbers—and they are drawn out from the front of that box and put in at the back. Hence I do not know—no individual can know—what juror will sit in a particular case. I don't know that myself. Having the power, though, to assign him in the case, it is exercised in such a way that I shall not know. The calendar —the non-jury cases—are assigned by me by an order to the Clerk of the Court to assign so many cases by rote to these certain judges. Hence I don't know, and no one else knows, what particular case will go to a particular judge. The jury cases are assigned from a monthly jury calendar, and as a judge calls for cases each judge takes off ten or fifteen or twenty cases from that calendar. Whoever is first through calls for the next cases. I don't know—no one else knows—what particular case will go to a particular judge; and yet it is an important provision. A witness may live here, in New York City or outside of the jurisdiction of the Court and far from Chicago. It may be necessary for that case to be tried on a particular day. On agreement of counsel it is generally set for a particular day. It may be advanced by the Chief Justice on special cause, on agreement or without agreement, on a proper showing. So, it is well to have the power to act in the Chief Justice, but it is important that his actions be such that they are not open to suspicion that he may be exercising those powers in the way of favoritism.

BY CHAIRMAN PAGE:

Q. I notice here the pictures of the assistants to the Chief Justice. What are their duties? A. Mr. Hayt, whose picture appears in the middle of the page, was Chief Clerk in the Recorder's Office of Cook County, and when the offices were examined by expert accountants the committee examining those offices reported that the Recorder's Office was the best managed office in the entire county. Mr. Hayt was Chief Clerk there. His duties in our court are to act for me in examining into the clerks' and bailiffs' offices, to look after the calendars and the purely business matters of the branch courts. He looks after the transfer of cases from one judge to another. For instance, a judge gets through, say, at 11 o'clock. He doesn't adjourn. He reports to Mr. Hayt that he is out of cases. Mr. Hayt's duty is to transfer from another judge having more cases than he can try a case with the witnesses and lawyers to the judge who is out of work. In that way about an average of twenty-five cases per day are transferred from a judge who has more than he can do to one who is ready to try it. That amount of business is conserved each day by this daily reassignment, over which he has charge. He has charge of making up the jury calendar especially, and he transacts the business between our court and the city in the matter of requisitions for supplies, and so forth. He passes upon those matters before I do. We have a general order of the court that all vouchers and requisitions for the expenditure of money must be O.K'd by the Chief Justice, because all the departments—the judicial, the clerks and the bailiffs—have requisition books in which they draw requisitions for supplies, signed by the Chief Clerk. Those are laid upon my desk, and I look over the requisitions and either O. K. them or refuse to O. K. them. And in that way hold down the expense, so that every item of expense for the court passes under my eye. Mr. Greene, the attorney, spends a large part of his time in drafting the court orders and, in conjunction with the Chief Justice, prepares those. He briefs them and presents his briefs and drafts to me, and as I am responsible, of course, I examine all orders carefully before they are O. K'd, and sometimes redraft them.

Q. Well, these orders are the orders of procedure? A. No; the orders of the Court in a particular class of cases. For example, suppose—well, in all classes of cases we have to do that because of our abbreviated forms. The scheme as originally planned was on the idea that any abbreviation would do that looked about right, so that the first orders prepared by the attorney for the committee that drew the law provided that you could use this abbreviation, or that one, or one like it; and I was of the opinion that since the court orders were abbreviations it became highly important that those abbreviations should be certain, it being a court of record, and hence the abbreviation must be exactly that abbreviation prescribed by the Chief Justice. That was my idea about it, which was different from that of the attorney who drafted the original law and prepared the first orders the Court began business with. And I think the law is defective in that particular, in which is provided the abbreviated forms. I think it should say—and we are going to ask the Legislature so to amend it so that it will provide that the entry of the abbreviated form shall in law be the entry of the full form and shall be so considered. The law now omits to say that in specific language. We have overcome that so far as we could by a general order of the Court to that effect. But the Supreme Court may say that is not sufficient. The matter has not reached our Supreme Court. It is an enormous task to prepare all these orders, based on the possibilities of what may be required. If there is not a prescribed form it is the duty of the Judge to see to it that a full form order is entered, in which case that order is spread in a general order book. And then, if it is a frequent order—that is, abbreviated by me, with an order to the Clerk that hereafter for the entry of that class of form he should use this abbreviation.

BY COMMISSIONER WINTHROP:

Q. Then your practice in any event is to have the orders of the Court embodied in the book? A. So near as they can be.

Q. In other courts it is the practice of the Court to have the orders of the Court filed away in a record of the Court, but not transcribed in a book, and your practice is to transcribe them in a book? A. The orders in the cases are transcribed in a book; the abbreviation of the orders.

Q. Yes. It is not the ordinary practice of the attorney handing up an order which is signed by the Court and then goes in the files of the court? A. Such an order would go upon the files of the court in full.

Q. It would be transcribed in full? A. Yes; in full, if it

was a special order for which no abbreviation had been prescribed. If it was a frequent order it would be my duty to abbreviate it, so that thereafter it would go in in an abbreviation. But generally there is a certain order. For instance: In these criminal classes there are orders covering every action the Court may take. If those orders are prepared correctly by the Chief Justice the work is done correctly in all of the branches of the court, and if incorrectly it is done incorrectly in all the branches of the court. Now, for instance, contempt proceedings are matters that are technical and require some care in the preparation of the order, and if one was not already prepared the Judge would have to take some time to prepare the order. With us he would turn to a certain page and turn to the Clerk. "Order No. 35," he would say. The Clerk may be busy and not able to write the order then. He may write "Order 35," and that order then is taken from the Order 35 in the prescribed forms. That order has been examined with care in the light of the authority of the Supreme Court of the State, and is more apt to be correct than one that the Judge in the hurry of the moment might prepare.

BY COMMISSIONER WINTHROP:

Q. Do you think in these minor criminal cases it is better to have the orders all transcribed into the Court's own book, rather than to have them filed away with the case on loose pieces of paper? A. I think the minor court ought to be a court of record. I think all these courts of first instance ought to be courts of record. They cannot be courts of record if the orders must be written out in full, on account of the volume of business in such courts, as they are in the general nisi prius courts. If abbreviated, however, it can

be done with a little expense, and that is the reason we
have been able to do it.

BY CHAIRMAN PAGE:

Q. Your practice in the nisi prius courts is that of having the court records in full transcribed in volumes; is it?
A. Yes.

Q. It differs very much from our practice here? A. Yes.

Q. Then there is the third assistant, Mr. Miller? A. Yes.
He assists in general office work—largely in the preparation of calendars. It is a big task to see that all the
names of the parties are correct—that this calendar is
made correctly—and it takes nearly all his time to look
after the jury calendar and to transfer these cases—the
cases from one court to another. Then I have a stenographer, and will have to have another. The correspondence
is so large and the complaints are so many, and my telephone is constantly ringing. In other words, the chief jus-
ticeship of the court is a fifteen or twenty thousand dollar
position and not a $7,500 position.

BY COMMISSIONER WINTHROP:

Q. Judge, I received the impression that before your
court was established the police justice courts were very
much in politics, and that since your courts were established that criminal administration has been altogether
taken out of politics. Is that impression correct? A. It is
correct to this extent: What I meant to convey was not that
they generally joined the Republican party or the Democratic party, except this—that they were in politics as affected by the desires of the Aldermen in the ward where

the principal courts were located. For instance, the First Ward in Chicago Alderman was always closely identified with the courts, and he frequently named the Judge who sat in those courts through his influence with the Mayor.

Q. Now, what feature of your new court has brought about this disassociation, do you think? A. Well, in the first place, the Judge who sits there is not named by the Alderman through his influence with the Mayor. He is an elected judge. For example: Alderman Coughlin, of the First Ward, otherwise known to fame locally as "Bath House," was arrested for breaking a newspaper man's camera at the Coliseum, on the occasion of the grand ball not long ago. He was put on trial at the Harrison Street Station. Two of the best judges of the Municipal Court were sitting at Harrison street at the time. He saw fit not to take a bench trial and demanded a jury. The jurors are not picked up around the "barrel houses" in the neighborhood by the alderman's henchman, the bailiff, but selected from the body of the county, the same as the jurors are in other courts. They might come from the aristocratic suburbs of Evanston and Oak Park, *et cetera.* And he chose a jury trial. He had a jury trial and was acquitted, and possibly, I think, rightfully. But the mere fact that the Alderman of the First Ward had a speedy trial and preferred not to have it at Harrison Street, where formerly he had great influence, was a terrible example to a great many residents of that ward that he hadn't any "pull" there.

Q. So political activity does not constitute a proper defense? A. No, I suppose there will be political activity, and we are constantly watching that, and I think now there are men representing the Aldermen who are on guard with bail bonds for defendants, and the courts are now considering what may be done——

Q. You do not have official bail commissioners? A. No.

BY MR. BUCK:

Q. How are the judges nominated? A. They are nominated by the political parties. When the court first was elected there was the Republican ticket, the Democratic ticket, and the Independent Party ticket; Judge Gilbert, who drafted the Municipal Court Act for the Commission, was the Democratic nominee, and Judge Garnett, a former judge of the Appellate Court, was the nominee of the Independent party. He was a Republican in politics theretofore. So that there were two Republicans nominated, and one Democrat. This last election all the Republican judges were elected, by about 30,000.

BY CHAIRMAN PAGE:

Q. You have had in Illinois, haven't you, a minority representation. A. Not in the judiciary.

Q. I know; but have had it in your members of the Legislature? A. Of the Legislature; yes. The judges were formerly selected half from one party and half from another. But latterly the parties have been nominating each its own candidates. Generally the older judges are elected, whether they are Democrats or Republicans, and partisanship doesn't cut much figure, so far as our courts are concerned. The fact they are Republicans is a mere accident, so far as I can see, in the administration of justice. Our judges do not take part in politics. They do not make political speeches. One of them has been a committee man for a short time, and I understand he is going to resign.

BY COMMISSIONER FRANCIS:

Q. There is no law against holding a district leadership or the position of committee man? A. There is no law against that, but it is frowned down by the Court, the judges are even adverse to presiding at a political meeting.

BY CHAIRMAN PAGE:

Q. What would you think of the applying of a minority representation to the judges of the court, where there is a large number to be elected, as there are in your court? A. Well, I don't think it makes any difference, if the Judge administers the law as it ought to be administered, what his politics are.

BY MR. BUCK:

Q. Are the judges nominated by a convention made up of delegates or are they nominated directly? A. Well, we have now a direct primary in Illinois. I don't know whether it will be sustained by the Supreme Court. It is now pending before the Supreme Court. The Direct Primary Law has been declared unconstitutional once by our Supreme Court, and there are those who think the present law will be. But the last judges were elected at a direct primary. The party places its nominees on the ticket, and others can go on the ticket by petition. Of course, the party nominees have this advantage—that all the "hustlers" are voting for the party nominees in all the districts of the city, and they constitute a margin of from fifteen to twenty thousand to start with. But one of our justices was not nominated by the political parties. He was left out of the list. He filed his petition, and he received the highest number of votes at the primary, and at the election he led all the others.

BY COMMISSIONER WINTHROP:

Q. Your old police justices were nominated; were they? A. The police justices were designated by the Mayor from those recommended by the judges of the Circuit Court to the Governor; they were appointed by the Governor.

Q. Your old police justices before this court? A. Yes.

Q. Were appointed by the Governor? A. Appointed by the Governor on recommendation of the Circuit Court, and designated as police judges by the Mayor.

Q. And they were local? A. Local.

Q. They were appointed from local districts? A. From the County of Cook, and they had jurisdiction throughout the county.

Q. But they sat always in their own localities? A. Sometimes, out in the country, in their own houses and adjoining some nearby saloon, as an adjunct to it.

Q. Does your court have full contempt jurisdiction—I mean the power to punish for contempt? A. Oh, yes.

Q. Both civil and criminal? A. Yes; the same as any other court. I think it were better in drafting a court act like this, rather than divide the jurisdiction up in five or six classes, to make the jurisdiction in one or two sentences.

Our act could just as well have said that the Municipal Court of Chicago shall have jurisdiction in all classes of cases within the City of Chicago, that the Circuit Court has, except—and name the exceptions, so as to make the different classes.

CHAIRMAN PAGE: We will suspend now, to resume at half-past two.

AFTERNOON SESSION.

February 5, 1909.

HARRY OLSON, recalled.

BY MR. BUCK:

Q. Judge Olson, can you describe to the Commission the system of records that are employed in your court? A. The Municipal Court Act provides—Section 44—"that the Clerk of the Municipal Court shall keep on hand and furnish to suitors and attorneys on application printed blank forms of præcipes, summons, entries of appearance, affidavits, bonds, attachment writs, replevin writs, petitions for changes of venue and all other necessary papers for the use of the parties to suits in such courts. Forms for such papers shall be prescribed by the Chief Justice of the Municipal Court, who shall also, from time to time, prescribe and cause to be printed forms of statements of claims to be used in said court." Section 62 reads as follows: "It shall be the duty of the Chief Justice of the Municipal Court to superintend the keeping of the records of said court and to prescribe abbreviated forms of entries of orders therein, which abbreviated forms so prescribed shall have the same force and effect as if said orders were entered in full in the records of said court. When any certified transcript of the record, or any portion thereof, of any suit or proceeding in said court is required the same shall be written out in full from such abbreviated forms and duly authenticated according to law." The judges of the court considered that not sufficient to cover the necessities of the case in this particular; that it did not provide that an entry of the abbreviated form should in law be the equivalent of the entry of the full form. Hence, under a general order of the Court an order was made to cover that, and we are going to amend that section of the law. In view of that provision of the law the duty falls upon the Chief Justice to prescribe the forms. I can illustrate that, perhaps, as quickly as I can tell it. Take a sixth class case. I have in my hand a book of court orders in sixth class cases, which contains directions to the Clerk. It contains an index of the various form orders. For instance, in bastardy. These orders are prepared from the sections of the statute, and cover all that could be foreseen as necessary in that class of cases. There is an order for warrant, order for recognizance to appear from day to day, order for commitment for refusal to enter into recognizance to appear from day to day, child not yet born, preliminary examination, case continued, preliminary examination, defendant discharged, motion of defendant to dismiss overruled and execution, child born dead, suit dismissed for costs, et cetera, et cetera, carefully drawn from each section of the statute, as to what could be done with a defendant, or on any motion of counsel. These abbreviations appear in the index opposite the order. These abbreviations in the index are complete, so that if the Court, for instance, finds that a defendant is dead, the death of the defendant suggested, suit dismissed, he may say to the Clerk, "Order No. 13." If the Clerk is busy he can write that number 13 on his pad and he can prepare the order later, or he can write it out at the moment, and the abbreviation is right in the index. The clerks are providing themselves with rubber stamps with these abbreviations, so that a clerk sitting in the Criminal Branch will have when the system is completed a box of stamps in bastardy cases, numbered with the corresponding number in the index, and there is no chance of his writing an improper order or one that is not correct. If on appeal, the record is required, the Clerk prepares the corresponding full form order which is prescibed in this book. Here is, for instance, an order of "judgment as an instalment bond"— mittimus order No. 28. The Court orders will occupy one line, or at most two lines, of the record sheet. It is provided: "Judgment on verdict or finding, judgment paid so much, instalment bond for...... Mittimus issued." The full form order occupies nearly two pages of the same book, where the abbreviation occupies two lines. That saves expense. If we were to hire clerks to write these full form orders in all these cases our staff would have to be ten or twenty times as large as it is. Perhaps more than that. It is expeditious. In the minor cases very few are appealed. As we have seen in criminal cases less than one-fourth of one per cent. have been appealed, and hence less than one-fourth of one per cent. of these abbreviated orders have been expanded for the examination of the higher court. That is a necessity in a court of record having a large volume of business such as ours has, 124,000 cases this last year for instance. It also brings about uniformity in the orders of the Court. They are prepared according to the statutory requirements, or the requirements of the Supreme Court—that is the intention but of course errors may be committed. If they are correct, the Court then operates its business in the light of the decisions of the Supreme Court, with accurate orders. In some of our state courts, especially out in the country districts in the State of Illinois, the clerks find great difficulty in preparing orders of the Court. The records that come to the Supreme Court from some of the districts are very poorly gotten up. At the last session of the Association of the Court Clerks of the Circuit Courts of Illinois the question of the abbreviation of their records, and especially the question of providing prescribed forms, came up, and I understand they like the system that enabled our clerk to get up an accurate record. Resolutions were adopted to examine into this method. That is particularly true in the country districts. In the City of Chicago in the Circuit and Superior Court clerks' offices there are two or three men who are expert record writers.

Q. Is it a part of your record or a part of the police records to keep track of the individual cases, so that you can tell whether there has been a previous conviction and what disposition has been made of each case? A. Yes, the minutes are entered on this half sheet, a copy of which is in the record here. That half sheet is not treated as a record of the Court, but as a memorandum from which the record is made, and the orders upon that half sheet are entered in the regular record book by the record writers. Those are filed, and a card is indexed, plaintiff's

index and defendant's index. We have a new system so that any case can be found in less than half a minute. One man has charge of the indexes. He waits upon the public, we have a recently patented system, so that he can turn immediately to the case and give the parties the numbers; they can go to the file room and get the number of the case or go to the record books of the court and get a copy of the record. If he desires to have that in expanded form, by ordering a transcript, it will be expanded in each case as prescribed in the book of orders given to the clerk by the Chief Justice. To illustrate I can show you. Here for the guidance of the clerks and for their instruction there is prepared a chart. This chart is headed "Judgments of Guilty in Criminal Cases." "Judgment on Pleading, Verdict, Finding, Defendant Guilty of.........
On............, Amount." Then there is a provision for second and third offenses if it is charged in the complaint. Then "Defendant Sent to County Jail, House of Correction for Term of............, Cumulative Law, Concurrent, and the numbers of the Mittimi to be used by the clerk, 84 and 85, Sent to the County Jail for a Term of, either Cumulative or Concurrent, or fined so many dollars, and taxed so much, to stand committed therefor until paid, with the number of Mittimi in each case, Sent to House of Correction for a Term of.........or fined." All possible orders that can be entered are on that sheet, so that the clerk can follow up to their legitimate ends all orders necessary.

BY COMMISSIONER HAMILTON:

Q. Suppose you wished to look up the record of John Doe in your court, could you find how many times he had appeared before the criminal part of your court, and the disposition of these previous arraignments? A. Yes. We would call for the index of defendants, John Doe, and by referring to the page of the docket giving the number of his case we could locate the case. If he was brought into court the second time we would find his name in the index a second time. The records of our court would only show that John Doe was there twice, I don't think they necessarily would show that it was the same John Doe. It would not unless he was charged in one of the complaints with a second offense. The records of the Police Department, however, if the offense was a criminal offense, would show that this was the same John Doe. In other words, the identity of the defendant is gathered through the Bertillon System, now largely the Thumb Print Method.

BY COMMISSIONER SMITH:

Q. In computing the number of persons arraigned in a year, if a man came up three times would he count as three different men or the same man? A. If he came up during the year he would count—John Doe would be on our record three times. We would not know whether he was the same man or a different man so far as our record is concerned unless he was charged with a second offense, and it was alleged in the complaint that he was charged before.

BY CHAIRMAN PAGE:

Q. These seventy-four thousand cases in the Criminal Court, that means that there were persons arraigned 74,000 times? One man might have been arraigned two or three times? A. Yes, he might be in on several charges, though there are fewer charges now than formerly. If you will let me see the report I will indicate to you a diagram which shows that. Opposite Page 42 of the Annual Report of the Court. That shows that matter. The black line shows the number of offenses committed, the red line shows the number of offenders. The distance between the black line and the red line is quite large under the justices of the peace regime. That meant that these offenders committed a large number of offenses. Under the Municipal Court regime those lines are closer together—in other words, the individual offenders commit less offenses.

BY MR. BUCK:

Q. Have you a statistician connected with the court? A. We have a system of statistics in the court. It was found necessary to know what the court was doing in its various branches in order to administer it properly, and I began to call upon the clerks for information, more particularly on one occasion because I had to make an address before the State Bar Association. The clerk said to me, "Are you going to ask for this information often?" And I said, "Probably I will," and he said, "We will then have to have some method of keeping it." I laid the matter before the judges of the court, and they concluded it was essential that we should keep complete judicial statistics of the court for the information of the public and for our own information, and we gave the clerk additional help so that he might be able to furnish us with the facts of the court's business, and furnish that to us in detail, as it appears in this annual report.

BY COMMISSIONER HAMILTON:

Q. What expert assistance did you have in drawing up the present system of report? A. The deputy clerks who were appointed. Some had experience in other courts, others had not, the majority had not, but we selected from the other courts some of their best men; for example, one of the clerks in the Criminal Court had been there some eighteen years. He was a lawyer, and he had had that large experience, he was a very efficient man. We found our criminal records not very well kept by one of the clerks that was in charge, and the matter was called to the attention of the chief clerk, and he said he would like to get a good man if he could find one, and I suggested to him this clerk in the Criminal Court who was a lawyer, and the man relied upon for all important information in the State's Attorney's office and by the Criminal Court. That man received $2,000 a year there, and we told him that we would fix his salary at $2,500 a year if he would come with us. The clerk agreed to appoint him, and we entered an order making the salary $2,500 a year and we got the man. That man took hold of the criminal records, and he was able to devise the system by which he reports, as you will notice in this annual report, the number of new suits filed of the various kinds, the different judges sitting in the court, the disposition of the case, the character of the case. He did that in all the criminal courts of the city, so that you will find in this annual report those seventy-five thousand cases divided up as to what courts they originated in, as to what judge handled the particular cases, and the percentages of discharges by each judge can be figured from that report, of all the cases handled in the criminal branch of the court. That man did that work.

BY CHAIRMAN PAGE:

Q. The tables to which you refer are found at what pages of the annual report? A. The tables are found pages 61 to 67, both inclusive. The figures are important for this reason, for example, let me illustrate. I find here that of the criminal and quasi-criminal cases and preliminary hearings there were discharged 55.4 per cent.; there were fined 22 per cent., sent to the House of Correction or County Jail 17.8 per cent., held to the Criminal Court 4.6 per cent., to the Juvenile Court .2 per cent. In other words, there is a large percentage of discharges. The number of discharges are not to be arrived at solely from these statistics for the reason that one man may be charged we will say with four offenses. He may be tried on only one of these and discharged on the others. In that case a defendant is held, and there appears three discharges. That often happens. Besides that many of these complaints have been made by police officers, and they have been improperly presented to the Court and no case proved and they were discharged. Many times raids are made and vagrants are gathered in. Vagrancy is hard to prove, and there was failure to prove vagrancy in many cases and there were many discharges on that account, so that the percentage of cases discharged on a full hearing would be much smaller than 55.4 per cent. Nevertheless that figure indicates that there has not been enough care taken in instituting criminal proceedings or quasi-criminal proceedings against citizens, and it is a warning to the Court to act with care. For example, it appears here that there have been 1,150 pardons by the Mayor. The Mayor in our city has the power to pardon for violation of city ordinances. That is a large number, and the fact appears in the report, so that all who may be interested can see, including the Mayor and the Court. The expenses are shown, and just where the money has gone is exhibited to the taxpayer down to the last cent. In that way the judges of the court and the City Council, the aldermen and any one interested can see how the money is expended, and if there is extravagance it may be complained about, and the judges may act upon it. On the other hand it shows whether or not crime increases or diminishes, it shows, for example, the character of cases. We have a table of misdemeanors, felonies, and violation of city ordinances. This table shows the various character of offenses, and it can be noted by the Police Department and the State's Attorney, by public officials, what classes of crimes are on the increase and what classes of crimes are on the decrease. All of these facts are important to know on the part of all those who have to do with the administration of justice.

It is necessary information for the Legislature in the matter of providing new legislation to meet conditions as they arise. Professor Pounds of the Northwestern University Law School told me that he had occasion to write to the various courts of the country in the matter of obtaining information about the cases disposed of in their courts, and in courts of appeal. He stated that he could get but little information anywhere regarding that matter, and I know that I have tried to get that information from the circuit courts throughout the State. Many of them could give me the number of cases brought and disposed of, but many could not. We think it is important to keep these judicial statistics.

BY COMMISSIONER HAMILTON:

Q. How large a territory is covered by the criminal courts contained in that single court house? A. About half a mile to the east, about one-quarter of a mile to the west, nearly a mile to the south, and about three-quarters of a mile to half a mile to the north.

Q. About what population does that contain? A. Well, I should say the population would not be over three or four or five hundred thousand perhaps, but it contains two of the principal levee districts of the city. It is the intention of the Court to draw a district about a mile to the south, a mile to the north, a mile to the east, and a mile and a half to the west, which will include the principal levee districts, and about 65% of the criminal business of the city, and to bring that into one court.

Q. How many parts, criminal parts, will be contained in

that one building then? A. At least four to begin with, and possibly six, if we try the felony cases surely six.

Q. At present how many parts did you say there are scattered over the city, criminal parts, besides those contained in that one building? A. There are two courts at Harrison Street, which is the principal court in the city; one at Desplaines Street, on the west side, taking in the west side levee. Those are the three principal courts. The Maxwell Street Court is a court for a district of about 300,000 population. That is one of the large courts. The West Chicago Avenue is another of the large courts. That is located about a mile from the center of the city. The Maxwell Street Court is about a mile and a half, and the Harrison Street Court is right in the center of the city. Then there is one a mile and a half south, Thirty-fifth Street; one at Englewood, four miles; one at Hyde Park, six miles south, and one at South Chicago, fourteen miles south. There is one on the north side about half a mile or three-quarters of a mile from the center of the city, and one still further out about two miles beyond the West Chicago Avenue Court. I think we will always have to have a number of outlying criminal courts, perhaps five or six, in addition to the four or five in the central building in the heart of the city.

Q. How many does that make a total of? A. That makes a total of ten criminal branches now.

Q. Counting the Central Court House as one only? A. No, the Harrison Street Court has two branches.

Q. And the rest one? A. The rest one.

Q. What system have you of providing for your Central Bureau of Records and having the records sent in from these outlying courts? A. The clerks every night bring the half sheet into the central building, if the case is disposed of. If the case is still pending, the half sheet remains in the branch court until it is disposed of, and then the records come in for the purpose of being written up.

BY MR. BUCK:

Q. Have you official interpreters connected with that court? A. We have not, but we ought to have, and we will have in a year or so.

BY COMMISSIONER WINTHROP:

Q. There is one remark you made this morning which perhaps you may be willing to explain. You said you did not approve of volunteer probation officers—what are your reasons for that? A. Well, quite often many of those who volunteer to act as probation officers have notions of their own as to how other people should live and act. A young lady whose antecedents are from Vermont or New England might think that the Russian Jews do some things they ought not to do, and that the Poles do some things they ought not to do, and that the Scandinavians do some things that they are accustomed to doing, that they ought not to do, and as long as they are volunteers many of them may seek to impose their ideas of behavior on these citizens of foreign extraction and foreign customs, their own ways of thinking and living. That causes some trouble. For instance at one of our night courts a number of people, social workers, assembled to see the operation of the court, and a great many of the foreign population took exception to that.

They said they did not like being paraded before other people from other parts of the city and held up as citizens who were a curiosity in the minds of others. They did not like it. We have of course in Chicago a population that is cosmopolitan. Five hundred thousand of our people are foreign born; a million are of foreign extraction, and there is in such a vast conglomeration of nationalities, antecedents and interests—there is apt to be a clash if you undertake to supervise them by anybody who might volunteer to do it. Then probation work if it is to be effective must be consistently carried out. It is important therefore to pay the officer and see that the work is properly attended to. A volunteer officer may or may not look after it. On the other hand, it is important that a probation officer be connected with the court officially. Sometimes there will be disputes between the probation officer and the party on probation and his friends as to the facts, and if the probation officer is a volunteer officer he has not that standing that he would have if he was a recognized official. Those are the things that come first to my mind.

Q. What do you mean by volunteer officers? Officers who are acting without appointment or officers who are acting with an appointment but without pay? A. Both officers who are acting because they have volunteered without appointment and without pay, and those who volunteer and act with pay. While on this subject of probation I would like the Commission to have on the record the language of our Superior Court regarding the probation, or the release of a defendant on his own recognizance. The decision is in 202 Illinois, page 300. The Court said in a case where a defendant was allowed to go on his own recognizance: "Whatever may have been the practice at common law, or whatever may be the practice in other states of this country in regard to the suspending of sentence for the purpose of giving the accused a chance to reform, and thus virtually reprieving him, the Legislature of this State has adopted a different method to give persons convicted of crimes the opportunity to reform, by providing a system of parole and boards to administer the same, and in view of the expressed policy of the Legislature of this State we are disposed to hold that the trial courts do not have the power to suspend the imposition of the sentence indefinitely after conviction or to do such acts that virtually amount to an indefinite suspension of sentence, or to release the prisoner on parole. As said in People *vs.* Allen, 'If such power remained in the court three years it would continue indefinitely and might be exercised at any future time, and that, too, without any reason for doing so except such as might exist in the mind of the Judge causing the rearrest and pronouncing judgment. The State has a right to demand, and the welfare of society requires, that those who are convicted or plead guilty to violations of the law shall be promptly and certainly punished.' The rendering of judgment and the final sentencing of the defendant cannot be made a mere matter of discretion with the judge or the public prosecutor, nor to depend upon the subsequent conduct of the convicted person. If it were so, what subsequent conduct would demand or justify the pronouncing or the withholding of the sentence? And who would determine its character? Such conduct might be innocent in itself yet offensive to those in whom the power to apprehend or punish resided. The liberty of the citizen cannot in a free country be made to depend for its security on the arbitrary will of any public officer; it can be taken by due process of law only."

BY COMMISSIONER WINTHROP:

Q. What is that reference to boards to administer parole —what are they? A. The indeterminate sentence board, the State Board of Pardons appointed by the Governor. There are one or two matters that might interest the Commission in regard to features of the law, some of which are new in our jurisdiction and not in others. I can briefly summarize them by combining them as follows: The administrative plan of the court; its organization on modern business lines; with a superintendent in charge with adequate authority, in view of the results to be obtained; its provisions for giving to the judges wide discretion in the matter of adopting rules of practice and procedure; abolishing written pleadings in a large class of cases. Written pleadings may be abolished in civil cases where the sum involved is less than $1,000, and the Court has power to change the pleadings on the preparation of rules to that effect, but it has gone slow.

BY CHAIRMAN PAGE:

Q. You have the common law form of pleadings?
A. Yes, sir; in first class cases. (Continuing.) Restricting courts of review to reversals on the merits; returning to oral instructions to juries; limiting the examination of jurors to ascertaining bias or prejudice; permitting interrogatories that must be answered under oath. Each side may file interrogatories to be answered by the other side, but only to ascertain such facts as are necessary to sustain his own case. In other words a defendant may file interrogatories to obtain answers to sustain his case, and the plaintiff may file interrogatories to obtain answers to sustain his case. That is for the purpose of eliminating controversy before the trial, so the issue will be clean-cut at the trial. (Continuing.) Allowing the calling of the adverse party as a witness without being bound by his answers. In a great many cases where defendants desire to make trouble for the plaintiffs it is difficult for the defendant to prove facts on the plaintiff's side of the case when they are not really in dispute. In such cases in our court the plaintiff says, "I desire to call the defendant himself under Section 33 of the Act." The defendant is put upon the stand and he may be cross-examined as to those matters, and the plaintiff is not bound by his answers. That shortens many trials materially a whole week is saved by three questions at times. (Continuing.) And the most important feature I think is having a court of the first instance as a court of record, with wide jurisdiction and salaried judges, elected by the whole city for long terms.

CHAIRMAN PAGE: On behalf of the Commission I wish to express our thanks to you for having come here at some inconvenience to yourself, and for having given us this most interesting line of testimony as to the method of dealing with these cases in Chicago.

JUDGE OLSON: I assure you I am very pleased to be here, and hope I may have been of some use, but that of course depends.

———

FREDERICK ALMY, being called as a witness, being duly sworn, testified as follows:

BY MR. BUCK:

Q. You are secretary of the Charity Organization Society of this city? A. I am.

Q. And you have been secretary for how long? A. 14 years.

Q. And your work in connection with the society has brought you in contact with the poor and unfortunate classes in the City of Buffalo? A. Yes.

Q. Have you any opinions that you would like to express or views that you would like to bring before the Commission in regard to the morning courts, or the Buffalo Police Court, or the Municipal Court? A. I think it would be better if we had not several judges holding court all day. The morning courts are open from 8 until a little after 9, and these minor positions are at the foot of the ticket, and we don't always get the men, and it would be better if they could be consolidated. The difficulty of course is we need to have more than one court in session at that hour to let men who are arrested get to their work, but I don't know whether the Commission has looked into the Massachusetts Probation Law, where the probation officers are given quite large powers with first offenders, so that like deputies, they can have the matter recorded, the offense entered in the books, and the man released on probation, the Judge afterwards looking over the action and ratifying it.

Q. Have you any idea what proportion of the men who come before the morning courts are doing work so that it is important for them to get away early? A. I don't know, I suppose a good many.

BY CHAIRMAN PAGE:

Q. Do you approve of the Massachusetts System? A. I don't know it well enough, I should like to study it, but I mentioned it because it is interesting. It appeals to me as I know it, but I am not posted.

Q. Well, without knowing it, it does not appeal to me. I think it would be a pretty dangerous power to put in the hands of probation officers. A. It needs very good officers.

BY MR. BUCK:

Q. You may continue? A. I was expecting questions. In regard to probation again—of course, we need a detention home here badly, and also I hope the Juvenile Court and the Police Court will always be kept in separate buildings. There was some talk lately of putting the two under one roof, and that would undo a good deal that has been accomplished.

Q. Do you believe that it would be desirable to have one judge who would do nothing but hear the juvenile cases? A. My impression is that way.

Q. Do you know how many volunteer probation officers there are here now? A. A good many. I used to know how many, but of late years, the last two or three years, I have not been so closely in touch with the Juvenile Court. I believe in volunteer probation officers but only in connection with paid probation officers who can see that the volunteers do what they undertake.

Q. Have you an adequate number, in your judgment, of probation officers here at the present time? A. I think we only have a good beginning.

Q. How many more do you think we ought to have? A. One or two more.

Q. That is, in the Juvenile Court? A. In some juvenile courts they have two probation officers, sometimes one for boys and one for girls, but I don't know whether the business here would warrant two now or not.

Q. How about the probation officers in the Police Court? A. I would say to the previous question that to develop good volunteer officers calls for some good paid officers, and two paid officers can secure more good volunteer servants than you could get otherwise. In answer to the last question—I am not acquainted there, I very seldom go there.

Q. Have you any recommendations to make in reference to the Police Court? A. No, I think not.

BY COMMISSIONER FRANCIS:

Q. Not as to the physical condition of the courts?
A. Oh, certainly, everyone knows that is bad now. It was so obvious that I didn't think it necessary to mention it.

BY CHAIRMAN PAGE:

Q. We are from New York, and are not as familiar with it as you are here. A. I saw in the papers that you had been there and I did not want to cover what you have seen.

BY MR. BUCK:

Q. Have you any further suggestions that you wish to bring before the Commission? A. No, I don't think I have.

Q. How do you think the probation system is working here from your observation of it? A. I think well, but as I said before I am now only occasionally in the courts and my knowledge is hearsay. When the system began I was in the court as a probation officer myself, and had much to do with the beginning of the plan. My impression is that it is going quite well now with the new paid officers.

BY COMMISSIONER WINTHROP:

Q. How long were you a probation officer? A. Two or three years.

Q. In the Children's Court? A. Yes, sir.

Q. Were children placed on probation with you? A. Yes, sir.

Q. By an order of the Court? A. Yes, sir, I was chairman of the probation officers.

Q. Your theory now is that they ought to be placed on

probation, not with volunteers, but with paid officers?
A. I have always felt that paid officers are needed to make volunteers responsible—we get some good volunteers and some bad.

Q. Volunteers you would use more as assistants to the paid probation officers? A. Yes, sir, and keep the volunteers on probation.

BY COMMISSIONER FRANCIS:

Q. Do you think there should be a state wide system for the appointment of probation officers, or do you believe in local regulation of appointments by local authorities?

BY CHAIRMAN PAGE:

Q. What Commissioner Francis means is should they be appointed from a state civil service list or taken from a local civil service list? A. I don't think it makes any difference as long as it is a civil service list.

Q. As long as it is a civil service list? A. I believe in a civil service list.

BY MR. BUCK:

Q. What do you think of the proposition for the trial of ordinary cases of drunkenness and disorderly conduct, a layman can be secured at a moderate salary, and that he is good enough? A. I should question it a good deal, I don't know.

BY CHAIRMAN PAGE:

Q. Have you had any experience with your morning courts here? A. Hardly any except by hearsay, and the visitors of the organization society who report to me.

BY MR. BUCK:

Q. Have you any further statement to make—if you have we would be very glad to hear it? A. I think not.

———

MARTIN McDONALD, being called as a witness and duly sworn, testified as follows:

BY MR. BUCK:

Q. You are connected with the Charity Organization Society? A. Yes, sir.

Q. What is your position with them? A. District visitor.

Q. Does your work bring you in contact with the morning courts? A. Yes, sir.

Q. Just what are your duties at the morning courts? A. Well, I may have cases there of some family that I am interested in, and also with the class of begging cases, people arrested for begging, and boys that I am interested in at Elmira that are out on probation.

Q. Then you are a probation officer, are you? A. Yes, sir.

Q. What do you do with the men that you are interested in? A. That depends on the circumstances of the case, what he is arrested for.

Q. Have you any recommendation that you would like to lay before the Commission in reference to morning courts? A. Why, there is one thing, I should like to see the women prisoners remain in their cells until after the men were disposed of in the court room, so they would not be brought out in full view of the spectators and of the men that are there under arrest.

Q. At the present time are all the prisoners brought in indiscriminately? A. I think so, but in some cases women are allowed to remain until the men are disposed of—I don't think that is always done.

Q. Is that in one particular station house that that is done? A. Well, no, I don't think that it is any particular one.

Q. Is there any further recommendation that you would like to make? A. If Acting Judge Collins is right in his recommendation that the non-support cases be taken from the Police Court and placed in the hands of the morning justices, I should say that I was very much opposed to that.

Q. What would you say to the proposition that a layman at a moderate salary is good enough to try the ordinary cases of disorderly conduct and drunkenness? A. If he is a good man, yes.

Q. Are you brought in contact with the Police Court? A. Yes, sir.

Q. Have you any recommendations that you would like to make in connection with that court? A. Nothing more than to have a better building.

Q. How many probation cases have you in charge? A. About 120.

Q. Both boys and men? A. Boys and men—when I say that I am speaking of the boys from Elmira and Rochester and the cases that I have in the Police Court.

BY CHAIRMAN PAGE:

Q. Do you consider that a boy that has been committed to Elmira is on probation with you? A. How is that?

Q. Do you consider that a boy who has been sent to Elmira to be incarcerated is on probation with you? A. He is on his good behavior for six months while he is out on parole, yes, sir.

Q. On parole? A. He is out on parole for six months after he has been temporarily placed—he is allowed to come out for six months' trial, and if at the end of that six months his behavior is such that his absolute release can be recommended the Board of Managers then discharge him.

Q. That is a system of parole and not probation, isn't it? A. Yes.

Q. You know the difference? A. Yes, I say I have the three classes.

Q. How many cases on actual probation do you think you can handle properly in a month? A. I should not care to handle over a dozen.

Q. When a case is put with you on probation what do you do? A. Well, it depends on what is necessary to be done. The first thing, if the man is out of employment I try to get him work, if he is a man. If he is a drinking man I try to make an arrangement with his employer to pay his salary to his wife, and try to get him into a class of associates, away from his old ones, where he will improve his surroundings.

Q. Do you require the probationers to report to you? A. At times, yes, sir. Not always.

Q. Have you any particular rule for dealing with these cases or do you deal with each case as the individual circumstances seem to suggest? A. Yes, sir.

Q. The latter? A. Yes, sir.

BY MR. BUCK:

Q. How would the proposition strike you to have the morning courts in this city done away with and another court created with the rank of the Police Court? A. I don't catch that.

Q. What would you think of the proposition to have a court created with the same rank as the Police Court to handle all the cases that are now handled by the morning courts? A. Well, I believe if we were always as successful as we are at the present time, with the present judges they could handle that just as well as the Police Court.

BY CHAIRMAN PAGE:

Q. Then you think you have a bad system with good judges—is that it? A. I think the present judges are doing good work.

Q. That is what I say, a bad system with good judges? Good judges can operate under a bad system and probably produce better results than bad judges under a good system? A. Well, the man that is in the Morning Court is not put to as much inconvenience as he would be in the Police Court. His trial takes place at 8 o'clock in the morning, there is not so much notoriety, there are not so many spectators and reporters about, and that class of thing.

Q. What class of cases are put on probation? A. Well, largely wife desertion, non-support.

Q. Do you have cases from the Juvenile Court also? A. Not now, no, sir.

BY MR. BUCK:

Q. Did you ever receive any instructions as to the duties of a probation officer? A. No, sir.

Q. You are an employe of the Charity Organization Society? A. Yes, sir. I acted as a volunteer for about three years under Judge Murphy.

Q. And you are now a volunteer probation officer? A. Yes.

BY CHAIRMAN PAGE:

Q. You don't report then to the State Probation Commision? A. No, sir.

BY COMMISSIONER FRANCIS:

Q. How are you supervised? A. By Judge Nash at the Police Court, and the Board of Managers at Elmira and Rochester.

Q. Do you always report the termination of cases, the final disposition? A. Yes, sir.

BY COMMISSIONER WINTHROP:

Q. You have been regularly appointed by the Police Justice as a probation officer—as a volunteer? A. Yes, sir.

Q. You have taken the oath of office? A. No, sir.

BY CHAIRMAN PAGE:

Q. Well, let us see just what you are. You say you have been regularly appointed as a volunteer, that seems to be a contradiction of terms. Now are you a volunteer probation officer who is recognized by the Judge by his giving the cases into your charge, or have you been appointed a probation officer without compensation? A. The conversation was in this way—my last conversation in this matter with Judge Nash was that he asked me to serve, and I told him that I would take two or three cases that he felt that I could do something with, but I would not act as a thoroughly authorized probation officer, that I did not have the time to do it.

ANNA E. GAFFNE, being called as a witness and duly sworn, testified as follows:

BY MR. BUCK:

Q. Mrs. Gaffne, are you now a probation officer? A. I am, in the Juvenile Court.

Q. And you are regularly appointed by Judge Nash? A. Yes.

Q. And took the oath of office? A. Yes.

Q. Did you ever receive any instructions from anyone as to the duties of a probation officer? A. Why, yes, I have. I acted in the court when Judge Murphy was judge of the court, in fact for the past seven years I have been in the court, and he gave me my instructions then.

Q. What was the nature of the instructions? A. Well, that I should take charge of the children given to me and perform the duties, visit the homes, investigate the cases, and do all that I could for the betterment of the child.

Q. Did you not have some supervision of the volunteer probation officers? A. No, we did not during that administration, we were all volunteers, did just the work that was assigned each one. For four years I was secretary of the court.

Q. What were your duties as secretary? A. To record all the cases and to keep track of the work of the probation officers as far as I could.

Q. That is, you record the names of the persons to whom individuals were assigned to be taken care of? A. Yes, every case that was tried in the court was entered in the card cabinet by me, and then I kept track of the children assigned each probation officer, and sent notices to them with reference to meetings or asking their opinion as to the work that we should perform, and all the duties which were assigned I tried to keep track of.

Q. Did the probation officers send to you reports as to the progress of each case? A. They did as far as they could but in volunteer work you know you cannot expect the same results as you get when they are paid officers. They reported as often as they could I believe.

Q. Have you any recommendations that you would like to make as to how the work of volunteer probation officers might be improved? A. The only recommendation I can offer there is that I have always thought that there should be a number of paid probation officers that would keep— that would follow up these cases, and in that way aid the probation officers in the cases in which the probation officer, the volunteer, would not have the time to devote to, that these probation officers appointed by the Court for that work should do the work that the volunteer would not have the time to do. It has been my experience that unless you keep after these cases daily the work is not a success, and you cannot expect that of volunteers at all times. There should be someone appointed to do that work. We have investigating officers now who I believe investigate the matter before the case is brought into court, but there is no one appointed to follow up the cases after they are placed on probation with the officers.

BY COMMISSIONER FRANCIS:

Q. You believe in strict responsibility attaching to the appointment of probation officers? A. I do. These cases should be followed up daily, and unless they are the success is not as it should be.

BY MR. BUCK:

Q. You are not secretary now for the probation officers? A. No.

Q. So you are not in touch at the present time with the way the work is going? A. I know something about the work, how it is going, but of course I would not know the details, I know the court has two paid officers and they investigate the cases very thoroughly.

Q. Have you any cases in your care now? A. I have three.

Q. Are there any recommendations or suggestions or criticisms that you would like to make? A. I think the Juvenile Court should have a detention home just as soon as possible, that has been a long-felt want in Buffalo.

BY CHAIRMAN PAGE:

Q. You have been a volunteer probation officer as I understand you? A. Yes, sir.

Q. Without receiving compensation? A. Yes, sir.

Q. Were you appointed and did you take the oath? A. Yes, I was appointed by Judge Murphy to act, there was no form, I was not sworn in, but I have been since Judge Nash has been in. I have been working in the court for about seven years.

Q. And these paid officers of whom you speak were only used to make investigations prior to the person being disposed of by the Court? A. Yes, and then they have children on probation with them, but there is no one appointed to follow up the work done, follow up in detail the work done by the probation officers.

Q. Your idea is there should be a chief probation officer in charge of the probation officers? A. Yes, to report to the Court at regular intervals just what the probation officers are doing, and to assist them as far as possible.

BY COMMISSIONER WINTHROP:

Q. You are a volunteer now? A. Yes, sir.

Q. In addition to yourself how many other volunteers are there in the Juvenile Court? A. At present I cannot say because I am not familiar with the details of the work, but during Judge Murphy's administration we had 15, we always had 15.

Q. Volunteers? A. Volunteers.

Q. Now how many paid probation officers are there in that court? A. At present, two.

BY MR. BUCK:

Q. Are there any other suggestions that you would like to make? A. No, only I would like to urge that detention home project, I would like that carried out as soon as possible, especially for the girls. We found the necessity for that from the beginning of the work. I think that many cases would not be disposed of in the court as quickly as they are if we had a detention home to send the children to while further investigation was being made; but as we have no place of that kind, I think the Judge settles the case right away because he knows there is no place to send the children.

BY COMMISSIONER FRANCIS:

Q. You had one some years ago? A. Yes.

Q. And you then became well acquainted with the value of it? A. Yes, sir, I was secretary and treasurer of the society that maintained it.

Q. You realize that it is a distinct loss that it is no longer in use? A. It certainly is a distinct loss to the children.

BY CHAIRMAN PAGE:

Q. Do you know that in the City of New York the Society for the Prevention of Cruelty to Children maintains such a place? A. Yes, sir.

Q. That society here doesn't do anything of the kind? A. There was one, the Juvenile Improvement Association maintained it as long as the funds held out. Since then of course there has been no appropriation made and we had to discontinue the work.

Q. Were there appropriations made by the county authorities? A. No, none at all, simply by the subscriptions of the members of the Association.

Q. Nothing paid for the expense of maintaining the children while they were there? A. Not by the city or county.

BY COMMISSIONER FRANCIS:

Q. Do you know whether an appropriation was requested of the city authorities? A. I don't think it was. I think Superintendent Regan spoke of asking for it at one time but I don't think it was ever requested in an official way. It was talked of but nothing further.

BY CHAIRMAN PAGE:

Q. I think the County of New York gives the society $50,000 a year? A. I don't think there would be any trouble at all to get it from the City of Buffalo if it were put in the right way, because the citizens at large when appealed to responded at once. It costs a great deal of course to maintain a home of that kind, and there would be no difficulty in having the city pay something if it was urged in the proper way. There is no reason why the city could not afford to maintain a place of that kind.

———

FRANK E. WADE, being called as a witness and duly sworn, testified as follows:

BY MR. BUCK:

Q. Mr. Wade, you are a member of the State Probation Commission? A. I am.

Q. Can you tell us how many volunteer probation officers are connected with the Juvenile Court? A. Why, I understand that there are 40 who are occasionally working now, and about 60 who have been appointed. The volunteer system has been recently wholly reorganized. Up to last July there was no paid service in the Juvenile Court, the whole system was voluntary. That system broke down. Results were not favorable, the Probation Commission, which investigated conditions in the State reported against the conditions in the Buffalo Juvenile Court and in the beginning of the year an application was made for a paid probation officer, a chief probation officer in the Juvenile Court, and such an office was created, and after the Chief Probation Officer took office—I think he went into office in July,—he began to reorganize the volunteer force there, and according to my understanding it is still being organized. He informed me a while ago that there were I think 40 in active service, and about 60 who had been appointed.

Q. Were you connected with the probation work before you became a member of the Governor's Commission? A. Well, not directly with probation. I had been interested in social settlement and charity organization work for a good many years prior to my appointment.

Q. Do you think we ought to have a detention home here for the children? A. Oh, yes; assuredly. I would say in that connection that the State Probation Commission, upon the invitation of Judge Nash, met in Buffalo in January of 1908 and the State Commission investigated the conditions in all the criminal courts of Buffalo and Erie County, and at that time they drew up a set of recommendations; one of the recommendations of which was the necessity for the appointment of a chief probation officer in the Juvenile Court. And they also recommended that the city appropriate sufficient money to keep and maintain a detention hall. That was the official recommendation of the commission to Judge Nash. Judge Nash incorporated that recommendation in his communication to the Mayor and the whole proposition went up to Mayor Adam. And a number of us presented the situation to the Mayor, but I must say at that time there was a detention home here under private auspices. We thought that even that institution should be under the public direction and so we recommended. After our recommendation the detention home was closed on account of lack of funds. So since I think the first of July there has been no such place here. We tried to make an appointment with the Mayor along in July, and he went out on his summer vacation, went away to Europe on his summer vacation before we could present it to him, and the subject has not been taken up since. But I assure you that we intend to press it as strenuously as we can. There is great need of it. We have been engaged in the organization of considerable probation work here in Buffalo and Erie County and we haven't been able to do it all.

Q. Have you any other recommendations you would like to make to the Commission? A. Why, I think that the present conditions in the Juvenile Court are working in pretty fair shape. There is one man who is detailed from the Police Department—he was a desk sergeant there— who devotes his whole time to the investigation of cases previous to trial and I think he is a competent and good man. There is a chief probation officer in that court who has organized a volunteer service and is organizing it now and is devoting a good deal of time and energy to it and with these two men working together I think that the juvenile work is developing along proper lines. In connection with the juvenile work one recommendation I would like to make would be to urge strenuously the maintenance by the City of Buffalo of a place of detention for children. I would advise that such a place of detention be large enough to have the Juvenile Court in conjunction with it. I think that it would be better to have the Juvenile Court in the same building so that the children would not have to be transported some distance, when they are brought in for trial. I would also have the headquarters of the probation officers in the same building, and also medical inspection and other reform methods could be brought into it, for the headquarters—for the detention and trial of all the delinquent children. In connection with the Morning Court we have there a paid probation officer who is doing fair work, but he is overwhelmed by the number of cases. He is supposed to organize a volunteer force. He has organized some volunteers, but it is difficult to get the right kind of volunteers in that court.

BY COMMISSIONER WINTHROP:

Q. What is his name? A. Kelly; Edward F. Kelly.

Q. Have you an idea of the number of cases he has? A. Why, Mr. Kelly has under his personal supervision a hundred and fifty cases, and he also—I think there were a hundred and seventy cases on probation in that court and of those he has one hundred and fifty. He also collects fines. We are using the provision, I think it is 483 of the

Penal Code, of the Code of Criminal Procedure, 483 of the Code of Criminal Procedure which permits the collection of fines on probation, in the morning courts there is good opportunity for that work. A man arrested for drunkenness who ought to be punished somewhat will be fined ten dollars and be given three months or six months or longer to pay his fine and the probation officer collects it in installments. The State Probation Commission considered that the morning courts were good courts for probation work, that intoxication, disorderly conduct and the offenses of that kind would readily yield to probation, and it was upon their recommendation to the Board of Morning Court Justices that the application went in to the city for a paid probation officer in that court.

BY CHAIRMAN PAGE:

Q. What is the idea of this fining a man and then putting him on probation with some one to pay his fine and allowing him to pay on the installment plan? A. The idea is it permits a man to support his wife and children. Most of those men are poor and when they are sent to prison their family must suffer. By putting him on probation to pay his fine the man is punished to the extent of the payment of the fine, the family is not deprived of his services for their maintenance and I think it operates also toward his reform.

BY MR. BUCK:

Q. Do you know how many cases are on probation in the Police Court? A. The situation in the Police Court is unfortunate. I would like to say in explanation that I know Judge Nash is thoroughly in sympathy with probation work.

I have had a good many talks with him on the subject and he believes heartily in it. And he has devoted a great deal of time to the development of the Juvenile Probation work. He is enthusiastic over it and he appointed as his chief probation officer the first man on the eligible list, who is a Republican, although Judge Nash himself is a Democrat. He has not permitted politics in any way to affect him.

BY COMMISSIONER WINTHROP:

Q. Who is that? A. Judge Nash, the Police Court Judge, is the man I am talking about.

Q. Well, who did he appoint? A. Pfeiffer, Frederick W. Pfeiffer, the chief probation officer in the Juvenile Court. In the Police Court he shortly after his election had appointed a man probation officer. I think that he appointed that man before he understood fully the development of the probation work. That man took office I think the first of March. He was James Kean, who was a witness here. The State Commission believes that that office is a civil service position and the matter has been brought to the attention of the Civil Service Commission and they have, I understand, already taken action on it, and the probation work undoubtedly will be reorganized in that court under a probation officer, who will be appointed from the eligible list. At least that is my view of the matter.

Q. Is Mr. Kelly the only probation officer connected with the court? A. He is the only paid officer. There has been a start at it, at imposing probation at the Juvenile Court. Judge Nash was devoting his time to organizing the juvenile probation work and also has been trying very hard to get a detention hall. He has made a number of efforts, seen the Mayor a number of times and his whole heart is in the work. And in his police court he has let probation drift and as a case would come up that would be a probation—a certain probation case, he would put it on probation with the police captain or with some probation officer that might occur to him. It is not good probation. In fact it is about as poor probation as there can be and be called probation. There has been, as far as I could see when I looked over the records, there has been no report of these probation officers. But the exercise of probation is a judicial function. The State Probation Commission is desirous of working in absolute harmony with the judges. The greatest gain can be achieved in that way and we haven't taken any active steps to correct the conditions in the Police Court because it was our position that it was up to the Civil Service Commission to take action. And I personally have brought that situation in the Police Court up a number of times and action has now been taken by the Civil Service Commission. Pardon me, did I make any suggestions as to more probation officers in the morning court?

BY MR. BUCK:

Q. I don't think you did? A. Well, I would recommend that there be at least one and, if possible, two more probation officers in the morning courts. I would recommend that there be a probation officer appointed from the eligible list of the civil service examination in the Police Court who will take hold of the situation there and organize the probation work.

Q. Do you think it would be best to have enough paid

probation officers to handle that work? A. Paid probation officers would give the best service, but it is slow work getting paid probation officers and until that time comes we will have to work with an efficient organization of volunteer probation officers under certain—under paid supervisors, paid probation officers, who will organize the volunteer force. If there were paid probation officers in the Juvenile Court it would require probably eight or ten of them to do the work properly, and the city at the present time would not give us those officers upon request. That would be a matter of growth. It is the desire of the State Probation Commission to get as rapidly as is consistent with the judgment of the court as many paid probation officers as possible in this State. Of course we work through the courts. If the probation system infringes upon the judge, and judges don't like to be dictated to and we 'don't propose to dictate to them, as far as the State Commission is concerned we never act unless we had an invitation from the Court to act in the way of extension work. Of course in the way of investigation work we have a duty there to perform which we do independently. I also think there ought to be a paid probation—a paid woman probation officer who will organize the cases of women placed on probation in the Police Court and Morning Court. I think one woman could handle all those cases and look after all the women cases and girl cases. At the present time we have no paid woman probation officer here. But with a good man in the Police Court the whole criminal system of Buffalo and Erie County would be guided by some paid supervision.

BY COMMISSIONER FRANCIS:

Q. Are any of the cases of females placed on probation now with adult male officers? A. I could not say as to that. They are placed on probation with woman probation officers, volunteers. Mrs. Rose Smith, who is here, or Miss Rose Smith, has a number of cases in the Police Court of that kind.

BY COMMISSIONER WINTHROP:

Q. At the present time you have two probation officers in the Juvenile Court, paid—— A. We have the chief probation officer, who is paid $1,200 a year. There is detailed from the Police Department to the Juvenile Court a desk sergeant whose duty it is to investigate juvenile court cases before trial. He has a record of every case prepared for the Judge and when the juvenile is brought before the Judge the Judge has his history, which has been gathered by this investigator.

Q. So that you have only one probation officer in the Juvenile Court who does work after conviction? A. Only one, yes.

Q. Only one that does strictly probation work? A. Yes.

Q. And then you have this number of volunteers in the Juvenile Court and in the court for the trial of adults you have Kane, the only probation officer? A. Yes.

Q. Now in the morning justice courts you have how many? A. We have one.

Q. One? A. Edward F. Kelly. He is the paid officer. This is all, all this paid service has been developed here this last year; up to this last year there hasn't been any paid service.

Q. Well, do you approve of children being placed officially on probation with a volunteer or do you think they ought to be placed on probation with a regularly appointed probation officer and then he work through volunteers?. A. Well, these volunteers are regularly appointed probation officers. They are appointed by the order of the Court and they are sworn in as volunteers—as probation officers. They have all the functions of the paid officer. I think with a thoroughly organized system that the chief probation officer can regulate that work probably better than the Judge. The Judge will put him on probation with the chief probation officer and he can designate the volunteer to whom this boy will be sent.

Q. But officially, so far as the court records go, the paid probation officer is the one with whom the child would be placed on probation? A. I think that would be a good system. I think now that they are put directly on probation either with the paid officer or with a volunteer, but it is the duty of the chief probation officer to supervise this volunteer service and he does. He gets the reports from the volunteer officers. I think that Mrs. Gaffne was mistaken when she testified that there was not any such supervision. Mr. Pfeiffer does give that supervision. Mrs. Gaffne hasn't been connected very closely with the work within this last year. He does supervise the volunteer work.

BY COMMISSIONER FRANCIS:

Q. Have you given any consideration to the thought advanced here that it is not sound law or good process of law to penalize for a breach of promise to the Judge rather than for the offense committed in the first instance? A. You mean the testimony of Judge Olsen?

Q. Yes? A. I had a talk with Judge Olson after he left the courtroom about that and it doesn't impress me that the reasoning of the Supreme Court of Illinois is good. It seems to me that the cancelling of the probation goes back every time to the offense itself. The placing upon a suspended sentence is the exercise of judicial clemency. That is the conscience of the Court. The Court may be right or the Court may be wrong about it, but the law gives him that right. Now he imposes certain penalties. The imposition of those penalties follows the exercise of his discretion in placing them upon suspension of sentence, and the violation of any of those requirements which the court asks from the probation brings it back again initially to the first offense. I don't believe that the punishment follows the breaking of the promise, but it seems to me the punishment follows the violation of the act of clemency.

Q. Well, in case of the pledge being exacted by the Judge and then the breaking of the pledge subsequently? A. Well, I don't believe that the cancelling of the probation and the commission of the man to prison is due directly to the violation of that pledge. It is due to the fact that he hasn't behaved himself in accordance with the judgment of the Court in the way the man should behave himself to avail himself of the clemency of the Court.

Q. Do you know that your State Commission has ever given that subject any thought? A. No, we have not—I don't think that question has ever been raised.

Q. It might undermine the entire practice of the probation system? A. Yes, I don't think it will be raised here and I think the reasoning in the State of Illinois is not good. At least that is my view-point.

I would also state that in connection with probation it would be a good thing to have a statute permitting restitution under probation. That is allowed in the State of Massachusetts. They have there a method of restitution. The offender is placed on probation, during the period of his probation he pays to the party whom he has wronged the damages of their wrong. Of course it is wholly controlled by the Judge. The Judge will fix the amount of restitution and in that way he repairs his wrong and his punishment is in the doing of it. I think——

BY CHAIRMAN PAGE:

Q. Is that using the Criminal Courts for the enforcement of a civil remedy? A. Well, we have now permission up to the time of conviction to compromise misdemeanors.

Q. Yes? A. It is merely an extension it would seem of that same principle. I don't think it would be anything unconstitutional and I think it would work out to advantage. This whole probation problem is largely unsolved yet.

BY COMMISSIONER FRANCIS:

Q. I was going to ask you if there is any state that has given it a trial such as would prove its worth? A. Of probation?

Q. Yes? A. Why probation has been in active operation in the State of Massachusetts for over twenty years and the results have been most satisfactory. The effects of probation in juvenile correction has passed the experimental stage and is proven. It has also been demonstrated in the minor offenses to be a splendid method of correction, intoxication and non-support. When you go to Rochester you will find there a probation officer in non-support cases who collects, I believe, something like three or four thousand dollars a year, collects this money from the man and gives it to the family. And in such cases in different parts of the country it has proven a great success. In felonies it is still in its experimental stage, but a great humane system that has operated effectively with children and with the minor offenses cannot fail to operate when we come to the more serious offenses, especially for the first offenders. Now we have here a peculiar situation in Buffalo. We have a large Polish population, anywhere from eighty to a hundred thousand Poles, right through the Polish section the railroad runs and they have their freight yards all around there. There cars are sealed very insecurely and there is a constant temptation there for these young Polish boys, with not a very high standard of morals to break those seals and get into those cars, and they are doing it in large numbers. Now, that is felony. Many of those boys are sent to Elmira Reformatory, many of them are punished severely for that crime and there is a demand that they be severely punished because many people think the railroads must be protected. Now in those cases probation ought to operate well, because many of them really are—it is the first offense and the temptation is strong and their standards of life are low; they ought to have at least one chance to redeem themselves, and we have now a salaried probation officer in the supreme and county courts who will take over a good many of those cases. Those are felony cases.

BY CHAIRMAN PAGE:

Q. Well, it seems to me there is great good to be accomplished through probation if you do not let it run to seed before you get it started by using it for a whole lot of purposes that it seems to me would be entirely aside from the main object of probation? A. Well, for instance, what?

Q. Well, it seems to me this having a man fined and putting him on probation to pay his fine on the installment plan, loses sight entirely of the purpose of probation. The idea that you have got to make it easy for the offender, I don't look at it as being a part of probation to soften the rigors of the law for a man that is really an offender? A. Of course, if the man did not have the opportunity to pay his fine he would go to prison and his wife and family would suffer.

Q. I know it. Either don't impose a fine or—— A. The State gets its fine and the man supports his family and he has the advantages of probation.

Q. Well, the State can get along very well without the fine? A. I don't—I think that about $120.00 has been collected in the morning courts through fines so far. It has not been imposed very much, but personally I am inclined to favor it.

Q. Well, I have given no consideration to it until it was mentioned here, because I have never heard of it. It strikes me that the probation must have something to do with the final reclamation of the person that is put on probation and make him a better citizen? A. That is the——

Q. ——to save them to society, whereas if they are sent to a reformatory institution or a penal institution they are much more apt to become hardened criminals; to save society from that condition and save the person? A. That is the object of it.

Q. Now, when you go and apply to that the system of selling justice on the installment plan I don't know whether it will work out well or not? A. Well, the object of probation is reformation.

Q. Yes? A. The object of probation is to reform a man in society, give him another chance. The effect of the prison system as in the correction of the individual is totally broken down. It is proven, I think, that outside of the reformatories the prisons make men worse instead of making them better. They are maintained at a very great expense to the community and the results are not the kind that—are not the best for the community. I think a good percentage of the men who come out of State prisons and penitentiaries and such like return again and they prey largely on society. Now the object of probation is to take the first offender, take him before his mind and habits are set in criminal ways and reclaim him and reform him. That is the purpose of probation. But it naturally will radiate in other directions. It is a human problem and like all human problems it has many sides.

BY COMMISSIONER FRANCIS:

Q. Would you limit judicial discretion in the matter of probation or set hard and fast rules for its exercise? A. Not at the present time.

Q. Well, I favor the practice, but throughout this entire investigation I have not been impressed by its operation? A. Well, we have—the system rests on the judges and it cannot be very much better.

Q. And the probation officers? A. It rests on the judges and the probation officer and it cannot be very much better than the Judge and the officer whom he appoints. For that reason I personally would strongly urge the appointment of probation officers from civil service lists. I believe that the judges are just as much influenced by political pressure as any other class of men and that when there is a paid probation office created the men with the greatest influence are the most unfit men and the tendency is for the Judge to make such appointments unless there is a limitation placed upon it. You cannot put—it would not be advisable to put any kind of statutory limitation on it, but the civil service work will operate in that direction. There ought to be a mental examination which will show that the probation officer has a certain average of intelligence. A certain degree of intelligence is required by the probation officer. Then at least 50 per cent ought to be allowed for personality and experience. The widest range should be given to the character and the kind and humane nature of the applicant.

BY CHAIRMAN PAGE:

Q. To whom would you have given the rating of 50 per cent. for personality? A. Sir?

Q. Personality, I believe you put it; personality and experience? A. And experience, 50 per cent.

Q. In whom would you vest the discretion of deciding? A. I would place it in the Civil Service Commission.

Q. Not in the man that has got to appoint and who would be responsible for the action of the officer? A. No, I think that the Civil Service Commission will do their duty fully in that respect. I think it is the mixing up of powers—if you are going to put it under civil service it ought to be under civil service. The Judge has the choice of the three names that are submitted to him.

Q. Yes. If you had seen some of the products that have been produced before us, men that were certified as number one on the civil service list and others that were very high you might not be impressed in the wisdom possibly of the civil service. The examination produced here the other day by your local commission would seem to me to be a very fair examination and one that probably would produce excellent results. We haven't as yet seen what kind of an examination is given in New York County and the greater city, but it is to be judged by its fruits that it must have been pretty poor? A. Well, that is the problem, of course, we have by civil service——

Q. Especially when it works out through an arbitrary system of examination, the production of a proper probation officer where so much depends upon temperamental character and the peculiar fitness of the person for that line of work. A. Well, if the——

Q. (Continuing.) A man may not be able to spell correctly or write correctly or figure correctly, for that matter, and yet make a most excellent probation officer, because he has the human element so largely developed. A. Well, it seems to me there ought to be a certain level of intelligence that can only be gotten by some test. Probation is something that must be studied. It is not a simple thing. It has a good many features to it. Now we take a person who prepares to be teacher, he has got to go through some course of instruction. The professions require a course of preparation of some kind, and probation work is along that nature, somewhat like the work of the teacher. It ought to require a certain amount of preparation and a certain degree of intelligence, which will only come through education. Now tests to get that level I think are advisable. Beyond that level it should be left to the personality. Whether the final test of personality is in the Civil Service Commission or in the Judge is an open question. It should be—it is an open question. Personally, I think it ought to be in the Civil Service Commission. Of course, there are good and bad civil service commissions and there are good and bad judges. All these problems are human, and they must be worked out relatively and there will never be the best results until men are made better.

Q. What would you think of a system to have a certain examination standard that any candidate must pass in order to become eligible, have that in the Civil Service Commission to rate them according to their intelligence, and then certify the entire list to the appointing officer and let him select out of that list? A. That would have some advantages. That is a question that would be open for discussion.

BY COMMISSIONER FRANCIS:

Q. Do you believe in a hit or miss examination, or rather the puzzle system? A. I think the Civil Service Commission should prepare themselves for such an examination, and if they do not prepare themselves it is not a fair test.

Q. My idea would be living up to a certain standard of examination that all might be aware of as necessary for qualification as probation officer, in addition to a personal qualification that would be sufficient. Why wouldn't that be better than this system of puzzle examination? A. Why, I don't like to say a system of puzzle examinations. I hope there won't be any such system. I hope the Civil Service Commission will give fair questions.

Q. Take a matter of fact, take a list of three names that have been handed to the head of a state department under the present administration, the names of men whom they certified, supposed to be the fittest of the fit, and who proved to be when the list was finally submitted No. 1, a morphine fiend; No. 2, dead, and No. 3, totally unfit? A. I am not making an argument here for civil service, gentlemen. I don't know much about the civil service system, but I do think that the work like probation work under present conditions ought to be put under civil service, because I know the judges are moved by political pressure in their appointment, and even if you get a poor examination and a poor lot of men recommended by the Commission, I think that the system can be improved, whereas the appointing power under our political system does not seem to improve. Political pressure is such that the judges would yield. Now, I have in mind a certain probation position that must be created and is supposed not to be under civil service examination, and the men that were the most active and started out with the most influence were the men who were absolutely unfit for the work. Now, it is possible that some of those men might have had enough pressure to secure the appointment.

BY COMMISSIONER MURPHY:

Q. Do you mean to say that because a man has political pressure that he has not ability that a man may have who has passed a civil service examination? A. Oh, no; I believe that everything else being equal the man who has done political service ought to be preferred as a principle, believing that principle.

Q. Well, he has got that ability? A. I think he has that ability, but I do not think it works out that way. I think that it is—that in a great many of our appointments it is the man who has either got the—has done political work himself or has clients who have done it and demand recognition.

———

ROSE SMITH, being called as a witness and duly sworn, testified as follows:

BY MR. BUCK:

Q. You are a volunteer probation officer, Miss Smith? A. Yes, the past seven years I have been a volunteer.

Q. Do you devote your entire time to that work? A. Yes.

Q. Are you connected with any local society that is interested in that work? A. No. Previous to being a volunteer officer I was a missionary for fifteen years, doing slum work in the morning courts and police courts.

Q. This is purely a volunteer work on your part? A. Yes.

Q. What class of cases do you have? A. Well, in the morning courts I take care of the entire cases, until last September, until the paid probation officers—I think it was September they went in, and in fact all of the women of the three courts, 8, 3 and 1, and then I take care of the cases in the Police Court.

Q. At the same time? A. Yes; because the Police Court followed the morning courts, the Morning Court is at eight o'clock and the Police Court at ten.

Q. And you are engaged now solely with the Police Court? A. Outside of the Salvation Army I am the only woman probation officer in Police Court and the only missionary, and therefore besides the cases she takes I take all the remaining cases, or what I don't take she takes.

Q. What time do the morning courts meet now? A. At eight o'clock.

Q. Did you ever receive any instructions as to the duties of a probation officer? A. No, because I started the work myself some twelve or fifteen years ago, just had ordinary slips for the morning courts, and the discharged cases were all turned over to me, and then the officers were always kind enough to call me and tell me at what station houses the women arrested were located, and that gave me an opportunity to investigate my cases and have them ready for the morning, and therefore it was really a system of my own. I have never received any instructions; I volunteered my services.

Q. At the present time there are how many in the Morning Court to look after the women? A. There is one man, that is Mr. Kelly; of course he is a regular probation officer.

Q. He takes care of the men, doesn't he? A. Yes.

Q. I mean the women? A. I am really the only probation officer for the court. There is a missionary, Mrs. Ross, but she doesn't take any cases.

Q. Are there any voluntary probation officers? A. No woman in the Morning Court; I am the only one. The Salvation Army woman takes one court in the morning and I take two, but she takes the public or non-Catholic cases.

Q. Are the cases in the Morning Court now handled as

they ought to be? A. Well, there are so many cases that are not subjects for parole or probation. As a rule a woman that comes up in the Morning Court is usually an habitual drunkard or an ordinary woman, a prostitute, and to parole a woman like that—it is sometimes impossible to do anything with them. This is my fifteenth year, I think, and I spent seven years almost constantly with them, day and night, in the hospitals and in the houses. In the morning they would put a woman like that on probation with me. If she came from a house of prostitution or a saloon she has no other home than a public rooming house, and about seven-eighths of the women are so physically demoralized after you handle them three or four years that I really don't approve of probation, because sometimes they go back to rooming houses and in a week or two I would have three or four women with perhaps the same disease, making it impossible to parole that class of women from the morning courts; but in 1905 and 1906 we started to send them to the local institutions here in Buffalo. For instance, the Protestant women went to the Ingleside or Salvation Army and the Catholic women to the Good Shepherd's. Then they were physically taken care of and it made a vast improvement, so much so that where I would have one woman perhaps fifteen or twenty times in a year, and sometimes as high as thirty times in a year, after 1906 I have had her perhaps three or four times in seven and then in eight I had her, well, I guess once, no twice; once in Morning Court and once in Police Court, but she was in condition to be put in some place to work. If they are physically wrong of course you can't ask a nice family to take them—therefore the Morning Court is very hard to deal with. A man must be very well versed both in morality and physically, because they are often harder to handle than the Police Court cases. The Police Court cases are easier to parole, because in the Police Court they have larceny cases and all public cases, and a girl will perhaps be well employed and still have a little fault and be arrested; but the Morning Court cases are usually old offenders—very seldom you will see a disorderly conduct case, perhaps one out of every ten. It is impossible to parole them, owing to the fact that there is no place to place them or put them.

BY CHAIRMAN PAGE:

Q. From your experience do you think that probation is proper to use with a woman that has been plying the trade of a prostitute for a number of years or for a long period of time? A. No, I do not unless she is placed some place where she can be watched—it is impossible. It is almost impossible to watch the juvenile offenders—well, the first time it is all right. You take young girls, the first time you may be able to parole them, but the second time they come in you cannot, because you cannot live with them. I have often taken them to my own home—for seven years I had a detention home—I used my own home for that. It was all right while they were with you, but of course I could not keep them there all the time. They were not prisoners, and the consequence would be that it was almost impossible to watch them. I would rather take a boy juvenile offender the third or fourth time than a girl the first time.

Q. Do you believe that it would be desirable to have a detention home for girls? A. Yes, I do; for one class of girls. You take where they have trustworthy parents it is all right if those parents after the child has been arrested take them home, it is all right because, as a rule, they want to do the best they can for their children. Take the Polish and Italian classes, and it is harder to handle them because there is no place to take them after I close my home—we had a great deal of sickness and death—and I was obliged to take them to the Society for the Prevention of Cruelty to Children, and down there they usually stayed for a day or two, so it really is necessary that we have a detention home for that class of girls.

BY COMMISSIONER HAMILTON:

Q. Where is that society's place here? A. 62 Delaware Avenue.

BY MR. BUCK:

Q. Mr. Churchill is superintendent? A. Yes, sir.

Q. Do you consider that at the present time there are sufficient probation officers for the women in the morning courts? A. While I am there, yes. I don't know how long—my police court work is getting very heavy for me now; I am the only probation officer in Police Court, and I also take women from the upper courts and from the District Attorney's office. I have been so many years at it—I don't know if I will be able to cover that when—as the Judge said of me, I am getting to be quite an old maid. I cannot cover the field and do it conscientiously.

Q. How many cases have you? A. I have at present only one from the Morning Court, only one, because the rest were discharged, and nine from Police Court, and two from the Juvenile Court, and then I have missionary cases that have been discharged and just turned over to me with slips. I think I have thirty-two of those, thirty-one or thirty-two.

Q. From the Juvenile Court? A. No, from the Morning Court and Police Court cases where there is not sufficient evidence to convict them and they were discharged and still had no place to go, and the Court just simply turned them over with a slip to my address.

Q. How many cases can one probation officer handle properly? A. Well, to speak for myself—I have a system to work on—I can easily handle twenty-five women very nicely, if I don't have to spend so much of my time in court. All the cases that are held over from Police Court to the higher courts, I take the records from the Police Court and transfer the women to the higher court and keep those records, so therefore it takes until two or three o'clock in the afternoon with my Police Court work; but if I didn't do that, and didn't feel it my duty to stay there and wait for the women to be discharged or their cases taken care of, I think I could. That would make about four cases a day to visit. You are supposed to visit them once a week, and they visit us. I allow them to visit me once and then I visit their homes once a week. And then, whatever church they attend I feel it my duty to see that the pastor or minister of the church knows of the cases, so I perhaps make my work a little harder; but I think it makes a great improvement in either a man, a woman or a child, because they get into the society there and they know that they can be improved. Every church is always willing to assist me, so working on that system I have found a great improvement.

BY COMMISSIONER FRANCIS:

Q. Do you believe that your presence in court is necessary? A. Well, yes; we have so much to do that the men cannot handle. I am obliged to examine these women, and do that work.

Q. You have no assistants under the present system? A. No, the Salvation woman is there. Of course, I do the heavy part; I have been so willing to do it, I suppose that is why I do it, maybe; I have never asked.

BY MR. BUCK:

Q. Are there any recommendations that you would like to make to the Commission, Miss Smith? A. We are very much in need of a new police court. We are in an awful way there; we have no accommodations for our women, and we are obliged to use the same lavatory for both, and it makes it very embarrassing for me, that is to handle the women, and it is also embarrassing when the Court adjourns a case half an hour or twenty minutes for me to decide whether a child has made a true statement, having no place to go to unless I go to the Judge's office or where the prisoners are kept, or to the men's lavatory.

BY COMMISSIONER WINTHROP:

Q. Are the women placed in the iron cage in the Police Court—there is an iron cage there? A. Yes, sir; just men; we have the women over in the corner.

Q. They are placed in a different part of the room? A. Yes, sir; they are seated on the chairs with me.

Q. In the case back of the court—are men and women placed there? A. No.

Q. Only men? A. Just the men. I stayed there with the women until they have finished with the court.

BY COMMISSIONER HAMILTON:

Q. Are all of the judges of the morning courts and the Judge of the Police Court here apparently as much interested as yourself, for instance, in forwarding the work of probation? A. Oh, yes; I am positive—this class of men. We did have, four or five years ago, I had great difficulty, but in 1906 and 1905 we started to make new courts. That was the heaviest work, because the Court did not see the necessity of having a woman watch the women. So many of the runners came in and paid the women's fines, and the men paid the fines and took the women right away again, and the judges did not see fit to give me jurisdiction, but now the judges do. They are very anxious always to learn from me. These men that have been in the habit of paying fines for women always get an allowance—if they paid a $5 fine they got $2, and they are always anxious to do it.

Q. Are these men runners for houses? A. Yes, we are quite well cleaned of them now, but if I am absent two or three weeks from court—I was away four weeks and I found a few when I came back. The judges are very much interested in the work and especially our Police Court Justice—we have almost an immaculate court there. We need improvements, of course, but it is so we cannot make them.

BY COMMISSIONER SMITH:

Q. Where are the women kept that are not bailed out? A. In the district north, they are kept at No. 3.

Q. I mean, are they kept in the station houses? A. Yes, sir.

Q. What kind of accommodations are there there for women that are kept over night? A. They have better accommodations now than we used to have, but still they are very crowded since No. 1 was burned down, because it brings the six station houses and headquarters' women into three, and eight accommodates all the South district, and that is mostly Poles.

Q. Are there any matrons there, what we call matrons in New York, women in charge of the female prisoners? A. Yes; No. 8 has a woman—she is there for three weeks and then she is relieved; No. 1 has a matron, and No. 3 has a twelve-hour matron, from seven in the morning until seven at night, and another matron from seven until seven in the morning. When we had the three station houses they were each on three weeks and then relieved one week. The same matron was on day and night.

Q. No. 8 has one woman, day and night?

BY COMMISSIONER HAMILTON:

Q. Do you think the accommodations in the three morning court stations are decent and adequate at the present time, the accommodations for women? A. Well, there could be improvement, owing to the number of women that are placed at No. 3. I think after we have our No. 1 station, and whatever accommodations there will be at headquarters it will relieve these districts. It is at present too crowded because it brings too many women and too many different classes of women in the one room. For instance, we have three or four vagrants, and four or five charged with prostitution, and we dislike very much to have a young girl eighteen or twenty years old, who is arrested coming from a dance perhaps, on a charge of vagrancy. They cannot make a division at present because they are so crowded. Ordinarily the regular drunk goes down to a cell if she is too intoxicated to take upstairs. There is a division inside of the men and the women.

Q. Do you mean to say that a young girl coming from a dance is arrested and held over night at a police station? A. They often come home at 2 or 3 o'clock in the morning, girls 18 or 19 years old, and if she has been walking Main Street for a half or three-quarters of an hour, the policeman brings her in, and until recently I was always notified.

Q. At once? A. Yes, but in 1907 the present superintendent took that privilege from me—I was not to see any more female prisoners without permission from the matron, so that made it very hard—the men had no more right to notify me.

Q. What is done with those girls? A. Well, they are kept there until morning, until one of the missionaries or I come.

BY CHAIRMAN PAGE:

Q. You don't mean to say they would arrest a girl that way without she had done something to show that she was a street walker, would they? A. Well, we have a class of girls that frequent the dance halls, and after 12 o'clock make a practice of just walking the streets to meet whom they may, sometimes to earn fifty cents or a dollar, and other times just for the amusement. Previous to 1906 they made very few arrests on the street, that is, of that class of girls, but our hospitals commenced to fill up so, and the maternity wards, and our orphan asylum, it was almost impossible, and in 1905 I asked that if any girl was found and her parents could not be found to bring her in and I would take care of her. Sometimes the parents refused to come. We generally notify them from the police station and tell them that they are there, and very often they won't even acknowledge that the child is theirs.

BY COMMISSIONER MURPHY:

Q. Are these dance halls allowed to run yet? A. Oh, yes, they are not as bad, of course, as they were, but they are still in existence.

BY COMMISSIONER HAMILTON:

Q. A good many have been closed up? A. Yes, sir.

BY COMMISSIONER MURPHY:

Q. Are there drinking places in connection with them? A. No, not since 1906. We had a raid then. I have the evidence that I gave to the Mayor, 38 pages, I had thought of bringing it down with me, and the dance halls and houses with saloons attached were closed. I don't think they have many of them now.

BY COMMISSIONER FRANCIS:

Q. Is there a matron at the court who has charge of the women there? A. Yes, sir; there is.

Q. A paid matron? A. Yes, sir.

BY COMMISSIONER HAMILTON:

Q. You think then that it serves a useful purpose to arrest these women and take them to the station houses instead of examining them for instance where they are known, and permitting them to appear the next day? A. Well, yes; very often you will summon them, and you will be unable to find them for weeks, and then you will find them in the rooming houses.

BY CHAIRMAN PAGE:

Q. If you are going to save these girls you have to act quickly, don't you? A. Oh, yes.

Q. Because in a short time they will be beyond saving? A. Yes, it is much harder to work with the women and girls than with the men, much harder.

CHAIRMAN PAGE: The Commission will stand adjourned until to-morrow, Saturday, February 6, 1909, at 10 A. M.

BUFFALO, N. Y., Saturday, Feb. 6th, 1909, 10 A. M.

The Commission met pursuant to adjournment.

HARRY L. TAYLOR, called as a witness, having been first duly sworn, testified as follows:

BY MR. MAYER:

Q. You are the County Judge of the County of Erie? A. Yes.

Q. In that capacity do appeals come to you from the Police Court? A. They do.

Q. And also from the courts which are called the Morning Courts? A. They do.

Q. In other words, from the justices to the police or justices of the peace as they are variously called? A. Yes, morning courts they call them here.

Q. Have you any idea of the number of appeals that have come to you annually? A. Well, I haven't—I haven't looked that up, Judge. I can give a pretty close estimate of it though.

Q. That will do? A. Why, I should say 150; now that may be 25 out of the way, or it may be more. That is from all the four courts, the three morning justices and the police justice.

Q. Do you recall or can you approximate how many of them came from the Police Court? A. Why, I should say not over a third.

Q. So that by far the larger number came from the morning justices? A. Yes, of course there are more of them.

Q. There are more because—— A. There are more of them, I believe they have two running each morning, or three.

JUDGE JUDGE: Three.

A. You say they have three running every morning.

BY MR. MAYER:

Q. Now, will you in your own way, Judge, state to the Commission the general character of the cases that come before you on appeal and the questions involved or pre¹ sented in these appeals, so that the Commission may see the character of the cases in which litigants appeal to a higher court from these lower courts? A. Well, generally, the percentage of cases in which appeals are considered squarely on questions of law and decided as such are very few—is small. It puts itself into what you might call an equitable proposition, largely. That is, an affidavit comes up for an appeal and the appeal is invariably allowed; that merely allows the appeal: Then in a large share of the cases, vagrancy, small crimes like that, in a large share of the cases an application is made for a modification of the sentence; that is to dispose of it summarily; and we have a system now, these morning courts and the Police Court and myself, whereby in such cases I always refer that back to the Judge who tried the case and let him investigate the matters raised on the appeal, and if he believes that the sentence should be modified, I don't feel bound to modify it but as a general proposition I do modify it then to the time served. So that a large share of these appeals are determined in that way. Now as to the matters that come up, questions of law, I should say the reversals

—well, they run about half and half I should say, but the returns indicate to me mainly that these judges have too much to do, that they have not time to properly consider the merits of the cases that come before them. I don't believe they have proper facilities for having testimony preserved—taking testimony, preserving it and thereby making up a legal return. I think that the mistakes that are made result largely from that. I don't know as I could say more except—it isn't any benefit to you but it is a good time perhaps for me to say that we have the nicest and best kind of co-operation, that these morning justices and the Police Justice I think are very high-minded, conscientious men, all of them, and are doing their best, and we have no friction or trouble and we are continually co-operating by correspondence and otherwise to improve situation in dealing with these minor crimes.

Q. In appeals from determinations of the morning jus tices there are no stenographer's minutes as I understand? A. I don't know.

JUDGE JUDGE: We have no stenographers.

BY MR. MAYER:

Q. Well, the appeal comes to you in the shape, I presume, of an affidavit alleging error? A. Yes.

Q. And, then, is the Justice under the practice required to make return? A. The Justice is required to file the return within ten days and that return as a strictly legal proposition should show a case.

Q. Yes? A. From the information to the commitment.

Q. Yes? A. Complete, and with their facilities you can see how easy it is to have error in it.

Q. Well, does that return merely show the Justice's version of the case as it came before him? A. Oh, sometimes
there was a police—the Police Judge has a stenographer,
hasn't he?

JUDGE JUDGE: Yes.

A. Then it is his cases where the testimony appears. The
returns from the morning courts are, we might say, a statement of the Judge as to what occurred, what testimony was
offered, and so forth.

BY MR. MAYER:

Q. So that from the morning courts there never comes
to you a strict transcript? A. No.

Q. Of what occurred? A. I venture to say I could if I
wanted to reverse pretty nearly every appeal from the
morning courts, if I wanted to be absolutely——

Q. Technical? A. Strict and technical, for that reason.

Q. Well, now, with your experience as practically an appellate court for these courts, is it your opinion that it
would tend to a better administration of justice to have a
system whereby the testimony is perpetuated? A. Why,
most assuredly so that they would have time to give these
—this class of cases the same consideration which—what
is called the higher class gets.

Q. How long have you been County Judge? A. A little
over two years.

Q. Was there any other suggestion that occurred to you
as the result of your judicial experience in connection with
these cases? A. Why, no; I don't know what suggestions
I might have if we had different men in those positions,
but I think that our present system works very well. As
I say, there is so much of this modification of sentence in

crimes like vagrancy for a large share of them are fairly and properly disposed of that way. An idle man is sentenced, for instance, by a morning justice for six or three months for vagrancy, on the theory that such a condition exists. He finds out afterward, after a month, say, the man has been down, or two months, upon looking into the matter, that that is sufficient. He recommends it to me, and invariably it is modified; that is, often, I mean.

Q. Well, what is the basis of the recommendations, are these recommendations on the theory that the person convicted has paid a sufficient penalty for his offense, or is it that some facts have been discovered which would indicate that that vagrant had relatives or friends, or—— A. Well, both, and very often there may be a legal mistake, but the representative of this man is willing to let it go at that, so to speak.

Q. Well, what kind? A. Additional facts, generally it is a case of additional facts, for the reason that the Morning Justice hasn't had time to consider it. A policeman brings a man in—I suppose, I don't know much about it— the testimony is given hurriedly, and he will say "thirty days" or something, without having time to fairly try the case.

Q. And to get fully the facts? A. Yes.

Q. And which might have tended to another judgment? A. Yes, I think that is the situation.

Q. Well, now, you said something that if the men who now administer justice were not men of as high character and as competent as they are, that you might have a suggestion? A. No, I don't know that I meant it just that way.

Q. Perhaps I misunderstood. A. I said with them there I thought we had a very good working system here now in this city, that is what I meant to say.

BY CHAIRMAN PAGE:

Q. As I understand, Judge, the bar and the people of Buffalo find a great improvement in the judges, those now on the bench, over those that were there before. A. I don't want to say that, I don't want to reflect on anybody that has been there before. I think the people are very well satisfied with this corps of judges, and the lawyers so far as I know. I would put it that way. In fact, I hear nothing but good reports. Indeed, I find that these judges, if I may say so, are very willing to have me make suggestions to them and to do anything that they can to improve their handling of these matters, so that there will be as few errors as possible and right handling as much as possible. I have never had the least friction with them in any way, and I haven't hesitated to reverse where I thought they should be reversed.

BY MR. MAYER:

Q. Now, do you recall the character of the errors of law, I mean, have you in mind any general classification of errors, or perhaps some specific ones? A. Oh, they claim everything, you know, in these affidavits on appeal, but very often the testimony isn't sufficient to show that any crime has been committed. For instance, an officer will say that he picked up—"I picked up this man, so-and-so, such a place, and he had a gun on him," and that is all the testimony there will be, and he will be sent down for carrying concealed weapons without a permit. Sometimes—it is like that very often—and sometimes there is nothing, it doesn't appear that an information has been sworn out, it doesn't appear that there is a warrant, it doesn't appear a crime was committed in the presence of the officer, and such matters as that ordinarily——

Q. Then it is a sort of an informal disposition? A. Yes, it is most informal.

Q. Rather than in accordance with legal procedure? A. Yes.

BY COMMISSIONER WINTHROP:

Q. When you talk of modifying sentences, your court acts as a court of appeal only, doesn't it? A. Yes, I have a right, though, to modify the sentence to the time served, at any time. These judgments of these justices I can modify at any time to the time already served, if I want to; but I never do that without having them first—without having them take the additional facts first to the Judge who tried the case and saw the witnesses, and find out what he thinks about it. Then, if I find he think it should be modified, I modify it if I see fit, or I sometimes do if he doesn't want to modify it; but I get him to first look up that matter.

Q. And in the last instance you can discharge any prisoner? A. Yes, I can do it, absolutely without them, if I want to do it, but I think it is proper they should consider these additional matters first, always.

Q. When you say that the lower courts haven't time, do you refer to the Police Court or the Morning Court, or both? A. Well, I say that these appeals and these returns indicate that they don't. Now, I don't know from practical experience, except I have been—while I was practicing, I have been in the Police Court, oh, perhaps half a dozen times in all. I know they are rushed in the morning, when

I have been there, but whether they are all day I don't know.

Q. I suppose the morning court has time? A. It doesn't appear so. If they sat all day I suppose they would have time, but they don't sit only a certain number of hours, do they?

Q. Start in, as we understand, at 8? A. A couple of hours, as I understand. I don't believe it is the intention that these judges sit all day, at all, is it?

Q. No, we understand not? A. I don't know what the law provides as to that, I am sure. I know it is their duty to sit about two hours in the morning.

BY MR. MAYER:

Q. Do you have many applications for the release of girls or women committed to homes in connection with some offense relating to the social evil, such as street-walking or prostitution? A. Very few; very few. I haven't had half a dozen in these two years.

Q. Then I assume you have no knowledge of what the conditions were prior to your taking the office of County Judge? A. No, I have not.

BY CHAIRMAN PAGE:

Q. Judge, this Commission is appointed to inquire into the operation of the criminal courts and to make any suggestions that might be necessary to correct any existing conditions that need correction. Have you any suggestion of any kind to make to us in regard to the courts of Buffalo? A. Do you mean as to remodeling them?

Q. Anything? A. Well, I have general views as to all the courts here.

Q. If you think they would be of any value to the Commission we would be very glad to have them? A. Why, they would probably, be amateurish, compared with the knowledge and the opinions you gentlemen already have.

Q. Well, we may not have any yet, Judge? A. Why, I have read suggestions about having a new system that would combine the criminal and civil jurisdiction and have enough justices, similar to that talked of by Judge Olson. It seems to me it would be better than this. We are in a peculiar situation here in Buffalo. It involves the civil side, too, and that you don't care to bother with. For instance, I get appeals from these morning courts and the Police Court and from the justices of the peace around the county, both civil and criminal, and we have a municipal court here that tries civil cases up to a thousand dollars, and they try penalty cases under the ordinances, they can ask to go over there and try it out civilly and when they have finished they appeal from the Municipal Court to the Supreme Court. But a judgment of the Municipal Court that is docketed in the County Clerk's office becomes a county court judgment. I have nothing to do with the appeal from there, and the result is a most mixed up state of affairs. The law won't tell us sometimes and we don't know. The Municipal Court can't grant a stay, but it is a county court judgment after the return if filed. The result is we have a very much mixed up system here. It ought to be simplified in some way.

BY MR. MAYER:

Q. So that the appeal should go to one place, one court? A. Why, it seems to me we ought to have a system of inferior courts covering the whole system, civil and criminal, and have all the appeals go to somewhere, and if a judgment in the Municipal Court is docketed have it a judgment of that court, so that there is no nonsense about it nor complications.

Q. Have you given any thought to the question which was under discussion yesterday as to a system of inferior courts having both criminal and civil jurisdiction? A. I say I think that would be a good idea, it seems to me it would, and shift the judges.

Q. Now, if I may ask you, in your experience as a county judge, do you find it helps you to have both jurisdictions, I mean is there value in the variety to you? A. Why, it is much more interesting, yes, I like it.

Q. That is what I mean? A. Yes, I certainly do, I think it is an excellent thing.

Q. I mean as a matter of personal equation and personal experience, do you think the variety is a desirable and useful thing for the Judge? A. Oh, certainly I do. I never— this proposition of disposing of criminals who are convicted is of course very difficult for any human being to handle, that isn't pleasant, but I don't object to it and I like the variety.

Q. You feel, speaking for yourself and based on your own experience, you can do better work if you turn from the criminal to the civil side and then back again? A. Oh, yes; it is certainly freshening, anyhow, if nothing more.

Q. Have you any idea, for instance, how many cases come before you in the course of a year? A. What kind of cases?

Q. Well, civil cases and criminal cases? A. Well, I don't know, I am working all the time. I have thirty-four weeks, I think it is, of actual term, of jury work, and then all these proceedings, sale of infants' property and——

BY CHAIRMAN PAGE:

Q. Foreclosures? A. (Continuing.) So many I can't—adoptions and committing people to the insane asylum, all kinds of proceedings running all the time.

———

DANIEL J. SWEENEY, called as a witness, having been first duly sworn, testified as follows:

BY MR. MAYER:

Q. Daniel J. Sweeney. You are one of the morning justices? A. Yes, sir.

Q. And you, as I understand, are not an attorney? A. No, sir.

Q. And what has been your occupation? A. I was City Clerk for two years and I am a newspaper man by——

Q. Well, as a newspaper man have you come into considerable contact, in the course of your work, with matters relating to courts? A. Yes, very extensively.

Q. And also with the persons who come into the courts, whether as prosecuting officers or defendants? A. Yes.

Q. Is that so? A. That is right.

Q. Now how long have you been a morning justice? A. A year the first of this year; about a year.

Q. Yes, and ordinarily how long do you find it necessary to sit each morning? A. Well, as a usual proposition, about two hours.

Q. From 8 to 10? A. From 8 to 10 I am generally there. Of course, I have run up to noon.

Q. You and your associates sit in rotation in the three station houses? A. Yes.

Q. What is your own view as to a station house being a

proper place to hold court? A. Well, I am not in favor of the station house as proper for it, but it should be near the station house. As it is now we are in the station houses probably that have the largest number of prisoners, the most important station house of a specified district of the city; now, I think, the Court should be near that center.

Q. Do you think you should have stenographers? A. Absolutely.

Q. As it is now you have no clerks at all excepting a desk sergeant? A. A desk sergeant, that is all.

Q. And that sergeant varies, doesn't he? A. Yes, every week he changes, they are changed every week.

Q. Do you keep any records? A. We have a police record or docket. The only record we keep is the name of the prisoner and the name of the witnesses, their plea, our verdict and the sentence.

Q. The character of the crime? A. Yes.

Q. Do you make any report to anybody? A. No, of course, there is a police report goes in every day, the desk sergeant takes a report from our docket, a typewritten report, which he sends to the Chief of Police.

Q. But you as justices don't make any report? A. No, we don't make any report—yes, we do, of the cases that we commit.

Q. What I mean is you make no annual report, or monthly report? A. No annual report or monthly report; no.

Q. The reports are practically taken from your dockets? A. Yes.

Q. By the police? A. Police officials.

Q. Police officials and they are the ones that keep such records as may be kept? A. That is all.

Q. Now, what would you say was the general run of cases that come before you? A. My experience in the year has been that seventy-five per cent. of the cases before me are cases of unfortunates who have committed no—really committed no offense, who are brought in largely because they are out of work. Perhaps a great number of them charged with intoxication, too, don't you know, but their condition is such that they are really unfortunates; some of them physical wrecks, others wrecks from drinking, that are incapable of keeping employment after they get it, many of them. My experience has been the greatest trouble I have is finding something to do with these men. How can I take care of them? What can I do for them? How can I save them in any way? Not how to punish them. That certainly has been my experience.

Q. Are these men charged with vagrancy, most of them? A. Vagrancy, jumping on railroad trains. There is a city ordinance prohibiting jumping on railroad trains. I cite one example: I had 118 prisoners one morning and I think 85 or 90 of them were charged with jumping on railroad trains, men who came into Buffalo here on railroad trains and officers had been stationed through the yards and picked them off as they came in and brought them into the station house. A great number of them were men looking for employment and going from city to city. Others were confirmed tramps; derelicts.

Q. What disposition do you make of these cases? A. Seventy-five of those that morning I formed in line and sent to the Erie County Lodging House to get something to eat, and if the keeper of the lodging house could help them find employment, all right; if he couldn't, they could get something to eat and a night's rest and get out of town again.

Q. And do you find any cases of this kind that you place on probation? A. No.

Q. You have a probation officer? A. Yes.

Q. How long has he been in your service? A. Since the first of July, I think it was.

Q. 1908? A. 1908.

Q. What class of cases do you place on probation? A. Well, I place the drinking man who has a family and has got employment. I place the wife-beater sometimes, if he has got a family and is willing to work. Some of them are men who won't work, and the family—the wife does the washing and supports the family, and that fellow, if he is continually hanging around and getting a little money to drink with or beating her or abusing her, I send him to the penitentiary.

Q. Do you place your cases on probation with the probation officer? A. Yes.

Q. Does the probation officer report to you? A. Yes, sir.

Q. Do you follow your own cases? A. Well, to a certain extent we do. We have No. 3 station as general headquarters for the probation officer. Among the three justices we have agreed that the probation officer shall stay at No. 3. Now, at certain periods, when the terms of probation of a number of them have run out, whatever judge is sitting in No. 3 station, he brings them before him, and the Judge discharges them or continues their probation, or makes such disposition as he believes to be warranted.

Q. Have you had any opportunity to ascertain whether the probation system as applied to persons found guilty of intoxication works out satisfactorily? A. Well, it does in certain cases that we have had, where the probation officer has reported that the man is steadily employed and takes care of his family, and the wife has not complained—the man has not been in an intoxicated condition since. Of course, I don't always tell them to abstain from the use of intoxicating liquors, I tell them to abstain from the excessive use. Many of them offer to take the pledge with me, but I tell them that if they are Catholics they should go to their priest and arrange with him. I do not believe in having a man take the pledge before me, because I don't think that they keep the pledge in any way—his word is as good as a pledge as a general thing with me.

Q. How about these cases of wife beaters? A. Well, such cases as I have had the reports have been very satisfactory.

Q. Do you require them to pay something to their wife? A. I require them to support the family and tell the wife to send in a complaint to the probation officer unless he is doing that.

Q. How long do you put them on probation? A. From two to six months. Quite frequently I put a man on probation for a week—a young man, maybe who I think is a pretty clean man, and I would not want to see him go to the pentitentiary; I will fine him and put him on probation and ask him how soon "Can you pay this fine?" Maybe he would say, "I can pay it in a week," and then I will say, "You are on probation for one week." That permits me to allow this man to go on probation to get the money. If he has employment he keeps his position.

Q. Then there are quite a number of cases where, after you fine a defendant, you place him on probation to give him an opportunity to pay the fine? A. Yes, sir; I have. I have quite a large percentage of such cases.

Q. How successful is that? A. It has been very successful, as the probation officer reports, they have paid most of the fines. Of course, some of them do not get employment, or are employed only temporarily, and they come in and ask if I will extend the probation, and so on. Eventually we get the fine out of them, and they have not been arrested again. In fact, I cannot recollect a single case that I have on probation where the probationer has been arrested again and brought before me—it may have been that he was brought before some other judge. I have no case in mind where he was brought before me.

Q. Do you think that you are able to give a full hearing to the persons brought before you in the limited time that you have to give to them—when I say you, I mean any justice of the court? A. Yes, we have the time, certainly have the time to do it. I don't know of any case where I have not been sufficiently impressed from the evidence advanced to give a decision on it—whether the facts are erroneous or not that is something that your judgment has to tell you. Maybe the officer is not telling the whole truth, the prisoner may be absolutely lying, all the way through, which is usual in these cases to a great extent. One has to form his judgment as he goes along.

Q. Do the police make arrests which you think are unjustified? A. I have not found any such, but there have been such arrests made, as I notice from looking at the evidence in the case, or from reports, one of the judges may tell me, but from my own personal experience the number is so small that it is infinitesimal.

Q. Have you had any cases before you where a prisoner has been detained for a longer period than over night? A. No—I have detained prisoners myself.

Q. In your capacity as judge? A. Yes.

Q. But I mean where the police have detained prisoners? A. No. Of course, the cases that are before us are not crimes, misdemeanors, and they are brought out the next morning.

Q. Not felonies, simply misdemeanors referred to in the statutes? A. Yes. Of course, we hold court Sunday morning, and all prisoners that are to be tried in the Police Court are brought before us Sunday morning, and we notify them of their right to counsel before they plead to the charge against them, of their right to witnesses, of their right to an adjournment for a reasonable time to get witnesses, and then commit them to jail for examination in the Police Court on Monday morning.

Q. You don't try any of those cases? A. No, just commit them to jail.

Q. So all these persons must remain in jail over Sunday? A. Unless they get bail, and they have to look for a police judge to get bail. I am annoyed every Sunday by people asking that I give bail—they cannot find a police justice. I suppose they are urged to death with persons trying to get bail.

Q. To repeat, if a man is arrested Saturday after police court is closed and is unable to obtain bail he is sure to remain in jail until Monday morning? A. He will remain in jail until Monday morning, that is in police court cases, of course.

BY CHAIRMAN PAGE:

Q. You have no power to admit to bail? A. We have no power to admit to bail, of course we don't need power for our cases, because the police have power to admit to bail in every case that is triable in our courts, and the police are always there.

Q. Well, you have power to examine and hold to the Police Court for trial? A. Yes, we have power to examine.

Q. You can hold a man but you cannot take bail for his subsequent appearance? A. We get those cases of course on Sunday morning.

BY MR. MAYER:

Q. I think you were here when some testimony was adduced recommending that more persons, more judicial officers, be permitted to take bail, were you not? A. Yes, sir.

Q. Do you think that would be a proper power to confer upon the morning justices? A. Well, I don't think that our powers should be extended beyond the cases in which we have jurisdiction. I don't think we ought to be entrusted with a problem—say a man held for highway robbery or something—I don't see why we should be trusted with the power of admitting that man to bail, or for any crime that is bailable—I don't think we ought to be entrusted with those powers. I am speaking personally—I don't see any reason for it.

Q. Well, take many cases which are technically over the line of misdemeanor, and not as serious as the crime to which you have referred—perhaps a case of a woman soliciting, or where a man has stolen $26 instead of $25. Is it not a hardship—— A. It is a hardship for the man. Of course in petit larceny, the police take bail, and to solve these problems I presume that they sometimes make it $25 where it is $26, and sometimes they make it $26 when it is only $25. I have had experience with a case of that kind where three young men were arrested on the charge of stealing three sheep from a railroad train, valued at $27, I think. The police had no idea what the value of those three sheep were, and as a matter of fact the three young men were taking the sheep back. There had been a wreck, and these sheep had gotten away from the train. A cattle car had been broken in the collision, and the three sheep were in a lot, and the men were taking them in a wagon when a railroad detective arrested them and charged them with grand larceny. Of course on Monday morning they were let out when the case was called, for I immediately discharged them, but I thought they had to spend a day in jail and it was really a hardship on them.

Q. Are there many cases which come before you where the defendant has asked for a trial in the Municipal Court? A. Very rarely, once in a while an attorney will ask me by telephone to hold such and such a case for the Municipal Court.

Q. When a police desk sergeant acts as clerk is he assigned to that duty by the Police Department or by the Justice? A. By the Police Department.

Q. So that the justices have no control whatever over anything except the adjudication of cases before them? A. That is all.

Q. From the experience you have had both as a judge and as a newspaper man, do you think it would be better to continue this system or to enlarge the number of police courts? A. I think it would be better to continue this system, and I don't say this simply as a layman, but I say it as a practical proposition. Of course we have had here in this town sometimes a conflict between the bar and the lay as to whether lawyers should not be judges of the morning courts. As a practical proposition the Bar Association —I am not saying it in any disparagement to the individual members—the Bar Association knows no more about the morning courts than they do about the biography of angels, because they are never there.

Q. It is a little early for them? A. Yes, a little early for them.

Q. I suupose you mean that the morning justices deal with human propositions as distinguished from questions of law? A. Yes, questions of law. I think our jurisdiction should be made so we could commit to almshouses—we have no such jurisdiction. If I could commit a man to the almshouse instead of sending him to the penitentiary so that he could get medical attention and something to eat, it would be a great help to our courts. There was a law passed that these cases had to go to the poor officers and be investigated. It would be better to give a man something to eat and then investigate him afterwards. After a great deal of trouble and correspondence with the Charity Organization Society and the Superintendent of Police, an order was issued directing the captain of each station to give the morning justices a patrol wagon. The policy had been that nobody but a prisoner could ride in a patrol wagon. If they picked up some poor fellow who was unable to walk, they would throw him onto the policeman, and then the policeman would throw him onto us; there he leaves him, and charges him with being a vagrant—the man could not work if he had work, he is only a cripple. Men like that should go to the almshouse, but we have no way to send them there. The only thing I can do is to send him for ten days to the Erie County Lodging House. They have a doctor there to look after them. I know he has got to get medical attention—the other way we could not do that.

Q. I thought I understood you to say that the Police Department had issued an order that you were to have a wagon? A. That is now, it is new, we can put him in the patrol wagon and send him up to the poor office, but the system that requires all that red tape—may have a wagon at the poorhouse you know—the city ought to have enough wagons to take the men up there. If I could send them to the poorhouse and let them investigate afterwards, even if a hundred of them were not worthy, if there is one that needs medical attention, he ought to have it, even if the other 99 are not all right.

Q. Where is the poorhouse? A. Away out on Main Street.

Q. It is in the city, is it? A. Yes.

Q. Have you from your experience any suggestions which you would like to make to the Commission? A. Well, I think that our defects are largely in the physical make-up of our courts. Of course we have a city of 415,000 people, and for the past three years we have made great strides in correcting the financial management of the city. The streets were not kept up, the police stations were not kept up, money was not used in proper channels. But under the administration of Mayor Adam we have made great improvements. We now have $13,000,000 to our credit on the debt limit. The debt limit is $30,000,000.

Q. Do you know what the debt limit is in Buffalo? A. I think about $30,000,000.

Q. No, I meant do you know where the debt limit is? A. Of course you have your troubles in New York, I suppose, different from ours, but we have $13,000,000 that we can expend. Now, the improvements that are being made must come now, because the past three years of this administration has been devoted to correcting the financial system, we have not made many improvements, and I think we have to have more police stations, we have to have new schools. Of course we have to expend a lot of money, and in connection with these improvements, we have to have new courts. We have to have police courts and morning courts. Of course this Commission, I don't suppose, can correct any physical defects of our condition here. It is largely municipal. As to the personnel of the Court there have been many nice things said about the morning judges here, and the general tone seems to be that it is improved somewhat. Of course most of the former morning justices are dead now, and it would be ungracious for me, even if they were living, to say that they were good or bad, but the general assumption is around the town that it is improved. I don't know but what the members of the Legislature can settle the problem by giving us the direct nomination system here—that might help.

Q. Let me ask you this, Judge Sweeney, have you had any occasion to form an opinion in regard to the necessity of a detention home for children? A. No, of course we don't have any children's cases. As a general proposition, do you mean?

Q. Yes. A. I think it is absolutely necessary.

Q. Have you not visited the place where the Children's Court is situated? A. I have not recently, no.

BY COMMISSIONER FRANCIS:

Q. What is the salary of a morning justice? A. $1800,

and if I did not have some other business it would not be a very attractive place. Of course the judges have other work to do.

Q. What is the idea of changing the Police Sergeant weekly? Is that simply a matter of routine? A. It is under the three platoon system, they run from eight to four and four to twelve, and twelve to eight. In the morning from eight on there is a new man there each week.

BY COMMISSIONER WINTHROP:

Q. On Sunday morning do you exercise increased jurisdiction? A. Just to commit men. I presume as a practical proposition they do not want to keep them in the police station, they don't want to keep these prisoners there, and they bring them before us to commit them to jail for their examination in police court, to change them from the police station to the jail.

Q. Do you examine them? A. No, we do not examine them. I have made it a practice when a prisoner is brought up before me to state the charge and advise him that it is his legal right to have the aid of counsel before he pleads to this charge, or any time during the course of his hearing, that it is his legal right to have an adjournment of his case for a reasonable length of time to get witnesses and counsel.

Q. That it is his right to have an adjournment when the case is to be heard in the Police Court? A. Yes.

Q. But it is not heard before you? A. No.

Q. You would not examine into his case to see whether he really ought to be held for the Police Court or not? A. No.

Q. Just a routine matter of transferring prisoners from the station house to the jail? A. Yes, just a transferring from the station house to the jail where they have better accommodations.

BY MR. MAYER:

Q. I want to ask you this question, if you can, eliminating the personnel of the gentlemen who are acting as morning justices at this time. What judge, from your point of view, if any, what advantage is there in having the Morning Court as against a sufficient number of police courts with a comprehensive jurisdiction and a requirement that the Police Court must sit as, for instance, is required in the City of New York, every day in the year, holidays and Sundays included, and open at nine o'clock? A. Well, the cases show such a vast difference between the Police Court cases and our cases. We have no, or very few, criminals, very few—police courts have all who are criminal, who have demonstrated some criminality in them. Our cases are for the most part the derelicts, and outside of them the fellow who gets drunk and makes a mis-step and falls into the hands of the police. Maybe there might have been a hundred persons drunk and only one of them fell into the hands of the police, and the others are just as guilty as the one who was arrested.

Q. But you have a power that is given to very few courts in the land, of being courts practically of last resort? A. Well, we have, yes.

Q. There are a very few appeals as against the total number of cases? A. Very few.

Q. And a man when he appears before a morning justice in the Morning Court is getting about all the trial he will ever get? A. About all, yes.

Q. Why, isn't that a matter of very great importance?

A. It is a matter of great importance because we have the liberty of the man at all times in our hands.

Q. How many cases in a year come before the morning justices? A. Well, I cannot estimate, I know one month I had over 2,000 cases.

Q. 2,000 cases before you alone? A. Yes.

Q. Is there any way in which you could get the statistics as to the total? A. I think the Chief of Police could give it to you.

Q. Would you say that in the course of a year 15,000 cases come before you? A. Really I cannot estimate, Mr. Mayer, because I have not thought—some days I have only four prisoners, and another morning maybe 118 or 120.

Q. At any rate some thousands of prisoners? A. Yes.

Q. Come before each of you? A. Yes. I know this, that the keeper of the lodging house down there informed me that in six months I had around 1,000 men that I sent to the Erie County Lodging House.

Q. Do you not think it wise, if some system were devised, whatever it might be, whether it be an extension of the jurisdiction of the morning justices or an enlarged police court system, or a combination of civil and criminal, whereby every case that comes before a court should be fully tried, with an opportunity to have stenographer's minutes, with the fullest opportunity of the defendants to be heard, and with the most careful statistics in regard thereto? A. That would be a great improvement, it would be a most marked advance in our system. We will take, say, 100 cases in our courts, there would be 80 of those which are not of a legal character, there may be twenty cases that morning who plead not guilty, and protest their innocence and want a trial. Now, if I try these cases and get all the facts that I can, if I think there is additional evidence I hold it over for a day and ask them to bring the witnesses. If in one of these 20 cases I sentence one of them, a month afterwards an appeal may be taken and I get served with a notice of appeal. Maybe I have tried 1,000 cases since that time, I have absolutely no recollection of what took place at that trial, whether I violated any of the legal procedure or denied them any rights to which they were entitled. The only thing I can do is to go to the record and find who the police officer was, or what witnesses appeared, and notify the police officers to give me an affidavit as to what they testified to, and then I make out my return to the appeal from the testimony. After I get that testimony I may recall some features of the case, but really that prisoner is at the mercy maybe of my recollection, which is a very serious situation to be in, and nine times out of ten, I will give the prisoner the benefit of the doubt.

Q. On the question of time, is there any special advantage in the hour or the hour and a half between eight o'clock and say nine, as a police court might be required to sit? A. There is this advantage in the financial proposition to the city. The city does not give these men any breakfast. These prisoners that are tried in the morning courts, the city does not have to pay for their breakfast. If they are held for the Police Court they have to furnish them with breakfast. There is that expense. Then again many of the prisoners go to work after they leave there—of course they are a little late, but they go to work.

Q. But if you have a large calendar of course you are liable to run on to half-past nine or ten o'clock? A. Oh, yes; we are liable to run on, but the policemen often tell me that they have a man who is employed somewhere and has got to go to work, or something of that character, and we try him first.

BY COMMISSIONER WINTHROP:

Q. Would you have a stenographer take every case? A. No, I would not have him take every case.

Q. Only cases where the defendant requests that stenographer's minutes be taken? A. No, where they want a trial. Most of the, 75 per cent., will plead guilty, and say, "Yes, I was drunk," or "I did this."

Q. Wherever the plea is "Not guilty" you would have stenographer's minutes taken? A. Yes, have stenographer's minutes taken.

Q. Would that delay the trial of cases to any great extent? A. No, because we hear all the evidence anyway, and if the stenographer was there he would take it.

BY COMMISSIONER HAMILTON:

Q. If you had three courts sitting as the morning courts sit now why wouldn't it be better to enlarge their jurisdiction so that they would be busy all day? A. I don't think you would get men to sit all day.

Q. I mean, of course, with corresponding increase in compensation. A. Well, I don't—we sit until we have disposed of the business.

Q. I mean increase the jurisdiction. A. Well, you could increase the jurisdiction. I talked with Judge Brennan, he submitted a statement to the Bar Association to take in petty larceny and the minor assault cases, and so on. That was before I knew about this Commission, and I agreed with him, and I told him the way to do it was to draw a bill and send it to the Legislature. I told him we might talk about it until doomsday and nothing would come of it, but that if he would draw a bill I would do all I could to advance it in the Legislature.

Q. But you don't think there is any special advantage in having three courts that only sit two hours, do you? A. Oh, yes, there is. It would be wrong to mix them up with the Police Court cases. You have no idea what a class of men we get in these courts as a general proposition, outside of No. 3. Of course each court is different. No. 3 is the Tenderloin precinct. There we get lots of women and men who are found in disorderly houses. We get the man who is arrested for intoxication and generally he is a man who has employment. In No. 8 we get the car prisoners, not those who are found guilty of car burglary on this occasion, but who have been convicted three or four times and are found hanging around saloons and refusing to work. We get the wife beaters out there also. In No. 2 we get the men that are coming in on the freight trains, and then—what is known as the Towline Gang. It seems that they get a man down there and stick with him until he spends all his money. The three courts are vastly different in the character of the men you get in them. How you are going to mix these with the Police Court cases I don't know.

Q. Well, I understand that you do favor increasing the jurisdiction to the extent that you speak of? A. To the extent that I said, because they are minor cases. Take disorderly conduct, sometimes a policeman will have a man who might be properly charged with assault, yet he charges him with disorderly conduct and brings him on that charge alone rather than wait until the Police Court is held and charge him with assault. Maybe it is a fellow who could be charged with petit larceny. I tried a case within a week, from lower Main Street, from a lodging house down there, the man stole an overcoat from some other tramp, and he was intoxicated at the time—he didn't want the overcoat, he just picked up this other fellow's overcoat and walked away, and he couldn't explain to the policeman where he got the overcoat. He might have been charged with petit larceny instead of intoxication. The policeman charged him with intoxication. I knew the man, I have had him there 20 times before me, he is a confirmed drunkard.

Q. When a prisoner is brought before you what do you say to him as to his rights? A. I advise him that he is entitled to the aid of counsel before he pleads to the charge against him, advise him that he is entitled to witnesses and to an adjournment of his case to get witnesses.

Q. Is he advised that he need not testify? A. He is advised that he need not testify. Well, they never do testify. Always after the evidence is in I tell him that he can make a statement, that he is entitled to make a statement. Of course the practical working of the thing—sometimes it amounts almost to a riot in the station houses, everybody talking in the reserve room, policemen come in dragging a drunk across the room who is hollering and bellowing, and three or four Italian women shouting that they want their Jimmy out, and officers stamping and telling them to shut up and keep still here, and all this. The theory of this thing and the practical working out of it is a different proposition in most of our courts, especially where we get the foreign element. We get the Polish element in No. 8 and the Italian element in No. 2.

BY CHAIRMAN PAGE:

Q. Don't you think it important that a court in which that foreign element comes should be conducted in a dignified manner and surrounded with all the majesty of the law? A. It ought to be, absolutely ought to be. It is very embarrassing at times to find yourself in the position that we are found in now, and the Court can only stop, instead of adding his voice to the tumult, can only stop proceedings and let them quiet down.

BY MR. MAYER:

Q. Well, in a word then, the holding of these courts in the police stations tends to everything pretty near, except order and dignity? A. Yes. It is an awful place to hold court as a rule, from the personal convenience standpoint.

Q. You have no control, I suppose, over the room? A. Only that the officers who are in there, the sergeant of police is detailed to keep order in that court, and we have a number of policemen around there, but we cannot do very much with them, because they are packed in there so. Some mornings I have gone into court when the police had to open an alleyway to enable me to get up to the Bench.

Q. Do you think it would be of any service to have a representative of the District Attorney in those courts? A. Yes, it would be. Of course, I don't know—it might be for a week he would not be required—it runs that way, but it would be a great thing for me. I would like to see lawyers come into the court—I could sit back and let them ask the questions. It gets very tiresome to ask the questions there for two hours every day. When I see lawyers in the court I am delighted, but they so rarely come. When the Bar Association says something, I don't pay any attention to it because I know they don't know.

BY COMMISSIONER FRANCIS:

Q. Bar associations are not always infallible, are they? A. Well, there was a case in the paper that I got a little note from about two men who kicked the janitor down the stairs and beat him up, and the paper said that Judge Sweeney fined each of the two men two dollars. I got a letter—it looked like a lawyer's letterhead, although it was unsigned, and it said, "Shame on such justice." As a matter of fact, those two men had nothing to do with this assault, but they were in this dance hall, they had been arrested for intoxication, and the janitor was assaulted at the dance hall, but these two men had nothing at all to do with it. I think that many people get their opinions from statements like this.

BY MR. MAYER:

Q. Being a newspaper reporter, you assume that the reports are not always correct? A. He was misinformed, the reporter was; he did his best, did the best he could under the circumstances.

BY CHAIRMAN PAGE:

Q. It made a better newspaper story? A. Yes, if you get too many facts you spoil the story.

———

FREDERICK W. PFEIFFER, called as a witness, and duly sworn, testified as follows:

BY MR. MAYER:

Q. You reside in the City of Buffalo? A. Yes, sir.

Q. And you are the chief probation officer in the Juvenile Court? A. Yes, sir.

Q. When were you appointed? A. The 15th of July, 1908.

Q. Did you take a competitive civil service examination?
A. I did.

Q. Were you at the head of the list? A. Yes, sir.

Q. What had been your occupation prior to this? A. Newspaper man.

Q. Connected with a newspaper in Buffalo? A. From the Buffalo Evening News for eleven years.

Q. Had you had occasion to be around children and study the subject? A. I was the police reporter for the News and assigned to police work at the courts for nine years. I was in the Police Court and the Morning Court and the Juvenile Court daily.

Q. So that you were familiar with the way in which the courts were run? A. Yes, sir.

Q. Will you state to the Commission the general character of your duties as chief probation officer of the Juvenile Court? A. You want our system as we have installed it, my method of doing business?

Q. Yes, I think perhaps that is better. A. Well, I will start right in at the beginning, as we get the prisoner, and go right along, and I will explain all the forms and our system. I think that will be the best way. I have an annual report that I have compiled, but I have not submitted to Judge Nash yet and I won't submit it in evidence, but I will read the part dealing with delinquent children.

"BUFFALO'S METHOD OF DEALING WITH DELINQUENT CHILDREN.

"Each complaint against a delinquent child is investigated before the child is brought into the Juvenile Court for trial. The name of the offender, the age, the address, the nature of the offense which he is accused of having committed, and the name of the complainant are furnished to the Chief Probation Officer by the police. When arrested the child is taken to the nearest police station and detained in the reserve room. His parents are immediately notified and one or both, or an older member of the family goes to the station. The boy is then released in their custody, no bail being required. In cases where parents refuse or fail to call, or where the child is an orphan, and living with relatives or friends who are neglectful of him, it is left in the discretion of the police captain in charge of the station as to what should be done for the child. If it is the child's first offense, he is usually allowed to go on his own recogizance with the understanding that he is to appear at the next session of Juvenile Court. If, on the other hand, the boy is known to the police to be a bad boy who has been arrested several times, he is locked up. If the captain were to release him, as has been the experience, the boy would not only fail to appear in court when wanted, but would run away from home in an effort to avoid the authorities. In some cases boys have left the city and been gone for weeks at a time. In most of the large cities there is a detention home, maintained by the city, where delinquent children are sent and held pending their trials, but it is with regret that I am forced to admit that Buffalo has no such institution, of which she is sadly in need.

"The boy and whoever calls for him at the station house are informed by the desk sergeant that the child is to present himself at the next session of the Juvenile Court. Two sessions of court are held weekly, on Tuesday and Friday afternoons. It is held in the Medical Examiner's office, at 241 Terrace.

"Upon receiving the name of the delinquent, Mr. Maloney, or the Chief Probation Officer, goes to his home to investigate the home surroundings. The investigator asks the correct spelling of the child's name, if there is an alias, his age, where he was born, his creed, the date of his arrest, and whether or not he goes to school, or has employment papers, and if the former, to what school and in what grade, and if the latter, if he is working and where, the name of the church he attends; if he has ever been arrested before, if so, for what offense, and the disposition of the case in court; if he has ever been in the truant school, the orphan asylum, or an institution of any kind.

"The probation officer also obtains the following information at the home of the delinquent: The given names of both parents, if they are alive, where they were born, and if dead, how long; how many children in the family and their condition, the employment of the various members of the family, and their financial standing. Whether they own their own home, and if they live in rent, how much they pay and whether or not they keep boarders or roomers. If the investigator finds that the family is poor, he asks whether or not they are receiving aid from the poor-master, the charity organizations, or any other source. He gleans all the information possible in regard to the family, and especially the boy, and then goes to the school the child is attending, if he is going to school. The probation officers talk with the child's teacher and the school principal in regard to his attendance, deportment and scholarship.

"A copy of the above information is furnished the Judge at the time of the delinquent's trial, and after hearing the evidence of the complainant and the child's defense, he always refers to the finding of the investigation made by the probation officer before deciding the case."

Q. Who is Mr. Maloney? A. Mr. Maloney is a desk sergeant in the Police Department detailed by the Superintendent of Police, at the request of Judge Nash, to assist in the probation work in the juvenile courts.

Q. Now, as I understand you, before the child is tried for the offense with which it is charged, you and Mr. Maloney make an investigation? A. Yes, a thorough investigation.

Q. Now the results of that investigation or the facts ascertained are placed before the Judge prior to the trial of the child? A. After the child has been arraigned, after he has pleaded, and the evidence has been heard, and the child's defense has been heard, then the probation officer is asked to tell the Judge his findings as to the investigation.

Q. Does he state that in the presence of the child? A. In the presence of the child.

Q. In open court? A. In open court.

Q. And can a person representing the child question the probation officer? A. He can.

Q. And is what the probation officer says taken down by the stenographer, or is there any stenographer? A. There is a stenographer.

Q. Is the report of the probation officer taken down by the stenographer? A. I believe it is.

Q. Do you know? A. I am not sure, but I believe that all the evidence is taken down by the stenographer.

Q. Do you know whether what the probation officer reports is taken as evidence in the case? A. I know that it is taken—the Judge considers it in making his decision.

Q. As to the guilt or innocence of the child? A. Not as to the guilt or innocence.

Q. As to what? A. As to his disposition of the case.

BY CHAIRMAN PAGE:

Q. Do you make any investigation into the facts alleged in regard to the commission of the crime? A. We do in some cases, not in all cases.

Q. Does your report to the Judge contain statements that have been made by other people as to the facts of the commission of the crime? A. Yes, sir. For instance, I want to explain that thoroughly. We get the name of the boy, it is his first offense, we go to his home and get all the evidence about the boy and the family and the home surroundings and all that, and if it is a serious crime, a felony, we will go to the complainant, and if it is the boy's second offense we will go to the complainant, or the third offense, and if there is any doubt as to the arrests of the boy, oftentimes the Police Department investigates to see about the cases, and we will go and look up the complainant. Sometimes the boys are arrested on warrants, and we look up the complainant. In that way we investigated every point of the case.

BY MR. MAYER:

Q. What we want to get at is this, see if I can make it clear to you. Assuming that the boy is charged with petit larceny, that he is about to be tried on that charge on next Tuesday afternoon. Now, do you, before that trial, investigate the facts surrounding the charge that the boy has stolen something? A. Only from the boy and his people, if the boy is at home when I call to talk with him about it.

Q. Now, when you go before the Judge do you, as probation officer, tell him anything about the facts as distinguished from the condition of the boy and his home surroundings? A. If the boy has admitted to the probation officer that he stole the thing he is alleged to have stolen, we state that to the Judge.

Q. When you go to the boy what do you say to him—how do you represent yourself? A. As the chief probation officer of the Juvenile Court.

Q. How do you get information from the boy? A. Why, I tell him that I am the chief probation officer from the Juvenile Court and that I want to talk with him about the crime that he is alleged to have committed. We sit down and we talk the matter over, I ask him, I ask him if he has ever been arrested before, and then I will ask him if he stole the article that he is alleged to have stolen, and how he came to be mixed up with the gang, and in that way we get the information; and then the parents, the mother or father, or older members that are at home, they are always on hand to defend the boy and say he was not guilty, that it was due to Johnny Smith, who was the ringleader of the gang, and that their boy was always a good boy.

Q. If that boy says to you that he did steal the goods, then afterwards do you state that to the Judge before the Judge has determined whether the boy is innocent or guilty? A. Yes.

Q. In other words, you present the admission or confession of the child as a part of the evidence on which the Judge makes his finding? A. Yes, sir.

Q. Do you ever warn the child that he need not say anything to you or tell his parents that he has a right not to say anything to you? A. No, sir.

Q. Do you ever advise the parents that it is the child's right to be silent, and that anything the child says may be used against him? A. No, sir. I advised the parents not to permit the boy to lie to me, I tell them that he should tell the truth. Oftentimes the parents will try to get him into another room and will not permit him to talk.

Q. Do you ever tell the boy that if he will tell the truth things will go better with him? A. No.

BY CHAIRMAN PAGE:

Q. Do you ever tell him that if he doesn't tell the truth it will go harder with him? A. No.

BY MR. MAYER:

Q. Do you know what rights a child under sixteen has where it is accused of crime? A. I don't know, not as regards the law.

Q. Do you know whether the child has precisely the same rights under the laws of this State as an adult? A. I believe he has.

Q. Do you know what the rights of an adult are, or what the precautions are which the law has thrown around any person charged with crime as to confessions or admissions? A. Yes, I do.

Q. What are they? A. I know he is entitled to counsel, and that the police are to instruct him or advise him that if he is to make a confession it will be used against him, and that he is entitled to bail, and that he is not compelled to make a statement.

Q. Now, do you know whether those same rights are accorded to a child under the laws of this State? A. No, I don't know.

Q. And as a matter of practice you have never warned or advised a child in the manner you have stated in regard to admissions? A. No.

Q. So that you have gone to the child's home to ascertain all the facts as best you can from the child and its friends and parents? A. Yes, from the child and the parents, and the school teacher.

BY CHAIRMAN PAGE:

Q. If I understand you, if it is the second offense, or if the child is charged with the commission of a serious crime, a felony, you then go to the complainant? A. Yes.

Q. And you inquire of him as to what he has to say in regard to the commission of this offense? A. Yes.

Q. And if he says there are other people that knew of the matter you go to them—make a thorough investigation? A. Yes, sir. The probation officer under our system acts as the boy's counsel, looking after the interests of the boy——

Q. Well, hardly. Let me show you where you do not. Then after you have gathered all this evidence from these different people you tell the Judge those facts, don't you? A. Yes.

Q. His counsel would not do that. A. No, that is true, they would not, they would withhold them from the Judge and try to free the boy.

Q. Isn't there occasion, sometimes, when the person who has told you these facts is not in court? A. No, not to my recollection; I don't recollect a case of that kind, only in regard to the boy's attendance at school and his conduct and behavior in school. We will ascertain that from his teacher or the principal of the school, and they are not present, and we use that in considering the case against the boy. Judge

Nash will ask his school record, will ask if he is going to school, and whether his record is in the boy's favor. If he is a bad truant that goes against him.

BY COMMISSIONER WINTHROP:

Q. And you also report to the Judge in this way the neighborhood reputation of the boy? A. Yes, we do, what the neighbors say.

BY CHAIRMAN PAGE:

Q. That you gather from talking to the neighbors? A. Yes.

BY COMMISSIONER FRANCIS:

Q. From what sources, if any, did you receive instructions to inquire into the guilt or innocence of the boy charged with an offense? A. Why, I have taken it from the recommendations made by the State Probation Commission that the duties of the probation officers in investigating these matters are in the interest of the child, and we want to determine whether or not the facts as stated by the police are true.

Q. Does the State Probation Commission recommend the propounding of any questions bearing upon the guilt or innocence of the boy or juvenile? A. I don't believe it does, no.

COMMISSIONER FRANCIS: Probably the practice is prevalent elsewhere.

CHAIRMAN PAGE: It seems to be the idea of a great many probation officers that this system of probation is to supersede the courts, and remove all the safeguards that have been thrown around the citizen when he is brought before courts. It might be well to have it ventilated quite thoroughly.

BY MR. MAYER:

Q. As I understand you, you start in with an investigation of the child's case from the moment, practically, that the child is arraigned—is that correct? A. The moment he is arraigned?

Q. Yes? A. No, the moment he is arrested.

Q. And your investigation includes an inquiry into the facts surrounding the offense? A. Yes.

Q. Now, when the Judge—if the Judge finds that the child is guilty of the offense, what is the procedure then? A. Why, if this is the boy's second or third offense, he takes into consideration the boy's previous record. We keep a record of each case, whether discharged, allowed to go on suspended sentence, committed, or placed on probation. We have an index system, and we have the name of every boy arraigned in juvenile court, and if he is placed on probation he has a number. If he has been on probation we present the card to the Judge.

Q. Then the Judge determines what to do upon all the facts that are presented to him before and after conviction? A. Yes. The Judge considers the evidence of the probation officer and the boy's previous record after the child has been convicted, in making disposition of the case.

BY CHAIRMAN PAGE:

Q. How do you know if it is given before conviction that he has not used it in arriving at his decision as to the guilt or innocence of the child? A. We are not called upon to testify if the boy is discharged or if he is allowed to go on suspended sentence. It is only in cases where the Judge places the boy on probation or commits him.

BY MR. MAYER:

Q. We are evidently talking about different things—that is what I have been trying to find out. After the boy is convicted, the Judge determines what to do with him? A. Yes, sir; our evidence is used in the disposition of the case.

Q. Is your evidence ever used by the Judge when the Judge is trying the boy to determine his guilt or innocence? A. No.

Q. Is your evidence given during the trial of the boy? A. Not until after he is tried, not until after all the evidence on both sides is in.

Q. What do you mean by "after the evidence on both sides is in?"—after the evidence is in and before the Judge has decided the case? A. Before he makes disposition of the case.

Q. Before he has decided whether the boy is guilty or not guilty? A. No. You see we stand right back of the Judge, we are right there at his desk. We know if the boy has not been convicted, we know that if he is discharged, or if he is discharged on suspended sentence, and if he convicts the boy he then calls upon the probation officer as to what disposition he will make.

Q. That is entirely different from the impression you have given the Commission. I will repeat the question. Here is a boy before the Judge, charged, if you please, with having committed the crime of petit larceny. The complainant and his witnesses state under oath the facts to the Judge upon which that charge has been made? A. Yes.

Q. The child tells his story? A. Yes.

Q. The child has pleaded not guilty? A. Yes.

Q. The child then tells its story—the witnesses and the

child tell their story. Now what happens then? Before the Judge decides as to the guilt or innocence of the child, does the Judge decide upon that evidence, or does he first ask you or the other probation officer what you know about it? A. Well, he is in the habit of asking the probation officers what they know about the case.

BY CHAIRMAN PAGE:

Q. At that point? A. At that point.

Q. And then he determines whether the child is guilty or not after that—is that correct? A. Yes, sir.

Q. Having determined whether the child is guilty or not guilty, he then decides, in the event of guilty, what to do with the child? A. Yes.

Q. As a part of the trial of the child—you know what I mean by that? A. Yes.

Q. Do you as probation officer testify as to whether the child has been previously convicted or not? A. Yes, sir.

Q. And you base that testimony upon your records? A. Yes.

Q. Do you base that testimony also upon admissions of the child? A. Yes.

Q. Now on that trial, if you get what I mean—and I think you do—do you testify, for instance, that the child, for instance, has told you that he stole the bananas? A. We do.

Q. And the Judge takes into consideration in determining the guilt or innocence of that child your testimony with all the other testimony? A. I believe he does.

BY CHAIRMAN PAGE:

Q. And also the fact that the child has been convicted of a similar offense? A. Yes.

BY MR. MAYER.

Q. Now, is this kind of testimony admitted? You understand we are just endeavoring to get the system? A. Yes.

BY CHAIRMAN PAGE:

Q. And we want you to very clearly distinguish the testimony as admitted before the Judge has announced his decision of the case? A. Yes.

BY MR. MAYER:

Q. The distinguishment between the practice prior to the time when the Judge makes up his mind as to the guilt or innocence of the child and the—after such finding and disposition by the Judge. That is what we want you to bear in mind. A. Yes.

Q. Now, then, with that explanation, is this permitted, that you find out from some man that you may regard as reputable, some facts regarding the specific crime, some reputable business man who said he saw Johnny Jones take the bananas from the fruit vendor's stall, and do you tell that to the Judge? A. We don't, no.

Q. Then is your testimony as to the offense confined to what the child has told you? A. And what his parents will tell us, yes.

Q. And what the parents will tell you? A. What the parents tell us and what we learn from the school.

Q. What you learn from the school? A. Yes.

Q. That is to say on his record from the school? A. Yes.

BY CHAIRMAN PAGE:

Q. What do you do with the information you get from the complainant? A. We very seldom use that, we are very seldom called upon.

BY MR. MAYER:

Q. But suppose you have been called upon? A. I have never been called upon by the Judge to testify as to what the complainant had to do about the case.

Q. Well, now, the school teacher isn't in the court, I assume? A. No, she is not.

Q. And you report that the school teacher at number so and so has told you that the following is the child's record in school? A. Yes.

Q. And that is before the child is convicted or acquitted? A. Yes.

Q. Now, you said you reported as to what the children— as to what the parents of the child may say. For instance, what? A. Well, if I find that the parents try to shield the child and that they told him to lie to me, I inform the Judge to that effect.

Q. Before the child is found guilty or innocent? A. Before the child is found guilty or innocent.

Q. The Judge has, it would appear, great confidence in you? A. Yes.

Q. And you make up your mind as to whether the child's parent is trying to shield the child? A. Yes.

Q. And you give your impressions to the Judge? A. I do.

Q. So that what the Judge has before him is not merely the evidence, but your impression? A. My impression, yes.

Q. And you say to the Judge, I assume, and if I am wrong you correct me, "I examined—talked to these parents and my conclusion is that they were trying to induce the child to lie to me?" A. That is correct, I will say that the boy was inclined to tell the truth, but the parents took him out of the room and told him not to tell me anything.

Q. And, undoubtedly, I assume from your knowledge of the Judge, that fact must have some influence on his mind, doesn't it? A. I believe so, yes.

BY COMISSIONER FRANCIS:

Q. In that instance, you really act as an investigator for the Judge? A. For the Judge, yes.

BY MR. MAYER:

Q. And partly as Judge, don't you? A. Well, we don't tell the Judge as to what disposition to make of the case.

Q. No, but you tell him your impression? A. We are working as—in the interests of the child.

BY CHAIRMAN PAGE:

Q. Well, the Judge usually concurs in your decision, doesn't he? A. Yes, I believe so.

BY MR. MAYER.

Q. I certainly have no doubt as to your personal earnestness, Mr. Pfeiffer. **We are getting at the system.** A. Yes.

Q. Now, has the State Probation Commission advised that procedure? A. I don't know; I am not just thoroughly clear on that matter, whether they advised questioning the boy as to his guilt or innocence or not. I know the State Probation Commission desires that every case be investigated, every detail of it, that a thorough investigation be made of the crime of which the child is accused.

Q. Well, now, how did this system develop, I mean, for instance, how did you know that such were your duties as you understood them? A. I followed out the system as adopted by Mr. Maloney previous to my assuming office.

Q. Well, you followed out then—— A. A system installed by Mr. Maloney.

Q. He had been in office before you? A. Yes, he was appointed to taake effect January 1st, 1908. I didn't go into office until July 15th, 1908.

Q. How many children's cases—— A. I have a table made up here of the number of children we had. I offer that in evidence to show the disposition of each case (handing paper to counsel).

MR. MAYER: I offer in evidence the paper referred to by the witness and it will take Exhibit number 71.

(Said paper was marked Exhibit 71.)

I will read it to the Commission (reads Exhibit 71).

BY MR. MAYER:

Q. In the paper, Exhibit 71, which is offered in evidence, and under the heading "Table C," you have "Violation of City Ordinance." Do you recall what those violations were? A. Why the greater number were sounding false alarm.

Q. Well, here is "Sounding false alarm of fire, 4?" A. That we enumerate there. Violation of city ordinance.

BY COMMISSIONER FRANCIS:

Q. Playing ball in the streets? A. Playing ball in the streets, and so forth. I don't believe we tried boys there for shooting craps or corner lounging, we don't have them there——

BY MR. MAYER:

Q. Then, as I understand, during the year 1908, 470 male children under 16 and 20 female children under 16 were placed on probation? A. Yes.

Q. How did the periods of probation run? A. The average period is three months.

Q. Well, does the Judge place the child on probation in the first instance for three months? A. Usually he stipulates the times. Some children are placed on for three months, others he will say six months and some a year.

Q. In the first instance? A. Not at their first offense in court, but when he sentences them, yes.

Q. Well, suppose a child has been found guilty. Now, for how long a period is the child placed on probation, generally? A. Three months.

Q. Three months. Now, during that three months the child doesn't come to court, doesn't report to the Court? A. No, he reports to a volunteer probation officer or to Mr. Maloney or myself.

Q. Now, you have a system of volunteer officers, have you? A. Yes.

Q. Will you briefly explain that to the Commission? A. We have sixty volunteers, forty of which have been sworn in by Judge Nash and their commissions forwarded to Albany. They are made up of a cosmopolitan group of ministers, school principals, truant officers and philanthropically inclined people, women—both men and women, secretaries of the Y. M. C. A., and so forth. They are in different localities of the city and of the different religions.

Q. Do they report, these volunteers, to you? A. They do, monthly; that is they are supposed to. It is hard to get all the volunteers to report on all cases. Some of them report regularly on their cases, make a written report to me.

Q. When you turn a case over to a volunteer do you follow up that case? A. We do.

Q. I mean do you go to the home? A. No, I only follow up——

Q. You follow up the volunteer? A. Follow up the volunteer.

Q. How many cases do you personally handle? A. Well, I have had——

Q. (Continuing) On probation? A. Well, I have on probation now twenty. This is my annual report—or monthly report (indicating) to the State Probation Commission. I had a number continued under my probation or oversight from the month of December, 10; number placed under my probationary oversight this month, exclusive of those transferred from other probation officer, 14 young girls; making a total of 24; 4 completed their probationary oversight last month; 2 were discharged with improvement and 2 were rearrested and committed, making a total of 4 passing from my oversight and leaving 20 remaining under my oversight.

Q. Well, now, how many cases do you think that a probation officer like yourself, devoting his whole time to this work, can handle at one time and do justice to the cases? A. Why, the smaller the number the more attention we can give the child.

Q. I understand that, but—— A. (Continuing) I would say that not more than 30 at one time.

Q. Not more than 30? A. No.

Q. Now, does that involve visits to the home? A. It does.

BY COMMISSIONER FRANCIS:

Q. You have had 1138 cases since July? A. Since the 1st of January, 1908.

Q. In one year? A. In one year.

Q. All on probation? A. Oh, no; 470 on probation in the year.

Q. Could you give—1138 is the entire arraignment of all children during the year? A. Yes. Table B shows the disposition of each for the month.

BY MR. MAYER:

Q. Of Exhibit 71? A. Those allowed to go on suspended sentence.

Q. How many cases do you think you could handle in a year, of course, how many altogether? A. Well, that is a hard question to answer; now, for this reason, I may have 20 boys on probation to me and they report regularly and obey all the rules of probation and at the expiration of three months they are discharged with improvement, and I may have 20 other boys whom I have got to follow up every week or every other day, and I will have them on probation with me for the entire year.

Q. Well, then, put it this way, how many for three months, which seems to be your average period? A. Not more than 30, I would say.

Q. Not more than 30 a month? A. Not more than 30 a month, 90 in three months.

Q. Now, as I understand it, you do all this investigating in addition to your probation work? A. Yes.

Q. When a child is placed on probation with the volunteer, what is the child required to do? A. We give that child a card containing the conditions of his probation. And he is instructed by Mr. Maloney or myself to go to—that (indicating) is the card the child is furnished when he is placed on probation.

MR. MAYER: I offer in evidence the card referred to, being Exhibit 72.

(Said card was marked Exhibit 72.)

BY MR. MAYER:

Q. Now, do you, in addition to giving the card, explain the contents of the card to the child? A. We do; tell them to read it and read it over with him, so that he will understand it, and tell him to go the next day to the address of the volunteer probation officer, which is on the card, and report to him and to take instructions from the volunteer as to what time he should report, and so forth.

Q. Now, who instructs the volunteers? A. The chief probation officer.

Q. Well, now, how much of a check do you have on the volunteers, I mean, may not some of the volunteers be perfectly well meaning people, but people with notions and ideas? A. They are, yes. The volunteer service is a very unsatisfactory service, a very unsatisfactory system.

Q. Not to unnecessarily use a word very well known to perhaps everyone, are some of them cranks, with particular notions? A. They are. If we find such cases, why the chief probation officer and Mr. Maloney, we sort of try and eliminate them; we don't give them any further cases. If they have notions about different things that boys ought to do and how many times they ought to go to church or this and that, why we try to refrain from giving them any further— any more boys.

Q. Well, now, do you think a system where you employ a great number of volunteers, who cannot possibly be under personal supervision, is a good system? A. The question again, please.

(Question read.)

A. I don't, no.

Q. And as the system is now practically operated, the persons who take these children on probation merely do it because they are interested in the work? A. Interested in the work.

Q. And want to help out? A. That's it.

Q. There is no obligation on them to attend to the work? A. No; no, sir, none at all.

Q. And I deem some of them do not? A. Some of them do not, they are very lax in the work.

Q. And you have no means of compelling them to do so? A. None at all. It is the best we can do under the conditions.

BY COMMISSIONER FRANCIS:

Q. Do they all try to do what you seek to perfect by the probation system? A. Yes, they do, to the best of their ability.

BY MR. MAYER:

Q. Well, it is the best you can do on account of the limited help, you mean? A. The limited help, yes.

Q. What is your salary, Mr. Pfeiffer? A. Twelve hundred a year.

Q. That is fixed by the Common Council? A. Yes, sir.

Q. Are you allowed any traveling expenses? A. We are not allowed a penny; not a penny has been appropriated for this work in the Juvenile Court.

Q. Yes? A. We are now compelled to pay our own car fares for investigating these cases. We have no money, have to pay—buy stationery, to buy stamps; the volunteers are compelled to pay their own postage and we have no money for filing cabinets, of which we are sadly in need, and if we were to have five hundred or a thousand dollars on which to perfect our system, it would greatly aid in improving the work.

Q. Well, you have reported in Exhibit 71 a certain number of cases successful? A. Yes. Of those on probation.

Q. I mean those. Now, from your personal contact are you convinced that the system is a desirable system for the working out of a permanent reform of the children? A. No, I believe that we ought to have paid probation officers.

Q. Devoting all their name to the work? A. Devoting all their time to probation work. I believe that we ought to have, in a city the size of Buffalo, at least eight probation officers.

Q. But you are convinced that probation is a most desirable arm of the court? A. I am.

Q. Yes, now do you—do you place these children in touch with the local religious authorities; for instance, a Catholic child, do you inform the priest in that neighborhood? Or a Protestant child? A. No, a Catholic child is placed on probation with a volunteer of his own faith and the Protestant child, and so forth, you know; a Jew child, Hebrew child, is placed in the oversight of the Hebrew probation officer, and, in fact, a State law compels us to place children in——

Q. That is, wherever practicable? A. Yes.

Q. Then you leave it to these officers to get in touch with the religious centers as they please? A. Yes, the volunteers are furnished with a church blank, you know, to keep track of the child's church attendance, and also furnished with blanks to make monthly reports, and so forth.

Q. And do you make monthly reports to the State Probation Commission? A. I do. I make a personal report and as chief probation officer. The report as chief probation officer, I believe this is the report for this month (indicating).

Q. Well, you have already read the substantial parts of that, have you not? A. Yes, I read my personal report. That is the report of the chief probation officer for the month ending January 31st, 1909.

Q. Oh, I see, this (indicating) is what you read before? A. It was my personal report.

Q. Was your individual report. Now the copy of report which you hand me is your report as chief probation officer? A. Yes, sir.

Q. Well, I will offer that as Exhibit 73. A. Well, Mr. Mayer, that is a part of my records of the court and we are compelled to keep a copy, a duplicate, you see, so three months from now I will use that in making out my report at that time.

Q. Instead of offering it as Exhibit 73, under the circumstances I can read the principal parts. To what month does this report refer? A. January.

Q. January, 1909? A. 1909.

Q. Well, the number on probation as of January 31st, 1909? A. Up to that time, yes.

Q. Well, that shows number carried over from preceding month, 116 boys and 8 girls; number placed under probation January, 1909, exclusive of those transferred from other probation officers, 64 boys and 5 girls, making a total of 180 boys and 13 girls; number passed from probationary oversight during January, 44 boys and 1 girl; number remaining under probation at close of January, 1909, 136 boys and 12 girls.

Classification of offenses.	Boys.	Girls.
Assault	1	0
Burglary or robbery	4	0
Larceny	40	3
Malicious mischief, breach of peace or disorderly conduct	8	0
Truancy, including prosecution under head of vagrancy	2	2
Violation of local ordinance, not included above	10	0

Well, I think you told us how many volunteers there were, didn't you? A. 60; yes.

Q. Do you know how the Judge selects these volunteer officers? A. Why, the chief probation officer goes to the various people who are interested in the work and talks with them and tries to interest them and asks them to volunteer, such as ministers and business men. Oftentimes they come in and volunteer.

BY COMMISSIONER WINTHROP:

Q. Let me ask: These volunteers, do they report to the Court in open court the result of their probationer's conduct or do they report to you? A. They report to me. They have a blank which is furnished by the chief probation officer, and they report the number of visits by officer at home, number of other visits by officer and where, has probationer reported as required and how often, has probationer obeyed all other conditions, does child take probation seriously and try to do right. Home record: Condition and influence of home, conduct of probationer as reported by family. School record: Attendance, conduct. Employment record; church record, and then there is a blank left on the side for remarks; and he files that.

Q. That is sent in by the volunteer probation officer? A. By the volunteer——

Q. Officer to you? A. Yes, sent to me.

Q. Well, do you speak to the volunteer probation officer yourself, or do you rely on those reports exclusively? A. We rely on the reports. If there are any remarks to make he puts them in the margin and I go and see him or call him up on the telephone.

Q. And then you just transmit that to the Judge? A. When the boy's term of probation has expired, yes; when the term has expired I notify the volunteer to the effect, I send him a postal card to this effect.

Q. The volunteer doesn't meet the Judge to discuss the case? A. No; on some cases, aggravated cases, the volunteer does meet the Judge, makes it a point to come into court and explain it.

Q. And do you see the volunteer during this probation period? A. At least a half dozen times; some cases I don't see the volunteer in six months, but the most of the volunteers I see a half dozen times during the course of three months; they come into court, every session of court we have a dozen or more of the volunteers attend. The truant officers, especially, they attend each session of the Juvenile Court and they act as volunteer probation officers.

Q. If the boy isn't doing right the volunteer reports to you? A. Yes.

Q. And you report it to the Court? A. I report it to the Court.

BY COMMISSIONER HAMILTON:

Q. Does this annual report which you have show how

many of the children placed on probation were so placed for the second time or the third time? A. No, it does not.

Q. Do your statistics show that, your records which you keep? A. Our records do, yes.

Q. You keep the record of each child separately, do you? A. Separately.

Q. Could you estimate how many children last year were placed on probation who had been placed on probation before? A. Why, without going over the records, approximately, I would say, that there were about 60 that had been placed on probation before.

Q. How many times is the greatest number of times that a child has been on probation, placed on probation, in your experience? A. Not more than three times and we only have—not more than a half dozen of those cases. In the Juvenile Court, previous to Judge Nash assuming office, the Judge was in the habit of allowing a boy to go at least nine or ten times on probation. But if we find a boy will not correct his habits and improve under probation, after he has been released a second time, why we believe that the proper place for him is in a corrective institution. But we are handicapped here in Buffalo in regard to the Protestant boy and the Hebrew boy, the incorrigible child and the truant. We have no place to which to send him. So far as the Catholic boys go, we have Father Baker's and can send them there. But take a Protestant boy between the age of 10 and 14 and he commits crimes, one right after the other, and the only thing we can do with him is to keep him on probation. We can't commit him any place. We can't send him to the Truant School; only holds 35. It ought to be enlaraged so that it would take care of 200 children, and we ought to have the power or have a bill passed so we could commit children to the Truant School for incorrigibility or larceny. Make it for the children, maintain such an institution, corrective institution.

BY MR. MAYER:

Q. Suppose that you simply could not take a Protestant or Jewish boy on probation and had to send him somewhere, where would he be sent? A. Well, we would have to make application to the George Junior Republic and ask them if they would kindly take this boy, that he is a bad boy and in need of a corrective institution.

Q. Does the George Junior Republic get any compensation for that? A. Two dollars and a half a month, I believe. I am not sure as to how much they get, but——

Q. So there is practically no reform school for such, for children of those two faiths? A. For a Protestant, no; we can send a boy from the ages of 12 to 18 to Rochester, providing he commits crime, but not an incorrigible child or truant. Up until——

Q. In your report, Exhibit 71, you do not set forth the religious faith of the children? A. No, we haven't decided to; I intend to ask Judge Nash as to the advisability of stating the faith, when he returns. Some of the chief probationary officers in other cities do it, but I don't know what his opinion is as to that.

Q. Might it not be very important as a basis of statistical information? A. I think it is important, but I want his opinion on it. Our figures would show that 80 per cent. of the children arraigned would be Catholic and we do not—I want his opinion as to whether we should put that in our report or not. You see the Polish people cause that figure to go so high. Most of the Polish people are Catholics and the majority of our cases are Polish cases; that is due to the railroad's temptation.

Q. Well, in order to ascertain how much necessity there may be for an institution for Protestant and Jewish children, if you had those statistics they might be of service to you? A. Yes, it would.

BY CHAIRMAN PAGE:

Q. Judge Nash is the Judge of this Police Court, is he, and also of the juvenile part? A. Yes, sir.

Q. Where is he now? A. Some place in the South. He is away on a vacation. I don't know.

Q. When did he leave? A. He left about two weeks ago, I believe.

Q. When will he be back? A. Expect him back Monday. I don't know, I just asked the clerk of the Police Court.

Q. When did it become known that this Commission would be here at this particular time? A. Not until about a week ago. Judge Nash spoke about the Commission coming here and——

Q. He was not here a week ago? A. No, he spoke about the Commission coming here some three or four weeks ago, possibly longer, five weeks ago. Had he any idea—I asked him at that time when he thought the Commission would be here and he told me he didn't know, but he said he thought they would be here about the latter part of February, and so I then went on to make up my figures to be ready for the Commission; and I believe that it was Judge Nash's opinion that the Commission would be here the latter part of February. I know that if he had thought for a moment that the Commission was to come here during his absence, he would have remained home, because he was very anxious to appear before the Commission.

CHAIRMAN PAGE: Well, he may still have an opportunity.

———

CLARK H. HAMMOND, called as a witness, having been first duly sworn, testified as follows:

BY MR. MAYER:

Q. You are one of the justices of the Municipal Court of the City of Buffalo? A. Yes.

Q. Now, generally stated, what is the jurisdiction of that court? A. I haven't one of our pamphlets with me.

Q. My question is, more generally stated, what is the jurisdiction of your court? A. Well, we have civil jurisdiction to a thousand dollars in certain specified cases. We have jurisdiction of ordinances, trials for violations of ordinances of the city.

Q. Are those actions for penalties? A. Those are actions for penalties, when tried against individuals if the penalty is not paid a body execution is issued and the person sent to the penitentiary. Then we have jurisdiction in summary proceedings, even if the amount involved is more than a thousand dollars, when it is here in the City of Buffalo. And that, briefly, is our jurisdiction. I can give it to you more in detail if you want it.

Q. Now, what kind of cases come to you from either the morning justices or the Police Court? A. Violations of the city ordinances, when they demand a trial in the Municipal Court.

BY COMMISSIONER HAMILTON:

Q. Well, the Morning Justice can also send them to you at his own option, irrespective of such demand, can he not? A. Yes; in other words, if the Judge didn't want to try it, it could be sent to the Municipal Court. That is right.

BY MR. MAYER:

Q. Now, how long have you been Judge of the Municipal Court? A. I am now serving my sixth year; I have been here five years.

Q. During that time, do you know how many such cases have come from these police courts? A. During the whole five years?

Q. Yes? A. I really couldn't tell you.

Q. Well, would your clerk know, do you think? A. Well, he has prepared a summary, at the request of Mr. Buck, simply for about one year.

Q. Well, that—— A. (Continuing) But five years, it would be a pretty hard matter to go back and get anywhere near an accurate report for that length of time, without a good deal of work and labor.

Q. Well, now, in 1908, how many of such cases were there? A. I don't know this personally except as the clerk tells me he has ascertained this from the record.

Q. Yes? A. (Continuing) That there were ordinance cases about 884.

Q. Well, do you know how many of those came from the morning courts and the Police Court? A. No, I couldn't tell you that. Our record wouldn't show; in other words, as I recall it, whether or not they were sent there or whether they were brought in in the first instance in our court.

Q. Have you given any thought to the question as to the advisability of consolidating the inferior courts of minor jurisdiction? A. Why, here in Buffalo, yes.

Q. I mean as to the City of Buffalo? A. Yes.

Q. Do you think it is a wise or unwise plan? A. Why, I found some thing that I thought should be remedied in the Municipal Court. I took the matter up with Assemblyman Weimert and we acted in conjunction with a committee appointed by the Bar Association and that matter was gone into at that time. I believe it was the general opinion of most of the members of that committee that it would be advisable to combine all of the courts of inferior jurisdiction. But that was not done at that time, for the reason that a delay was thought necessary in order to perfect any proper plan, and we needing some remedies there at once, this new Municipal Court Act, so called, was passed to simply fill in during the interim.

Q. Well, now, as a matter of principal, looking at the question from the standpoint of a system, do you think better results could be attained, assuming that you had a sufficient number of judges, if the civil and criminal jurisdiction were combined? A. Well, that would be simply my personal opinion; yes.

Q. As a judge, you sit entirely in civil cases, excepting—— A. No—except these ordinance cases.

Q. Except these ordinance cases? A. Penalties.

Q. In those cases isn't the action a jury action? A. That is covered by our Municipal Court Act, which provides that they may demand a jury trial; if they don't, it is waived and the court tries it.

Q. Now, then, is the result of that action a money judgment? A. In the ordinance violations?

Q. Yes? A. It is.

Q. And imprisonment follows only upon a return of the execution unsatisfied? A. Absolutely right.

Q. So that there is no system where a man who is found guilty is fined ten dollars or ten days, in these ordinance cases? A. Not ten dollars or ten days, but if he is found guilty a fine is imposed of ten dollars, and, that fine not being paid, a body execution issues and he is committed.

Q. He is taken then by the Sheriff? A. He is taken then by the Marshal of the Municipal Court to the penitentiary, turned over to the penitentiary and the penitentiary gives the Marshal a receipt for him.

Q. Now, if the defendant in such case doesn't pay, is there any execution virtually issued against his property? A. No.

Q. Well, then, if the jury finds against the defendant and he has not the money, then and there, or cannot satisfy the court that he can get it, then sentence of imprisonment is imposed? A. That is true, too; very often we have a man go out and telephone; he asks us to telephone. We grant him those permissions right along.

Q. I understand that. A. (Continuing), To get the money if he can, but if he says he can't get it, then the body execution is issued at once.

Q. I mean a long, formal execution against the property? A. No.

Q. And the return of that execution? A. No.

Q. So that it is, in substance, ten dollars or ten days? A. Well, it would amount to that.

Q. Yes, that is the alternative, then? A. Yes.

Q. How do these fines run, in amount? A. Well, they are all the way from one dollar, I believe, to one hundred, under the ordinances.

Q. Do you find these men demand jury trials, the defendants? A. Very infrequently. I don't recollect, in the five years I have been there, that there has been more than two or three jury trials demanded in ordinance cases.

Q. If there was a combination of civil and criminal jurisdiction, would there be a necessity, under present conditions, in your opinion, of more judges? A. There certainly would.

Q. I mean to cover—in order to take in the civil part only, without considering, for the moment, the criminal part? A. There would.

Q. Now, will you state, for the information of the Commission, then, on this subject, the number of actions started and other general statistics for the year 1908, in the Municipal Court? A. In 1908, there were 7,793 actions started in the Municipal Court; summary proceedings, 2,352; ordinances cases, 884, making a total of 11,029 actions started in the court during the year. Of those cases, 875 cases were tried by the judges.

BY COMMISSIONER WINTHROP:

Q. You don't mean the others are still pending? A. How's that?

Q. You don't mean the balance is still pending? A. I mean they are either still pending or have been disposed of by settlement, dismissal or otherwise, default judgment, any way you please.

BY MR. MAYER:

Q. Are you able to give us any approximation of the number of cases for violation of ordinances which have come to the Municipal Court from the morning justices or the Police Court—and the Police Court, I should say? A. Well, the Police Court doesn't——

Q. For one year, 1908? A. Well, that was the question I thought we were discussing. I couldn't recollect only three.

Q. We were discussing it informally? A. I can't recollect only three. The clerk says five or six. I am informed that by the clerk.

Q. Well, do you think, if the present system were continued, of separation between the criminal and Civil Courts, that that class of cases should be tried by the Police Court or the morning justices? A. There are some cases, violation of ordinances, like a case I just finished yesterday for a speed violation by a railroad crossing a crossing, that a man who is a lawyer certainly ought to preside at that trial. It took us a day and a half to try that case and there was able counsel on both sides.

Q. Well, that was a case of much importance? A. Yes.

Q. But how about minor violations. For instance—I don't know whether you have such here—but a merchant obstructing the thoroughfare with his goods or a hackman driving the wrong way, and things of that kind? A. Well, those violations, such as turning short corners and being on the wrong side of the street, vehicles obstructing the passage of a street car or remaining in the track, and things of that kind, I believe that those could be properly disposed of in the morning courts. I do. Because very often it gets to be simply a question of fact on those matters, the determining who is right in the matter.

Q. Now, is there anything that occurred to you that you could suggest to the Commission, in connection with the administration of these criminal courts? A. I have not given any time to that, except as I was interested in benefiting or making changes that I thought was advisable to make in the Municipal Court. But there is one thing I would like to say, and that is this: Suppose, under the violation of an ordinance as we have here in Buffalo, a boy is brought in the first instance for the violation of the ordinance in turning in a false alarm, to the Municipal Court. We find that it is pretty much of a farce, because that boy may be seven or eight years old. All that we can do is to try him, and if he is found guilty ask him to get his parents to send the money in, and if he can't get it, all we can do is to send him to the penitentiary, and they won't take him. Now that is the actual situation we are in here in Buffalo.

Q. Does that occur often? A. Well, that has occurred within the five years I have been there, at least half a dozen times, where we have found that we really haven't any power to do anything bcause you don't get any results.

Q. Then, in other words, you would suggest that all children under 16, charged with violation of ordinances, should be tried by the Police Judge? A. On small matters, yes; that is, where there isn't some great question involved or some large penalty; that is what I said. But you take, like these railroad cases——

Q. I am talking of children only? A. Yes.

Q. Why not have all children tried in the Juvenile Court? A. I think that would be a good idea.

Q. We are very glad you called our attention to the matter. I don't believe any of us knew about what you suggest? A. That is the actual situation faced, in actually working it out that thing has happened to me. You try this boy, find he has violated the ordinance and turned in a false alarm, and you can't do anything because the boy's parents won't send in the money and you can't commit him to the penitentiary. What are you going to do?

BY COMMISSIONER FRANCIS:

Q. Does it encourage false alarms? A. Does it encourage false alarms? Well, I can't say that, no; but yet this situation isn't known generally. If I hadn't been there the length of time I have, I probably wouldn't have had it brought to my attention. I don't know as Judge Hodgson, in the time he has been there, has had a case of that kind; nevertheless it is a fact and I have to say to the Corporation Counsel or his representative, "What can you do? All you can do is simply bring this boy in, give him a good lecture and let him go." That's all you can do.

BY COMMISSIONER WINTHROP:

Q. Do you have many children under ten years of age brought into your court for violation of a city ordinance? A. A good many; picking flowers in the park, playing ball in the streets, riding bicycles on the sidewalks—all those things.

Q. Into your court? A. Into our court, brought right there in the first instance, because these morning courts are not in session. They arrest them and knowing they are violating city ordinances they have a right to forthwith arrest them and bring them to the Municipal Court.

Q. How many such cases have you in a year; have you any idea? A. I couldn't tell you as to this last year, but I should say, as a general proposition, in the five years I have been there there have been **fifty or sixty of** those cases, where we simply couldn't do anything because they were children. Sometimes we get the parents to send up the money. Sometimes—I remember particularly one motherly woman coming up, finding her boy up there and giving him a very sound thrashing. But when you get the result otherwise, what do you get?

Q. But a person charged with violation of a city ordinance is arrested? A. Oh, yes.

Q. Arrested? A. Yes, given that authority right by the ordinances of the city, in the charter.

Q. He is arrested? A. Arrested.

Q. And if it occurs in the afternoon or evening, after your court has gone for the day, he would be taken to the station house? A. Taken to the station house and either locked up or bailed out; and I have lots of them come in there looking very badly in the morning and saying they couldn't get any bail and had been locked up all night; and many times I have said, "For this small violation you have been punished a great deal more than the violation," and let them go.

BY MR. MAYER:

Q. Well, of course, all of that ought to be out of your court, ought it not? A. Well, I—that is why I say I think these matters ought to be tried by the morning courts or by that branch. I don't think—with these ordinance cases, if I am trying a lawsuit involving a thousand dollars, with a jury of twelve men sitting there, and some little urchin is brought up, I have to stop the business of the court and hear that proceeding; keep the witnesses, the lawyers, the jury and every one waiting, until I dispose of that little boy's case.

CHAIRMAN PAGE: The Commission will stand in recess to 2:30 P. M.

———

AFTER RECESS.

2:30 P. M.

CLARK H. HAMMOND, recalled:

BY MR. MAYER:

Q. Before recess you were telling the Commission of some of the cases arising under violations of city ordinances which come before your court. During recess have you had an opportunity to make a summary of some of those cases? A. I have.

Q. Will you state them to the Commission? A. Do you want me to state them all?

Q. If you please? A. Not having legal scales for selling of coal and wood, etc., driving loaded wagons in parkways, using short unsealed weights and measures, failure to take out licenses for plumbers, bakers, auctioneers, pedlers, billiard and pool rooms, bill posters, hackmen, hucksters, running steam boilers without licensed engineers, failure to take out licenses for pawnbrokers, junk dealers, for selling of milk; then under the health provisions, sale of unwholesome bread, flour, meats, unsanitary condition of premises, such as cesspools on premises, unsanitary condition of meat markets, adulteration of milk, violation of quarantine when contagious disease is in a house, destroying placards put on a house by the Health Department indicating that a contagious disease is in the house, not reporting a contagious disease either by physicians or others, the conduct of funerals publicly when they should have been conducted privately because of a death by contagious disease, unmuzzled dogs, dogs not having tags, tenement houses not complying with orders of the Health Department as to their sanitary conditions and as to the certain number of windows in rooms, partitions, etc., resistance to the orders of the harbormaster; then under disorderly conduct, indecent exhibition of animals, begging in the streets, having bonfires in the public streets, drunkenness, houses of ill fame and assignation, playing ball in the streets, using profane and obscene language in public places, resisting an officer, immoral soliciting in the streets, displaying of obscene pictures, posters, postal cards, improper exposing of the person in public places and creating a noise or disturbance in the street. That briefly covers the ground that I went over during recess.

Q. So if a police officer were to arrest a woman for soliciting on the public streets for purposes of prostitution, he could bring her before your Court? A. Yes, and has done so lots of times.

Q. And then you must interrupt the work of the Court, whether it be a jury trial or not, if the case in which you are sitting has a jury, to hear such a case? A. That would be so, except that we have rules over there running with jury term, so it would not interrupt a jury trial, but it would probably without a jury.

Q. Then you have cases of disorderly conduct brought before your Court? A. Lots of times. I may add to those I have already stated the "contributing to a house of ill fame or assignation, to its support."

Q. Such cases have come before you? A. Often.

Q. And all these cases necessarily take up time and interrupt the business of the Court? A. They certainly do. Some of these trials that I recollect now have taken half a day to dispose of.

Q. Those of these ordinance cases? A. Yes, sir.

BY CHAIRMAN PAGE:

Q. I suppose that comes under subdivision 14? A. That is it exactly.

Q. The ordinance prescribes the penalty? A. Yes, sir. I want to correct my testimony of this morning. I said up to $100—I find it is up to $250.

BY MR. MAYER:

Q. What is your daily calendar now? A. Our daily calendar, consisting of cases on the day calendar with and without jury, is about 250 cases waiting for trial.

Q. And there are two judges to dispose of the calendar? A. Two judges to dispose of it and do all the *ex parte* work and try these ordinance cases.

Q. You have no doubt then that that class of cases, so long as there is a division between civil and criminal jurisdiction, should not be in your court? A. I am certainly of that opinion, very emphatically.

BY CHAIRMAN PAGE:

Q. What do you think of the regularity of the procedure, commencing a civil action for the recovery of a penalty by arresting the defendant and bringing him into court? A. That power is given us by the charter of the City of Buffalo, which is an act of the Legislature, and as I explained to one member of the Commission, there is a reason for it. Suppose you don't know where you can serve a summons on the man who has violated the ordinance, how are you going to get him into court? You know there is a violation there, but if you can't arrest him, you can't get him to court.

Q. I mean what do you think of commencing this action in the civil courts by summary arrest and arraigning the prisoner before the Court? A. I say that power is given us, as I understand it, in the Charter, and the reason is, as I stated, that if it were not so you would not be able to get these actions for penalties against these people in a great many cases, because you would not be able to find them.

GEORGE JUDGE, called as a witness and being duly sworn, testified as follows:

BY MR. MAYER:

Q. You are one of the morning justices, so called? A. Yes, sir.

Q. And how long have you been such? A. I have served during the year 1908.

Q. Prior to that, what had been your occupation? A. For fifteen years previous I was a desk sergeant of police.

Q. And you were elected and took office as a justice on January 1st, 1908? A. Yes, sir.

Q. Now, you have heard the testimony of your two associates before the Commission? A. Yes, sir.

Q. What suggestions, if any, have you in regard to improving the procedure of the court as now constituted? A. Why, I agree entirely with them, that the court should be held in a separate place aside from the police station, thereby removing it from police influence, and I believe that proper clerks should be afforded and better facilities.

Q. What is your view as to having a stenographer, so that the testimony can be preserved? A. I think we should have a stenographer, for the reason that in cases of appeals we have nothing except our recollection of the affair, and it becomes a question of veracity between the defendant and the Justice as to which is right.

Q. And sometimes those appeals are taken only after a considerable period has passed? A. Yes, I have had them right up to the limit, nearly 60 days.

Q. Sixty days is the limit within which an appeal may be taken? A. Yes, sir.

Q. Do you think that the morning justices should be empowered to take bail so as to give citizens an opportunity of having more officials before whom bail may be given? A. I cannot conceive any advantage in that for the reason that the police authorities, the police captain or police sergeant, is empowered to take bail in all cases of misdemeanor.

Q. How about felony cases—you think the jurisdiction should not be enlarged? A. I don't think so.

Q. What is the reason for that view? A. Why, I suppose one reason is that it is taking bail for a crime which we have no jurisdiction to try, and possibly another one, a personal reason, we would be bothered at all times by people looking for bail.

Q. Do you think that some method should be devised whereby a person over whom the Morning Justice has no jurisdiction, but who is arrested after the close of the Police Court on Saturday afternoon, should have an opportunity to be heard before Monday morning? A. Yes, sir.

Q. Do you regard it as a hardship that such a person has no opportunity now to be heard? A. I do, yes, sir.

Q. Do you think it is desirable that somebody in addition to the police justices and the justices of the Supreme Court should have authority to take bail in felony cases? A. I think it would be well. Of course, there are quite a number of Supreme Court judges, and one County judge, who are empowered to take bail in cases of that kind.

Q. As a matter of fact, do you know whether applications are often made to the Supreme Court judges in such a case?

A. I have no personal knowledge, but my impression is that there are not many.

Q. Would you leave the jurisdiction of the morning justices where it is now, or would you enlarge it? A. I think that it could be increased with propriety.

Q. In what cases? A. Petit larceny as a first offense, assault, and those cases enumerated under Section 56 of the Code of Criminal Procedure.

Q. Well, you mean by assault, assault in the third degree—simple assault, so called? A. Yes, sir. for the reason that many cases of disorderly conduct which are brought into the Morning Court are really cases of assault in the third degree, such as a person striking another, and so on.

Q. How are they treated now? Do the police make a complaint of disorderly conduct? A. When the offense is committed in the presence of the officer, an arrest is made and the defendant arraigned in the Morning Court on a charge of disorderly conduct, a violation of Section 5 of Chapter IX. of the Buffalo City Ordinances, which provide that no person shall create or assist in creating a noise or disturbance on the street, and so on.

Q. Do you think that the morning justices should have jurisdiction over the violation of ordinances relating to public breaches of the peace, like disorderly conduct and women soliciting and the like—exclusive jurisdiction? A. I don't know that I quite understand that—they have that jurisdiction now.

Q. Do you think that the opportunity of the defendant to go into the Municipal Court ought to be cut down? A. As far as I am concerned, I think that I am competent to try such cases.

Q. In your experience, have you had many cases where the defendant has demanded to be tried in the Municipal Court? A. To the best of my recollection, I have had four of those cases during 1908.

Q. Were there any special points about the cases? A. One of them, as I recall, was a disorderly case, which occurred on a street car, and the man asked that his case be transferred to the Municipal Court, and I granted it, and it was tried there; I think it was tried by a jury in the Municipal Court. Another case was of resisting an officer and the ground for that was that the attorney had not time to acquaint himself with the evidence, and the Municipal Court sitting, say at ten o'clock, it would give him more time to prepare his case, and it was taken to the Municipal Court. The other two cases were cases of houses of ill fame.

Q. Do you find that your experience as a police officer is serviceable to you in judging the cases that come before you—I mean as a matter of experience? A. I think so; yes, sir.

Q. You are not an attorney, I assume? A. No, sir.

Q. Do you place cases on probation? A. Yes, sir.

Q. What class of cases? A. I have placed some cases of intoxication, disorderly conduct, boys charged with street corner lounging; in fact, nearly all the cases over which I have jurisdiction.

Q. Have you had any opportunity to see how this system works? A. Yes, sir.

Q. What do you think of it? A. I am very favorably impressed with it.

Q. Do you place cases on probation where you have imposed a fine and you believe the man can pay the fine if given an opportunity? A. I have; yes, sir.

Q. How does that work out? A. The probation officer has collected considerable money.

Q. How do you find those cases working out where husbands are concerned, husbands and wives? A. Why, I think they work well. If you will allow it, I will detail a case I had the other morning of that character.

Q. Yes, go ahead? A. This man was charged with intoxication. He appeared to me like a bright, intelligent man, not an habitual drunkard, by any means, and I suspended sentence upon him, and the next morning he appeared again in court on a charge of intoxication. His wife appeared there in the role of a witness, and I went on with the examination, and the wife had to testify that the husband had slapped her, and she appeared to me to be rather vindictive in her attitude toward the defendant. I determined upon an investigation and postponed the case until the following morning, giving the facts in my possession to the probation officer, Mr. Kelly, who investigated and rendered a report on the following morning which went to justify me as to the opinion that I had formed as regards the woman, that she by her conduct had aggravated her husband so that he went out and possibly did take a few drinks more than was good for him, not because he was an habitual offender, but on account of the aggravation. I got both of them together and talked to them the best I could, and they both left the court united and apparently happy. Now, I have placed that man on probation for a period of six months.

Q. What did you require him to do? A. Required him to report to the probation officer, or the probation officer visit them at their home to see what their conduct has been.

Q. Have you any idea of how many cases come before these morning courts in the course of, for instance, the year 1908? A. I have a general idea from the statistics which have been furnished by the Police Department as to the total number of arrests in the city.

Q. What is your idea? A. I should say 25,000.

Q. Coming before you three men in these morning courts? A. Yes, sir.

Q. You stated in answer to one of my questions that you thought it desirable to have these courts away from the police stations in order to be away from the police influence. Just what did you mean by that? A. Well, in the first place, the Police Court is held in the back room of the police station——

Q. You mean the Morning Court? A. Yes, and there is a police atmosphere there. You enter the station and you go behind the police desk in the station house, and you are naturally brought in contact with police officers, and you are entirely surrounded by a police influence. In other words, we do not feel the idea of independence that we would feel if we had a place that we thought was our court room—we are there by sufferance of the police virtually.

Q. Well, the police officer not infrequently is desirous of getting a conviction—isn't that so? A. Yes, sir.

Q. And you mean, to some extent the atmosphere of conviction and keeping up police records—is that what you have in mind? A. Yes, somewhat.

Q. And you have no control over the courtroom, I assume, practically no control? A. We, I suppose, have the right to enforce order there, but we have no officers of our own with which to do it. The only help we have are policemen who are on reserve duty that day, and they assume charge of the court room.

Q. Do the police and the justices co-operate in regard to the daily administration of those courts? A. I have never had any trouble.

Q. Your idea is that the court room should be separated from the police station? A. Yes, sir.

Q. Was there anything else that you desired to say? A. You questioned Judge Taylor this morning on the number of appeals. I want to speak about that. The number of appeals that I have had during the past year has been eight, and four of those were from a conviction upon which sentence was suspended, three from a fine which had been imposed, and one from a penitentiary sentence which the County Judge affirmed, and the man served his term in the penitentiary. I have not had one man released from the penitentiary that was sentenced by me to the penitentiary.

Q. Nevertheless, do you not think it would be better if there was a record taken of the proceedings? A. Oh, yes, very much better.

BY COMMISSIONER WINTHROP:

Q. You have no female probation officer—you have one male probation officer only? A. Only a male.

Q. You have no female probation officer? A. No, sir.

Q. You put the female prisoners on probation with the male probation officer? A. I never have.

Q. Do you think that it is a good system? A. I do not.

Q. Does it often occur that there is a female prisoner that you would like to place on probation? A. Why, I have never discovered any. In the cases of young women under eighteen or nineteen years of age, it has always been my custom to send for their parents and have an understanding between the parents as to whether she is incorrigible or whether anything can be done for her.

BY CHAIRMAN PAGE:

Q. How about a young girl that has come in from the country and has no relatives or home in this city? A. I have never sent one of those to the penitentiary.

Q. But you never put any of them on probation? A. I have had one or two cases of that kind, and I turned them over to the police with instructions to notify their parents as to the facts of the case, and the parents have generally come to the city and taken them back to their respective homes.

BY MR. MAYER:

Q. Have you any other occupation, Judge, besides this work? A. Nothing regular; no, sir.

Q. So that you give all the time that is necessary to these duties. A. Yes, sir. I was going to suggest that there is too much work in this probation system for one man in these morning courts on account of the great number of cases, and I have favored the idea of having three probation officers, one for each of the courts, and that man would also act in the capacity of a clerk, so that we would have our own clerk, and then there could be an interchange of reports between those three men every month, and we would have a knowledge of what has been going on in the other courts by that interchange of reports.

BY CHAIRMAN PAGE:

Q. You sit in one particular court room all the time? A. No, we rotate—there are three districts and we change each month.

BY COMMISSIONER FRANCIS:

Q. Do you find it very wearing on you to try these criminal cases all the time? A. It has never bothered me so far.

BY MR. MAYER:

Q. Do you have a sufficient number of cases of women to require, in your opinion, a woman probation officer—when I say women I mean girls and women? A. Why, I hardly think there is any necessity for that at present.

Q. Are most of these cases women of the street? A. Most of them.

———

DEVOE P. HODSON, called as a witness and being duly sworn, testified as follows:

BY MR. MAYER:

Q. You are one of the two judges of the Municipal Court of the City of Buffalo? A. Yes, sir.

Q. How long have you been judge in that court? A. Three years in January.

Q. Do you think it desirable to have these violations of corporation ordinance cases tried by the Municipal Court or tried by either the Police Court or the Morning Justice's Court? A. Well, that is a great, big question. There are a great many of these cases that ought not to be brought to the Municipal Court, because that it a very busy civil court, trying a great many important civil matters, particularly now since the increased jurisdiction last year. I know of no reason why a great many of the ordinance violations should not go to the criminal courts.

Q. Take the violations such as Judge Hammond has referred to, of women charged with soliciting for the purposes of prostitution, and disorderly conduct cases, and the like? A. I have never had any of them.

Q. Have you had the cases of any children charged with violating some ordinance like picking flowers in the park, or anything of that sort? A. Yes, and sending in false alarms and the like.

Q. Do you think those cases ought to interrupt the business of the Municipal Court? A. I have never permitted those things to interrupt the trial of a case yet.

Q. Do you think it would be better to have those disposed of by these smaller minor courts? A. I think it would be preferable.

Q. Have you given any thought to the suggestion of a system of inferior courts having both civil and criminal parts, which is being agitated? A. I have given a good deal of thought to it.

Q. What is your view as to that question? A. That is also a great, big question. I was present at meeting of the Bar Association at which Judge Kenefick presented his views, which was about the time the Chicago Act went into effect, and his views, I think, were quite in accord with the Chicago Act. Although I don't look upon the trial of cases in a criminal court with any favor, I never did that kind of business and don't think I would like it, yet I am very quick to say that in a city like Buffalo the most natural solution of the whole trouble that can possibly be made —I don't see any better solution of the thing. I think Judge Kenefick's plan is to give the City Court civil and criminal jurisdiction, with enough judges so that they may rotate from one business to another, and from one court to another, holding regular terms of civil and criminal matters, very much as the Chicago plan is enforced now.

Q. Then, as I understand you, you think such system would be good for the City of Buffalo? A. I don't believe there could be anything better, and yet my personal predilections are against the proposition.

Q. What do you think, briefly stated, as you view it, are the advantages of such a system as applicable to this city? A. Well, I think, in the first place there is nothing that would do the administration of the criminal law so much good as to dignify it. I have not any patience with the cry which is very often made by some people that it is a degrading business—I think it is the duty of the court to elevate it and not to permit the business to degrade the court. A court properly constituted and conducted would elevate the business, purify the atmosphere, do the business properly, if it be that it is improperly done. I don't believe that that kind of business ought to drag any court down, so that my notion is that the consolidation of the two kinds of business, civil and criminal, would dignify the administration of the criminal law in the city, and not be harmful at all to the civil branch of the court.

Q. Do you think it would give a greater elasticity in the use and assignments of judges? A. Specifically, what do you mean?

Q. I have in mind that if you had a sufficient number of judges, you would always have available the Judge necessary to try—— A. Why, my notion in a city like this— this is a provincial city, it is not as big as New York or Chicago—my notion would be that with four or five judges, that you could assign Judge Smith for January criminal term, and Judge Williams for February criminal term, and so on, during the year, or, have one judge take the criminal term say, according to the number of judges, three or four times a year, and the other judges hold civil trial terms or civil special terms monthly. I think that is the natural, sensible and logical solution of the trouble in this city.

BY CHAIRMAN PAGE:

Q. Is there any further suggestion you would like to make? A. If it is not done, and I don't urge it, I simply express my opinion. If that is not done I believe that if the criminal courts were to remain as they are, that they should take from this civil court, which has got to be a court where the same cases are tried at the Circuit every day and take away from it these little matters—the pestering ordinance matters. That is the only suggestion I would make.

BY COMMISSIONER FRANCIS:

Q. Do you believe any more dignity could be employed under the present situation with the quarters now assigned to the judges in the morning courts? A. No; I think from what I have heard these gentlemen say that it is disgraceful—the manner in which the City of Buffalo requires the police justices to hold their courts, and something must be done. It is entirely out of the question to expect a court of justice to be maintained in a place surrounded by police influence, and police agitation—what the Chairman suggested, or the Attorney General, I believe—earnest for a conviction. Every police officer who has a case before the Judge there is anxious to make a record and get a conviction, and that feeling is present with the Judge constantly. I may say this to you in explanation of my personal opinion in regard to the trying of cases: I like to try a case where it depends upon precedent and judgment and not so much upon sentiment and sympathy, which necessarily moves a criminal court in very many cases. I am so full of it myself that I am afraid that I would be moved pretty often. I would not want to leave here any impression that I find the least fault with the present justices in the police courts. I think I may safely say, and it is the concensus of opinion in this place, that we never had better police justices, regular and morning, than we have to-day. I think the system is bad and should be corrected in very many respects.

MICHAEL J. REGAN, called as a witness and being duly sworn, testified as follows:

BY MR. MAYER:

Q. You are the Chief of Police of the City of Buffalo? A. Superintendent of Police—the same position, only a different name.

Q. You are the head of the administrative part of the Police Department—of the police end of the Police Department? A. Yes.

Q. Have you had prepared for us the data showing the number of prisoners taken before the justices in the morning courts from January 16th, 1908, to January 16th, 1909? A. Yes, sir; this is it.

Q. And the paper that I show you is the paper containing this data? A. Yes, sir.

Mr. MAYER: I will offer this in evidence.

(Paper marked in evidence Exhibit 73).

Q. Now from the standpoint of police administration do you think it desirable to have the morning courts? A. Yes, sir.

Q. Now, will you tell the Commission what your view is as to that? A. Well, I think the morning courts ought to convene earlier than they do.

Q. Well, what time do you think they ought to convene? A. I think about five o'clock in the morning.

Q. The purpose of that would be what? A. Well, the majority of the people that are brought before the Morning Court are poor people and have to work for a living, and by taking them before the Morning Justice at five o'clock in the morning they would have time to get to their day's work at seven o'clock in the morning. Now, they are not tried until eight o'clock and of course they lose their day.

Q. Are there large numbers of people arrested for drunkenness and disorderly conduct? A. Yes, sir.

Q. What do you think about these courts being held in police station? A. Well, I think it is all right.

Q. Don't you think they ought to be held away from police station? A. I don't see any reason why.

Q. What good reason is there why they should be held there? A. Well, in the first place a man is arrested and he is brought to the station house, and then he is paraded through the streets again to go to the court. It would save him a little by being tried in the station.

Q. Wouldn't it be better than if the courts were perhaps next to the station or there was a special room for the court where the judges could run their own court room —wouldn't that help? A. I guess they do that now.

Q. But they seem to think that they don't? A. Well, I think they do.

Q. What would you think about having no Morning Justice's Court and have more police courts? A. Well, I would not think of that at all—I think that would be bad.

Q. Why? A. Well, it takes up too much of the police time, and another thing you would have to have three or four police courts here to try them.

Q. In other words, if I understand you to dispose of the 26,782 cases in addition to what the Police Court has already

now, you would have to have three or four police courts?
A. I think so.

Q. And you think that is the most economical system
for the City of Buffalo? A. Well, I think the most economical way was the way we used to do it before this new system
was inaugurated. The municipal justices used to visit all
the stations, not hold court in any one regular station, but
in all the stations, and make a delivery of all the prisoners confined there. That I think was the better way.

Q. How many stations have you? A. Thirteen.

Q. How long would it take a man to get through on
that basis? A. Sometimes there are not any people arrested in the stations for the morning justices.

Q. With your three stations do you have to carry your
prisoners any great distance? A. Yes, sir.

Q. What are the numbers of these three stations where
they hold court? A. It was up to the time of the fire No. 1,
No. 3 and No. 8; now it is No. 2, No. 3 and No. 8.

Q. Station No. 2—do you have to carry your people far?
A. Yes, sir; we take all the people from all that district
here, one, seven, nine and two.

Q. Where is No. 2 situated? A. Seneca near Louisiana.

Q. And how about station No. 3—do you have to take
the people far? A. Yes, sir; we have to bring them from
thirteen—away down in the extreme northern end of the
city.

Q. How about station No. 8? A. At eight, we don't
have very far to take them. They have them from, I think,
4, 11 and 12. It is a smaller distance there—it is longer to
No. 3 than any other place.

Q. Do you keep any classified records of those 26,782 arrests? A. Oh, yes; it is in our book, but that isn't in shape yet. Here is our book for last year, our annual report.

Q. You mean as to the character of the offenses? A. Yes, sir.

Q. And is the book which you have handed me a copy of the annual report of the Board of Police for the City of Buffalo for the year ending December 31st, 1907. A. Yes, sir.

Q. Do you remember the total number of arrests last year? A. 27,000 some odd—I think you will find it there.

Q. The total arrests for 1907 were 27,125? A. That is every person arrested.

Q. So that this year of 1908, to get the correct total of all persons arrested you would add to the 26,782 brought before the morning justices, the additional persons brought before the Police Court? A. 35,525.

BY CHAIRMAN PAGE:

Q. Not 35,879 arraigned in the Police Court, but the total is 35,525? A. That is pretty close to it.

Q. That includes in addition to the morning courts and the police courts also cases of persons arrested on bench warrants, I suppose? A. Yes, sir; everybody arrested for the year.

BY MR. MAYER:

Q. From your point of view, then, the present system works all right, excepting that you think these courts ought to open, these morning courts, at 5 o'clock in the morning? A. I think it would be better.

Q. Are many cases brought into the Municipal Court? A. Well, a man can elect a morning justice, to be tried by a municipal judge, if you want to; they are mostly taken up in civil cases.

Q. Are there any cases the police bring in the Municipal Court? A. Yes.

Q. What are they? A. Well, peddling without a license, anything of that kind, violation of a corporation ordinance.

Q. Why are they brought there instead of the Morning Court? A. Well, sir, because the Morning Court isn't in session the time they are arrested and they are taken direct to that court.

Q. So, if I get it rightly if one of your police officers arrests a man for violation of an ordinance like peddling without a license, say at half-past ten in the morning, that man is taken to the Municipal Court? A. Yes.

Q. And if arrested at seven in the morning, would be taken to the Morning Justice? A. Yes, he can elect himselt the manner to be tried.

Q. I am talking about the police end? A. Yes, that's right.

Q. So where a man goes for a smaller violation depends on the time of day he gets arrested? A. Yes.

Q. And he has a different kind of judge, depending on the hour he violates the ordinance? A. He has a different judge, yes.

Q. Do you make many such arrests that go in before

the Municipal Court? A. Well, I couldn't just tell you that off hand, we did make quite a few.

Q. Do you keep a record of those? A. A complete record, see in that book you have in your hand.

Q. You refer now to report for 1907? A. Yes.

Q. When will your report for 1908 be ready? A. Well, it goes to the Common Council, according to our charter here, the first Monday in November. Then they will refer it to a committee and have it printed. I suppose it won't be done until about the first of April.

BY CHAIRMAN PAGE:

Q. It is in such shape, then, Chief, your clerk could give us any specific information we might want? A. Yes.

Q. Now? A. Yes; oh yes, it is all made up, except it is not in book form.

BY MR. MAYER:

Q. Let me ask you also, Chief, in this annual report that you make up, do you keep a classification of the different kind of things; that is, how many arrests for violation of corporation ordinances, how many for burglary, how many for larceny, and so on? A. No, there is a list at the back end there, all of the cases that go to the high court there.

Q. I see, this here? A. Yes.

Q. Yes, I understand that, but do you keep a record of the—— A. Of what court disposes of that?

Q. No; do you keep a record of the offenses? A. Oh, yes.

Q. The small—— A. (Continuing), That is there in that book.

Q. Yes, in your annual report? A. Yes.

Q. Are you familiar with the fact that in some of the European cities a person is not arrested for some of these minor offenses, but he is summoned, or told to go to a court in the morning; you have heard of that, haven't you? A. Heard of it.

Q. Well, now, suppose—get your mind off serious crimes like burglary and such matters? A. Yes.

Q. And think for a moment about violations of ordinances, such as a licensed peddler selling contrary to law? A. Yes.

Q. Or a hackman turning a short corner or an automobile driver exceeding the speed limit. Thinking of that class of cases, do you think you could work out a plan by which the large number of arrests for these minor offenses could be cut down? A. Well, now, my instructions to the men is this—it will come in the same line here—that if a man is slightly intoxicated and can find his way home, provided he is not near a dangerous locality, near a railroad, or water so he is apt to get drowned, let him go home, if you want to. Now those automobile drivers, why they are pretty cute fellows, you know. There are quite a few of those gentlemen that have wrong numbers on their machines. You take their number and notify them to come to court. You would be there and he wouldn't.

Q. Well, that is what we want to get at; we want to get at your practical experience as police chief? A. I tell you what I think. I think he ought to be arrested on sight for any violation and then taken to the station and if the offense doesn't amount to much, say violation of a corporation ordinance, by him putting his name down he should be let go and told to appear in court in the morning, if they haven't time to try him at that time. That I think would be a good way.

Q. Well, what classes of cases would you treat that way? A. Well, these violations of corporation ordinances; that is, some of them, not all. I think that a foul-mouthed man on the street using very bad language, I think that fellow ought to be kept there until somebody goes his bond, to make sure he will come around in the morning. I think a man that has got a family and is peddling for a living, I think it is all right to take his name down and tell him to be at whatever court you wish to try him at in the morning, the proper one, and have him go there.

Q. Well, now, in a city of this kind you could follow those men up pretty closely if they didn't turn up, couldn't you? A. A majority of them you could. Some, of course, you couldn't.

Q. Well, now, when I talk of violation of corporation ordinances I haven't in mind what you call disorder on the street or disorderly conduct? A. No.

Q. I mean different rules like traffic regulations—— A. Yes.

Q. (Continuing), Or merchants putting goods on the street or persons shaking a carpet in the street, something of that sort? A. There are very few of those arrests made you speak of, goods on the street.

Q. Then you have very few arrests? A. Of that class.

Q. Well, how much further would you go? You state you would extend that system, that you think it could be extended to cases of violation of corporation ordinances; what other classes of cases? A. Well, the automobile drivers; I think they could be the same class, but you would get fooled occasionally, because there are quite a few of them come through here that don't belong in the city.

Q. Yes, that is true, but suppose you had some State law which would require every automobile driver to carry a card of some kind? A. Well, that law is now he has got to have a tag on.

Q. No, but a card of his own? A. Well, the license, the chauffeur has got to have a tag.

Q. (Continuing), But on which the Judge would stamp a record of conviction, if he was convicted? A. Well, now, you would be surprised. We found some very well-to-do people here with wrong numbers on their machines in Buffalo.

Q. Accidentally or purposely? A. No, no; I don't know whether accidentally or not; I guess you better put it that way.

Q. But the wrong numbers were there. Well, I suppose Buffalo is so near the border that they can take a little advantage here, but, still, most of them would turn up, wouldn't they? A. Yes, but people that belong out of town they may not come around, they might get away.

Q. Well, don't you think it could be extended to cases of mere violations of the speed law as distinguished from a case where an automobile was being driven in such a reckless manner as to endanger life? A. Well, we keep those gentlemen in until somebody goes their bond; but there is very little of that done in Buffalo since Judge Nash has been elected. He puts $50 fines on all of them. It doesn't make any difference who the person is, $50, if you show he violated the ordinance. But he isn't very rabid about it; if a man goes ten or fifteen an hour he doesn't care, if the street is not in a congested state, something of that kind; but if a fellow gets wilful and careless and drives that way he soaks them.

Q. That is what I am getting at. Suppose what is merely violating a special ordinance as distinguished from driving his machine outside the rate and in a section of the city where he is liable to injure life, in the first instance do you think it would be wise to trust such a man to turn up the next day? A. Well, we do caution first those fellows first, before he is arrested he gets cautioned two or three times.

Q. I understand that, but looking at—— A. If he shows he belongs in town it is all right, yes.

Q. If he is a resident of the town? A. Yes.

Q. How many people, how many officers, have you in the Police Department here? A. We have 607 patrolmen.

Q. All told, officers and men? A. No, we have 13 captains, we have 39 sergeants, 39 desk sergeants, 3 inspectors and the superintendent and the clerk of the Board— that is all of the police force.

Q. The 607 then are patrolmen? A. Yes.

BY COMMISSIONER FRANCIS:

Q. Chief, it has been testified here persons have been de-

tained over the time necessary to produce them in court.
A. Yes, I have heard that myself; I would like to be in and
ask the Judge what person that was.

Q. You sanction nothing of the kind. A. No, sir; the
only man that is kept any length of time is—well, he is
kept with the sanction of his attorney, of the District Attorney, as a man that commits murder. Sometimes he is
left in the station two or three days, but that is understood
by everybody, by his counsel and the District Attorney
and all concerned.

BY MR. MAYER:

Q. Mr. Collins said that one case had been called to his
attention where a young man was detained 6 or 7 days and
the officer was asked whether that was so and he said
yes. Do you know anything about it? A. I have no recollection of that, anything about that. The doorman of the
Third Precinct, where headquarters are located, has each
man make out to him every morning, after the Morning
Court is over, the number of prisoners in the station house,
he has got that there. I have no recollection of anybody being held one day. Sometimes a man is held there from out
of town. For instance a man is wanted in Chicago and
he is brought there, and if the Chicago authorities say
they will be after them right away, why then we keep them
there, and if they must make out a requisition for them
we send them to jail and charge them with being fugitives
from justice.

Q. Were you Superintendent when Judge Murphy was Police Judge? A. Yes.

Q. Well, I understand he testified before us to the same effect. Do you remember any cases during his administration? A. Well, the police and the Judge didn't get along very well together.

Q. Well, do you remember any cases? A. No, sir.

Q. Then, as I understand, you would not permit any such detention? A. Why, no; there is a rule in our book here that says you must not allow any such thing.

Q. Well, there is a good deal of difference, sometimes, Chief, between a rule and living up to it? A. Well, that's so, only if they all lived up to the law they wouldn't need any policemen, either.

Q. The only question is whether there is any such practice as that sanctioned here? A. Well, sir; a man may be detained to-day, but I don't know about any further. Now, we have been up here under a Grand Jury investigation; here less than a year ago there was some man down here thought the police force was entirely rotten. The Grand Jury investigated the police force at that time and couldn't find anything. Here a short time ago there was the Bar Association, through a complaint made of a branch of what they called a sunshine society in Buffalo, that investigated the police force and what they called the third degree. Now the Bar Association here—I think there are some of you gentlemen in that association—they couldn't find anything wrong with us, the police force. So I think when we go through two ordeals of that kind we are pretty near it. Now there may be a few people detained there for the purpose of scaring them, by a man's father or parents or something of that kind, but there is nothing to all this business they are talking about, this third degree, and that.

BY COMMISSIONER MURPHY:

Q. You think it is a bad practice to get in the habit, to allow the police to start it, if it should be started? A. Oh, I don't think it is fair to the man. I think he ought to be taken to court and let the Court dispose of him.

BY MR. MAYER:

Q. Would kindly have your clerk send me for the year 1908 the classification of offenses as they appear on page 118 of your annual report of 1907? A. Yes.

Q. Together with the exact total of persons arrested during the year 1908 and their disposition? A. Yes.

———

GEORGE C. PRINCE, called as a witness, having been first duly sworn, testified as follows:

BY MR. MAYER:

Q. Mr. Prince, what is your present occupation? A. The record clerk of the Department of Superintendent of the Poor.

Q. Is that a county department? A. Yes.

Q. Superintendent of the Poor elected—— A. Of Erie County.

Q. (Continuing), In this county, is he? A. Yes.

Q. Now, in that capacity do you come into personal contact with the courts, here, the police courts? A. The Police Court.

Q. Yes? A. Very seldom with the morning courts.

Q. Do you take charge of the prosecution of bastardy cases? A. I do occasionally. That work is usually looked after by the County Attorney. I prepare the case and then give the facts to the County Attorney and he usually attends to the trial. But there are occasions when he is unable to attend and then I look after them; I prosecute them.

Q. You are not an attorney, are you? A. No, sir.

Q. How long have you been connected with the Superintendent of the Poor's office? A. Ten years last September.

Q. Well, now, there were some technical matters which I think you wanted to call to the attention of the Commission, and I shall be very glad if you will do so now. A. For twenty years or more it has been the custom of trying these bastardy cases before the Police Justice without an Associate Justice, as required by the Code of Criminal Procedure, Section 848. When Judge Nash became Judge, a year ago last September, he raised the point that they were not conducted in accordance with the requirements of the Code of Criminal Procedure. From that time on he has required to a greater or less extent the association with him of one of the morning justices. Not very long since the question was raised as to the jurisdiction of the Morning Justice in such a case as this. I then took it upon myself to look up this question and examine the Charter and found that in my opinion the morning justice jurisdiction extended only to cases who were found in the Police Court or in the police stations, been arrests without warrants. Do you want me to read that section?

Q. Is it a section of the Charter? A. Is a section of the Charter.

Q. You refer to Section 385? A. Section 385.

Q. Of the Charter? A. Of the Charter. Then at the same conference with the Judge in which this point was raised, he stated that it had always been a question in his mind, as well as in the mind of Judge Murphy, as to the jurisdiction of even the police justices in such cases, for the Charter as I recollect it gives the jurisdiction of the trial of these cases to the Police Court. The question arises, what is a bastardy case? Is it a criminal case or is it a civil action? It is a quasi-criminal action. Does a case of that character come within the jurisdiction of the Police Court under the present Charter?

Q. Well then, in a word, you think—yes, go on? A. In a word, to make it appear that the Police Court—or that there was no way of trying a bastardy case in Erie County or in the City of Buffalo, without having it started in either the County Court or Supreme Court if either of those courts have jurisdiction.

Q. Has this question ever been raised on appeal? A. It has not been raised on an appeal until a case that came up about three weeks ago. An appeal was taken on the ground that one of the judges had not—no that case was taken upon the ground that the—let's see, that case was partially tried before one justice, it being stipulated by the defendant's attorney that the case should be tried before one justice. Mr. Sullivan, the attorney, raised the question that that was not proper and later had part of the evidence that had been taken read before two justices, Judge Nash and I think Judge Judge were sitting.

Q. Judge Judge, the Morning Justice? A. Judge Judge, the Morning Justice, yes, and an order of affiliation was entered and an appeal taken from that upon the ground that the Judge—or that the trial was not proper, it was irregular. That case is to be argued next week in the County Court and Mr. Sullivan has asked the attorney for the defendant or the appellant to raise the issue as to the jurisdiction of the Morning Judge in this case. The question has never been adjudicated to my knowledge.

Q. Well then, you think that that whole question of jurisdiction should be made clear? A. It certainly should.

Q. Now, is that all you thought of in connection with that subject? A. That is all, yes.

Q. In the Police Court does the Judge place certain classes on probation with you? A. The Judge—yes, the Judge has placed quite a number of cases with me, in a manner, on probation, I believe their records show that he has placed six cases with me on probation. I have charge of the work of the Children's Court in the Department of the Superintendent of the Poor, and that necessitates my conducting or prosecuting the cases for non-support, a good many of those cases I ask the Judge to adjourn the case from time to time so as to keep the case open as it were and instead of actually disposing of it by placing the man, the person, on probation. That has been done to a considerable extent, and not only done with Judge Nash, but was done with Judge Murphy when he was still on the bench.

Q. Well, you then have the cases adjourned from time to time? A. Just simply to keep them open on the record.

Q. And have the husband keep on paying? A. And look after his family, and finally afterwards discharge him if he does well, takes care of his family as he should or his children, finally discharge him; if not, report to the Court what his conduct has been and have him placed under bonds, and that means commitment to the penitentiary unless he does provide bonds.

Q. Well, those are not, technically, cases of probation? A. They are not technically cases of probation, no, sir.

Q. But the whole system is— A. Amounts to that.

Q. Amounts to that? A. Yes.

Q. Do you know whether those would be returned in the records as cases of probation? A. No, sir, they would not be.

Q. What is the system here in Buffalo in the case of a woman who is not being supported by her husband? Does she first go to the Charities Department, or may she first go to the Court? A. She can go to the Court direct, as a usual—quite frequently, though, when an application is made to the Court, the Court refers it to either the Overseer of the Poor, the City Department or particular department.

Q. For investigation? A. For investigation.

Q. Do you have quite a record of families throughout the county? A. Yes, we keep a careful record of every case that we have anything to do with.

Q. So you are in a position to have a record of offenders? A. Yes.

Q. Is the number of cases of abandonment or non-support growing in the city? A. No, not in the city, I don't think, I think that that—the careful watch that we have had over those cases for some time, especially in the abandonment cases, had diminished. Those cases we have prosecuted thoroughly. Whenever a case of abandonment has come up we have obtained an indictment if that was necessary and prosecuted to the fullest extent we could, brought them from anywhere we could find them.

Q. How about cases of non-support? A. Non-support, I don't know whether there is a particular decrease or not, I think it runs along just about the same practically all the time.

Q. Well, you have not been attracted by any increase sufficient to make an impression on your mind? A. No.

Q. Now, do you think—you get sometimes into the Morning Court, as I understand? A. I think I have had one case in the Morning Court in four or five years. Those cases are—the non-support cases are not usually brought into those courts.

Q. When Judge Sweeney spoke about a plan this morning of feeding a defendant first and investigating him afterwards, did that refer to your department? A. No, sir.

Q. That is the overseer of the poorhouse? A. No, that

usually comes within the limits or the jurisdiction, or whatever you may call it, of the Lodging House.

Q. The Municipal Lodging House? A. The Municipal Lodging House, yes, sir.

Q. And under whose jurisdiction is that? A. That is Mr. Krug's.

Q. I know, but what is the department? A. Well, it is the County Department, the county office, but there is no particular department that has it in charge further than the Lodging House, so far as I understand.

Q. Now, from your observation in police court work, as I understand you have done it quite frequently, have you any suggestions to make to the Commission; we are talking now of systems and not of men? A. I think the probation system could be extended to good advantage.

Q. Well, thus far in the adult court there is practically no probation system, is there? A. That is the situation.

Q. And what classes of cases would you extend probation to? A. Non-support and those of intoxication where it seems as if there was a possibility of reforming them, unless they had gone to such an extent that you had got to incarcerate them in order to get them straightened up to do something with them. Vagrancy——

BY CHAIRMAN PAGE:

Q. Do you think there is an increasing amount of intoxication among women? A. Not with the cases that we have had, I don't think, not with those that come in my particular department, no, sir. They find an increasing number, it seems to me, of young girls who are going astray, that is girls—only last week or the week before there were seven, I think it was, pregnant girls came to our department for help and of that seven there were five girls under 18; one of them 15. But whether they were not—there were part of them that had become acquainted with the men who had ruined them in either—they had been enticed into saloons or found in dance halls; that is, they had been taken into saloons, they had gotten them to drink wine or something of that kind and then had ruined them afterward. But as to an increased amount of intoxication, I don't know as that—I don't see as there is any particular increase in it.

Q. Well, among married women? A. How many of those cases have we?

Q. No, I say among married women have you noticed any increase in intoxication? A. I don't know of any particular increase in that. I know that our records show that if drink could be eliminated from the cases of destitution we would be saved pretty nearly 75% of the pauper children that we have to take care of, that is the primary cause of their destitution. Fully 75%. I don't know that it is on the increase, but it has been that about ten years that I have been in that department, I noticed it ran just about 75%.

Q. Do you have much of a tenement house population here? A. There is considerable. But the tenement houses are in better shape now than they were a few years ago. There were, I think it was four years ago that—or five years ago, there was a movement started in the Charity Organization Society, clearing up the tenement houses or putting them in more habitable shape. Before that they were—there were women or families living eight or ten families living in quarters where there ought not to be more than three or four. And those things have been cleared up, which is the work of the Charity Organization Society and the Board of Health, working in conjunction with each other.

BY MR. MAYER:

Q. You think, as I gather it, that a very valuable work in probation can be done in the cases of men not supporting their wives? A. Yes; in fact I know it.

Q. And that under the proper control, proper system, they can be made to pay? A. Pay and support their families.

Q. And in many cases live with their families? A. I have one instance now in mind. It is a family for fully ten years that I have known—well, the case came up when I first went into the Department of the Superintendent of the Poor, and I don't know but they had known something of it before that. There was the mother, an old lady, who had—there were three and she, and she had two sons and one daughter. One of the sons had three children and the greater part of the time those children were living with this old woman in an old, dirty shack. He was a worthless— he was drunk repeatedly, drunk habitually, the father of these small children drank heavily and had been in the penitentiary repeatedly. Finally we removed them and they are now out at homes and are doing well. Later on this one son murdered the wife and he is now serving a life sentence I believe in Auburn State Prison. The other son left his wife. He had two children and went away with another woman. We had to care for those two children, for some considerable length of time, and then they grew to be old enough so they could get along at home, out of the orphan asylum. The daughter was a feeble-minded woman, while she was not feeble-minded to the extent that she could be committed to an institution for the feeble-minded, and she married and they had—they have five children. A year ago last fall that—I think it was, I had that man—the Society for the Prevention of Cruelty to Children went to the—this same old shack where the mother had lived and found this wife and small children in the most deplorable condition, and brought them to the Shelter and sent for me, and I went over there and sent the older children to the orphan asylum and the mother and the two young children to the Erie County Hospital, and got them cleaned up and had the man arrested. Had him on probation for some time, could do nothing with him and they had him rearrested and sent to the penitentiary. He was directed to furnish bonds and couldn't do it. He was there for a few weeks and then—until I could get him straightened up, get him over his drunk. And then I went to the County Court and asked them to release him as I had found a place for him to work. And the man had agreed to pay into the Department of the Superintendent of the Poor one-half of his wages and have it deducted from his pay by his employer, and upon that understanding the Court released him. That man—the order was granted

May 12th, last, and since then he has worked steadily. He was a scooper and Mr. Griffin, who is the Paymaster for the Lake Carriers Association, says there hasn't been a more steady man on the whole force of scoopers than that man has been. And one-half of the money has been deducted, under that court order, and turned over to the Charity Organization Association, and the family has been kept in good shape and doing well now and getting along nicely. It was the probation in the first place, but finally —the severe handling later on brought him to his senses; but he is doing well now.

Q. From your observations at the Police Court, have you any suggestions to make to the Commission, have any occurred to you beyond what you have already stated? A. Nothing more than simply the extension of that—of these things.

Q. Do you think there can be any effective probation with police officers from the Police Court, I mean police officers who are busy with other things, got other things to do? A. I think the probation officers who give their entire time to it, and a sufficient number of them, would be much more efficacious than police officers who have their other duties to perform.

———

GEORGE A. LEWIS, called as a witness, having been first duly sworn, testified as follows:

BY MR. MAYER:

Q. Judge Lewis, you were a judge of the Municipal

Court? A. I was one of the two judges who inaugurated that court in this city in 1880.

Q. How long did you serve? A. Two terms, twelve years.

Q. You are now a practicing lawyer? A. Yes.

Q. You are also, I think, a member of the State Board of Charity, is it? A. No, sir, I am vice-president of the New York State Training School for Girls at Hudson, 28 miles below Albany, and was one of the managers when that was still the Hudson House of Refuge. I am also a member of the State Prison Board of Paroles and Pardons and have been connected with some work in connection with the paroles and probation, somewhat, in this city. I have a general knowledge of a good many things connected with the subject matter of your investigation, but more particularly, perhaps, with the matter of the treatment of juvenile delinquents and truant and neglected females, juvenile females.

Q. Well, now, I am going to ask you to tell the Commission, in your own way, any suggestions that have occurred to you on the line of improving the administration of the inferior criminal courts? A. I consider that the work of probation, strictly speaking, in the juvenile courts, in regard to girls, is extremely limited in its proper application. The field of usefulness of probation as such for juvenile girls is—I mean to give them that course and compel them to report is very largely a farce and—my experience in that direction is derived from the fact that I have been in the position of legal adviser of the Good

Shepherd and Magdalene Institutions in this city. They formerly received a good many commitments of girls under 16 years of age, and I attended the morning courts here for the purpose of observation and study, eight o'clock courts, for a very long time, eight or nine months, with Sundays included. And I have been familiar with the work of very experienced and competent officers; Volunteer Officer Miss Rose Smith, who I would couple with Miss Miner of the night courts in New York, as one of the two or three leading experts I have ever known or heard of in handling the cases of young girls and young women. And I have often discussed this matter with such experts as Dr. Hortense Bruce, Superintendent of the Training School at Hudson, a woman whose position took in jurisdiction over women and medical education, and also the head of the House of Refuge, and I find those people who know most about it say that when a girl of tender age has gotten far enough away from her mother to be arrested and brought into a court, that it is time to segregate her from the occasions, approximate occasions, of her difficulties, and that you cannot profitably parole her, because she escapes from you in so many ways, and her loss is irretrievable. When she falls she falls far and hard. You never hear anybody talking about a fallen boy of 14 or 15 years of age, but they do speak of fallen girls of that age, and when a girl is once before the Court, the notoriety of the very fact in her neighborhood makes her a mark for the pursuit of all the industrious boys in the neighborhood who are looking for trouble with girls. I have seen some monstrous evils in a very limited way in my own experience from the effort to parole, place on probation, girls of that tender age who are threatened with becoming prostitutes. They usually do, when they are paroled, in my judgment. However in the latter class of women, the interference of the woman probation officer is very vital in very many ways, because there is such a frightful thing may happen from a mistake if the Judge mistakes; if there happens to be a woman come along and get arrested and she really is a virtuous woman, and is treated like a prostitute, it is a frightful calamity to her, much more than if a respectable man had spent the night in the station house unjustly or received some petty punishment unjustly. And the work of the woman probation officer in the Police Court in the Juvenile Court, as far as the investigation of cases is concerned and conditions concerning the children, the females, that are brought before the Court, I regard as most forceful, highly effective and desirable in all ways. In all ways women can find out things men can never find out, about girls and young women. They will do very well with the women, when they cannot talk with a man. And if anybody has ever observed Miss Miner's operations—I have sat in the Night Court in New York and seen her do her work and I have been told, too, by the judges there; you probably have heard them tell of the character of the services of Miss Miner and her like.

Q. On that point, then, as I understand, you would recommend steady employment of the female probation officer? A. Wherever possible.

Q. Both in the Police Court and in the morning courts and in the Juvenile Court? A. Wherever possible. Oh, the Morning Court, yes, that is a question, it is a question whether you may get too much of a good thing. The work men do I think in one court as another. I have been in our morning courts morning after morning when there was no occasion for the services of a woman, six or eight or ten days running. Then the next morning she would be badly needed. I feel—I heard the testimony this morning, the remarks of one—on the part of a gentleman who is probation officer in the Police Court, touching the expenses. He receives a salary and I know perfectly well that a probation officer, man or woman, who has got 20 or 30 cases to look after, that are now—that are already on probation, without regard to the investigation of other subject matters which are before the Judge, must expend fifty cents a day for street car fares alone. Well, that means a very large hole in even a $1,200 a year salary, that is 25% of the salary gone for official expense, not private expense in any way. I feel that the city should cover all those things and pay a living wage beside.

Q. Well, of course, what the wages or salaries shall be must necessarily be a matter of local administration? A. Local control, but it is——

Q. And the question would be to impress the local authorities with that, with the importance of the work, I assume? A. I only mention it because I heard some testimony on the subject here. I understood the Judge from Chicago remarked yesterday he didn't believe in the em-

ployment of spinsters as women probation officers. Well,
I don't know what he would define by a spinster for his
purposes; strictly an unmarried female, but perhaps he
refers to women of uncertain age and narrow minds and
bellicose dispositions. But both of these rather eminent
women in their work are unmarried women, Miss Smith and
Miss Miner, and they are among the most remarkable
women I have ever seen engaged in the work.

Q. In regard to these cases of violation of ordinances
triable in the municipal courts, do you think that the most
of these minor violations should be tried in the municipal
courts? A. They are, I believe.

Q. I mean do you think they should be? A. Oh, certainly.

Q. Well, do you think they could be disposed of in the
Police Court? A. Well, I was thinking in my mind, the
Municipal Court, as compared with the Morning Court, the
early Morning Court, the Police Court has no jurisdiction
of it at present.

Q. No, I am talking of the Municipal Court? A. They
should be disposed of in a day court, not an early morning
court, and I don't know why they should not come into
the Police Court.

Q. I mean don't you think they should be disposed of in
some place other than the municipal courts, where the Municipal Court is busy with the trial of causes? A. That
is merely a matter of convenience.

Q. Well, isn't it a matter of— A. Waste of time?

Q. (Continuing.) The proper disposition and the char-

acter of your business? A. Well, I don't see why. I think
the Police Judge is as competent as the Municipal Judge,
or vice versa, to dispose of ordinance cases. These cases
are usually begun by summons from the Corporation Counsel's office and issued in the regular way. The arrests are
relatively infrequent, for violations of ordinances, and they
usually occur in the daytime and are brought into court
and the Corporation Counsel notified.

Q. Have you given any thought to the suggestion that
there be one court of inferior criminal and civil jurisdiction? A. I have heard the subject discussed at the Bar
Association meetings, and while I would not undertake to
deny anything that an advocate of those measures might
propose, I think it is rather a revolutionary proposition
and it is very chimerical in its present shape, as there is
nothing to compare it with, I know of, around this part of
the world. Why the scheme, as I understood it, included
the transference of the Judge from time to time from the
Police Court into the Municipal Court and back again. I
should see no reason why such a scheme should not work
and be excellent, in the long run, in the administration of
justice. It would involve several radical changes of the
present laws, of course.

Q. Oh, yes. Is there any other suggestion you thought
of in regard to the morning courts or the Police Court?
A. No, I—excepting in regard to the question of hour of
holding court. Some people think that the court should
be held at 5 in the morning. Now I don't think that is
particularly convenient for anybody excepting the patrolmen who make the arrest. Out of all the people that you

will find in the morning courts there are mighty few of them who have got a 7 o'clock job yawning for them. Very few people, or a very small percentage of the people arraigned in the morning courts would be the least inconvenienced by being held until 8 or 9 in the morning, rather than being released before 7. The women don't work at 7 A. M. They work after 7 P. M., that come into the morning courts, usually.

————

JOHN P. MALONEY, called as a witness, being first duly sworn, testified. as follows:

BY MR. MAYER:

Q. Mr. Maloney, you are a police sergeant? A. Yes, desk sergeant.

Q. Desk sergeant; what is the salary of the desk sergeant? A. Ten hundred and twenty a year.

Q. And does he get more, dependent on the length of service, or is that a fixed salary? A. Fixed salary.

Q. Now, you are assigned to the Juvenile Court? A. Yes.

Q. And you do probation work entirely? A. Yes.

Q. No other work? A. No.

Q. And who assigns you to that work? A. The Superintendent of Police.

Q. Before you began this, had you any experience in probation work? A. No, sir.

Q. Well, were you interested in it or how did you come to be assigned? A. Why, the Judge requested my assignment to the court.

Q. I see. Do you act under the orders of Mr. Pfeiffer?
A. And the Judge; yes.

Q. And the Judge. Now, what do you do? A. Why,
Mr. Pfeiffer and I do practically the same work. All the cases
of children arrested are reported to No. 8 Police Station.
I go there every morning at 8 o'clock and get all the cases,
and we divide them up, he takes half and I take half, and
then go out and make an investigation into the home conditions and character and environment of the children and
learn all we can about the child and its home conditions.

Q. Well, do you make inquiries as to the crime, as to
the facts surrounding the commission of the act?
A. No, sir.

Q. Then, are your inquiries confined to ascertaining the
child's home conditions? A. And the character of the child
and its habits and all that sort of thing.

Q. About his record in school, and with his employer?
A. Yes.

Q. Now, there seems to be some little confusion perhaps
on this question, which you may be able to answer. Prior
to the time that the Judge, after the hearing or trial of
the child, makes up his mind as to whether the child is
innocent or guilty of the offense charged, does the probation officer testify before the Judge? A. No, sir.

Q. Well then, Mr. Pfeiffer, if he gave the Commission that
impression, was mistaken, is that it? A. Yes.

Q. When is it that the probation officer informs the Judge
as to the surroundings and other results of investigation?
A. After the Judge has determined as to the guilt or in-

nocence of the child, if he considers the child innocent and it is discharged, we make no report at all, but if he finds the child guilty, why then he calls upon us to give all the information possible in regard to the child, its habits, home conditions, and everything, in order that he may determine what is the proper disposition to make of the child after its conviction.

Q. Well, you are quite sure about that? A. Yes.

Q. So that, if,—using the same illustration I did with Mr. Pfeiffer, you were to see a child before its trial and the child were to confess to you or state to you that it did the act charged, you would tell the Judge about that? A. No, sir.

Q. You are quite sure about that? A. No, sir.

Q. I say you are sure of that? A. I am sure of it, yes.

Q. You would not say anything about it? A. No, I never considered it was in my province to work up a case against a child or secure the evidence. I take it that is the duty of the officer making the arrest; that my duty is to learn all about the child from the first in order to enable the Judge to determine what to do with it after conviction.

Q. Whether to suspend sentence or— A. Probation or commitment.

Q. Put on probation or to commit? A. Yes.

Q. Is that right? A. Yes, the Judge is advised of children who have been led to the commitment of the offense on account of wretched home conditions.

Q. Yes, exactly, and then all of this inquiry is solely for the purpose of advising the Judge when he is to make

final disposition of the child in the event of conviction?
A. Yes.

Q. Now, how many cases can you handle a month, to do them justice? A. Well, with all the investigating?

Q. Yes? A. Investigating we have to do—oh, I have sixteen on hand and that is plenty to do justice.

Q. Sixteen on probation? A. Under my personal supervision.

Q. And that doesn't count the cases you have investigated? A. No, we are constantly investigating cases every day.

Q. And does this take up all your time? A. All of my time, yes, sir.

Q. And who assigned you to Judge Nash, the Police Superintendent, the Police Commissioners? A. Well, application was made to the Police Commissioners and they gave their consent and then the Superintendent assigned me.

Q. How long have you been at this work? A. Seventeen years as desk sergeant of police.

Q. I mean as probation officer? A. Oh, a year, a little over a year, a year the ninth of last January.

Q. Well, seventeen years might sound old on the record, so I am going to ask you to give your age? A. 39.

Q. Do you like the work? A. Very well, yes.

Q. Do you think you are getting results with the children? A. Yes, we would get of course much better results if we had better facilities to work with. We are working under such miserable conditions that it is pretty difficult to get the results that we would like to get.

Q. Well, what do you mean by that? A. Well, we have no office and no appropriation for expenses, no detention home and not a sufficient force to properly do the work.

Q. You are not enthusiastic about volunteer officers, I assume? A. It would be better if it were possible to have a sufficient corps of trained paid officers. We have a great many very good volunteers who are doing good work, but if it were possible to have enough trained officers, paid men, under the direction of one man and compelled to do as he directed, it would be better I think.

Q. How many children are on probation now, do you know? A. I think it is 460. That table shows (indicating).

Q. I see, and they are distributed between Mr. Pfeiffer, yourself and these volunteers? A. Oh, I am in error there, Mr. Mayer, the number of children on probation at the present time is about 140.

Q. Oh? A. That was the total number put on probation last year, that I just gave you.

Q. But these 140 children are distributed as I say among— A. Among the volunteers and Mr. Pfeiffer and myself.

Q. Now, do you have any control over the volunteers or is that Mr. Pfeiffer's duty? A. Mr. Pfeiffer's.

Q. Then your work is investigation and taking care of the children placed with you individually on probation? A. Yes.

Q. Do you regard the present quarters as a proper place to try children? A. No, sir.

Q. Do you regard it as desirable or necessary that a detention place for children should be had in the City of Buffalo? A. Yes.

Q. As a police officer, do you know whether or not children have been detained in police stations? A. They have.

Q. And are they being detained right along where there is no parent to take the child? A. Yes.

Q. And are they locked up in cells? A. Sometimes.

Q. And that is a matter that is going on now, I assume? A. Yes.

Q. And that is because the police have no other place to put them? A. Yes.

Q. Do you regard that as proper for present civilization? A. I do not.

Q. Is there any suggestion that you would like to make to the Commission from your personal observation, in addition to having a proper detention home, and a proper place to hold the Juvenile Court? A. No, sir. I have heard nearly all the testimony that has been brought out in this matter and I think it has been covered very thoroughly. I don't know of anything more I could suggest.

Q. I want to ask you a question, do you find your work with the children is getting results? A. Why, we are getting results, doing good. We would do much better if we had better facilities to work.

Q. You visit the children's homes? A. Yes.

Q. Keep track of the school records? A. They bring a report from their teacher each week and then at the end of each month they bring their monthly report showing their standing in each subject.

Q. Do you get any neighborhood record at all, is that feasible here? A. Only in the first investigation, we go around among the neighbors and inquire.

Q. Well, I mean suppose a boy is placed on probation, is it feasible to hear what his neighbors say about him, whether he is getting along all right, whether he is a pretty good boy in the neighborhood? A. Why, I don't think so. Some people might be prejudiced and others friendly to him would tell you he was good.

Q. Well your police officers change posts from time to time—what is your system here, does a police officer keep on one post a long while? A. No, change weekly.

Q. Different posts? A. Different posts, in some of the precincts, I believe in the 10th and 5th, I don't know whether that is still in force or not, they did try that, of keeping a man on the same post all the time, but I don't know whether they are doing that now or not; but generally they change every week, a different post each week.

Q. There is a sufficient amount of change so that a police officer would not be in a given neighborhood long enough to know what a child's reputation was? A. No, sir.

Q. So you depend upon his conduct and reputation at school or at his employer's as the case may be? A. And at home.

Q. And at home, and upon his obeying the orders of the Court and the probation officer? A. Yes.

Q. And I suppose upon his general appearance, the way the child acts? A. Yes.

BY COMMISSIONER FRANCIS:

Q. Do you ask the same character of questions as to guilt or innocence as testified to by Mr. Pfeiffer, of juvenile persons, after the Judge has sent you out on an investigation? A. I don't make any investigation as to the guilt or innocence. I don't go into that part of it at all. There is one exception to that. I found, after I had been at the probation work for a little time, that some officers seemed to be trying to take advantage of the fact a child was on probation to arrest it on the slightest provocation. That was principally railroad subs. The railroads have a big force of men here and some of them are a pretty unscrupulous lot of fellows and they would arrest a child on the slightest——

BY M. MAYER:

Q. Special officers? A. Special officers. On the slightest provocation, sometimes without any provocation at all, and I have—in investigating cases children told me they had been arrested wrongfully and in those cases I did go into the matter of their guilt or innocence very carefully, and where I found they had been wronged I acted as the child's attorney in case of proof of its innocence.

Q. Quite right? A. In any case where I thought a child treated wrongfully I have always gone into the merits of the charge very carefully and reported it to the Judge, and the Judge has gone so far in two or three of such cases as to threaten commitment to the workhouse to the officer making the illegal arrest.

Q. Have you many special officers in the city? A. Oh,

the railroads must have 30 or 40 of those men. I don't remember such a case among our regular officers in the Police Department.

Q. These special officers are paid by the railroads? A. Yes, they are just sworn in as officers, they are in the employ of the railroads.

Q. I see, so that in fact the purposes of your investigation have been to see whether the child has been wrongfully accused? A. Yes.

Q. And if you think it has you feel it your duty to practically represent the child before the Judge? A. Yes.

Q. And let the Judge have the benefit of that information? A. Yes.

Q. But, as I understand you, you never appear either as a prosecutor against the child or as a witness against him in the trial of an action? A. No, only in cases where I have to bring a child in for violation of his probation.

Q. Yes, of course that is an entirely different matter? A. Yes.

Q. But in the original matter? A. Oh, no, in the original offense, where an officer makes an arrest we put it up to him to prove his case.

Q. Do you make reports to Mr. Pfeiffer or to the State Probation Commission? A. There is a monthly report which I make to the State Probation Commission, and as I said before, Mr. Pfeiffer and I divide up the office work.

FREDERICK W. PFEIFFER, recalled, testified as follows:

BY MR. MAYER:

Q. First, as to records, do you employ the system of records which is prescribed by the State Probation Commission? A. Yes.

Q. That is a system of colored cards and so on? A. Well, the little colored tabs, a system of mine, just—aside from that the system is recommended by the State Probation Commission.

Q. Do you know Mr. Graveur of New York? A. I don't, no.

Q. Well, your colored tabs are for purposes of indexing, are they not? A. Yes, I will explain it to you briefly. Each color is a different month.

Q. Suppose you get it right up here (indicating Chairman's desk)? A. Each color is a different month and as you see they are abbreviated, October, April, January, February and so on, for the entire year, and July and so on. Now the different positions on the card denotes the week. Divide the card into four sections, that would mean the first week of May, 1909, that his probation will expire, and the center of the card would be the second week and the third division the third week and the last division the fourth week. That aids me in keeping track of the live cases. I just run over the cases, if I see—now here, when I come by the second week in April I will see I have got a number that will expire the second week. I send the volunteer a notice, postal card, that the probation term is expiring and if the probationer has lived up to the rules of probation and if in his opinion he is ready to be discharged kindly have him ready at the next session of the Juvenile Court. Then when he reports I take out the card and it is marked "Discharged with improvement" or "Discharged without improvement," or whatever the results might be. I take the little tab off and put the little tab back in again and replace in the box. The tabs are my own

BY CHAIRMAN PAGE:

Q. Did you devise that system? A. I did, mine.

Q. In that way you can readily keep track of each case? A. Of each case of the live cases. Those cards without tabs are cases that have either been committed or pass out.

BY MR. MAYER:

Q. Cases that have been disposed of? A. Cases disposed of, yes.

Q. I understand that you desire to make yourself clear on the point as to the production of testimony by you before the Judge prior to conviction? A. I do; yes.

Q. Now, you may make such statement as you think proper? A. I desire to make myself clear, that the information gathered about the juvenile offender is given to the Police Justice after he has decided whether the child is guilty or innocent, and that only for the purpose of enabling the Justice to determine whether or not he will release the child on suspended sentence or place him on probation or commit him.

Q. Well, now, in the outline of the work that you gave this morning, in which you read from the proposed report do you recollect that you said to the contrary? A. You asked me whether before he made the final disposition.

Q. When you said that he, meaning the Judge, "Always refers to the finding of the investigation made by the probation officer before deciding the case," what did you mean? A. That must be corrected.

Q. You really meant to decide what he would do with the boy after the boy's conviction? A. Yes, sir.

Q. So that the use of the words "Decide the case," is inapt? A. Yes.

Q. And you desire to make it clear that what you mean is that all the information which has come to you or which is gathered is laid before the Judge after the case has been tried? A. Yes, sir.

Q. After the Judge has decided that the child is guilty? A. And never before.

Q. And after the Judge decides that the child is not guilty—if the Judge decides that the child is not guilty, what do you do? A. We never testify, he never calls upon us.

Q. So that you are quite clear about that now? A. I am.

Q. And your confusion arose as you stated? A. Between the words "Final disposition" and "Final decision." That is where I became confused.

BY COMMISSIONER FRANCIS:

Q. Is the Judge's declaration of guilt or innocence publicly recorded, verbally or otherwise, before he hands this to you? A. We stand at his shoulder, and he has a docket which I will show you. He has the book laid out in this manner (illustrating). We stand right at his shoulder, we are standing right here, we notice that he records, "Plea guilty," and then he announces that he intends to place the boy in an institution or on probation, or something to that effect upon our recommendation. That is where I became confused this morning.

Q. Before he makes any other record then he places the boy on probation to you? A. Yes, if he places the boy on probation.

Q. What record is there that would show that he has found the boy guilty? A. Just the plea there.

MR. MAYER: I beg to inform the Commission that I have received from Doctor Carpenter, Municipal Civil Service Commissioner, the memoranda showing the value given to each question in the competitive Civil Service examination for probation officer. I may say, to summarize, that fifty per cent. is given to the technical examination, twenty-five per cent. to the examination for experience, and twenty-five per cent. for what is calld the oral examination, or the impressions of the Examiner as derived from the appearance of the applicant and the various questions which they asked orally. The percentage given to each question will appear on this exhibit opposite the question.

(Paper marked in evidence as Exhibit No. 74.)

————

EDWARD F. KELLY, called as a witness and being duly sworn, testified as follows:

BY MR. MAYER:

Q. Mr. Kelly, are you a paid probation officer in the morning courts? A. Yes, sir.

Q. How old are you? A. Twenty-five years of age.

Q. What was your occupation before? A. I was doing

newspaper work, and investigating work for the Lacka-
wanna Steel Company.

Q. What is the salary that you now receive? A. $1200.

Q. Did you take a competitive Civil Service examination?
A. Yes, sir.

Q. The same one as Mr. Pfeiffer? A. Yes, sir.

Q. Where did you stand on the list? A. Second.

Q. When did you enter on your duties? A. July 18, 1908.

Q. At what morning court are you situated? A. At No.
3 Court. Third District Court.

Q. How do you get cases from the other two courts? A.
The judges presiding at the other two courts send me reports of cases that have been placed on probation that
morning. I receive them within half an hour.

Q. Do you keep a record of the probation cases? A. Yes,
sir.

Q. How many cases have you had since July 18th when
you entered on your work down to say, January 1st? A.
About 300.

Q. Have you an exact record? A. I would say 300 up
to January first.

Q. Have you an exact record? A. Yes.

Q. Have you made any classification of the cases? A. By
classification, what do you mean?

Q. Kind of offenses? A. I keep a record of the offense
that each one is charged with.

Q. Have you any of your books with you? A. Yes, sir
(witness produces books). That is a card record of the
active cases.

Q. You keep a card record of the active cases? A. Yes,
sir; of all cases.

Q. And that shows what? A. Number, docket number, name, alias, address, age, creed, offense, date of arrest, complaining officer, number of children in family and condition, employment and character of vocation, financial condition of family, address, precinct, number and disposition.

Q. On the obverse side of these cards what record do you keep? A. Number of previous arrests, church environment, previous probation record and a blank for remarks.

Q. What other record do you keep? A. Report card showing dates on which the probationers have reported, and visits made by me to the homes of the probationers.

Q. And this report card is made out in accordance with what form? A. The form prescribed by the State Probation Commission.

Q. Do you find these forms very useful? A. Very useful, they could not be improved on.

Q. And convenient? A. Very convenient and satisfactory in every respect.

Q. Do you find that the judges and yourself are willing to have suggestions from the State Probation Commission? A. Most decidedly.

Q. And you act in co-operation with them? A. Yes, sir.

Q. Now, what else do you keep? A. A book in which the names of the probationers are filed alphabetically in order to find the list of persons on probation.

Q. That book shows you to the card? A. Yes, sir. The cards are filed numerically and the names are kept in the book alphabetically.

Q. So that you have practically a cross index system? A. Yes, sir.

Q. And this book is also suggested by the State Probation Commission? A. It has been suggested, it was in use in the Juvenile Court before I took office.

Q. What else do you keep? A. We also keep a cash book showing the amount of fines.

Q. Are there many cases in which the judges place a defendant on probation to give him time to pay a fine? A. There are a few cases, yes.

Q. How does it work out? A. Fairly well.

Q. Well, have you kept any record? A. Yes, I have. We have collected about one-half the amount of fines, and owing to the commercial depression we are unable to collect the remainder.

Q. What is done with the men? A. The persons are still on probation until the fine is paid.

Q. Do these men explain why they cannot pay the fine? A. They explain, and I also investigate, and I have them report every week how much they pay, whether they have paid anything on the fine or not.

Q. Well, now, can you tell us what sort of cases the morning justices place on probation?

BY CHAIRMAN PAGE:

Q. You have used the term probation in regard to these cases where a man is allowed to go and required to report and pay his fine. That is not probation, is it? A. Certainly.

Q. The men are really paroled in your custody? A. No, it is probation.

Q. What permanent improvement are you making in those men? A. We have a direct oversight over that man, and we guide his steps while he is in our care.

Q. The effect of guiding his steps is to see that his steps have been guided in such paths as will produce a certain amount of money? A. Well, it has been my practice where a man is placed on probation, to pay a fine, that he must also live up to the conditions that would be imposed upon him if he was simply released on probation without a fine. If that man was arrested for intoxication, whether the Judge said so or not, I would see that he refrained from drinking to a certain extent. I apply probation to every case that is turned over to me whether it is to collect a fine or to see that he carries out his term of probation.

Q. Whether the judge puts him on probation or not, you do? A. If they are turned over to me I consider it a probation, because I am not a parole officer.

BY COMMISSIONER WINTHROP:

Q. Would you keep him after he had paid his fine, or would you see that he was discharged? A. If his habits were good and he paid his fine I would recommend to the Court that he be discharged.

Q. But if you did not think his conduct was satisfactory before he paid his fine and he paid his fine, would you then report the case to the Judge, and he might or might not be discharged? A. I would report the case to the Judge with the idea of having an extension of probation until such time as I thought he would be fit to be discharged from the oversight of the probation officer.

Q. When such a case pays his fine, what happens—is he brought before the Judge? A. When the fine is paid they are not brought back before the Judge.

Q. But where his conduct has not been good then you have him brought back before the Judge? A. Yes.

BY CHAIRMAN PAGE:

Q. On what charge? A. On the charge that he has violated the probation.

Q. As I understand it the Judge convicts the man, sentences him to pay a fine of say $5; he is then turned over to
you to see that he gets that five dollars. He pays it. Now,
is there any other term or condition imposed by the Judge
at the time he turns him over to you? A. As I understand
it there is. He is also under probation to behave himself
and conduct himself properly, and I see that he does so.

Q. I know, but what is the condition of the sentence—
that is what I am trying to get at. The Court sentences
him to pay a fine and says, when the man states he has
work and if given an opportunity he can pay the fine, "I
will put you on probation with Mr. Kelly, and you pay that
as soon as you can," or he places some definite amount that
he is to pay. Now, when he has paid that fine he has satisfied the condition of the sentence? A. The Judge I might
say in every case imposes a condition with that man, to do
this or not to do that, in connection with paying his fine.

Q. Besides paying the fine? A. Besides paying the fine.
I have never had a case turned over where I was simply to
act as a collection agency.

BY COMMISSIONER FRANCIS:

Q. But if a man had the cash there would be no conditions attached to the sentence? A. If the fine was paid immediately—no, I have never had such a case.

BY CHAIRMAN PAGE:

Q. He would not have the power to, would he, under the
law? A. To place a man on probation?

Q. Yes, after he fined him? A. No, I don't believe he would.

BY COMMISSIONER FRANCIS:

Q. You and Mr. Pfeifer passed what I consider a very favorable, a very good examination by the Civil Service Commission, so you must have some sentiment regarding the system of probation; don't you think it is a kind of prostitution of the probation system to use it as a legal covering for such cases? A. As a legal covering for the collection of fines?

Q. Yes? A. No, I believe it is a very good part of the probation system to allow a man to be placed on probation and given time to pay his fine.

Q.-Agreeing that the theory is all right, don't you think it should be kept apart altogether from the question of probation? A. No, I cannot say that I would want it kept apart.

Q. You must remember that you are one of the pioneers in the probation field and you have got to look into that? A. I understand that.

BY COMMISSIONER HAMILTON:

Q. You think whatever the theory is, that it is good sound sense in practice, don't you? A. I think probation itself is a very good system.

Q. No, I mean the use of the probation system in paying these fines—it works out all right in practice? A. It works out all right.

Q. In a good sensible way? A. So far I don't believe it could have been any more successful than it has been.

BY COMMISSIONER WINTHROP:

Q. You think it is an advantage to the community that that man should be given an opportunity to pay his fine instead of being sent to jail? A. Yes, it is an advantage to the community and it is a saving to the City of Buffalo.

BY CHAIRMAN PAGE:

Q. Wouldn't it be better if the Judge in convicting these men should impose the highest term of imprisonment that he could, and place the violator on probation with you during that period? Wouldn't that give you a better control over him and wouldn't it work out better in the long run, don't you think? A. Probably the conditions surrounding the case would not permit that.

Q. As I understand it, that is what the law provides for probation. Wouldn't it be better to enforce the law as it is written in the statute book, and then apply to the Legislature if you think you have some improvement, rather than setting up some system of probation of your own? A. I honestly believe that we are carrying out the idea of probation in every respect when we conduct our system as we have been doing it.

BY COMMISSIONER HAMILTON:

Q. It is a better lesson for a man to be compelled to pay a fine, even if he is given time, than it is to have a sentence of imprisonment suspended on him and not have to pay anything—isn't that your opinion? A. No, I can't say that it is. The mere fact that a man is under the jurisdiction and oversight of the probation officer is enough to show him that he has to observe certain conditions. While he may come around every week with a dollar or fifty cents, still if he has to come and report, and live up to certain conditions, it is humiliating enough for the man, and serves to satisfy the Court.

BY COMMISSIONER FRANCIS:

Q. So that probation in that case is simply interest on his fine. He gets that in addition to the fine? A. Yes. He is entirely responsible, for he has brought it on himself.

BY MR. MAYER:

Q. What class of cases are placed on probation by the morning justices? A. Cases of intoxication and disorderly conduct generally.

Q. Just how do you make these investigations yourself as to the environment, and so on? A. Personally in every case.

Q. And you are the only officer who has charge of probation? A. The only probation officer in the three morning courts.

Q. You do all this work yourself? A. Every bit of it.

Q. How many cases do you think you can handle per month? A. I have carried and can carry 150 cases a month and make my own investigations and look after the report.

Q. And go around to their homes? A. Yes.

Q. You work at it all the time? A. Day and night, seven days a week.

BY COMMISSIONER WINTHROP:

Q. You mean 150 new cases a month, on an average of 50 cases a month, cases take on the average three months, don't they? A. Yes.

BY MR. MAYER:

Q. Do you have to pay your own carfare and small expenses of that kind? A. I pay my own carfare and all expenses connected with the office, stationery and postage, etc.

Q. You have paid for your own stationery and postage? A. Yes.

Q. How much does that cost you? A. About $17 a month, besides a little charity work which has to be done here and there which will be another five dollars.

Q. So it costs you $200 a year anyway? A. Yes, I would allow $250 a year as the smallest sum.

Q. And that reduces your salary to a matter of perhaps $900 or $950? A. It reduces the salary, but the salary is not the idea of the proposition, it is the work. I look at the benefit that will be derived from the work.

Q. Do any outside societies pay you anything, any charitable organizations? A. Not a cent.

Q. You are interested in the work? A. Very much.

Q. Is it your intention to spend your life at the work? A. It is if I am allowed to do so.

Q. It is the career you have chosen? A. It is my chosen career.

Q. You like it? A. Yes, sir.

Q. And you feel that you are doing a lot of good? A. I do.

Q. How do you find these cases work out, do you see cases of improvement? A. Ninety per cent. have been satisfactory, good results.

Q. And you and the judges act in co-operation? A. First rate.

Q. Are the judges—do you find that they are interested in the probation work? A. I find that the three of them are, not one any more so than another.

Q. And they like to have reports from you, do they? A. They do.

Q. Are many of these cases of apparently decent men who just commit one little breach? A. Yes, about 60 per cent.—cases of good character who have made a misstep.

BY COMMISSIONER WINTHROP:

Q. Of the three hundred cases how many are males and how many are females? A. I have not more than six females on probation at the present time or at any time.

Q. Do you find that you can treat those cases successfully? A. I find that I can, but I don't approve of females being placed on probation, especially the class that you get in the Morning Court. They are nothing more or less than common prostitutes. Probation will do them no good.

Q. But if probation is to be tried with that class of prisoner would you think that females would do better than males as probation officers? A. No, I don't think so. I don't think that a female probation officer, even if appointed and paid as a female probation officer, could exercise the proper authority over the female probationer. I don't think that they would pay the attention to them that they would pay to a man, to a man that they know represents the Court, even if a woman did represent the Court, they would not take her as seriously as they would take a man.

Q. Do you have your probationers report to you? A. Personally to me.

Q. Where? A. At police headquarters, at my home, and at No. 8 police precinct.

Q. You have no office? A. I have no office, no facilities of any kind.

Q. Do they all report to you once a week? A. Some twice a week, some only twice a month. If they have been on probation two or three months and are getting along first rate I allow them to report twice a month.

Q. How many do you have reporting in one evening on the average? A. About sixty.

Q. And these you have to see in police headquarters somewhere? A. I have to see them in police headquarters, in the corridor, which is practically an absurd place to talk probation to anyone, and it is a bad practice to bring them back to the station houses when you are trying to keep them away from the station. It is absurd to suppose that really belongs to the Police Department. When the officers come in for roll call I have to bundle them out like a herd of sheep into a dark hallway. It is no place whatever for keeping records or for confidential work on probation.

Q. That must interfere with your work? A. It does.

BY COMMISSIONER HAMILTON:

Q. Do females and males report at the same time and place? A. The same place but not at the same time.

Q. Did I understand you to say that you did not think there should be a female probation officer connected with courts? A. Not with the morning courts. In the first place, I don't think there would be enough work for them, and I don't think they would derive much good from it.

Q. Aren't there occasionally cases that really demand a female probation officer's help? A. There are cases that would demand a female child worker, but I don't think it demands a female probation officer.

BY CHAIRMAN PAGE:

Q. Are there many women brought in for intoxication in the morning courts? A. Quite a few, but generally the class that would not be placed on probation.

Q. Generally the class? A. I will say always the class.

Q. You don't find them in this jurisdiction that they are frequently young married women brought in for intoxication? A. As a first offense?

Q. Yes. A. I have only seen one case there since I have been in the court.

———

WILLIAM C. JORDAN, called as a witness, having been first duly sworn, testified as follows:

Q. You are a sergeant of police? A. Yes.

Q. How long have you been in the service? A. As a sergeant?

Q. No, altogether. A. Fifteen years.

Q. And as a sergeant? A. Thirteen.

Q. What are your duties as sergeant? A. To take care of the platoon that is under my charge, attend morning courts.

Q. So you are in attendance at the morning courts? A. Yes.

Q. Are you a desk sergeant or—— A. No, sir; I am a sergeant.

Q. There is a difference between the word "sergeant" and "desk sergeant"? A. We are the sergeants.

BY CHAIRMAN PAGE:

Q. Just to make that clear, because we have come from the Greater City, which hasn't this distinction, the sergeants there rotate in charge of the desk, you have sergeants and desk sergeants? A. We don't rotate. The desk sergeant was formerly called a doorman. He is an operator and he was made a desk sergeant by act of the Legislature for the purpose of accepting bail and I don't know for what other purpose.

Q. He keeps the blotter, I suppose, the record? A. He keeps the records of all that comes into the station house.

BY MR. MAYER:

Q. Well, now, what morning court are you in attendance on? A. I am in the Third District Court.

Q. No. 3 as it is called? A. No. 3 Station, yes.

Q. And how long have you seen the Morning Court assemble? A. I have been in attendance in the First District Court and the Third District Court for about nearly twelve years.

Q. Do you think it is desirable to have these courts in the station house? A. If the room were suitable it would be, in my opinion.

Q. Well, you have a suitable room in No. 3? A. Not in the condition it is in now. We have headquarters located there and we are overcrowded.

Q. Do you think it is desirable to have a member of the police force act as clerk of the court as the desk sergeant does now, and should not the police force in the magistrates' courts be entirely separate? A. I don't think that a desk sergeant ought to act as clerk of the court. His duties are enough to occupy his time.

Q. Do you think that the police force ought to have its affairs attended to by its men and the magistrates their affairs by themselves, and proper clerical help? A. I should say yes.

Q. What system of identification do you have here in Buffalo? A. In respect to what?

Q. Well, suppose you wanted to find out whether a man is a second offender. A. We have a record of offenses committed kept at police headquarters.

Q. Well, I know, but do you employ the Bertillon system? A. Yes.

Q. Do you employ the finger-print system? A. No, sir.

Q. You don't employ it? A. No, sir; the Bertillon system only.

Q. As yet the finger-print system has not been tried? A. I haven't ever seen it.

Q. When a man is arraigned before a morning justice and found guilty of one of these minor offenses, more particularly vagrancy, has the Morning Justice any means of knowing whether that man has been convicted of the same offence before, other than the police recollection of him or his own recollection? A. If he were convicted in the same district court we could trace the record back.

Q. Suppose he was convicted in one of the other courts? A. Well, I don't know how you would find it out, unless that it could be stated by the officer that arrested him on that date, that he was convicted in the other court, and referred to that record.

Q. Yes, but ordinarily, unless the police officers who were concerned in the arrest remembered the man, there would be no means of identifying him, would there? A. Unless they went back over the records of all the courts.

Q. I am talking now of the better disposition of business?
A. No, sir.

Q. So whether the man is an old offender or not really depends on the recollection of the Judge and the police officers who have arrested the man or individual in the station house? A. The man arrested on those charges, the charge of vagrancy are generally arrested in the same district.

Q. Well, I understand that? A. At different times.

Q. But not always, are they? A. I wouldn't say—no.

Q. Is the question as I put it to you correct in its assumptions? A. Yes, as far as I know in that respect.

Q. Do you take Bertillon measurements of vagrants?
A. No, sir.

Q. You take Bertillon measurements of what criminals?
A. Of felons, suspicious persons.

Q. Well, what is a suspicious person? A. A man that we have knowledge has committed a crime in another city.

Q. That is that you have information he committed a crime? A. Yes, that we have information.

Q. But you don't take measurements of misdemeanants?
A. No, sir.

Q. What class of misdemeanors would you say that the police have most difficulty with in the City of Buffalo, misdemeanants? A. Intoxication and disorderly conduct.

Q. Have you many vagrants? A. Not for the population, no.

Q. Do you know of many cases where men have been detained without being arraigned before magistrates or the Police Judge? A. No, sir.

Q. Did you know anything about the case to which Judge Collins referred? A. I do not.

Q. Or any of the cases to which Judge Murphy referred?
A. I do not. ' None came under my observation. They don't
occur in the Third Precinct.

Q. Now, is there any suggestion that you have to make
as an experienced police officer in attendance on these morning courts about those courts or the police courts. A. Nothing further than you have requested an answer to in reference to the judges having their own clerk.

Q. Do you agree with the Superintendent that these
courts ought to be open earlier? A. I think it would be a
good idea, yes.

Q. Would that be advantageous to the police? A. I don't
wish to make milkmen out of the judges, or anything of
that kind, and I think it is not advantageous to the police,
the police suffer no inconvenience during the late court, they
are allowed time off in the evening for attending at the
Morning Court.

Q. Do you think the time off in the evening tends to unnecessary arrests by the police? A. No, sir; I do not.

————

THOMAS J. GILLIGAN, called as a witness, having
been first duly sworn, testified as follows:

BY MR. MAYER:

Q. What is your full name? A. Thomas J. Gilligan.

Q. Of what precinct are you in command? A. Third.

Q. You are an officer in command of that precinct? A.
Yes.

Q. Have you heard the testimony of Sergeant Jordan?
A. Yes.

Q. Do you agree with him that the employees for subordinates of magistrates in the Police Department ought to be separate? A. I agree that the magistrates ought to have their own clerk in the Morning Court instead of a desk sergeant, which does their work now.

Q. Do you think it is desirable court should be held in a station house or would you think it ought to be held somewhere else? A. Well, it is all right in the station house but they ought to have a different court room, a separate room from the room that is used by partolmen as a smoking room and rest room.

Q. And a room over which the Magistrate should have full control? A. Yes.

Q. Do you agree with some of the magistrates, that there is a police atmosphere in the trial room? A. Well, I don't know if that has anything to do with the court or not. The police around there a good deal—it is a room for lounging around.

Q. It is not very big is it? A. No. There ought to be more dignity to that court.

Q. It wouldn't impress a person who had never been in a court before? A. No.

Q. As being the place for a court, would it? A. Ought to have something fixed up more respectable than that court is, the Morning Court; some furniture there.

Q. Don't you think a great many of the people brought in are people of foreign birth, in these morning courts? A. The majority of them are.

Q. And from your experience on the police force and as a man who knows the City of Buffalo, don't you think they get very bad impressions about a court from that—— A.

I do, I think we ought to have something more dignified.

Q. Do you think it would contribute to the better administration of justice? A. Yes.

Q. If the Morning Court were held at a different—in a separate room at any rate? A. Well, it could be held in the same building, but have a room fitted up as a court room for court purposes.

Q. Do you think the three divisions as now laid out are laid out with due regard for the convenience of the city? A. I think they are.

Q. And for the handling of the police business? A. I do.

Q. Is there any suggestion that has occurred to you as a police officer? A. Well, the Superintendent made a suggestion there about holding the morning courts at 4 or 5. I was going to make the same suggestion myself for this reason——

Q. That is what we want to know? A. Now, there are many times I take bail for a man who is arrested, usually for disorderly conduct. He gets in a scrap or argument on the corner, the policeman overhears him and brings him to the station house. His friends come to bail him out. We accept bail. Well, when he signs that bail bond, ''Now you are bailed with the understanding that you will be in court in the morning at 8 o'clock.'' ''My God, have I got to be here at 8 o'clock in the morning?'' ''Yes.'' ''Well, I am going to lose my job. I can't show up here at 8 o'clock. I go to work at 7 o'clock.'' Now, I think if we had the session of the Morning Court 4 o'clock or 5 in the morning those men would come there, and we would try them and they could go home and get breakfast and be working at 7 o'clock.

BY CHAIRMAN PAGE:

Q. What would you think of having one Night Court, where they could all be brought in during the night? A. Well that would work all right, I guess.

BY MR. MAYER:

Q. Would that take your officers off post to an extent that might interfere with your police system? A. Well, yes, it would to the extent; yes, it would. Unless a——

Q. You have got the three platoon system here? A. We have got the three platoon system, yes.

BY COMMISSIONER FRANCIS:

Q. Does it work very well? A. It works good. It is the only system.

———

WESLEY C. C. DUDLEY, called as a witness, having been first duly sworn, testified as follows:

BY MR. MAYER:

Q. Mr. Dudley, you are the District Attorney of the County of Erie? A. I am.

Q. You took office on the first day of this year, I believe? A. I did.

Q. Prior to that time you had been a practicing lawyer in the City of Buffalo? A. Assistant United States Attorney.

Q. Assistant United States Attorney. Have you had sufficient opportunity to have an opinion as to the advisability of the District Attorney being represented in the Police Court? A. I think it would be a very good idea.

Q. How would it be helpful in the administration of justice? A. Well there are a great many cases that come to the District Attorney's office, held for the Grand Jury, that would probably never reach there, that would be disposed of in the Police Court, although I think it would require more police justices than we have in the City of Buffalo at the present time.

Q. Well, as a matter of good administration do you think that the District Attorney's office should be represented in the Police Court? A. I think they should.

Q. Now, what do you think in that regard as to the Morning Court? A. I don't think it would be possible hardly to have the District Attorney's office represented in all the morning courts unless we had double our staff of employees down there.

Q. Of course, that I understand, but I mean if you can eliminate for the moment the question of expense, would it be desirable to be represented in the morning courts? A. It might be well, but I hardly think it necessary.

Q. Have you looked into that court? A. No, I haven't made a study of it.

Q. You don't think the class of cases requires it? A. I hardly think so.

Q. Now, as a matter of fact, the history of the Police Court here is, that many important cases have come before the Police Judge, is that not so? A. Oh, yes.

Q. Would you say that the number of police courts should be increased here? A. I think so, I think it should.

Q. To what number? A. Oh, I don't know what number, but, I don't care how good a judge we have over in the Police Court the number of cases that he has there he cannot dispose of and give them the proper consideration, I don't believe. In other words, he can't take the testimony, in case of appeal and in his return they are not as full as they should be. It would be impossible for him to make them as full. In other words, he would not be able to dispose of the cases.

Q. Well, would you do away with the morning courts, I am not speaking of the justices? A. I don't know as I would say that. I haven't given it study enough for that. I think perhaps the morning courts in these minor cases, it might be a good thing. Still if we had more police justices, they might be able to take care of those cases and perhaps give them better attention. What I have seen of it myself the morning courts and the Police Court are crowded with cases and they cannot give it the time or each case the time and consideration I think a case deserves.

Q. Have you considered at all the question which is being agitated as to the creation of a court of inferior jurisdiction having both civil and criminal jurisdiction. A. I haven't, except what I have seen in the papers.

Q. So that you have not given the matter any study. A. No, I have not.

Q. I suppose you have not been District Attorney long enough to see the practical operation of these criminal cases to an extent—— A. No, I have not.

Q. (Continuing.) To enable you to give an opinion? A. No, I don't think so. The last—of course we have only been in office about a month now. We have had about 100 cases before the Grand Jury and we have had forty or fifty appeal cases from the Police Court.

Q. To the County Judge? A. To the County Judge. Then we have persons coming in before the trial Court, ask-

ing that bail be fixed, things of that sort, which in my
opinion should be attended to in the Police Court, if we
had a proper number of justices.

Q. Well, now, in the City of New York, as you doubtless
know, the jurisdiction of the Court of Special Sessions is
in all cases of misdemeanor except libel. Do you think it
would be advisable that the present jurisdiction of the Police Court Judge in the City of Buffalo should be extended
to take in all misdemeanors? A. I do, very much so.

Q. Would such an extension of jurisdiction greatly fa-
cilitate the trial of felony cases? A. There is no doubt of
it. The cases would be better disposed of, too. Now, for
instance, you have a great number of cases over before the
Police Judge every morning. Many of those cases are cases
of burglary, larceny and criminally receiving stolen property, some of the defendants are—it is their first offense.
That defendant is held for the Grand Jury and he is confined in jail until his case comes up. Then it takes the time
of the grand jurors and the District Attorney and the
stenographer to present his case to the Grand Jury. Then
he is held in jail if he is not bailed out of course until the
trial and a good many times the property value of what
he has taken is from two to ten dollars, and the Judge will
in the end suspend sentence or give him two to four months,
while if that could have been disposed of in the Police
Court with a sufficient number of justices, the person would
be sent down to the same length of time or perhaps a little
more. It would be better for the individual and the case
would receive just as good consideration. It would save
the trial courts——

Q. You don't mean felonies, of course? A. No, misdemeanors.

Q. You mean misdemeanors? Well that wouldn't include burglary? A. No, that wouldn't include burglary, but I mentioned that as——

Q. But would you have excise cases tried by the Police Court? A. Why, I cannot say in regard to that. I hadn't thought of it.

Q. Disorderly conduct cases? A. I think so.

Q. And the many misdemeanors in which imprisonment is not to exceed a year or $500 fine or both? A. I think so.

Q. As it is now do you as District Attorney find that there are many misdemeanor cases which you have come to you and which must be presented to the Grand Jury? A. Oh, yes, a great many.

Q. And if that was cut down you could do the more important work more speedily, I suppose. A. Oh, yes; I think it would be very much better.

Q. Do you have a criminal term here all the time? A. Well, we have, yes, every other month in the Supreme Court and two weeks out of the alternate months in the County Court.

Q. Two weeks in each month or only in the alternate months? A. The alternate months.

Q. So that there are spaces of two weeks when there is no criminal term? A. Yes.

Q. Could you have prepared for the Commission statistics showing the number of cases of misdemeanor presented to the Grand Jury last year? A. I will.

Q. And also the number of felonies? A. I will.

Q. And if you could possibly do so, also have the misdemeanors classified? A. I will try to.

Q. As to character of the offense? A. I will try to, Mr. Mayer.

Q. In New York, I might have stated, I assume you know, that the Court of Special Sessions in each division consists of three judges, while here, under existing law, the Police Judge is a Court of Special Sessions. Now, do you think it would be wise to confine jurisdiction of all misdemeanors to one judge? A. Oh, I think it would be better, if you are going to have three or four judges, or more than we have now, to give them all jurisdiction.

Q. I mean to say, would you make the Court consist of one man or three, as in New York? A. Why, I think one man is sufficient, that would be my opinion, without considering it very much.

Q. Now, did any suggestion occur to you in connection with these minor courts that you would like to present to the Commission? A. No, I don't think I know enough about the morning courts to express much of an opinion.

BY CHAIRMAN PAGE:

Q. Does the District Attorney make a report to anybody? A. Makes a report every year to the Board of Supervisors.

Q. I suppose that is printed? A. Yes.

Q. You can send us a copy of the 1907 report? A. Yes, I will.

MR. MAYER: If there is anyone here who desires to say anything, I wish he would step forward. I think we have covered the essential features of the administration of the courts of inferior criminal jurisdiction in this city.

CHAIRMAN PAGE: The Commission will stand adjourned to meet Thursday, the eleventh of February, in the City Hall, Borough of Manhattan, City of New York.

Proceedings

of the

Commission to Inquire Into the Courts of

Inferior Criminal Jurisdiction in

Cities of the First Class

Volume V

ROCHESTER, N. Y., Friday, May 21, 1909.

10.30 A. M.

The Commission met pursuant to call of the Chairman.

CHAIRMAN PAGE: This Commission was appointed pursuant to statute, to inquire into the manner in which justice is administered in the courts of inferior criminal jurisdiction in cities of the first class. The Commission has investigated the courts in the city of New York, also in the city of Buffalo, and it is one of the afflictions brought upon the city of Rochester when it became a city of the first class, that this Commission should be sent upon them.

JOHN H. CHADSEY, called as a witness, having been duly sworn, testified as follows:

BY MR. MAYER:

Q. Judge, you are the Police Justice of the city of Rochester? A. I am.

Q. And how long have you held that office? A. Seven years the first of January. This is now my second term.

Q. Is it required that the Police Justice should be an attorney? A. Yes, for at least five years.

BY CHAIRMAN PAGE:

Q. Is he allowed to engage in other practice, Judge? A. Yes, no limit.

BY MR. MAYER:

Q. Now, where is the police court situated? A. On Exchange Street; 137 Exchange Street, and it is in the first police precinct station; that is, it is the general offices of the police. The chief of police and inspector have their offices in the same building.

Q. But the court has a separate room? A. A separate department entirely.

Q. What time, generally, does the court open in the morning? A. Nine thirty.

Q. And how long do you sit? A. Well, according to the cases and according to the trials, and the length of trials, sometimes——

Q. Is court held? A. (Continuing.) Yes, sometimes— we oftentimes get through maybe at eleven o'clock if we do not have litigated cases, but if we have contested cases we will be there maybe until half past twelve or one. Sometime we adjourn until two and have an all day session.

Q. Does the Court sit every day? A. Every day.

Q. Including Sundays? A. No.

Q. Not Sundays? A. No, nor legal holidays.

Q. Who is empowered to take bail, besides the Police Justice? A. In that court no one, except the captains, when a man is arrested they can take a captain's bond.

Q. For misdemeanors? A. Yes, up to—for appearance the next morning.

Q. Well, in the case of a person arrested for a felony? A. They have to apply to the Police Justice. That is, the practice here is that if a man is arrested in the evening they telephone me to fix the bail, if it is a felony, and they give them the bond, what we call here the captain's bond. That can be the bond given, a bond before the captain or sergeant or lieutenant for appearance the next morning in court. They just give that bond and then next morning, when he is arraigned, there is a bond required of course on further adjournment.

Q. Is that in the case of felonies as well as misdemeanors? A. Felonies and misdemeanors as well.

Q. Well, under what provision of law may the captain take a bond for a felony? A. There is, I think there is, a provision, I could not tell you just where it is, that the captain can take a bond for the appearance in court the next morning of anybody that is arrested; what we call here a captain's bond. It is a regular blank.

Q. Well, under the criminal code, isn't that applicable only to misdemeanors? A. Yes, but they cannot fix the bail.

Q. No, but I mean can they—is there any special provision in the Rochester charter? A. I don't know, I couldn't tell you exactly as to that. The practice is that if a man— as I say he must be either arraigned before me and give bail, or sometimes, when they are arrested in the evening or night, instead of keeping them locked up, they telephone and I say "Fix the bail at so much," and they give them a temporary bail, or until the next morning.

Q. And that is done at the police station, I suppose? A. Yes, at the station. Then the next morning they are brought in court at nine thirty and then arraigned, the charge read to them and they are required then to give bail, whatever we take.

Q. Now, under your charter, when the Police Justice is away his duties are performed by the municipal—— A. One of the judges of the municipal court.

Q. Yes, and there are two judges of the Municipal Court? A. Two judges of the Municipal Court.

BY COMMISSIONER HAMILTON:

Q. Just a moment, in reference to bail, Judge. Do I understand, at whatever hour of the night a person is arrested for a felony, if he desires to give bail they call you up? A. Yes, I am disturbed sometimes not only by telephone but maybe by a party who comes down in a hack.

Q. And that is liable to occur at any time? A. That is liable to occur and if I am at my summer residence why I have a 'phone and they communicate with me there.

Q. Are you called up frequently at night for that purpose? A. Well, not so very; oh, it would average probably not over once a week, on an average; sometimes oftener. You see, if they are arrested any time during the day after court is adjourned, why they appear right before me.

BY MR. MAYER:

Q. Now, you hold the Police Court and the Children's Court? A. Juvenile Court, yes.

Q. Or Juvenile Court? A. Yes.

Q. And then do you have a separate time and place for hearing cases of women? A. Yes. I have adopted that. There is really no law for it, but then I have done it.

Q. You have done that as a matter of practice? A. Yes.

Q. Now, how do you arrange as to that; do you have a special day for hearing women? A. No. I might digress here to say that I understand in New York you have a women's court, but here we have no provision for a women's court. They are arraigned on the morning calendar with the men, but I found that it was a case oftentimes where I thought it would be best not to have the girls over sixteen in the adult court, brought into the regular police court; and we had a room upstairs on the floor above the police court, that we had formerly used as a juvenile court, and so I arraigned the women there. I do that after the morning calendar is called and disposed of. I hold the women, who are in the police station, up there all on the floor above. The women are not connected; the cells are not connected at all or anywhere near where the men are. The men are on the lower floor and the women on the third floor proper, and I go up there and arraign them in the old juvenile court room; take their pleas or try them as the case may be; but I do that right after the morning session of the police court.

Q. Have you any idea of how many women are arraigned in the course of a year? A. I tell you, I think the clerk will be able to give you a record of it. I don't know whether the clerk will be sworn here. He has a statement, I think, of all the arrests.

Q. How many are there? A. (Continuing.) And the police have a statement of all departments, of the arrests of women, the number arrested per year. I sent for it and expect it to be here.

CHAIRMAN PAGE: The Clerk will testify to those details.

MR. MAYER: I will ask him afterwards.

THE WITNESS: It is really the Police Court, but you know I hold it in a separate room apart, and if you desire I can tell you the reason I did it.

BY MR. MAYER:

Q. Yes? A. Now, for instance, notably on one occasion,

a young lady was brought in, about seventeen years of age, charged with vagrancy; a girl that had wandered around here; just came in from the country. Well of course the people that frequent the Police Court and the back part of it, taxpayers, etc., as we call them, why they rubbered a good deal, and as the girl was discharged and went out of the court room she was accosted by men on the street. And she was a respectable girl. Well, I thought it was about time to protect them from such an attack as that from any evil-minded man, and so I said we will arraign them separately and those people will not be invited to attend the Women's Court.

Q. How do you find it works? A. Nicely, nicely, as we have the women all on that one floor, the cells and a matron and all on that floor, so that when they are discharged they can go back and go down unmolested in the elevator and out on the street and get rid of the rabble.

BY COMMISSIONER HAMILTON:

Q. Do they go out by the same exit that is used for the other court. A. They do, but I hold court after the other court is adjourned, so that the others are supposed to have gone.

BY MR. MAYER:

Q. How often do you hold the Juvenile Court? A. Three times a week; Mondays, Wednesdays and Fridays.

Q. And that is in the afternoon? A. Afternoon at two o'clock.

BY CHAIRMAN PAGE:

Q. I would like to ask a question, if you please, in regard to this morning court: Do you find that there are some of these curiosity seekers that attend the sessions of the Women's Court upstairs? A. Very few; very few. The court room isn't very large and I—well, if anybody is interested, anybody wants to go there, of course they can. But the officers know these people and they generally inquire if they have any business in the Women's Court. Of course we can't stop them from going in, but we can very well by having an officer inquire, keep out a great many undesirable ones, and we do do it.

BY MR. MAYER:

Q. Now, referring to the Police Court, it appears from Section 468 of your Rochester Charter that the Police Court has exclusive jurisdiction in the first instance to try for all misdemeanors, practically? A. Yes.

Q. Now, as a matter of practice, are all misdemeanors brought to the Police Court? A. Yes.

Q. Are there many applications for removal? A. For what?

Q. For removal to the—— A. Oh.

Q. (Continuing.) So as to try the cases, present the cases to the Grand Jury? A. Oh, on the examination, no. You mean for misdemeanors?

Q. Yes? A. I don't think I have had a case of such since my term of office. They have elected, when they have been empowered to elect, sometimes they have elected to go before the Grand Jury, but never under Sections 468 and 9 to remove a case.

Q. Yes, that is what I mean. So that as a matter of fact your experience is practically all misdemeanors are tried before you? A. Yes.

Q. Now we notice also that a defendant may have a jury trial on demand? A. Yes.

Q. Is a jury trial often demanded? A. Once in a while, but I don't think we have averaged a jury once a week.

Q. What class of cases? Any special cases where demands were made? A. Oh, generally over city ordinances, violations, but once in a while assault cases, misdemeanors.

Q. You mean city ordinances that are large in their importance, such as—— A. Oh, sometimes something in the nature of milk cases and health ordinances and automobiles, or something of that kind, often times. I don't have many automobile cases, though, that they call a jury.

Q. Well, has the procedure whereby a jury trial is demandable by a defendant in this city, has that always existed? A. Always existed since, I suppose, the first.

Q. Well, where there is a jury trial, is there considerable delay? A. Very little. The law says they shall have eight days on adjournment and under our law we have to give the jury man three days' notice. We have to get our jury from the regular box, city box of jurors, that is made out by the Jury Commissioner, and we have just the same class of jurors as we would have in the Supreme Court.

Q. I meant, rather, do these jury trials block the business? Are they delayed? A. Oh, not very much. We generally set them down for a day when we can give the day, and of course it oftentimes will take all day. We have had some important cases where it has taken three days.

Q. Do you think it is desirable to retain that feature in the law? A. Oh, yes, I think that right to a jury should— especially in a city of this size; that is, I am a firm believer that the people have the right, although I don't know if the jurors always get a right conviction. They may differ from the Court, but no matter; they are entitled to it and we never deny it. There is a provision in the Charter that they shall demand a jury on the joining of issue. We sometimes enforce that when we think it is done merely for delay or something of that kind.

BY CHAIRMAN PAGE:

Q. In what classes of cases, Judge, do they demand jury trial? A. Well, we have one now, only one jury, that is a case of petit larceny, they charge. But the case that took us the longest, I think, since I have been in office, was a case of a nuisance, existing in a section where there was a phosphate factory, that was taken in when the city was enlarged, formerly in the Town of Brighton; and under the Charter the City Attorney, the Corporation Counsel as we call him, brought an action before me. They questioned the jurisdiction there and that case went clear to the Appellate Division, I think away up to the Court of Appeals, and they decided I had jurisdiction in this case. Therefore a jury was called and it took some three or four days, I think, before we got through with it, in that case.

Q. Well, then, there is no particular class of cases in which they demand jury trial? A. Oh, no; they have got the right.

Q. I know they have the right in any case? A. No, I couldn't say any one class particularly. Once in a while probably they might think they would have a better chance. They have the right to a jury and will demand it

Q. Do you have jurisdiction to try excise cases, violation of the excise law? A. Yes, we have to examine some.

Q. Yes, as a committing magistrate, but I mean as a magistrate to try? A. No, not to try and determine. That has been decided by a late decision. I decided that I could only hold to await the action of the Grand Jury. There was a case taken on appeal and that has been decided that I was correct, in that decision, that I could only hold to the Grand Jury, and I could not try and determine excise cases.

BY MR. MAYER:

Q. What is the title of that case, Judge, do you remember? A. The Prosecuting Attorney, Mr. Hogan, can give that.

Q. Bastardy cases are tried in the Municipal Court? A. In the Municipal Court.

Q. And two judges sit? A. Two judges sit, yes.

Q. Don't you think that those cases ought to be tried in the Police Court? A. Well, personally, I decidedly object to it, I think; and, another thing, too, under the law it requires two justices, and there is but one police judge, but there are two municipal court judges. And it is a quasi-criminal case, really, and therefore there was, I think, first there was an act giving the Police Court jurisdiction. I think that has been changed, as far as this city is concerned, and gives it exclusively to the Municipal Court. Judge Hebbard, who is present, can tell you more about it.

Q. Is there any other quasi-criminal action that is tried in the Municipal Court? A. Nothing only of this kind, as I understand it; but such cases, of course, whereby execution can issue.

Q. Oh, yes; but those are civil actions? A. No, I don't think any other except bastardy cases.

BY COMMISSIONER HAMILTON:

Q. No violations of ordinances? A. No violations—oh, when for penalties; if you bring a civil action for penalty, that is triable in the Municipal Court.

BY MR. MAYER:

Q. What salary do you receive, Judge? A. Four thousand two hundred.

Q. Is that fixed by the Common Council? A. Fixed by the Board of Estimate and Apportionment.

Q. The Board of Estimate of the city? A. Of the city.

Q. Do you find that you are able to attend to any other business? A. Very little. I find that, although I had a practice when I took this office and I am trying to keep up same, I have to have somebody else attend to it; that is about it. I have to turn my clients over. I am unable to appear in court for the reason my time is taken every day in the Police Court, and I cannot give much attention to private practice. I do some private practice. I don't want to lose it.

Q. Do you have the appointment of the Police Court clerk. A. Yes, the Police Court clerk and deputy clerk.

Q. And the Police Court clerk you can appoint at will? A. At will.

Q. How is the deputy clerk appointed? A. The same.

Q. Court attendants? A. The same; that is, the court attendant only, not the officers at the door; not those.

Q. No, I mean what is called in your charter the Police Court attendant? A. Yes, he is appointed and at will.

Q. Now, in addition to him, have you civilian or police attendants? A. Police attendants, court attendants.

Q. They are assigned by the Police Department? A. Yes, sir.

Q. And are they assigned at your request or upon the initiation of the Police Department? A. The Commission of Public Safety assigns them. They generally ask me, but I have no power to appoint; that is about all.

Q. How many probation officers are there? A. We have one male and one female probation officer in the adult court, police court.

Q. They are appointed by the Police Justice? A. No, sir.

Q. How are they appointed? A. They are appointed by the Commissioner of Public Safety, under the Charter. Under Section 11A of the Code, it gives the right; I could appoint, but I cannot appoint and fix the salary. Whenever the Board of Estimate and Apportionment fixes the salary, the appointment has to come from the Commissioner of Public Safety.

Q. Is that provided for in the Charter? A. In the Charter. That is one thing that I contend, that I have always said, that I think the judges ought to make their own appointments.

Q. Are these officers appointed with or without examination, do you know? A. With civil service examination.

Q. And they are selected from an eligible list? A. Yes.

Q. You refer to Section 318, which reads: "The Commissioner may appoint to hold office during his pleasure such number of probation officers as may be prescribed by the Board of Estimate and Apportionment, which number may include one or more female officers when so provided by the Board——" A. Yes.

Q. (Continuing.)—"and they possess the powers now or hereafter conferred by law upon probation officers and must perform such duties as may be prescribed by the Commissioner or otherwise by law"? A. Yes.

Q. So that the probation officers are not wholly subject to your jurisdiction? A. Yes, sir; that is the fact.

Q. And it is your opinion that the Police Justice should have the power to appoint his own officers? A. Yes, sir; not only the Police Justice, but I think any court should be held responsible for the conduct of his court, and the prisoners when he paroles them should not be subject to some other influence.

Q. Well, have you any idea how that provision got into the Charter, what the reason for that was? A. I couldn't tell you, sir; I don't know; only I suppose they have taken the ground that wherever the money was paid for it out of the city funds the Board of Estimate and Apportionment should name it.

Q. Is the Commissioner of Public Safety a member of the Board here? A. No, I don't think he is; I think he is not. He is appointed by the Mayor. (To Prosecuting Attorney Hogan:) He is not a member, is he?

MR. HOGAN: No.

A. (Continuing.) I think not, of the Board of Estimate and Apportionment.

BY MR. MAYER:

Q. Now, what are the names of the probation officers in your adult court? A. Alfred J. Masters and Mrs. William W. Armstrong.

Q. Now, have you any probation officers in the Children's Court? A. Yes, sir.

Q. Just before I refer to that: Is the work of the probation officers in the adult court divided between the attention of males and females? A. Yes.

Q. So that Mr. Masters handles the cases of males? A. Yes, sir.

Q. And Mrs. Armstrong the cases of females? A. Yes, sir.

Q. Now, generally speaking, as to males, what class of cases do you place on probation? A. A large number are those that are arrested for disorderly conduct under the section, what we commonly would call non-support cases; men who fail to support their wives or their families, disorderly persons under the section. Then we also parole quite a number of people charged with intoxication; and where children are, we might say—we might say persons arrested who are over sixteen, we have to treat them as adults in the adult court, and whenever I can save sending a child to the penitentiary, of sixteen or seventeen or eighteen, why I generally place them in the hands of Mr. Masters, the probation officer.

Q. Now, in the non-support cases, have you found probation to be successful? A. Very; very.

Q. Have you been able to bring about the support of the wife and family? A. In very many of them, and there has been a great deal of money saved. The manner in which it is conducted is this: The man is arrested and required to give a bond and an order is made that he shall pay so much per week to the Overseer of the Poor for the City of Rochester, for the support of his family.

Though possibly in the country, you understand, there is only a bond required; here by statute, in the City of Rochester—I don't know whether it applies to other cities or not—the Justice can fix the weekly allowance. On inquiry and finding what a man is earning, we make an order that he shall pay, say, a certain amount per week for the period of one year to the Overseer of the Poor and he shall give a bond in double that amount. Now, if he fails, suppose he is unable to give that bond, then we say to Mr. Masters, "We will place him in your charge" for as long a period as the law allows; the rule is six months; "and he shall pay that money over to you. If he fails to do so, why you bring him into court and we will have to send him to the penitentiary until the bond is given." Now, that is a great saving. We not only save the character of the defendant, but the money is devoted to the support of the family and we save the city in that respect. Mr. Masters, who is here, will give you the amount that was paid in during the last year, and I think it amounts to quite a sum of money.

BY CHAIRMAN PAGE:

Q. Don't you think the law should be changed so as to allow you to put that man on probation for a year instead of six months? A. It would be a good thing; yes. I wish it were. I can make them give a bond for a year.

Q. Yes, I know? A. But I can't put him on probation for over six months. I think it should be.

BY MR. MAYER:

Q. That would be a very great help, if you had control of such a defendant for, say, a year? A. Often; often.

Q. Do you find that the probation system results in either reuniting or more closely uniting the family? A. Many a time they are united and they are brought together, that are once separated over, maybe, some trifling affair. I wish to state, for your information, you would have seen it if you had been in court this morning. A man is arrested by the wife and brought into court. I say to Mr. Masters, the probation officer, "I wish you would take this man and wife right out in your room"—which we have provided for him—"and have a talk with them and see if you cannot get them together." It often results in their coming back into court and saying the case is withdrawn, settled and made up. Other times it will be made up during the probation period.

Q. Now, in the case of wayward youths, do you find probation to be successful? A. Yes; yes; very much so.

Q. Then you are a strong believer, I assume, in the probation system? A. I am, decidedly.

Q. You think it results in not only saving the persons but saving the County and State a great deal of money? A. Not only in doing a great deal of good—the fact is we have to send these young boys over sixteen, a day over sixteen, to the penitentiary. You understand that under the law, the special law, we must commit to the penitentiary. We don't commit to jail in this County at all. A great many don't understand that fact.

Q. That is under Section 477 of the Charter? A. Yes, and I guess the old law; it has always been the law here, for years. We don't commit to the jail for any offenses except certain offenses; certain ones, like under bond to keep the peace or something of that kind.

Q. Well, what classes of cases are committed to the industrial school? A. That is under sixteen years of age, juvenile cases.

Q. No cases over sixteen? A. No cases over sixteen.

Q. So that where you have a youth of upwards of sixteen, if you must commit, you are compelled to commit to the penitentiary? A. Yes, sir.

Q. And where is the Monroe County Penitentiary situated? A. South of the city, within the city limits I think it is; yes, I am very sure it was taken in.

Q. Well, would you think it would be a good idea if there could be a reformatory for misdemeanants of the ages of, say, sixteen to twenty-five? A. Why, yes; and I have been an advocate, I have spoken of it; I have spoken of it here in this city for the last two years or more and agitated it somewhat, that we should have an institution where we could send children, well, from the juvenile court as well as the adult court, up to, say, twenty-one years of age; what I call a sort of a shelter, or a place for a child brought in, say, that is going to school, maybe a boy of sixteen that is in the High School, or seventeen, where if he should be confined we could send him there for a limited time, maybe a few days or a month or two months; and then at that institution let him continue in his studies, similar to our public schools or parochial schools, and let him continue right there for a certain period of time. That will, I think, have a great tendency to save that boy.

Q. Well, then, in this part of the State, although you can send a person who has committed a felony, and who is between the ages of sixteen and thirty, to the Elmira

Reformatory, you have no place to send a person who has committed a lesser offense? A. No, sir; none whatever, only the penitentiary.

Q. So the person who has committed the graver offense gets the better opportunity to reform? A. He goes to the Reformatory at Elmira. The County Judge here has that jurisdiction; I don't.

Q. Would you favor a state reformatory for misdemeanants, which would take in perhaps all of the western part of the State? A. Well, I haven't thought of that question, but I merely thought for the city. The idea was, a great many boys are brought in and if I send them to the State Industrial School, they stay there only to be discharged by the Board of Managers of that institution. The rule is that they keep them there probably from a year to four years, according to their behavior. I think very few are released short of a year.

Q. In the cases of youths under sixteen? A. Under sixteen; whereas if we had them there where I could say, "Now, you go to the shelter for one month," why, that boy, on his release, probably would continue in his studies, with the encouragement he would get there and the advice he would get there, and probably it would be the thing for us; whereas you go to the State Industrial School, although it is an elegant institution, they come in communication with all from the western part of the State. The State Industrial School, they send them all there, and of course there are some pretty hard boys up there.

Q. That is situated at Industry, New York? A. Yes.

Q. And that is near here? A. In the Town of Rush, about ten miles, I think, ten or twelve, from here.

Q. Now, in the case of adult female offenders, where do you commit them—also to the Monroe County Penitentiary? A. Some of them, or if under certain charges, I can send them to the Western House of Refuge for Women at Albion.

Q. Well, when you say certain charges, you mean charges that have to do with sexual crimes? A. Yes, mainly.

Q. And are those the only two places where female adults may be sent? A. No, there is an institution called the Shelter, or Protection for Unprotected Girls, at Syracuse. They will take them until they are eighteen, there. I have sent girls between the ages of sixteen and eighteen there.

Q. Now, all of those cases of adult women, girls or women, are placed in charge of Mrs. Armstrong, I assume? A. On probation.

Q. On probation. A. (Continuing.) I wish to add, also, that I can send also to the St. Anne's Home at Albany.

Q. At Albany? A. At Albany. I can send anyone there from twelve years—I would say from sixteen years, to any ages.

Q. Now, in the juvenile or children's court have you probation officers? A. Yes, sir.

Q. Are those appointed by you? A. All without pay.

Q. Yes. So you have the privilege of appointing the officers who do not get anything? A. Yes, I can appoint all those volunteer officers, but those that receive a salary have to come through the Commissioner of Public Safety.

Q. Now, how many probation officers have you in the Children's Court? A. Well, we have one paid officer now, just appointed this month, the 10th of this month—Mr. Killup.

Q. Was he appointed by the Commissioner of Public Safety? A. The Commissioner of Public Safety.

Q. And was he previously connected with the Society for the Prevention of Cruelty to Children? A. Superintendent of the Society for the Prevention of Cruelty to Children.

Q. Have you any other probation officers there? A. Oh, I have a number; I think I had on my list about fifty.

Q. Volunteers? A. Volunteers.

Q. Well, do you remember the work they do? A. Well, for instance, Mr. Killup now is at the head. If a child is brought in, say from some section of the city where he attends, maybe, some parochial school, we will appoint or have in that church some priest who is a probation officer. We assign the boy to him. If it is in some other part of the city, or in some other religion, we have more around the city and they will take them, and we will let them report to them and they will make a report.

Q. Now, do those probation officers report to Mr. Killup or to you direct? A. They have heretofore reported to me, but now they will report to Mr. Killup.

Q. So that Mr. Killup will act really as a chief probation officer? A. Yes.

Q. And be practically at the head of the probation work in the Children's Court under your supervision? A. Yes.

Q. And I assume that your effort is, following the provisions of law, to parole or probation a child to a person of the same religious faith wherever practicable? A. Always; always.

Q. Well, do you find that these volunteers do the work? A. Well, some are active. Of course on this list of fifty there are some that haven't maybe had a case once a year, but they come in and are willing and offer to do what they can, and of course we will put them on the list. But I suppose there is about twenty what I can call active ones, twenty to twenty-five. They are very efficient, they attend strictly to it, I think they do good work; attend to it, make their reports, and see that the children report to them. Our probation officers consist of all classes in the community. The Honorable Judge Wm. E. Werner, Judge of the Court of Appeals, is one of my probation officers.

Q. How does the learned Judge perform his duties? A. Very well—he has had but one or two cases, and we have the clergyman of the church which he attends. We have a great many clergymen who are probation officers and some of the women who take an interest in this kind of work.

BY COMMISSIONER HAMILTON:

Q. Is Mr. Killup a paid probation officer? A. He is now, yes.

BY MR. MAYER:

Q. Just within a month? A. Appointed the 10th of May.

BY CHAIRMAN PAGE:

Q. You are placing him in charge of the volunteer probation officers, and the system of reporting to him was prescribed by you, was it? A. Yes, always heretofore— but now I say that we are just getting ready, and I want Mr. Killup to notify all these volunteer officers to report to him, and he will keep it. We have a card-index system. For instance, a boy is brought in and he is put on parole. We have that boy's record. He is brought in again, we have that. So that we know when that boy has been in. If he has been in three or four times, and it is necessary and he doesn't improve under probation, why then we can send him to the State Industrial School, or, to a certain age, to the Catholic Protectory at Buffalo, familiarly known as Father Baker's. We send a great many there up to the age of 14; no from 12 to—yes, they take them younger; but I really, unless they voluntarily go there, have no authority to commit until they are 12 years of age.

BY COMMISSIONER HAMILTON:

Q. Have you any house of detention or detention home for the children here? A. In this city? No, sir, none whatever, only what we call the Shelter here. That is maintained by the Society for the Prevention of Cruelty to Children. For instance, if a child is arrested by an officer on the street, his duty is to take him to the station, the police station, and there take his name and then immediately take him to the Shelter.

Q. So that all children arrested here are taken to the police station first? A. Well, they are supposed to be, yes; they are to be taken there and have a record taken, merely. Then, if the parents bail them out, the police captain is authorized to admit them to bail or parole them, otherwise they are taken immediately to the Shelter where they are kept and appear in court.

Q. Is that the course of action prescribed by ordinance or is it a mere custom of the Police Department? A. Well, yes, there is a law regarding juveniles that says they shall be taken to the station, to the police captain, first.

Q. Do you refer to an ordinance? A. No, I think there is a regular law in regard to that.

Q. A state law? A. I think there is; I think there is some requirement in regard to that. Mr. Killup, how is that, isn't it a regular law they shall take them to the station? It does not come under the city ordinance?

MR. KILLUP: No.

A. (Continuing.) No, I think it is a code provision. You will find it somewhere.

COMMISSIONER HAMILTON: It must be in the Charter.

CHAIRMAN PAGE: That a child shall not be detained in the police station?

COMMISSIONER HAMILTON: No, shall be.

THE WITNESS: When arrested, if an officer brings him in, he must, I think, take him to the police station, and there the captain or officer in charge can take bail or parole them. If not, then he must send him immediately to the Shelter. I think there is such a law.

MR. MAYER: Well, there is a general provision of law.

BY CHAIRMAN PAGE:

Q. What provision is there of law that a child shall not be detained in any police station? A. Well, I think there is also a provision that the children shall be kept separate and independent from the adults and other criminals. The same rule that requires that we shall hold a court in a separate room. I am very sure; I know that is our practice here, and I think that comes under the law.

Q. We found the practice was different in Buffalo. I didn't know whether there was any general provision of law. I think in New York it is under our charter; isn't it, Mr. Mayer?

MR. MAYER: Yes.

Q. (Continuing.) It is under our charter in New York. A. I rather think that that is the law here. I don't think it is under the Charter.

BY MR. MAYER:

Q. You mean taking to a detention house? A. No, that they shall,—when a child is picked up, for instance, a waif picked up and taken by an officer, he shall take him to the station and there the sergeant or captain can take bail, if a parent appears, or some other guardian, or he shall send him to the Shelter, what we call the Shelter here, that is, the rooms of the Society for the Prevention of Cruelty to Children.

Q. Now, Judge, did you want to supplement that statement? A. No. My Killup thinks that is the law and I know that is the way we do it here. There is a provision. I don't know but what I mentioned, in disposing of children under sixteen, I also can send them, you know, to the New York Training School at Hudson, and often do.

Q. For girls? A. For girls; yes, the girls. I think that is an amendment recently in regard to taking—I think it was amended within a year or two.

Q. Are you familiar with the bill for the City of Buffalo prepared by this Commission? A. No.

Q. Well, let me read you Section 92, which is supposed to be something of a departure or advance, because I desire to ask your opinion about it. Section 92 reads as follows: (Reads section.) In other words, this section seeks to deal with the child, wherever practicable, not as a criminal and not as being tried for crime, but rather as requiring the protection of the State. Now, does that section that I have just read strike you favorably? A. Very much so, for this reason, that we are virtually practicing that now, here. A great many times a child will be brought in, young, where maybe I have no authority to convict that child of a crime, unless it is shown that he knows the difference between right and wrong. He has got to be twelve years of age. Now, I will say to the parents, "This boy has got to be taken care of. Now, if you consent to this, you better send him to Father Baker's, up to Buffalo," or we will parole him, and oftentimes we parole him in care of some good person who will take him—whether it is law or not—if the parents consent. So now you have provided for just what I have often thought ought to have been provided and have given us some power to do it.

Q. Then, in other words, putting it generally, you favor any legislation looking to the treatment of the child not as a criminal—— A. Yes.

Q. (Continuing.) But rather as a ward of the State, that needs the State's protection? A. That is it.

Q. And I assume you would favor any legislation which, so far as was practicable, obviated branding the child with the record of a criminal? A. Yes, sir. Now I would like to ask you, what ages do you refer to?

Q. Well, those up to sixteen years of age. A. You don't limit the lower age of the child?

Q. No. A. Well, that's it. Now we often have a case where a child eight years of age is brought in for committing a burglary, and two or three of them will do as nice a job as an adult or an experienced person, and they sometimes are in more than once. They merely need a restraining hand, somebody to have some influence and guard over them. Now, what can I do with a child of eight years of age, under the present law, or ten years of age? Your provision there has provided for it. I think it is just what is needed. But that is not the law yet, is it? Is that an amendment to the charter of Buffalo?

Q. No; this is a new act, drawn by this Commission, passed by the Legislature, and approved by the Mayor of Buffalo, and now awaiting the signature of the Governor. A. Does it only apply to Buffalo?

Q. Confined only to Buffalo. A. I wish you would make it confined to the cities of the State. I don't think it would do any harm. It would do a great deal of good here.

Q. That is what we want to find out. Now, Judge, what would you think, instead of having a separate municipal court of civil jurisdiction and a separate police court, of having one court having both civil and criminal jurisdiction and practically amounting to a court of inferior civil and criminal jurisdiction, in which the judges could sit both on the criminal and the civil side, and having the judges devote all their time to the work of the court? A. Well, I haven't considered that question, but, at the first impression, I don't think I would favor that. I think a criminal court, as I have always been brought up,—of course it has been a great many years, we have always had the criminal courts and the civil courts. Now, the criminal law and the civil law cover a great deal of ground, and when you take some one that is brought up in the criminal and had that criminal practice, he is acquainted with that, whereas he might not be so acquainted with the civil, and the more so, if he is a civil judge, he is not as informed. I have seen a great many people who might be familiar with the civil law. And then there might be one other objection that I just think of; that is, that there are so many cases where people try to use the criminal law to collect a debt; and I find, many a time, that I have to say, "This case is not a case for the criminal court; it is a case for the municipal court, civil court. If it is a wrong, you can get a body execution there, but it is really a civil action; it is not a criminal action."

Q. Well, in your own case, were you practicing at the civil bar? A. Mainly, yes, but I was brought up in a criminal lawyer's office. I was somewhat in the criminal law as well as the civil. Here we do not have it such as in New York City, where they have made some specialty,— somebody that is called a corporation lawyer, for instance. Ours here is a general practice.

Q. What I am getting at is, for instance, from your own experience would you feel that, if you got a greater variety, it would be useful to your judicial development, if you had an opportunity of sitting, say two months, on the criminal side, and perhaps a month on the civil side? A. Oh, we can do it, we have always been in the civil practice, more so than in the criminal, but yet, as I say, we have had a good deal of criminal practice.

Q. Well, if you had such a court as that, might it not, for instance, relieve the single police justice, whoever he was? A. Well, the time will come in this city, probably, when they will have to have more than one, but heretofore, however, a man—it requires the attention of one, I assure you, now to take care of the business, especially the juvenile as well as the adult courts. I think the time will come when you will have to have another one who will act in the City of Rochester, one of them will act as juvenile court judge and also will have the authority of police judge and conduct cases. For instance, if a man is arraigned in the Police Court and he desires a trial set down for a certain day, why you can say, "Take this case to the other judge," just as you would in the county or supreme court, as long as you only have one jurisdiction over the whole city. I understand in New York you have districts and there is a police judge for a certain district as well as of the lower civil courts. It used to be when I was there,—I was admitted in New York and I was there seven years.

Q. Well, the judges rotate, however. A. Yes, you have got something new to me there; I never knew, until I saw it in the paper, that they get a vacation of two weeks and then serve two weeks. We can hardly get a vacation at all here.

Q. Well, now, suppose you had a court consisting of at least three members, with jurisdiction of civil and criminal cases, wouldn't that allow the courts elasticity in the assignment of the men, the arrangement as to the work? A. Well, I am not prepared to answer that. I think that the time will come when in the City of Rochester there will have to be more judges on the civil business as well as the criminal. In fact, I understand our courts, our municipal court, is pretty well occupied with business, two judges are kept busy.

Q. Well, now, have you thought of anything that you would like to suggest to the Commission, in the way of change of the law or improvement, or any suggestion? A. Well, I have thought of two ways to relieve the Police Court. In fact, I have to, when I take a vacation, call on one of the judges of the Municipal Court. The law provides that they shall take my place, whenever I am out of town or disqualified from acting in a case or ill. Now that is putting onto the work of the Municipal Court, it might put on, a great deal of extra work, and I have thought that there ought to be a bill passed in the Legislature, empowering, say, the mayor of the city to appoint somebody to take the place of the Police Judge while on vacation, or while ill, if he should be ill, or disqualified. On the other hand, I have thought that this city now really requires two police judges, or will in time. One of them should have the jurisdiction of the Juvenile Court, or *vice versa;* have, both, the same jurisdiction as police judges, but one of them pays attention to the Juvenile Court. My idea of that is that, a man who is familiar with the Juvenile Court, it takes some little time to acquire that knowledge of the manner of conducting the Juvenile Court. No man can step in there at first and know just exactly what to do until he has had experience. In Denver, I understand, they have one Mr. Lindsay there, who is the juvenile court judge, with the same authority as the Supreme Court over both the person and property of the minor. Here, if they do not come to that in this State—in the City of Rochester, I think the time will come when they will have two, who, as I say, can alternate, or let one be assigned to the Juve-Court, and then assist in the Police Court business when required.

Q. Well, I would like to call your attention to Section 9 of the so-called Buffalo Court Bill, that provides as follows: (Reads Section.) Now, would you think it desirable to give to your local legislative body the authority to add, from time to time, as your city develops, additional judges, while at the same time, you understand, that would not divest the Legislature of its power, but——
A. No, but I can see where questions might arise in such a case as that, if the Common Council,—questions might arise, depending a good deal, maybe, on the complexion of the Council.

Q. That is true, of course. A. (Continuing.) But I think that the judges should not be under any obligation, particularly, to any appointing power, unless temporarily.

Q. Well, this does not involve appointment, it merely confers authority upon the local body to provide for additional judges. A. Yes, recommend their election.

Q. Well, to make additional places. A. Yes.

Q. The question is whether it is not desirable to confer that power so that the city can avail of it, if it pleases, and thus save constant going to Albany for a new legislation to provide for increased service? A. Well, I must say that I am not in a position to answer that question. We have had here members of the Legislature, and the Legislature has been very fair, I think. I sometimes think that when you get it down to a local question, there would be more trouble with a local question.

Q. Then, in other words, you feel more inclined, as a permanent point of view, to trust the Legislature. A. Yes, it seems to me that is my first impression. I think, when you find that it is necessary to have the additional help, you can go to the Legislature and give them power to elect an additional judge.

BY COMMISSIONER FRANCIS:

Q. It is best to keep free from local partisanship. A. I rather think so, because you must remember that a judge of the lower courts often has many visits from aldermen.

BY COMMISSIONERS HAMILTON:

Q. Judge, are arrests made here customarily for drunkenness, unaccompanied by disorderly conduct? A. Oh, yes; yes. I don't want to criticise anybody, but we have a great many cases of arrests for drunkenness, and there are a great many first offenses.

Q. You spoke of cases of drunkenness in connection with your probation work? A. Yes.

Q. Are those partly cases of drunkenness that were not accompanied by disorderly conduct? A. Well, yes. I have placed with the probation officers men who needed someone to guard over their conduct. They are men that provide for their families, generally, but will spend their salaries in liquor, and if I can place him under a probation officer, and have him report to him, it oftentimes keeps him in check, and also, he dare not get drunk during that time, because he knows, if he does, the probation officer will bring him in for sentence. You understand, when we put them on probation, they are still under the jurisdiction of the Court?

Q. Certainly. A. The sentence is merely suspended. I don't place so many, but oftentimes there is a case when even the wife, in complaining, will ask that the defendant be placed on probation, because she thinks that will remedy the evil. I am sorry that it has got out that the city of Rochester has more drunkenness, in proportion to its population, than other cities. Now, the fact of it is, we have, I think, the cleanest city in the State, and they will bring them in, the officers. The police force is very efficient, and they will bring in a great many cases that are on our docket, in which I suspend judgment, for they are first offenses; but that is in the discretion of the officers entirely. It might be abused in other cities, but here it is merely their discretionary power. But when they come into court, as to-day, for instance, a large number were first offenses, and that is the rule, a great many of them. People from out of town will come in; they are brought in here, and they are really tramps or vagrants, people going through the city, and they will get drunk. They are brought in, kept in the station over night and sobered up by morning, and we let them go, let them go on, and we don't railroad them off without giving them a chance to be heard. I think I have disposed of a calendar of one hundred and twenty-five in one morning, and, every man, the charge has been read to him, he has been given an opportunity to plead, and demand an adjournment, and to be heard. But of course those who plead guilty are disposed of very quickly, and we can dispose of a great many cases. The trouble is in the trials; that takes up the time of the Court, as you all know who are lawyers, a great many times, in the cases that we give the election to have a trial, and they have a trial there the same as they would have in the County Court. When I took this office I found that it was qualified, we had our officers, we had our clerks and assistants, and I maintained that the conduct, the decorum of that office, should be as good as if it were a court of sessions or the County Court in the City of Rochester, or the Court of Sessions in New York. Now, for instance, we give them all the chance. We don't run it as some police courts are run—whether it is in New York or Buffalo, I don't know— but I lived in New York seven years, I was admitted to the bar there, and I knew years ago something about the manner in which it was done. I have no criticisms to make at all, only this, that we try to give them all a hearing and see that no harm is done, that the rights of everyone are protected. I would be very glad to have this Commission go over, if you are going to stay over, to-morrow morning. We open court at 9.30. But I would like you, in any event, to go this afternoon, if you have time, up to the police station, and they will show you the workings. The clerks will be there and show you the manner in which we conduct this system, our court system, and it can be explained to you by the other officers here.

BY COMMISSIONER FRANCIS:

Q. What is the population of Rochester? A. We claim now 215,000. 200,000 is what we always claimed, but they say now we have probably got up to 215,000. Of course, Buffalo has twice our population.

BY COMMISSIONER HAMILTON:

Q. Have you any writ or process that you use in practise in your court instead of a warrant, where you are doubtful about the advisability of issuing a warrant? A. We have no process, only I issue what I call a "Notify".

Q. What? A. No, we issue the warrant, but instead of bringing a man in under arrest, we mark that warrant "Notify", and that simply is to notify him to appear in court.

BY MR. MAYER:

Q. It is in the nature of a summons? A. It is in the nature of a summons, but if he does not appear in reply— it is merely a matter of courtesy to give that man an opportunity to come in himself in court.

BY COMMISSIONER HAMILTON:

Q. Do you think you should have the power, if some process should be provided for, to make it compulsory for him to appear in such case?

CHAIRMAN PAGE: A summons.

A. That is really a warrant, a man has to make a complaint first, every warrant has to be founded upon a complaint sworn to, and you know no person—we cannot even try an intoxication case without a complaint being filed. That has been decided by the Appellate Division, and so if a man makes a complaint against a party here in the city, of course, a business man or anyone that we do not think it is necessary to arrest, no one is going to escape, we will mark the warrant "Notify", and the officer will go to him, read the warrant to him, and ask him to appear in court the next morning. Now, if he fails to appear after that courtesy is shown him, we will take the word "Notify" off the warrant, and send out and bring him in. That is the way we do it.

BY CHAIRMAN PAGE:

Q. Then in practise, you have found that some method of bringing a man in court other than by warrant for his arrest is very desirable? A. Oh, very; very.

Q. Wouldn't it be better if we provided by law for some process in the shape of a summons that could be served upon a man and make it a legal procedure? A. Yes, sir.

Q. That is, legalize the process that you have been——
A. Yes, I think that would be a good thing. Of course, all I can do now, I say, "Why, here is a man arrested, a well known business man," maybe for some trifling offense, or some accident, or speeding, or something of that kind; why, we just mark on the warrant "Notify", and the officer goes and notifies him and asks him to appear in court the next morning.

BY MR. MAYER:

Q. Let me call your attention in that connection to Section 69 of the so-called Buffalo Court Bill, which I will read, and then ask you whether this meets with your approval. (Reads section.) A. Well, now then, I want to ask a question before I answer it. If, on that investigation, we find that a crime has been committed, then would a warrant issue?

Q. Then and there. A. Then and there?

Q. Yes. A. Well, we now carry out that provision in

the manner of subpoenaing, what we call a John Doe proceeding.

Q. Yes. A. That is, we send out subpoenas and bring
in parties, and have a closed examination, do not allow the
public in, you might say, nor the attorneys, merely ask
witnesses certain questions, then upon that we issue a
warrant.

Q. Don't you think this provision of Section 69 would
meet your plan of putting—— A. That would do, but I
am afraid we would be called upon to issue a good many
of them.

Q. Well, you would not have to? A. No, we would not
have to, but there are so many people we would turn down,
as we say.

Q. Well, wouldn't it be very much better to have, as
suggested by the chairman of the Commission, a method
which was unquestionably sanctioned by statute, to accomplish the very thing that you are seeking to accomplish
with the so-called "Notify"? A. Yes, I think we ought to
have some other, and I think that process would be a good
thing, but, as I say, it would make more work.

Q. Well, of course, that may be. A. (Continuing.) It
would necessarily make more work because there are a
great many people who come in now to the clerks and
prosecuting attorney. You see we have here a prosecuting
attorney that is appointed by the District Attorney.

Q. Who attends at the Police Court? A. At the Police
Court. He is deputy assistant district attorney of the
county. He is appointed there and his business is there to
see and investigate this.

Q. And you find his presence, I assume, very useful? A.

Useful? Why, we couldn't get along without him. In fact, we corrected that office—it was appointed, just as some student would be appointed in there years ago, but since I have been in office, we have had the Legislature pass an act authorizing the District Attorney to appoint, and they have given us qualified attorneys, young men, generally, but it has been a great school. Now, the present first assistant district attorney was my first officer under that, assistant in the Police Court, and the second assistant district attorney also followed him, and now we have another assistant, Mr. Hogan.

Q. He, in due course, I suppose, will move up? A. Yes, those officers, I tell them, have been initiated in my court, educated there, and now they are the first officers of the District Attorney's office, in the County. I am very glad to say that their record is such that I am very proud of them; I am very proud.

BY COMMISSIONER FRANCIS:

Q. What time do you close court on Saturday, as a rule? A. It is a legal holiday.

Q. In the morning? A. Yes, only up to 12.

Q. And a person unable to get bail must stay in a cell until Monday morning? A. Oh, no; oh, no; the police captain has a right, as I let them take that bail as a rule, and if not, I am within call, and if I am at——

BY CHAIRMAN PAGE:

Q. No, the question was, suppose a man cannot get bail? A. Oh, if he cannot get bail, of course he cannot avoid trial.

Q. He has to stay in jail if he is arrested at one o'clock Saturday afternoon, and stays there until nine o'clock

Monday morning? A. Yes, unless he gives bail, or unless they parole him, if it is a misdemeanor. It is according to who he is. The police captain generally acts in that respect, if he is arrested for a misdemeanor. If it is a felony, why I fix the bail.

Q. Does the police captain have power to parole a man? A. They take bail.

Q. I know, but you said take bail or parole? A. Or they put up temporary bail.

Q. You say, depending upon who he is. If it was a man that had a proper acquaintance with the police captain, the order would be parole without bail? A. I don't think that they have any authority to parole.. I think they merely have got to fix bail.

Q. Well, I misunderstood you. A. Well, they oftentimes will communicate with me, say, "Here is So-and-so." "Well, will you vouch for this man being here; do you know him; who is he?" And if that is so, I often say, "Well, we will parole him until Monday morning." For instance, a reputable attorney appears for a client, and he says, "This man is brought here"—they communicate with me—and I say, "Mr. So-and-so, will you say that man will be here? Now, you are known to me, but I don't know the defendant"—for a misdemeanor.

BY COMMISSIONER MURPHY:

Q. Paroled in the custody of counsel? A. Of the attorney. We get around that very nicely. This morning court, I don't think much of it myself, because I find so many cases now where drunken people are brought in, and they are not really sober when arraigned, and I won't have them in court drunk, and I generally send them back and tell

them, "When you are sober we will have you arraigned."
A man arrested in the night or early in the morning doesn't
get sober much before nine o'clock in the morning. I sometimes think that that is an accommodation for drunken
people; the sunrise courts, as they call them, merely an
accommodation for the drunks, a great portion, because
if it is a man that is not accustomed to getting drunk, he
can very readily get out, and very readily find somebody
to appear for him, where he can give bail. That is the
reason why I have never been in favor of sunrise courts.

BY COMMISSIONER HAMILTON:

Q. You don't see any necessity for any court sitting any
earlier in the morning than the opening of the Police Court?
A. No, sir; I am opening the court at 9.30 in the morning,
and I think that is giving—it is done then for the accommodation of lawyers who will come in and maybe adjourn
a case, or it will be discharged. But if a man is brought
in for intoxication, why he is not as a rule fit to go to
business at seven or eight o'clock in the morning. If he
is, and his employer wants him, why let him come up and
give bail for him.

BY COMMISSIONER FRANCIS:

Q. What is the extent of your vacation period, during
the year? A. Well, sir, the most I have had was last year,
and that was one month. Other years—the year before,
I think I had about a week or two. Before that I have
had about two weeks. The other courts in the city take
a longer period. I hoped that I could manage to have a
month vacation in a year, at least.

Q. You find the work in your court requires your having

a vacation? A. Yes, I think the work I am doing here and the constant attendance, if I had not been a man of physical ability, and also of good health—I think it has worn on me, but fortunately for me, in the summer time I have a cottage at the lake, where I go every night and come up every morning. We have arrangements so that we are only a few miles from the lake. That has, I think, been a great help to me.

———

DELBERT C. HEBBARD, called as a witness, having been duly sworn, testified as follows:

BY MR. MAYER:

Q. Judge, you are one of the judges of the Municipal Court? A. Yes.

Q. And what is the name of your associate? A. John M. Murphy.

Q. The judges of that court, I assume, are required to be members of the bar? A. Yes.

Q. And how long? A. I think the last is five years.

Q. What is the salary, please? A. Three thousand dollars a year.

Q. And are you permitted to practice? A. We are.

Q. And you hold court five days a week, I assume? A. Six days.

Q. Saturdays included? A. Saturday forenoon.

Q. And you alternate, do you? A. Yes, that is the general practice. We sometimes—we sit when the business requires it; we run double, both courts, when required.

Q. You have jurisdiction in bastardy cases? A. We do.

Q. Have you any idea how many cases you have a year, bastardy cases? A. Not more than five or six that are really tried out. A great many of them are brought in, but are settled before, so that we do not have to render any determination.

Q. How many times do you have to sit in the course of a year in bastardy cases? A. Those bastardy cases will average from three to four days apiece.

Q. When they occur? A. When they occur, not possibly whole days, but they will spoil three or four days.

Q. That is, you mean a bastardy case will do that? A. Yes, one will do that, it will run over; possibly that is a little too long, but we rarely finish one in one day.

Q. And they are usually bitterly contested? A. Yes, they are.

Q. When they are contested? A. When they are contested.

Q. And both of you Municipal Court Judges must sit, under the provisions of your charter? A. Yes.

Q. So that during that time the regular civil business must wait? A. Oh, yes; yes.

Q. Well, now; how many such trials have you had in the past year; I understand you to say you have had five or six? A. I should think that would cover it; yes.

Q. Well, are the other cases settled between the parties, or—— A. Settled.

Q. (Continuing.) Or with the overseer? A. With the overseer of the poor.

Q. Well now, do you think your court should have jurisdiction in these cases? A. Personally, I do not care. It seems a peculiar sort of matter of foreign substances, though, to have that kind of a case in a civil court.

Q. I am speaking now not so much of the individual feeling about it, but the principle involved? A. That is the only thing. It has always seemed to me as though those cases were out of place in a civil court, in a purely civil court.

Q. Now we have understood, I don't know whether correctly or not, that the business of your court is very rapidly growing? What is the condition? A. It is growing all the while. The last six years the number of litigated cases that have actually been tried before me has increased a third.

Q. What would you say was the total number of cases in the Municipal Court for the year 1908? A. Do you mean litigated cases?

Q. Yes? A. Between four and five hundred.

Q. And how many cases altogether have come before you in one form or another? A. I could not tell you, but it is away up in the thousands.

Q. Have you an annual report that you make? A. No, we make no annual report.

Q. Is there any clerk of your court that could get those data for us? A. Yes. It would be quite a job. I have gotten them together each year for myself, but I don't know that those would be of any assistance to you, it would be simply what I have charge of myself. Well, there is pending over there all the while in the neighborhood of 300 cases. Our daily calendars run from fifty to eighty or ninety cases a day.

Q. Well, that means summary proceedings? A. Everything.

Q. Defaults, issues joined—— A. Adjournments.

Q. (Continuing.) Adjournments and trials? A. Yes. Our two calendars, what we call the original and the adjourned calendars, will run from—some days it won't be eighty, but that is about the way it runs.

Q. Do you have many jury trials? A. We have a great many called but very few tried. In the last month there have been at least twenty jury cases called. I have tried one and I think Judge Murphy has tried three.

Q. Are you elected by the whole city? A. We are.

Q. You run then on a general city ticket? A. Yes.

MR. MAYER: Well, if you would let the Commission have such statistics as you are able, we should be very much obliged.

BY CHAIRMAN PAGE:

Q. Judge, I do not quite understand what you mean when you say a great many jury cases are called, but few are tried. Do you mean they are settled, or what? A. I don't know what becomes of them, but they call the jury, pay for the jury, it costs them $5.25, and they are set down, and when we call the calendar that morning, we discover that the jury case has been disposed of.

Q. How frequently do you hold jury trials? A. Last week we had four of them down.

Q. No, but I mean, do you have some particular days in the month for jury cases? A. No, we make no distinction that way. Whenever the attorneys and the parties agree upon a day, if there is nothing on our calendar to conflict with a jury trial on that day, it is put down for that day. Then it takes precedence over all other matters that may come on the calendar on that day, it is the first case on the calendar.

BY MR. MAYER:

Q. Well, the call for a jury trial is not infrequently a method of delay, I presume. A. Well, it would seem to work for that purpose. I think possibly that is one method.

Q. You have probably heard the questions that I asked Judge Chadsey as to a court of inferior civil and criminal jurisdiction? A. Yes.

Q. What is your view of such a court for this city? A. I should not be in favor of such an arrangement in this city, for this reason: We all know that a great many men are elected to do civil work, that are well enough for the—I don't know what you may call it, the duties of criminal—running a criminal court. I think I speak knowingly upon that subject, and I believe that I would not be a good man, I don't think the people of this city would be getting what they ought to get, if I were called upon to run a police court. Now, I have done it, and do it every year, do it in the absence of Judge Chadsey. That is the feeling I have of my limitations upon that work. I think the attorneys of this city would be opposed to it. That is really my view on that.

Q. Well how would you feel about holding court on the civil side three months, or perhaps all the year except one month? A. Why, when duty required it I would feel that I could run and would run the Police Court for a month or for any length of time, but it strikes me that a person who has not been in touch with that work, in a city of this size, would be ill at ease for the month that he is there. That is the way it has always worked upon me. In other words, a man who is presiding for a short period of time would be wholly at the mercy of his own guesses and the information that would be given him. He would not be in touch with the situation at all, wouldn't be able to deal competently with the so-called police court characters. He would not be familiar with them. He would be plodding away in a field where a man who knew the situation would be of much more value to the city and render much more, it seems to me, much more, valuable service.

Q. Has there been some agitation here for an additional Municipal Court Judge. A. I believe the Bar Association had that agitation up for a while, yes.

Q. On the ground of the amount of business? A. Yes.

Q. The Municipal Court judges are elected for six years? A. Yes.

BY COMMISSIONER FRANCIS:

Q. Is the calendar pretty well crowded now? A. Yesterday I think there were between 60 and 70 cases.

Q. Are you far behind in the trials; I mean by that is there a large number of cases on the calendar—— A. I think not.

BY COMMISSIONER HAMILTON:

Q. How long does it take a case to reach trial now? A. So far as the as the Municipal Court proper is concerned, any case can be tried within three days, that is my recollection of it.

BY MR. MAYER:

Q. What do you mean by municipal court proper, Judge?
A. I mean the court itself. Now the methods of adjournment, the methods of getting adjournment under the discretionary power we now have, are working at white-heat in some quarters. A man can come in with such a reasonable excuse for an adjournment that to force him to trial and render judgment against him would make proper grounds for a reversal of judgment, and when attorneys are not ready for trial they get their adjournment. And in a great many—sometimes for a week or two at a time we are congested, but when we are we double up and it isn't but a little while before everything is cleaned up.

Q. Well suppose both parties desire to have a speedy trial, they could have it within three days? A. They can have it within one day.

BY CHAIRMAN PAGE:

Q. Well, now, what do you mean by that? The summons is issued and returned for pleading? A. Yes.

Q. Now, if a man comes in and both sides are ready, the case can be tried that day or the next day? A. Yes, it could be. Of course, we alternate over there, or are supposed to alternate. But very often I am—we are both there always every morning and when that situation arises if there is any necessity for the trial of a case that morning it can be tried that morning.

Q. Well, that could be done if there were a hundred thousand cases on the calendar? A. Yes, sir.

Q. That doesn't convey much information to my mind. What we are trying to find out is whether you have any accumulation of untried cases? A. Why, I presume there are in the neighborhood of three hundred cases now pending in the Municipal Court.

Q. Yes? A. (Continuing.) That are untried now. How many of those will ever come to trial I don't know; a very small percentage of them.

BY COMMISSIONER HAMILTON:

Q. You mean to say, as I understand, that your day calendars habitually go to pieces to such an extent that when both persons are ready for trial you can arrange without delay? A. That is generally so, and if they do not, the other judge is generally around somewheres and if there is any need of it the cases can be tried.

BY CHAIRMAN PAGE:

Q. Now, you made use of the expression "the judges alternate?" A. Every other day, we sit every other day, that is actually engaged in the trial of actions every other day.

BY MR. MAYER:

Q. And the days you are not sitting I suppose you are practicing professionally, or trying to, anyway? A. Sometimes. Sometimes we get matters on the days on which we conduct trials that really require our attention next day. I got two of them yesterday.

Q. I suppose some of these adjournments are due to the fact that the defendant perhaps is delaying the plaintiff and it is carried along? A. Oh yes.

Q. What is your own opinion as to the desirability of having judges devote themselves entirely to judicial work, assuming, of course, that they are adequately paid? A. I think the city would get better service if that was done. I don't think there is any question about that.

Q. Now, as a matter of fact, the judges are constantly coming in professional contact with the lawyers who appear before them, I assume? A. Yes.

Q. And the salary, I suppose, you regard as inadequate for a man to devote all his time to judicial work? A. Well, with the present cost of things it is a close run, that has been my experience.

Q. Would you think it would be better if the judges were required to devote their entire time to their work? A. I think it would be better for the service.

Q. I mean better for the people? A. I think, possibly, it would not be so well for the Judge.

Q. No? A. (Continuing.) Although the income we have been able to get from our practice, that I have been able to get, from the time that I can devote to it, is exceedingly small. I make that perfectly frank statement.

Q. In other words, I suppose you find that people want lawyers that will devote their time to their clients' business? A. No, I don't mean that, I mean that I cannot give to law practice such time as would make it either safe or profitable, and do the work of the Municipal Court. That is what I mean.

Q. I see. Do you think that reflects Judge Murphy's view, too? A. Yes, I am sure it does. The easy matters that come in we attend to if we can. Anything that is hard is turned over. That has been my experience.

BY CHAIRMAN PAGE:

Q. How many hours a day does the Court sit? A. I

started in yesterday at ten o'clock and got through last night at a quarter of six.

Q. Is that an exceptional day? A. Yes, sir; five o'clock we usually get through.

BY MR. MAYER:

Q. Do you ordinarily sit from ten to five? A. Yes, sir.

Q. With an hour for recess, I suppose? A. Oh, we take longer, I quit any time before one and come back at half-past two. That rule I think was made originally for the accommodation of the attorneys. That lets our court convene half an hour after the other courts convene, so that if they have any motions or work at the opening of the other courts, that can be done before they have to get back for trials.

Q. You mean in the afternoon or both morning and afternoon? A. Come in the afternoon, we begin the same time in the morning.

Q. So that such a day, from ten to five, even with that extended recess, is practically a day wholly devoted by you to your court work? A. Oh, yes; yes.

Q. To your judicial work? A. Nothing can be done in this short intermission. Of course our jurisdiction is so large now that important questions are started, and final consideration of the proofs and the law after the cases are in, require a great deal of time if it is properly disposed of.

Q. You have jurisdiction up to two thousand dollars? A. Yes, sir.

BY COMMISSIONER HAMILTON:

Q. How long has your jurisdiction been up to two thousand dollars? A. What was the date, at the time of the adoption of the renewed charter—two years ago; it had been fifteen hundred for some time before that; two years ago last January.

BY MR. MAYER:

Q. That extended jurisdiction came with the charter of the City of Rochester? A. With the charter of the City of Rochester.

BY CHAIRMAN PAGE:

Q. Do you have a good many cases over a thousand dollars? A. Oh, yes; yes; a great many of the minor negligence cases are tried there now, those less than two thousand dollars, up to two thousand dollars, those are usually tried before a jury.

BY COMMISSIONER HAMILTON:

Q. Usually with a jury? A. Usually.

BY MR. MAYER:

Q. Well, I wish very much that you might be able to furnish us with a general outline of statistics, showing the total number of cases, if it were possible, and the cases tried, and any cases tried by jury, for, say one year, 1908, if that could be done? A. Well, that can be done. You would not want it to-day, would you?

MR. MAYER: Oh, any time.

BY CHAIRMAN PAGE:

Q. Could you give it to us to-morrow morning? A. Well, perhaps sometime to-morrow. It depends on how busy we are over there. There is no summary at the end of the docket. Every one of those cases, no matter what is done with it, a complete record is made.

BY MR. MAYER:

Q. Well, if that is not practicable, if you cannot get it for us by then, if you would have it prepared and let Assemblyman Phillips have it, he will be good enough to forward it? A. I prefer to have it right, make it correct, if we are going to make it at all. I can make an approximation. Last year I tried myself something like two hundred and fifty litigated cases. Now some of those cases took—I could try two or three of them in a day. Some of them took as many as eight or nine days, not right straight along, but they took up eight or nine days, started and adjourned, and I mean that eight or nine full days. A great many of them took four or five days. Yesterday we had a jury trial in the morning and tried two other cases in the afternoon, so we disposed of three yesterday.

BY CHAIRMAN PAGE:

Q. Your juries you obtain from the list of the Commissioner of Jurors? A. Yes, sir.

———

JOHN H. CHADSEY resumed the stand and testified as follows:

If the Commission please, I would like to correct one statement. Prosecuting Attorney Hogan states our jury trials have averaged the last year only one a month, about one a month. There have not been over twelve or so in a year, the last year. Now you are ready to adjourn, I see. Here is a statement prepared by the clerk, who is present, that will tell you the number of cases that we have had (handing statement to counsel).

ROY P. CHADSEY, called as a witness, having been duly sworn, testified as follows:

BY MR. MAYER:

Q. Have you prepared a schedule showing a summary of the work done by the Police Court for the year 1908? A. That schedule shows the number of cases, convictions, and felonies and held for the Supreme Court. That statement was prepared for the year 1908 by the Prosecuting Attorney and myself, for the special benefit of the District Attorney's office, but I brought it over here simply as a memorandum.

Q. Well, I will read this right into the record at this point (reading):

POLICE COURT.

SCHEDULE "D."

"This schedule is a summary of the work done by this office in the prosecution of criminal cases in the Police Court of the City of Rochester during the year 1908":

Number of cases in which a representative of this office appeared	11,099
Number of convictions in cases in which the District Attorney's office appeared	4,697
Number of trials in which this office appeared	525
Number of preliminary examinations in which this office was represented	170
Number of defendants held to await the action of the Supreme Court in cases where this office was represented	261

Q. The words "a representative of this office," which appear in the schedule just read, mean the District Attorney's office, do they? A. The District Attorney. That includes every case, because he is there for every case.

Q. Are these all Police Court cases? A. All Police Court cases, for the year 1908, appearances.

Q. Well, now, there were 11,099; convictions, 4,697; trials, 525; preliminary examinations, 170; number of defendants held to await the action of the Supreme Court, 261. The schedule just read in evidence, however, does not show the disposition of cases in which the District Attorney did not appear, does it? A. Why, that includes everything. You understand the District Attorney appears, although there might be an attorney appear for the prosecution and the District Attorney will sit with him. But that includes every case, taken from the docket, the book.

Q. You say your total here is 11,099. Now all your other data together only makes perhaps six thousand? A. That of course does not include a man who pleads guilty and judgment suspended. There is a record conviction. There may be lots of men discharged, cases withdrawn. That is not down here. This 11,099 means every case that is on the docket.

Q. I understand, but what we are trying to get at is how the 11,099 are disposed of. Can you get that for us? A. We can by referring to the books, we can show just exactly.

Q. I mean can you get us up a summary statement? A. Do you want to know in every case? (Referring to paper.) There were 8,125 male arrests for 1908 and 560 female arrests, making a total of 8,635 arrests during the year;

in the Children's Court there were 553; and that includes the number of arrests. Of course, this 11,099 includes cases that are adjourned. This is simply the appearances, the adjourned calendar of the regular docket, that includes every appearance in which the prosecuting attorney has appeared.

Q. Then that 11,099 may involve a repetition of the same cases? A. Oh, yes; yes, that may be. Yes, that's it. The District Attorney appears one day, a case is adjourned to a week from to-day, he appears on that day the same. So the schedule is made up to show how many times he appeared.

Q. It is greater than the total number of cases? A. Yes, the total number of cases would be 8,685 arrests.

Q. Male and female? A. Male and female, and that will show the number of cases on the docket.

Q. That is what we are trying to get at? A. Yes.

Q. Will you obtain that for us? A. I can get you from the Police Department a detailed statement of the arrests, convictions and everything else.

Q. Can you have that this afternoon? A. I think so.

Q. Now, you are the Police Court Clerk? A. Yes, sir.

Q. And you are a confidential appointee of the Judge? A. Yes, sir.

Q. Now, what records do you keep? A. We have the Police Court docket. That docket is prepared, for instance the Police Department, each precinct station has a card system, which they call the arrest blotter. A man is brought in by a policeman and charged with public intoxication. His charge is put down and name, and if it is a case of felony his pedigree is taken. That card is sent to the headquarters, every morning, and the arrests during the night—for instance, we will say all the precincts make forty arrests, those forty arrests are made out. The clerk, the deputy clerk who has charge of the docket, when he comes in in the morning, he gets these cards, which are made out in duplicate; one set to go to our investigator, which we call our court attendant, the other set to the deputy clerk. He takes that up and writes down those charges on the Judge's criminal docket. The Judge has that docket before him in the morning. The deputy clerk has the blotter. The investigator has the duplicate set. He takes that duplicate set, takes the name of every man, looks up in his card index system which he has, looks up his record, and makes out a statement to hand to the Judge before he is ready for court in the morning. The Judge has that statement showing the man's previous record before him, for every man that is on that docket, if he has a record at all. And the Judge, after disposition of the case, marks the disposition on the docket, and the clerk, after court is over, writes up the book, of course, for the next day and also puts down the adjourned cases. We have an adjournment book that we keep, of course; the attorney, the investigator and the clerk have the adjournment book.

Q. Are those books alphabetically indexed? A. No, sir.

Q. Suppose I wanted to find out when John Brown had been arrested or arraigned before the Court? A. Just step in the investigator's office and have the card index system and he can tell you in two minutes.

Q. I see. Your card index works out so that you may have quick reference? A. Yes, if a man comes up and says, "I want to get a record," for instance the District

Attorney often calls me up and says, "I want to get the record of John Doe, his criminal record," just go to the card index and it is down there; there is his record for the last two years. He might have eight convictions against him, and I advise the District Attorney of that fact. We have only had that card index system, I think——

BY COMMISSIONER FRANCIS:

Q. Two years? A. (Continuing) Two or three years, a little over two years. But previous to that we had another system, which we used to keep, but we didn't think it as good as this card index system.

BY CHAIRMAN PAGE:

Q. What is this system or index, if it isn't alphabetical? Have you any marks or any other thing? A. Why, this police blotter, arrest blotter system, is a new system. We used to have what we called a police night book. That is, every charge of arrest they would bring to the captain, the sergeant, and he would write the charge in the night book and we would transfer that to the Judge's docket in the morning. Now we have just the arrest blotter. We have no index, that is, the books are not indexed alphabetically, so if we want to know what day John Doe was arrested we refer strictly to the card index system.

Q. I know, but how would you get at it in the card index system, what kind of an index have you got to that? A. Well, they are all, each, A, B, C, D, like in a card index system.

Q. Well, then it is alphabetical, that is all? A. That is alphabetical, the card index system is alphabetical. I thought you meant our docket.

Q. No, I understood you to say that, by a system you had which was not alphabetical, you could arrive at this information immediately? A. Oh, no.

BY MR. MAYER:

Q. Have you a summary of the fines and forfeitures? A. Yes, here it is, for the year 1908. (Handing to counsel.)

Q. What is meant by forfeitures? A. For instance, a man will leave twenty-five dollars bail for his appearance in court and he fails to show up; under our charter that is forfeited to the Police Pension Fund.

MR. MAYER: I will read this in the record at this point. (Reading.)

POLICE COURT CLERK'S OFFICE,
ROCHESTER, N. Y., January 4th, 1909.

Hon. HIRAM H. EDGERTON,
    Mayor of the City of Rochester.

Dear Sir:

I have the honor to report the following sums received by me as clerk of the Police Court of the City of Rochester during the year 1908, for fines, forfeitures and other sums, as follows:

	Fines.	Forfeitures.
January	$490.00	$338.00
February	162.00	96.70
March	193.00	383.00
April	302.00	422.95
May	472.00	317.00
June	375.00	358.00
July	494.00	354.26
August	518.00	446.85

	Fines.	Forfeitures.
September	490.00	382.27
October	799.00	622.23
November	434.00	605.00
December	400.90	256.00
Total	$5,129.90	$4,582.26
Fines paid at Penitentiary	1,615.00	
Total fines	6,744.90	
Forfeitures	4,582.26	

Total fines and forfeitures.. $11,327.16

Auction sale, December 1st, 1908, receipts.... $204.01

Less expenses 11.50

Net receipts $192.51

Money left by prisoners as evidence and property uncalled for and unclaimed 35.39

227.90

Total receipts during year 1908 .... $11,555.06

Respectfully submitted,

POLICE COURT CLERK.

CHAIRMAN PAGE: The Commission will stand in recess to 2:30.

Adjournment to 2:30 P. M.

ROCHESTER, N. Y., Friday, May 21, 1909.

2:30 P. M.

The Commission met pursuant to adjournment.

DELBERT C. HEBBARD, recalled, testified as follows:

BY MR. MAYER:

Q. Judge Hebbard, I think you want to make a correction? A. In giving the figures of the actual trials this morning, for last year, I stated I thought I had tried nearly three hundred. That includes all the cases that were tried there in our court last year. There were two hundred and ninety-six actually litigated cases. Now I have prepared a statement showing the work of the court since 1904 and to the close of 1908, and that shows that in 1904 we had, defaults and trials, 1480, and last year we had 2202; which makes an increase of just about a third, as I said this morning.

Q. Well, is this paper that you now exhibit a summary of actions and proceedings for the years therein mentioned? A. Yes, down to the last, that represents the actual judgments that were rendered by default down to the last. Last year I have the actual number of processes issued, something over forty-five hundred. I haven't those for the other years. In the processes there shown a great many of them were missed on return or default, dismissed without the entry of judgment.

Q. So that, referring to the paper, for instance, for 1904, there are 860 defaults and 196 trials? A. Yes, sir.

Q. Which means actual trials of actions? A. Yes, actual trials of actions. Then there were summary proceedings.

Q. In summary proceedings, 416 represents defaults. and 14 litigated trials? A. Yes.

Q. And for 1908 you have also given the total number of summonses or præcipes issued out of the court? A. Yes, sir.

Q. The clerk, I suppose, issues the summons? A. Yes. I said this morning there was not a report made. I was in error there, because every year we do; the clerk reports to the Mayor.

Q. I see, and the paper that you now show, I assume, is an extract from that report? A. No. The paper that I show you now is my—what I arranged, for the first fiive years there. This last one is his report, the extract from his report. The other is what I dug out myself.

MR. MAYER: That will be read right in evidence (reading):

1904.

	Actions.	Proceedings.	Totals.
Defaults	860	416	1,270
Trials	196	14	210
			1,480

1905.

	Actions.	Proceedings.	Totals.
Defaults	892	409	1,301
Trials	196	14	210
			1,511

1906.

	Actions.	Proceedings.	Totals
Defaults	930	423	1,353
Trials	231	19	250
			1,603

1907.

Defaults	1,136	447	1,585
Trials	253	31	284
			1,869

1908.

Defaults, 1906 (N.B. This figure includes actions and proceedings, 1906) 296

2,202

Summons and precepts issued, 4,536.
Jury trials in 1904, 11.
Jury trials in 1905, 11.
Jury trials in 1908, 35.

——

JOHN M. MURPHY, called as a witness, having been duly sworn, testified as follows:

BY MR. MAYER:

Q. You are judge of the Municipal Court? A. Yes, sir.

Q. And have been such how long? A. Fourteen years.

Q. Trials in bastardy cases are conducted in the Municipal Court? A. Yes.

Q. Now, do you think that ought to be transferred to the Police Court? A. I do; always have thought so.

Q. What is your recollection of the total number of litigated cases of that character during the last year? A. Why, it would be pretty hard to determine, but they are not numerous. They are usually settled, those cases are, before they actually come to trial. They are not very many. They would not go over fifteen, ten or fifteen, in a year anyway at the outside.

Q. When they are tried do they take considerable time? A. Yes, they are slow and disagreeable. It takes both the judges.

Q. And while both the judges are busy with those trials I assume the other business of the Court is held up? A. It lags, yes.

Q. Now do you think it would be better for the city, assuming adequate salaries were paid, if the judges of the Municipal Court were to devote all their time to judicial work? A. Well, it might be better for the city, but it would not be better for the judges, surely. If they had an ample salary and a sufficiently long term to justify their giving up their practice entirely, they probably would be able to devote their time to the business of the Court more than they do now.

Q. As it is now, you practically alternate, as we understand? A. Yes.

Q. And you devote such time as you can, when you are not sitting or deciding cases, to your private practice? A. Yes. It is mostly an office practice. We can't get into court very much.

Q. You cannot? A. Oh, no, we find we can't take chances on that.

Q. Can't take the chance of being detained? A. Occasionally in the sumer time, when business is dull a little, or getting on to late spring or early fall, you can get into court once in a while. But as a rule we are practically prohibited from the trial of cases, practically so.

Q. Have you given any thought to the question of a court of inferior jurisdiction, both civil and criminal? A. I have not. I saw a report, I guess it was your committee that made some report, but I haven't given the matter any thought to speak of.

Q. Have you any opinion? A. I don't like the idea. I say candidly I don't like the idea of mingling the civil and criminal jurisdicton.

Q. That is what we are trying to find out? A. I doubt it's working well. There are two classes of people who patronize the Court, different people. People who have civil causes to try do not like to rub shoulders with those who are interested in criminal affairs.

BY COMMISSIONER HAMILTON:

Q. Maybe you have a misconception of our idea of combined jurisdiction. I don't think Counsel intended any combination that would bring two classes of litigants into contact? A. Oh. Do you mean then, is that opposing jurisdiction, civil and criminal jurisdiction, in the same parties, without reference to the place or the manner in which it would be conducted?

Q. Not necessarily in the same room? A. No.

Q. Now in the same—not on the same calendar? A. Oh.

Q. As at present except that the same judges would try both cases, say? A. Yes.

BY MR. MAYER:

Q. Or, in other words, suppose you had one part or court that dealt with civil cases? A. Yes.

Q. Over which in the month of May you would preside? A. Yes.

Q. And another part of the Court, dealing also with civil cases? A. Yes.

Q. The same month, over which Judge Hebbard, if you please, would preside? A. Yes.

Q. And a third part of the Court, dealing with criminal cases, over which the Police Justice would preside. And then make assignments whereby you would each, in due course, have your term in the civil side and your term in the criminal side, just as the Supreme Court does in—— A. Why, theoretically I think it is all right, but I think in its practical workings it would be a failure. I will tell you why I think so.

Q. That is what we want; we want a frank expression of your views? A. Well, it is a well known fact, there is no use discussing it, that there is a good deal of influence exercised in criminal matters brought to bear upon the Justice in reference to the disposition of parties accused of crime. And it seems a very wise thing to do, because often the Police Justice is more desirous of doing something that is a benefit to the criminal than he is to punish him in the interests of society. And very frequently he will listen to advice from outsiders in reference to the matter, and it has come to be a recognized mode of procedure, in reference to criminal trials in the inferior courts, that men of influence and standing in the community who are acquainted with parties accused of crime, approach the Police Justice and speak to him in reference to the disposition he proposes to make, or is liable to make, of those cases. Now if the jurisdiction is reposed—the same jurisdiction, civil and criminal jurisdiction is reposed—in the same judge, the man is liable to forget the dual character of the official and approach him in civil matters as well as in criminal. Now, that would not do at all. It is never done as far as the judges of the Municipal Court are concerned. It has come to be a recognized fact in this city that they cannot approach the judges of the Municipal Court to influence them in the slightest degree in the matters pending before them, because it different; it is a different thing. Two litigants come before me for the trial of a case. If I do not decide conscientiously and do what is right, I am simply taking money out of one man's pocket and putting it into another's. Whereas, sitting as a Police Magistrate, I would be very glad to have a man familiar with the history and character of a person before me charged with crime, and would dispose of his case with the view of bettering, perhaps, his condition, and rescuing him from the course that he is pursuing. I would be glad to listen to advice. Now I cannot listen to any advice whatever, sitting in the capacity of a Civil Judge. The danger would be, as I have stated before, that they would forget the distinct characters existing in one person, and try, unconsciously and unwillingly perhaps, and in perfect good faith, to exercise the same influence in civil matters they would in criminal matters. That would be the only danger I would apprehend from that. Otherwise it would be all right.

Q. Well, if that danger were eliminated from your mind, do you think that otherwise such a plan would be practicable? A. Why yes, I think it would be all right. But there is that danger that will always exist, in my opinion.

Q. Don't you think there would be greater opportunity if you had a court of civil and criminal jurisdiction with a sufficient number of judges, to avail of the services of the judges and at the same time give justices a fair opportunity for change and proper recreation and vacation? A. Oh, that might be so, but it is pretty hard, of course, to determine in advance how anything of that kind would work. It is so largely speculative that I would not, without careful thought, care to answer that question off hand. I have not given it the necessary thought. The other matter struck me very forcibly.

Q. How frequently have you sat as the Police Justice, in the absence of Mr. Chadsy? A. Oh, I have been over there quite a little in the past four or five years. It isn't a frequent occurence, that is true. If Judge Chadsey is sick—we gave him a vacation last summer of a month, but it came at midsummer. It was found it was pretty exacting on us to run both courts, and we think that there ought to be some arrangement whereby Judge Chadsey could have a vacation, but not at our expense. We hardly feel that we ought to do it, and the law requires it. We would like to accommodate him, but the task is really too heavy, at that time of the year in particular. But I have been over there probably not more than a dozen times a year, outside of that vacation time; probably not more than that and maybe not so many times.

Q. Well, from your experience there, is there any suggestion that occurs to you? A. I cannot think of any.

Q. (Continuing.) As to the law on the criminal side?
A. No, I cannot think of anything, I guess everything is
run very well over there, so far as I know. It is perfunctory service as far as we are concerned. We don't take it
very seriously.

———

JANE L. ARMSTRONG, called as a witness, having been
duly sworn, testified as follows:

BY MR. MAYER:

Q. Mrs. Armstrong, are you a probation officer, for female adults? A. Yes, sir.

Q. In service at the Police Court? A. Yes, sir.

Q. Now, your appointment came from the Commissioner
of Public Safety? A. Yes, sir.

Q. And were you on the eligible list? A. Yes, sir.

Q. And had you taken a competitive civil service examination? A. Yes, sir.

Q. When were you appointed, Mrs. Armstrong? A. I
don't remember just the date.

Q. Approximately? A. About a year. I think it was
a year the 15th day of April; I think I was appointed about
April 15th, 1907.

Q. Well, now, how many cases have you per annum?
For instance, what was your total number during 1908?
Have you the data with you? A. I have a report that I submitted to the Judge the first of the year. I might read it to
you, just as it is, Mr. Mayer.

Q. Very well, if you will? A. (Reading)

Rochester, N. Y., January 6, 1909.

Hon. John H. Chadsey,
    Police Court,
        Rochester, N. Y.

Dear Sir:—

I beg leave herewith to submit my third annual report for the year ending December 31st, 1908.

A.   GENERAL STATISTICS.

   I. Number continued under probationary oversight
       from preceding year 24
  II. Number placed under probationary oversight for
       the year 1908.................................34
 III. Number passed from probationary oversight dur-
       ing the year 1908.............................18
  IV. Number remaining under probationary oversight
       at close of year 1908.........................40

B. CLASSIFICATION OF OFFENSES OF ADULT WOMEN PLACED ON PROBATION DURING THE YEAR 1908.

   I. Vagrancy 8
  II. Vagrancy and Common Prostitution.............. 7
 III. Intoxication 10
  IV. Disorderly Acts and Language.................. 2
   V. Petit Larceny................................. 6
  VI. Burglary 3d Degree and Petit Larceny.......... 1
                                                    ———
                                        Total, 34

C. CLASSIFICATION OF ADULT WOMEN PASSED FROM PROBATIONARY OVERSIGHT DURING THE YEAR 1908.

I. Completed probationary period and discharged with improvement..............................11

II. Completed probationary period and discharged without improvement........................... 4

III. Re-arrested and Committed 3

Total, 18

D. CLASSIFICATION OF ALL OTHER CASES.

I. Interviewed at Police Station before disposition of case.......................................540

II. Letters written...............................174

III. Interviews after placed upon probation........480

IV. Calls to homes of girls upon probation......... 40

V. Interviews with young women who have never been arrested...............................138

VI. Calls to homes of young women who have not yet been arrested........................... 79

VII. Telephone interviews........................212

VIII. Employment procured for young women on probation 27

IX. Employment procured for young women not on Probation 87

All of which is respectfully submitted,

JANE L. ARMSTRONG,
Probation Officer for Adult Women.

Q. What is your method: For instance a woman is arrested, now do you interview her in the jail? A. Yes; at the police station, not the jail.

Q. At the police station? A. Yes.

Q. Before she is arraigned before the Magistrate? A. Yes, sir.

Q. And what is the general purpose of the interview, the general character of it? A. I might tell you just what I do.

Q. You just describe it in your own way. Take a woman from the first time you see her, right through? A. The officer who makes the arrest usually meets me at my office at the police station in the morning at nine o'clock, between nine and nine-thirty, and tells me of the facts that led to the arrest of the woman. Usually there are several people, some of the family and some friends, who are there, have learned of the arrest, and I talk with them. Then I talk with the woman and take whatever facts are brought out, and usually write a written report to the Judge, telling him only of the facts in the case as I find them. I seldom make a recommendation, but just give him the facts from as many sides as I can get them, or people, rather.

Q. Does this written report contain matters that relate to the commission of the crime or the alleged commission of the crime? A Yes, sir.

Q. In other words, you try to find out whether or not the woman, we will say, stole ten dollars, if that is the charge? A. Yes.

Q. And you give the results of your conversation with different people in reference thereto? A. Yes, sir.

Q. As well as her own statement? A. Yes and the

woman's character or previous record. Of course, if she has been there before several times I give him a record of her offense.

Q. Well, does he make known to the woman the contents of your written report? A. No, sir, I don't think so very often.

Q. Does he read that report before he tries the case? A. He reads the report as he comes into court. We have a separate woman's court, and when he comes up I submit these reports to him of the women who are on the docket for that day.

Q. But is the report read by the Judge before the defendant is tried? A. Yes, sir; yes.

Q. So that, as I understand it, the Judge gets your version of the matter, as you have been able to obtain it, before he tries the case? A. Yes, sir.

Q. Well, now, is it his custom to call to the attention of the prisoner the statement made in that report? A. No, sir, I think not. Sometimes he says, "You have been here several times before, the report of Mrs. Armstrong shows," and sometimes states the last date on which the woman has been at the police station.

Q. Well, suppose you have reported that you interviewed John Jones and John Jones stated that he had seen the woman take the ten dollars, and suppose John Jones is not in court. Now, that creates some sort of an impression on the Judge's mind doubtless. What I am trying to find out is whether the prisoner is told that here is a report which says that somebody saw her take the money in question? A. No, sir.

Q. Whether she is given an opportunity to refute it? A.

No, sir, I don't think the reports are used in that way. Of course, if John Jones saw her take the money and my report stated that he did, probably John Jones would have to come in and give his testimony; it might be adjourned for several days then.

Q. And then the report deals with the facts as you have gathered them, the record of the prisoner, and such information as you can get about the home surroundings? A. Yes.

Q. Well, now, assume that the prisoner is convicted, then what is the course? A. Well, if she is to be turned over to me on probation for a certain length of time, there is a certain record we take of the woman and a card that is issued signed by the Judge, telling her that she is placed on probation for a certain length of time, and on the back of the card are the months and a space left in each month; four spaces, I think, left.

Q. How long a period does the probation run to? A. I never have had over six months.

Q. How short are the periods? A. Three months is the shortest.

Q. Three months is the shortest? A. Three the shortest.

Q. So it runs from three to six months? A. Three to six.

Q. Now, what must the woman do after that? She is placed on probation with you; now what? Do you visit her or does she report to you? What happens? A. She comes to me once a week for a time.

Q. Where does she come to? A. She comes to the police station, I regret to say, and I visit her usually once a month in her home or wherever she boards.

Q. I suppose she comes to the police station because no other place is appointed to—— A. That is just it.

Q. And I assume from what you have just stated you are of the opinion that it is really not a proper place for her to report? A. I am very much opposed to having girls put on probation come back to the station for any reason whatever, either a first offender or what we call an old-timer. I think it is a bad thing to do.

Q. And then in due course you report to the Judge whether the case is one that merits suspension or other disposition? A. Yes, sir.

Q. Now, from the observation you have made, have you any suggestions you would like to make to the Commission? A. Why, I don't know that I have anything special. I have thought for some time that the appointment of the probation officer should come through the Police Judge. My appointment came through the Commissioner of Public Safety. I don't know that I see him more than once a year, and never talk over the matters with him, and am under the jurisdiction of the Police Court Judge, who has no power to appoint.

Q. Who has the power to remove, do you know? A. The Commissioner of Public Safety.

Q. So that the Judge has neither power to appoint nor to remove? A. No, sir.

Q. And how is the salary regulated—by the Board of Estimate? A. By the Board of Estimate and Apportionment

Q. What is your salary now, Mrs. Armstrong? A. Fifty dollars a month.

Q. Fifty dollars a month? A. And I get street car tickets

and postage stamps; about the only expense that the office incurs.

Q. How many women did you say you had as a total during 1908? A. I had thirty-four on probation.

Q. Thirty-four on probation? A. Thirty-four on probation; yes, sir.

Q. Do you know how many women were arraigned altogether during 1908? A. No, I do not. I know that I interviewed five hundred and forty women. The interviewing takes a great deal of time.

Q. Well, there is, then, no suggestion that you have to make, either as to the law or as to its administration? A. No, sir, I think not. The law seems to cover our wants very well at present.

BY COMMISSIONER FRANCIS:

Q. Are women well cared for under arrest while detained? A. Yes, sir; yes, I think they are very well cared for.

BY COMMISSIONER HAMILTON:

Q. Are the quarters provided here for the detention of women satisfactory to you from a sanitary point of view? A. Why, I think so. Of course, the station is undergoing changes at the present time which will make it much better. But the building is sanitary as far as I know.

BY CHAIRMAN PAGE:

Q. Are the women all brought to one particular station? A. Yes, sir.

Q. Or would they be taken to the nearest police station to the place where they were arrested? A. They are brought to the Central Police Station for detention. I don't—I hardly think that they are all taken to the different precincts before they are brought to the Central Station.

Q. I suppose there is a matron at the Central Station? A. Yes, sir.

Q. And probably not at the others? A. I think we should have a matron at the county jail, where women have to be detained for some length of time.

BY MR. MAYER:

Q. Is there none there? A. The wife of the sheriff does a certain amount of overseeing, but there is no regularly appointed matron.

BY COMMISSIONER FRANCIS:

Q. Are the younger women allowed to mingle with the so-called old-timers? A. Yes, sir, and I don't think that is—we haven't had room to regulate it very much. For instance, we have a girl at the station now, who is being detained as a witness, and she isn't locked up; she is just kept there, and goes into the cell room if she wants to. And I notice she has been visiting quite a little lately whoever comes in.

BY COMMISSIONER HAMILTON:

Q. How old is she—over sixteen? A. Oh, yes, she must be twenty-two or twenty-three.

BY CHAIRMAN PAGE:

Q. What has been the result of your probation in cases of those discharged—eighteen, was it, discharged during the year? A. Yes, sir.

Q. Did you report those as having satisfactorily completed their probation? A. I think there was only a very small portion of those, Senator Page, that were recommitted. Completed probationary period and discharged with improvement, eleven; completed probationary period and discharged without improvement, four; rearrested and committed, three.

BY MR. MAYER:

Q. That would account for the eighteen? A. That would make the eighteen; yes, sir.

———

JOSEPH P. HOGAN, called as a witness, having been duly sworn, testified as follows:

BY MR. MAYER:

Q. Mr. Hogan, the question was asked of Judge Chadsey as to whether the Police Justice had power to try violations of the liquor tax law. Are you familiar with the case in which that question was tested? A Yes, there was a case there entitled The People against Nicholas Kemmet.

Q. People ex rel.? A. That was when it first came into the Police Court.

Q. People against Nicholas Kemmet? A. (Continuing) And the defendant asked for trial in the Police Court, and Judge Chadsey denied the motion, and exception was taken, and he appealed from the decision to—I think he got a writ of habeas corpus and it then went up into the Supreme Court under the title of People ex rel. Nicholas Kemmet against Craig, Sheriff of Monroe County. And Judge Clark decided the Police Court had no jurisdiction to try the offense; it must be tried by indictment in the County Court. And that decision was appealed from to the Appellate Division, the Fourth Department, and the Fourth Department affirmed the decision without opinion; I suppose, following the decision of Judge Clark. And I understood from Mr. Bennett, the attorney for the defendant, that the case is now to be argued in the Court of Appeals, I think at the next term of court.

Q. That Appellate Division decision was 128 Appellate Division, 908? A. 908.

Q. Have you got a copy of Judge Clark's opinion? A. I have not myself, but I assume you can get a copy.

Q. You will get a copy and send it to us? A. I will get you a copy.

BY CHAIRMAN PAGE:

Q. It wasn't published, was it? A. It possibly is in the advance sheets, the 128th, just a memorandum of the decision. I suppose they affirmed Judge Clark's opinion without writing any opinion in the Appellate Division.

BY MR. MAYER:

Q. Was Judge Clark's decision published in the Miscellaneous Reports? A. That I could not say. I assume, probably, it was.

Q. You might look that up for us? A. I will endeavor to get you a copy.

Q. You are an assistant district attorney? A. Yes, sir; I am appointed by the District Attorney here and I draw my salary from the county, but the city pays half of it, as I understand. I prosecute city ordinances and then take care of the Grand Jury work for the county as it comes into the Police Court.

Q. Do you attend that Police Court every day? A.

Every day, yes. I am there in the morning, and in the afternoon in preparation of the cases for the following day.

Q. Now, just tell us, briefly, the kind of work you do there? A. Well, with reference to the city ordinances, of course, I have charge of prosecuting those. Also, if a defendant, or, rather, if a complainant, comes into court without an attorney, I prosecute the cases for the complainant, such as lots of women who come in there charging their husbands with non-support. I take care of the prosecution of those kind of cases. And so far as the Grand Jury work is concerned, I sort of try to sift out such cases as I believe it is not necessary to send over to the Grand Jury. It frequently happens that in cases of assault, where, at the time the defendant was arrested, the complainant was probably bleeding a great deal more than usual and it might look as though the assault would be second degree; upon examination and after being attended by a physician the charge could be really a charge in the third degree; whereas if allowed to remain second degree assault and the defendant pleads, there is nothing to do but hold the defendant to the Grand Jury, and the chances are he would never be indicted. Whereas, on the other hand, if the case is followed up, and I see the evidence rather warrants holding for third degree assault, I can accept a plea of third degree assault or else advise the withdrawal of a charge of second degree and putting a charge of third degree against him.

Q. In other words, your being on hand enables you to—— A. Somewhat save.

Q. (Continuing) To prevent a lot of minor matters going to the grand jury? A. Unnecessary cases.

Q. And taking up its time and the time of the prosecuting officer of the county? A. Yes, it does, in a way; it helps out. Sometimes it happens, as in a charge of grand larceny, if a complainant charges a person with stealing a watch valued at fifty dollars, where he cannot prove it is worth more than twenty, if the defendant pleads guilty and it goes to the grand jury, naturally there could be no indictment for grand larceny; whereas we could accept a plea of petit larceny in the Police Court, as we often do in those kinds of cases.

Q. Are minutes taken in all cases? A. Yes, a stenographer is there taking minutes in all cases.

Q. Are minutes taken in the—— A. Every case that we have over there of any kind minutes are taken down.

Q. No matter how trivial the case? A. No matter how trivial the case.

Q. So that in ordinary cases charging drunkenness minutes are always taken? A. Minutes are always taken.

Q. You do not attend at the Children's Court, I assume? A. Why, I do on some occasions. If there is a felony committed and the child or person charged appears by an attorney and they desire to have a jury, to put in a defense, I usually examine the officers and the witnesses over in the Juvenile Court. Under ordinary circumstances Judge Chadsey takes care of that part of it himself, unless a jury is demanded.

Q. Well, from your experience, **you think it is desirable** that there should be some representative of the District Attorney on hand at the Police Court? A. I think so. I think it is a great help in the preparation and prosecution of cases. Of course, if I am there in the afternoon, I can act in a certain advisory capacity to officers. It frequently happens that complainants come in and ask for warrants for persons far off in another State. Of course, we don't like to send out for such people unless it is reasonably sure they have committed a crime which we are reasonably sure of proving when we get them here. On an application for a warrant of that kind the clerk will refer him over to me. We usually investigate pretty thoroughly without sending clear off to California or some place for the defendant. I also follow cases up on appeals; if appealed I take them up with the County Court.

Q. Follow them right through. A. As far as possible.

Q. Appeals from the Police Justice are to the County Court? A. To the County Court.

Q. And by permission to the Appellate Division? A. To the Appellate Division, yes.

Q. Well, now, from your experience in the Police Court, have you any suggestions to make to the Commission? A. Why, no, I don't believe I have, except that I think one prosecuting attorney in a position such as mine is a very desirable thing to have, or a person to be in charge of cases of that kind. As I say, it helps out, mostly in this grand jury work, in a good many ways. That way it saves a large lot of cases.

Q. You have no suggestion, though, as to any change in the existing law? A. Why, I don't recall offhand. I have not looked up any such subject as to suggest any.

Q. Well, if anything impressed you, you would probably remember it? A. Nothing particularly at the present time.

ALFRED J. MASTERS, called as a witness, having been duly sworn, testified as follows:

BY MR. MAYER:

Q. What is your full name, Mr. Masters? A. Alfred J. Masters.

Q. Mr. Masters, you are a probation officer for male adult persons. A. I am, sir.

Q. And you act as probation officer also in the County Court? A. I do.

Q. Have you any data as to the number of adults placed in your charge during 1908? A. Well, I was not—I have during 1908, I have brought a copy of a report, but this is strictly from the Police Court.

Q. That is all we are interested in? A. I received in 1908 two hundred and thirty-five and carried over from 1907 seventy-three, making a total of three hundred and eight.

Q. Have you with you there a summary showing the disposition of these matters? A. I have of all of them, carried right through.

MR. MAYER: Well, then, I will read that in evidence (reading):

1908 REPORT.

	Brought Forward Last Report 1907.	Received 1908.	Released.	Probations Revoked.	Absconded.	Total.	Total Accounted For.
Assault 3d degree...	7	30	19	7	1	10	37
Petit Larceny......	18	45	40	7	..	16	63
Forgery 3d degree ..		2	2	..	..	0	2
Unlawfully Carrying Firearms....	..	1	..	1	..	0	1
Non-Support	29	50	45	23	3	8	79
Vagrancy	4	24	15	8	..	5	28
Intoxication	9	43	22	7	1	22	52
Disorderly Acts and Language...	3	19	17	2	..	3	22
Shooting Craps....	1	3	1	2	..	1	4
Fraud on Boarding House	1	1	1	1	..	0	2
Walking on R. R. Tracks	..	4	1	..	2	1	4
Malicious Mischief.	..	10	7	..	1	2	10
Exposure	..	1	1	..	..	0	1
Receiving Stolen Property	1	..	1	..	..	0	1
Abandonment	..	1	1	..	..	0	1
Misdemeanor	..	1	1	..	..	..	1
Total	73	235	174	58	8	68	308
Total		308			308		308

SCHEDULE B.

RECAPITULATION.

Held over (1907 report).. 73 Released 174
Received (1908)........235 Revoked 58
Absconded 8

308   240
240

68 Still on Probation.

Total amount of money received in non-support cases and paid out by me, $5,733.

Investigations, 135.

Non-support cases investigated and withdrawn, 43.

Interviews with probationers, 3,707.

Respectfully submitted,

ALFRED J. MASTERS,
Probation Officer.

Q. So, with the hold-overs from 1907 and the new cases of 1908 you had in all 308 cases? A. Three hundred and eight cases.

Q. And you disposed of all of those but 68? A. Sixty-eight.

Q. Those are now on probation? A. They were on probation the first of the year. Of course they are gradually working off.

Q. The first of January, 1909. A. The first of January, 1909.

Q. Now, of this total, 174 were released, 58 probations revoked and eight absconded, is that correct? A. That is correct.

Q. And you collected in all $5,733 for non-support cases? A. I did.

Q. You can let us have this, can you? A. Yes, you can have that.

Q. Now, have you any system here by which you collect a fine on probation? A. We have not. We never have used it.

Q. How long have you been a probation officer? A. I have been a probation officer in the County Court since March, 1901.

Q. Well, you have had, then, we will assume, an extended experience. Now, do you believe in any such system as that? A. I do not. I think if the man is worthy of letting out, the hardship comes on the family of the man paying the fine.

Q. Now, when a man is arrested do you make an investigation? A. I do not. We have a regular investigator here in the Police Court. In the County Court I always make it, or at least am requested, as a rule, to make an investigation by the Judge. I tell him all I can.

Q. What I am trying to get at is this: Before a defendant is arrested and gets his hearing, we want to find out whether any statement of the facts is made to the Judge out of court, as it were? A. No sir, not in the police court.

Q. Well, in other words, does the Judge have any report before him prior to the time the defendant is tried? A. He has the investigation of the Police Court investigator.

Q. Well, now, what is the nature of that investigation? A. Well, he gets a report from the police officer that arrests him, and also looks up and sees whether the man has a record or not, and finds out from the officer the nature of what the man has been arrested for, and the condition in which the man is brought in if it is an intoxication charge.

Q. Now is that laid before the Judge prior to the trial of the man? A. That is laid before the Judge prior to the trial.

Q. Well, does the Judge call the man's attention to the contents of that report? A. He does not, anything more than if he has been there before he has that record before him.

Q. Well, after a man is convicted and placed on probation, what is your system? A. My system is to take him to my office and tell him exactly what I expect of him.

Q. And where is your office? A. In the County Court House.

Q. Well, now, you tell him what he is to do? A. I tell him exactly what he is to do and what I expect of him.

Q. Does that involve reporting to you? A. It does.

Q. Where does he report? A. He reports in the Court House, my office there.

Q. How often? A. Well, as a rule, once a week, until he has been there a certain period of time. If I find he is doing remarkably well I extend the time.

Q. Then do you visit him? A. Well, only occasionally. We don't make it a practice to follow them up; if a man goes out and gets a position for himself we don't feel we are justified in following him up. If we find him a position we have no objections to go and inquiring how he is getting along.

Q. Of course your object in not going is not to let his employer know? A. Not to let his employer know about it, provided the man is doing well.

Q. Yes, but do you make investigation to satisfy yourself that the man is employed? A. Oh, we do in a great many cases.

Q. Well, suppose a man says "I am employed by Jones & Company," now do you take his word for it, or do you take some means of finding out whether he is telling the truth. A. Well, we very often make inquiries to find out whether he is telling the truth, if we doubt him at all. But in a great many of these cases they come so direct to us and we know pretty well when they come in whether they are telling the truth or not. I don't think I ever have in more than one or two cases found a man deceived me.

Q. And now what is the longest period of time these men are on probation? A. Well, in the Police Court six

months is the longest we can hold them. In the County
Court, of course, we can hold them during the time we can
sentence them.

Q. Well, that isn't the longest you can hold them in
cases where the punishment is a year or five hundred dollars fine? A. Well, the Judge generally places them on
probation for six months, it being the rule here to do that.

Q. Do you think it would be well to extend the time in
non-support cases to a year? A. I certainly do.

Q. That would be a desirable change? A. I think it
very desirable, in fact we started out doing that but ran up
against a snag and had to quit.

Q. I mean if the law were so amended as to cover a
year? A. I think it would be a great benefit.

Q. Now you take these 174 cases out of the 240, where
the men were released, were you satisfied with those cases?
A. I was.

Q. And you felt that the probation had done them good?
A. I do and it has done good in a great many cases, a
great many hold-overs; that is they will behave themselves
well during probation, but shortly afterwards will maybe
drop back again; but I find even doing them that much good
is—at least keeping them that long has done quite a little
good.

Q. What kind of cases do you find probation works most
successfully in? A. Well, most successfully, what we
would consider the best fruits, would be from boys sixteen
to twenty, who have just started out in going wrong, and if
we can bring them around and get them to earn an honest
living and behave themselves we think we are doing the
best work in that line.

Q. How is your work coming out in intoxication cases?
A. Well, I have had very good success in it. I think it is
fully—I don't believe we have lost over fifteen or twenty
per cent. of them.

Q. Do you think it would be desirable, somewhere in the
city, to have a reformatory for misdemeanants? A. I do,
and I have talked it here for the last three or four years,
in fact ever since I have been connected with the Police
Court. It is something we need and need badly.

Q. Do you find embarrassment in the Judge not being
able to send some boys to a reformatory? A. At times I
think it would be a benefit for the boy to go to the reformatory. But there is nothing here, nothing to do but send
them to the penitentiary, and I do hate to see a boy go to
the penitentiary.

Q. Now, in addition to the suggestions that you have
made, or the changes that you believe, in answer to my
questions, desirable, have you thought of any other changes
or suggestions.? A. No, I cannot think of any at present.

Q. Have you had anything with child probation at all?
A. I have not. In reference to the non-support cases, I
think fully forty per cent. of them are settled up before
they ever come before the Judge. Those are the only cases
I investigate. I always investigate those before they are
brought before the Judge, and about forty per cent. of
them are settled.

Q. Well, you mean you bring the people together? A. I
bring the people together.

Q. And seek to unite the——? A. Unite the home.

Q. (Continuing) The home, and you keep pretty close
watch, I assume, in those cases? A. We do. and in a good

many of those cases I ask the Judge to adjourn the case and parole them in my charge, and in the meantime I settle them up and have the cases withdrawn.

Q. Well, that is a branch of probation work that is really effective, is it? A. It has been very effective here.

Q. And it accomplishes the results that the Judge spoke of, I assume? A. Yes, sir.

Q. Do you find that the poor authorities co-operate with you? A. They do. They are all in sympathy with the work, and I find the police officers here gladly co-operate.

Q. Well in this whole administration of the criminal law relating to the inferior offences, is there general co-operation in this city between the different arms of enforcement, in the Police Department and the Court? A. Oh, yes, I think they all co-operate together. I know the police officers very often come to me and ask me to have a talk with a boy, or some boy is brought up and they think that the boy ought to be given a chance, and ask me if I will not intercede for them, which we do quite frequently.

Q. Now you were appointed also by the Commissioner of Public Safety? A. Yes, sir.

Q. And what salary is accorded you? A. Six hundred a year.

Q. And your carfare expenses, I suppose? A. And carfare expense.

Q. In addition do you get a salary for the County Court work? A. I also get a salary for my County Court work.

Q. What was your occupation before this, Mr. Masters? A. Well, I was superintendent in a factory for quite a number of years.

Q. Do you believe this probation work is accomplishing

results? A. I believe it has been very successful here. We have seen a great many cases where they have turned out splendidly.

Q. Now of these cases, are there many persons of foreign birth? A. Well I don't think the percentage would be very big of strictly foreign birth.

Q. Of course I mean by that—— A. You mean those born in foreign countries, not foreign parents?

Q. I mean foreign parents. How about cases where the parents of the persons are of foreign birth? A. Well, I think those are about fifty per cent.

Q. Have you an increasing foreign population here?

A. Yes, I think the foreign population is increasing, especially the Italian.

Q. The Italian? A. Yes.

———

JOHN H. CHADSEY, recalled, testified as follows:

BY MR. MAYER:

Q. There is one question I want to ask you, Judge. Where these investigations are made prior to the arraignment of the defendant, are they placed before you?

A. Yes, the investigator, Mr. Wiedman's business is—the police officers, every one of them, are ordered by the Chief of Police to report to Mr. Weidman. For instance, if a man is arrested, and he is arrested for some misdemeanor, he reports it to him and tells the condition in which he is found or how it was. For instance, take a case of intoxication, why, what was he doing, what was his condition; whether he was what we call a plain drunk, or whether he was excessively so, and whether he was fighting, whether there was disturbance. Then he looks over his record and he can tell whether that man has been arrested before or convicted before. He puts that on his pad and that is placed before me every morning, and as I call the docket, I can refer to his pad and tell whether that man has been in court, haw many times he has been in court, for a period now, since we have got the card system, of two or three years, but before that we had another system to follow it up. So that has been my custom.

Q. Well, now, does the statement have, as to the alleged offense—— A. Merely that he is an old offender, for instance, or something of that kind, but it is the minute—only the statement of the police officer. Now we will show you. These are the cards, Mr. Wiedman says, of those arraigned this morning that had criminal records. Now, for instance, a man comes up and pleads guilty to being intoxicated, and I say, "have you been arrested before, or convicted before," and he says "Yes" or he says "No." If he says "No," I can turn and tell whether he is telling the truth or not. He can't get out of it by lying.

Q. What I am trying to get at, Judge, is this: whether there is placed before you in writing, or stated to you verbally, the facts and circumstances concerning the crimes which are alleged to have been committed? A. Oh, nothing particularly, in fact I don't allow that; that is for the Prosecuting Attorney. I tell them to go to the Prosecuting Attorney. Lots of people come to me to tell me their side of a case. I say, "No, I will not receive it, but you go to the Prosecuting Attorney."

Q. Does Mrs. Armstrong lay such a report before you? A. Well, very seldom she might. I don't think as a rule, she merely has her pad and tells me whether they have been in and how many times they have been in, and whether the person is free to tell us as to her character, she notes, but not as to the identical offense which is specifically to be tried.

Q. Is the defendant prejudiced by any ex parte statement of the investigator or the probation officers? A. No, because her record is merely what she gets from her, from the defendant herself, and from her record that she keeps. She tells her story probably to Mrs. Armstrong, but Mrs. Armstrong doesn't tell me that, only sometimes she will say she claims this is her first offense, or the officer didn't treat her well, or something of that kind. Well that goes just so far, but it has nothing to do with the facts of the case. They will—it is a hard job to avoid it.

BY COMMISSIONER HAMILTON:

Q. Do you find this card system of records, showing the previous record of defendants greatly assists in determining what sentence to impose? A. Yes, I make it a rule to be governed somewhat by the number of times they have been in.

Q. Is there any system of identification used in connection with this record system? A. To know that you have got the same man?

Q. Yes? A. Yes, Mr. Weidman, I think, if you put him on the stand, Mr. Weidman, the investigator, will tell you just how that is done. Once in a while we get a man by the name of Smith and sometimes it is quite a puzzle to find out whether he is the man on record there. Mr. Weidman will ask him, where he has got his record as to his age and residence, maybe, "Why, you were here such a date?" "No, No, I never was here before, I am entirely another Smith." Well, now, oftentimes we have had officers come right up and identify the man and show that he was absolutely telling an untruth. But often in such cases we find the man is right, that the record shows John Smith was in a good many times, but not this John Smith.

Q. Then you have got a system of identification? A. The Bertillon system.

Q. Either the Bertillon or the finger print system? A. Not in the Police Court proper. Of course, a man arrested for a felony, they take him in the Police Department and go through that system which we have. We have a very elaborate system here in Rochester. I wish you could see it. I will show it to you.

BY MR. MAYER:

Q. You have the Bertillon system here? A. Oh, yes.

Q. Have you the finger print system too? A. I think they adopted that—haven't they got that yet? They are going to adopt that, but haven't got that yet, I think.

Q. Now is this card the card that the investigator lays before you (indicating)? A. He takes it from that card.

Q. He takes this record from this card? A. Yes.

Q. And this card is one of the cards in your index system? A. Yes, that is taken right out.

Q. And the card shows the name, address, age, occupation, distinguishing marks, date of arrest, charge, any remarks that might be made, and disposition? A. Yes.

BY COMMISSIONER HAMILTON:

Q. Judge, I want to ask you in reference to the shelter

that you spoke of this morning, that is maintained by the Society for the Prevention of Cruelty to Children here? A. Yes, sir.

Q. To what extent do you use that, in connection with your juvenile court work? A. Well, it is our only place of detention.

Q. How many children will it accommodate? A. Very few. Now, by the way, Mr. Killip is here and he has been superintendent of that and will tell you more particularly.

Q. Do you commit children to that? A. Oh, no.

Q. You have no authority? A. No, no authority to commit there. It is merely a place for them to stay until they are disposed of in court.

Q. Prior to disposition of their cases? A. Prior to disposition.

Q. Do you feel the need of any other place to which you may commit children, than such as you have access to? A. I feel the need of having a house or school of correction, as I call it; that is, where I can commit children for a short time.

Q. For a short time, that is what I mean? A. Yes, instead of sending them to the State Industrial School, instead of sending them to some place where it is optional with the institution to let them out.

Q. This refuge is of no use to you in that respect? A. Not after conviction. That is a suggestion I have made. But suppose we have a Catholic child and want to send that boy to Buffalo, to the institution there. Now if they are able to pay, the parents, we say to the parents, "you must pay for that child up there," which costs about two or three dollars a week. If not, if I commit them there, it has to be paid by the Overseer of the Poor. So the object is to save the expense if we can. If a parent brings in a child and says it is an ungovernable child, we say, "Why can't you take care of it? We don't want to take care of this child. If we do, I will have to send it to the State Industrial School. If you prefer to send it to Father Baker, up in Buffalo, a Catholic institution, you will have to pay for that up there."

Q. Well, have you any recommendations in reference to remedying that condition? A. I have what I mentioned this morning. I think there ought to be established in this city, whether it is a State institution or a city institution, a place where I can send children from the age of eight years to sixteen; some sort of a reformatory or shelter where they can be committed for a limited time, and while there, that they should be conducted in the same course of study that they had in the public schools, but being under that restraint they could not get out among their evil companions.

BY MR. MAYER:

Q. How much accommodation do you think would be necessary. I mean accommodation for how many children? A. I don't think but what accommodation for fifty children would, for this city. Going in and out, of course, I don't think there would be fifty at one time.

Q. A place then that would accommodate fifty children would be ample? A. I think so for this city.

Q. Would you have the administration of that place practically under the jurisdiction of the Court? A. Well, that is a good deal for me to say. I would not want to have the responsibility of it, but I think it would be well enough to have a little jurisdiction.

Q. Well, what we are getting at is, eliminating the personal element entirely? A. Yes.

Q. (Continuing.) And yourself, thinking of it as a Police Court? A. Yes.

Q. (Continuing.) Whether you think, for instance, the superintendent of such an institution should be appointed by the Court? A. No, I don't think that would be necessary. I don't think that, only I think the superintendent of the institution, when a child is committed there, should get his information in regard to that child from the Court and its officers, so he will know.

Q. You mean to have a close relation between the Police Judge and the institution? A. That is it, exactly. Of course, I don't think—I think it is an appointment that ought to be made either by the State or the City and which should not be an emolument of the Police Judge. I wish to suggest, gentlemen, in one respect; I have in my Court also, besides these probation officers, two stenographers. One is a confidential stenographer and one is a regular stenographer who takes down all, as you have had here to-day; every proceeding in court is taken down by the stenographer and transcribed whenever required. We also have an Italian interpreter under salary. We have a Polish interpreter, and in fact, a man who can talk seven languages, who is paid per diem for his attendance, that is, cases.

Q. By whom is the interpreter appointed? A. Those I hire, but the Italian interpreter being an appointee, is under civil service, appointed by the Commissioner of Public Safety, and he is not on my payroll, understand, neither are the probation officers on my payroll. They come under the police. I have sometimes said, but I don't know if I was asking too much, that I thought they could be made appointees by the Court, but under the present civil service examinations it makes very little difference. Of course, sometimes you can get a personality—a man who is adapted for that business, and it might be very hard, maybe, to answer all the questions that would be put to him by the Civil Service Commission.

Q. Where do appeals from the Municipal Court go, to the County Court? A. To the County Court.

Q. So the County Court passes on appeals from you and appeals from the Municipal Court? A. Yes, sir.

BY COMMISSIONER FRANCIS:

Q. Well, are the police officers attached to your Court permanently detailed there or are they changed from time to time? A. Just as the Commissioner sees fit, the Commissioner of Public Safety. But the officers that have been there—for instance we have a German interpreter, by the way, too, who is an officer, a detective, under the rank of detective, drawing the salary of a detective, and he is in charge there as an acting officer. They have two door-keepers now who are assigned by the Police Department, and three other officers, attending the courts and taking care, besides the police officers who are downstairs and bringing the persons up there, regular police attaches from the Police Department.

BY CHAIRMAN PAGE:

Q. Does the City pay the Children's Society here for

keeping these children? A. Yes, I believe they pay a certain amount, don't they, Mr. Killip? The city pays for sustaining the shelter, don't they?

MR. KILLIP: No, the county. The county gives a flat rate now to the society. The city pays one agent a salary of seven hundred and twenty dollars a year.

BY COMMISSIONER HAMILTON:

Q. Do the agents for the society make any reports to you as to the children's records, or keep children's records? A. No, that is why I insisted on having a juvenile probation officer who is a salaried officer. Now Mr. Killip is appointed, who was the superintendent. Now the system will be that they report and I shall receive the report. In fact I have assigned Mr. Killip his duties, inasmuch as he shall take charge of all these probation officers, other volunteer officers; and we have a system of cards, card system, to give to them, and on the expiration of their probation it will be returned. They have never been in the habit of bringing the child into court, but now I have adopted the system that they shall bring the child into court, and on the report of the probation officer, commend the child for his good work or continue his probation if they see fit.

BY CHAIRMAN PAGE:

Q. Judge, it might interest you to know, in regard to the City of Buffalo, we made this provision: (Reads regarding Children's Detention Home.)

I approve of that very much and I never saw where it had been thought of before. I know I thought of it here. I didn't know it was talked of in Buffalo. The only correction I think of is it ought to be more than thirty days.

I think they ought to make it at least three months. Now, in the State Industrial School they do not get out under a year, I understand, most of the time sixteen months or eighteen months if they are very good. And I sometimes think we ought to have a limit, we ought to have any time up to say at least three months or six months, because thirty days, it seems to me, is hardly long enough. I rather approve of ninety or a hundred days, rather than thirty. Of course, we would exercise that as we see fit, but not fix a limit of thirty days.

———

ANDREW WEIDMAN, called as a witness, having been duly sworn, testified as follows:

BY MR. MAYER:

Q. You are the Police Court investigator? A. Yes, sir.

Q. And are you attached to the Police Court all the year around? A. Yes.

Q. Do you get a salary? A. Yes, sir.

Q. What is your salary? A. Fifteen hundred a year.

Q. Now, what is the nature of the work you do, Mr. Weidman? A. Well, in the morning I get down there any time between seven and half-past, never any later than that. I generally keep a docket on a pad of all the charges, the names and the ages, and I hunt up the records and I go downstairs and have a talk with the prisoners, come upstairs, and by that time it is probably time for the officers to make their reports, and they come in and make their reports to me. Well, a case where a man may be charged with intoxication: For instance, this morning we had a young fellow about twenty years old. He was picked up on Front

Street trying to sell a watch. He was intoxicated, and they brought him to the station and locked him up for intoxication. This morning we came to find out the fellow had stolen the watch from someone in Buffalo. The fellow comes in and pleads guilty to intoxication. Of course, this the Judge had on his pad. The Judge gave him five days in the penitentiary. In the meantime we will investigate and find out what Buffalo wants to do with him. We have probably all the way from one to five a day or one to three a day, something of that kind.

Q. Now, when you have made that investigation, what do you do? A. Well, I go in and simply say to the Judge, "Here is John Doe, arrested by Officer So and So, and the officer's report was this man was picked up on Front Street trying to dispose of a watch, and he was intoxicated, so he was brought in and they put a charge of intoxication against him. This morning we find out the man stole this watch in Buffalo." The Judge sends him away long enough to investigate and find out what they want to do with him in Buffalo.

Q. Now, do you do any investigating after that? A. No.

Q. Do you keep this card index system? A. Oh, yes.

Q. And you keep track, then, of the number of convictions? A. Yes, sir.

Q. And the number of arrests also, I suppose? A. Yes, sir.

Q. So that comprises your work? A. Yes, sir.

Q. Are you able to identify prisoners except by memory? A. Well, a number of times. That is one of the reasons I like to have a talk with them in the morning. Now, they will come in there intoxicated and give some fictitious name, but I get to talking with them, and a number of times they give their right name. And I like to hear their side of the story, besides the officer's side of the story.

Q. That covers your work, does it? A. Yes.

W. A. KILLIP, called as a witness, having been duly sworn, testified as follows:

BY MR. MAYER:

Q. What is your name? A. W. A. Killip.

Q. You have been recently appointed probation officer for the Juvenile Court? A. Yes, sir.

Q. What is your salary? A. Twelve hundred a year.

Q. Before you were appointed probation officer, were you Superintendent of the Society for the Prevention of Cruelty to Children? A. Yes, sir.

Q. And did the city pay your salary in that capacity? A. No, sir.

Q. The county? A. The society paid me.

Q. How long had you been such superintendent? A. About three years, I believe.

Q. Is that society supported by private contributions? A. Yes, sir, and also gets a donation from the county.

Q. Appropriations by the county? A. Yes, from the county.

Q. And does the society get the fines? A. Yes, sir.

Q. (Continuing) Which are imposed in cases initiated by it? A. Yes, under certain conditions.

Q. (Continuing) Or prosecuted by it? A. Yes, sir.

Q. Well, now, does your Society for the Prevention of Cruelty to Children here keep records? A. Yes.

Q. Family histories? A. To some extent.

Q. But you don't furnish that to the Police Court? A. Not the family history. We might furnish the record of the boy or child that might be arraigned.

Q. Has the society a shelter for children? A. Yes, sir.

Q. And are the children brought to that shelter? A. Yes, sir.

Q. Now, What is the procedure? Suppose a child is arrested out here on the street by a policeman? A. Why, the policeman, I believe, first takes them to the office or the station house to which he belongs, then he is immediately brought to the shelter from the station house.

Q. He is taken to the station house to have a statistical record? A. To have the charge put on the book.

Q. To get his name, address, and so on? A. Yes, sir.

Q. Before he is taken to the society? A. In some cases. In some cases they take them direct from the street to the society.

Q. If he has to be detained then he comes into the society rooms? A. Yes, sir.

Q. The city, I suppose, pays the society for that? A. No. They used to put a bill in to the Supervisors for the number of meals served, etc., and they got so much per meal, but of late years the Board of Supervisors have provided a flat rate and the society extends all over Monroe County.

Q. Now, the society holds that child until the time comes for the next session of the Children's Court? A. Unless paroled by the Judge or the Police Department.

Q. Now, what do you do as probation officer? A. Why, I am supposed to investigate the conditions of the child, that is, as far as the doings, what the child did, and its surroundings. I am supposed to find out if the child is more to blame than the parent, or the condition is such that the child is criminal because the home surroundings are not right.

Q. You report to the Judge the result of your investigation? A. Of course; however, I was only appointed on the tenth of the month and have hardly got the thing running, but that will be the intention, to do it.

Q. That will be the procedure, will it? A. Yes, sir.

Q. Have you started in to organize this volunteer force? A. Yes, sir.

Q. And you are to have charge of that whole situation, are you? A. Yes, sir.

Q. Now, where will you make the children report? A. Well, we have had about twenty-five or thirty volunteer probation officers, and that child will be supposed to report to some one of those probation officers at least once a week, and at least once in two weeks, I believe, the chief probation officer ought to visit the child's home and also get in touch with the school authorities and find out whether he attends school regularly or not and whether he keeps good hours, and at the end of the probationary term he should come back to the Court to be discharged by the Judge.

Q. Do you know how long the Judge places a child on probation? A. Generally three months. There have been cases of six months. There has been one case that we received from Livingston County, from Judge Carter, for one year. A boy left this city and went up to Avon and committed a burglary, and was arrested and detained in the Genesee jail for a few weeks. Then the Grand Jury indicted him and he was convicted; and Judge Carter, on a letter received from me, sent him down to report to me for one year. He has been reporting now for about nine months, once a month.

Q. Have you the data as to the number of children arraigned in 1908? A. Yes. It is the society's report, of course. Five hundred and fifty-three.

Q. Five hundred and fifty-three? A. Yes, sir.

Q. How many boys? A. They were about 500. We haven't got them separated. This is from the society's report. There must have been something about five hundred and six or eight. There were 45 girls, or so, altogether, 35 or 45 girls, something like that.

Q. This paper you show me is an extract from your report as Superintendent of the Rochester society? A. Of the Rochester society.

Q. Of the Rochester Society for the Prevention of Cruelty to Children, from October 1st, 1907, to 1908? A. Yes, sir.

(Said paper marked Exhibit 98.)

Q. And of this total of five hundred and fifty odd there are only 45 girls? A. That is about all.

Q. What do you think of a detention home or shelter to which to commit children for short periods? A. I believe there ought to be such a place for those children between the age of eight and twelve years. I should think it should be more of a truant school than a place where they should be detained for truancy. In this city the children are seldom brought into court on a truancy charge or a vagrancy charge. Mostly the parents are compelled to bring them in as ungovernable children. From the fact that the boy does not attend school, the parent is compelled to bring him into court as an ungovernable child, and then, if he is over the age of twelve, he may be committed to the State Industrial School.

BY CHAIRMAN PAGE:

Q. The charge should be, probably, incompetent parents?
A. A great many times it ought to be improper guardianship, that is what ought to be the proceeding.

BY MR. MAYER:

Q. You heard me read Section 92 of the Buffalo Court Bill this morning, didn't you? A. Yes, sir.

Q. Do you think that is a good idea, do you remember what it was? A. No, I don't recall it. I heard you.

Q. That was the section which treats the child, not as a criminal, but rather as in need of the State's protection?
A. Yes, I believe that is proper.

Q. Now, from your experience, don't you think it is a good thing to gradually get to a point where, so far as possible, the child should not be regarded as a criminal? A. Yes.

Q. And if the child is ultimately set on the right path, so that its record as a child shall not stand against it in after life? A. I do.

Q. Do you approve of that? A. I approve of that.

Q. And I assume you approve—would approve or think well of any legislation which carried out that general thought? A. I do.

BY CHAIRMAN PAGE:

Q. Is there any truant school here where children are committed under the compulsory education law? A. No, sir. Some years ago, some ten or twelve or fourteen years ago, there was a truant school here, and it generally had from forty to forty-five boys in it, and I believe that during the time that truant school was being maintained by the city they also had outside truants that were boarded here, some from Watertown, and that there were a number of boys that would have been truant if it had not been for the fact that they knew there was a place where they might be sent if they played truant. The boys now are not considered truants; they are considered to be ungovernable children.

Q. What do they do then to enforce the compulsory education law, anything? A. They don't seem to. They have five truant officers, I believe, who follow up those cases. They have in some of the schools rooms set apart for what they call truant or deficient children, in several of the different schools. Now, a child might be asked to go from the most extreme northern part of the city to away up on Monroe Avenue, which would be two or two miles and a half, to attend a class of truants or a deficient class in that section, instead of having one right in their own neighborhood; and that child would have to travel there and come back, but they would go in at nine o'clock and get dismissed at half-past two. They don't keep them there very long, of course, just simply day time. Then when they are not in that classroom up there, the truant officer is notified, and I believe they come out and look them up. Many times a boy is playing truant and the parents cannot get him to go to school, and they do everything they can, and the parents are notified if they do not get the boy in school they will be arrested for not sending him to school. So the parents are in some cases given warning that the next offense would cause the truant officers to arrest the child and bring him before the Judge, charged with being a vagrant and truant, under some subdivision of 887. That has only been done recently, though.

Q. Well, now, from your long experience as Superintendent of the society, are there any suggestions you want to make to the Commission? A. Well, I believe that we have all had occasion to come in contact with those boys that are just too old to go to the State Industrial School, and, as Mr. Masters said, it seems almost a sin to send them to the workhouse with those old-time criminals. I think there ought to be a place, a reformatory, for those boys between that age and 21 or 22 years of age.

Q. Well, you regard the absence of that as a great lack, don't you? A. I do.

Q. There could be a reformatory that would take in all misdemeanants in this part of the State? A. Yes, I believe that matter of a reformatory for children the ages of eight and twelve, instead of being for Rochester and Buffalo alone, should be for the western part of this State. Now, I believe the boy being sent there should not be sent for any definite length of time, and I believe sometimes the fact he was sent there for a few weeks would be sufficient to cure many a boy of truancy, by being caught in time. I acted as truant officer in this town for four years and a half. A young man will graduate from a university this year who was brought from one of the public schools by me to the old truant school and detained three days. When I took him there he declared he didn't care how long we kept him nor what we did with him over there. This boy was being brought up in the slums of the city. His mother had deserted the family and gone to Buffalo and was there living with another man, as I was informed. At that time the truant officers had to go to the truant school and take any one after working all day on the street and spend an hour or two, and it was my turn that week that I locked the boy up over there. He begged of me to give him one more chance, when he was in there the second day, and the third day he cried and begged again, and I went to the superintendent and had him paroled. We never had any more trouble from that boy. He continued in school, and the high school, and this year he will graduate from the university. For that reason I believe sometimes a few days or a few weeks in many cases is sufficient to cure a boy of some of those small habits of truancy.

JOHN B. M. STEPHENS, called as a witness, having been duly sworn, testified as follows:

BY MR. MAYER:

Q. Judge, you are the County Judge of the County of Monroe? A. Yes, sir.

Q. And have been such how long? A. Since—well, this is the third year. Two years ago last January.

Q. Now, what misdemeanors, if any, are tried in your court? A. Excise cases.

Q. And only they, I mean outside of those which are occasionally removed from the Police Courts? A. Yes.

Q. Now, have you any idea of how many excise cases come before your court in the course of a year, from the City of Rochester, I mean? A. I cannot—I have kept a record of those which we probably could supply you with, but I havn't it with me.

Q. Well, you might do that, if you will, so we will get an idea. A. I could give you a record of the number of cases and the disposition of them, if you care to have it.

Q. Does it take up very much of the time of your court? A. Excise cases?

Q. Yes. A. No, it is a small percentage of the work.

Q. And I assume that the majority of that are acquittals by juries, are they not? A. No, I should say not.

Q. In the course of a year how many appeals came to you from the Police Court; of course I don't want it accurately, just approximately? A. Oh, I should estimate thirty-five or forty.

Q. And are they varied in character? A. Yes.

Q. And how many appeals from the Municipal Courts? A. Well, I should estimate them to be about fifty. Our present calendar, of the present term, which opened this week, contains twenty-eight appeals, but they have not all been taken, of course, since the last term.

Q. Now, of course, you sit both in civil and criminal term? A. Yes.

Q. Now, from your own experience, as bearing upon this general subject we are discussing, do you find it advantageous to have two kinds of jurisdiction? I mean the effect upon yourself. Do you think there is an advantage in variety? A. Not a particular advantage, I think. I am inclined to think that in the administration of criminal jurisdiction it is better to have it centered as far as possible in a single individual, by reason of the recurrent cases, persons who are charged again and again, perhaps, with crime. There is a good deal in understanding the personality of the criminal class in a community. I find it even helpful to me in the County Court, that I know men, their histories, where they came from and something of their earlier careers.

Q. Well, do you find it any relief at all in your judicial work that you do go from one class of work to the other? A. The criminal cases are easier for a judge than civil ones. It is a little relief sometimes in that respect, except for the additional nervous strain of dealing with the liberties of the citizen.

Q. How many criminal cases have you in a year? A. Well, that is merely a matter of estimation, founded upon a few data that I can just now recall. I should say we had from 125 to 150 indictments.

Q. You have stenographer's minutes, I suppose, returned to you in every appeal from the Police Court? A. Yes.

Q. And of course that is likewise true of the Municipal Courts? A. Yes.

BY CHAIRMAN PAGE:

Q. If a new trial is granted, does that take place in your Court or do you send it back? A. On appeals from the Police Court it is had in the County Court. On appeals from the Municipal Court, if a new trial is granted, it is sent back to that court.

BY MR. MAYER:

Q. Well, I am glad the Senator thought of that, because that leads to this question: Don't you think it would be advantageous, if a new trial is granted, to send it back to the Police Court? A. No, I think not. The cases are of such a character that they can be disposed of either one way or the other on appeal, and if the question involved is of sufficient importance to necessitate a new trial, I think it should be had in the County Court.

Q. Well, are those new trials in ordinance cases frequent? A. Well, I haven't known of but one in my own practice, extending over my own experience as County Judge and Special County Judge, a period of ten years, I think, in all. I haven't known of but one new trial being granted on an appeal from a Police Court.

Q. I see, only one new trial? A. Only one new trial during that period.

Q. I asked you this, I don't recall whether you answered: Do the appeals from the Police Court cover a variety of cases? A. Yes, sir.

Q. Cover pretty much a general range? A. Yes.

Q. You don't find them in any special lines? A. No.

BY COMMISSIONER HAMILTON:

Q. Judge, what advantage would it be to a Judge sitting in a Criminal Court, if he knew the record of the prisoner personally, over that of the Judge who had his record before him on paper and never saw the man before? A. Well, I spoke of recurrent cases. I had in mind, perhaps, more particularly, cases of non-support and cases of intoxication, where the complainant in each case is likely to be the same, and upon the trial of the case the Judge would be better able, in my opinion, to know the character of the evidence that was being given, if he had known something about the history of the cases before.

Q. Don't you think that any advantage, any such advantage, to be derived from continually sitting in the criminal part, is more than offset by the tendency to gradually become so accustomed to criminal charges that they cease to have importance in the Judge's mind, so that he becomes, as it were, hardened to them? A. Well, that is a question which involves certain relations, I don't know that I am competent to answer that question. It may be that the Judge does get hardened by hearing criminal business too much.

Q. And don't you think the constant sitting on the criminal side would bring about a wearing pressure on the Judge, from those elements that are most closely in association with crime, that would in time tend to wear out his mentality and general freshness? A. Well, I do feel sorry for a Judge that has to sit continually in criminal practice. I wouldn't want to do it myself. But, at the same time, if it has any tendency of that kind, you are not spoiling but one man at a time, if one Judge has all the work.

BY CHAIRMAN PAGE:

Q. But, on the other hand, supposing that after he sat there for a while he was turned into a new pasture, that is, the civil side, and allowed to refresh himself there, don't you think it might have the effect of restoring his equilibrium? A. Well, it might, no doubt. But still, in the administration of criminal justice, the attitude toward it has changed so much in recent years that I am inclined to think that a man gets an oportunity, even though he is dealing with criminal cases, to develop a side of him that would not be developed in the civil cases. The probation work is giving a new life to the administration of criminal law. The Judge does not stop with his interest in a case after the trial is concluded and the judgment recorded.

BY MR. MAYER:

Q. Judge, just one more question: In the City of New York, where there is a very great number of such cases, the excise cases, or violations of the liquor tax law, are tried by the Court of Special Sessions, which is, for the purposes of this question, the same as a Police Court. Now, do you think it would be desirable to confer that jurisdiction upon the Police Court, eliminating, of course, the question of the incumbent, and so on? A. Yes.

Q. Or as a matter of procedure? A. I think it might be a good idea.

Q. There isn't any difficulty in those cases, is there? A. Not that I know of.

Q. There is very rarely any profound questions of law involved? A. No, statutory crime is very easy to dispose of.

Q. And the Judge who tries a case of petit larceny presumably can try an excise case? A. I don't think it requires so high a degree of qualification to try an excise case.

S. P. BURRILL, called as a witness, having been duly sworn, testified as follows:

BY MR. MAYER:

Q. Are you the secretary of the Civil Service Commission? A. Yes, sir.

Q. And have you brought with you the questions that were asked in the examination for probation officer? A.

We never held but one examination, that was for probation officer, several years ago, at the time Mr. Masters was appointed. We have pending now an examination for probation officer in the Juvenile Court, which will be held on June 18th. What I have here are the——

Q. Questions of that first examination? A. Questions in the examination Mr. Masters took several years ago. That has nothing to do with the juvenile work.

Q. When was this examination of Mr. Masters? A. I cannot give the date unless it is on here. I presume it was about two years ago.

Q. Now does the paper which you show me contain the questions asked at the examination referred to? A. Yes.

Q. And does it also contain the answers as made by Mr. Masters? A. Yes.

MR. MAYER: I will read this in evidence (reading):

2778.   ALFRED J. MASTERS.   Parole Officer.

1. Q. How are probation officers selected, what is their term of office, and how is their compensation determined? A. Probation officers have been selected by the Judges of the various courts. My appointment in the first place came from Judge Sutherland. In the city, I was appointed by Judge Chadsey, who has power, under the code, to appoint parole officers. My present appointment was from Commissioner Gilman. The compensation is fixed by the Board of Estimates and Apportionment. There is no term of office specified, the position being held at the pleasure of the Court, or the officer who made the appointment.

2. Q. What are the duties of probation officers? A. The

duty of a parole officer is to take those who are turned over to his charge and keep a record of them and find out their condition and home surroundings and try to change their mode of living. We have a regular system; at first, they report to us weekly, then once in two weeks, then once a month and finally we let them go.

3. Q. What powers do probation officers have with reference to persons committed to their care? A. They have the power to re-arrest them if they are found not doing according to their instructions.

4. Q. What do you consider the chief purpose of probation work? A. To take young boys from sixteen to twenty years of age and get them to lead a good life.

5. Q. What do you consider the essential qualifications of probation officers? A. A man should be able to sympathize with people who are brought up in crime and try to do something to help them to get out of it.

6. Q. In what cases can a person be placed on probation under charge of a probation officer? A. Burglary, larceny, robbery, non-support and misdemeanors of the law.

7. Q. If directed by the Court to investigate and report as to the advisability of suspending sentence in any particular case, what investigation would you make, and to whom would you go for information? A. I should find out for whom they had been working and go and see the parents and get all the information I could about them and find out if there was any chance of bettering their condition.

8. Q. In case sentence were suspended and the probationer put in your charge, what general conditions would you impose? A. First, the boy must be perfectly truthful, and I should insist on his coming to me regularly. I should also go out and find out for myself if he had been telling me the truth. I should insist on his being perfectly honest with me.

9. Q. What co-operation would you try to enlist to help you in the work of reformation? A. In case the boy was a Catholic, I would go to the priest and ask him to look after the boy. If the boy is a Protestant, I sometimes go to the minister, but those of the Protestant faith seldom go to any church. Then I also ask the police to let me know if they see anything wrong.

10. Q. In case probationer violates conditions for probation, what would be the procedure on your part and on the part of the Court? A. I would go to the Court and explain the whole thing to the Judge and get a warrant and have the boy brought in.

Endorsed on back as follows: "Letters of recommendation were filed with the Commission from Hon. George A. Benton, Hon. J. B. M. Stephens, Hon. Arthur E. Sutherland and Hon. John H. Chadsey. These letters were returned to Mr. Masters at his request."

BY MR. MAYER:

Q. Did Mr. Masters stand first in the examination? A. Yes, sir.

Q. Now, in the examination, was something allowed for experience? A. The examination was rated, consisted, of two parts. Fifty per cent was given for experience and testimonials presented. Fifty per cent was given for answers to the questions which you have. It was an oral examination taken down by our stenographer. The answers there are the stenographer's answers, which he took and afterwards transcribed.

Q. Oh, then it was an oral examination? A. It was an oral examination.

Q. And no written examination at all, that is, no applicant had a written examination? A. No examination except that the questions were propounded to Mr. Masters and to the other candidates in turn and were taken stenographically.

Q. Was anything allowed for appearance or manner or anything of that sort? A. Well, in rating the fifty per cent. on testimonials and experience, the candidates are given several days to prepare their experience statement and to prepare testimonials. They then present those and are rated by the three members of the Commission. The Commissioners are guided by the testimonials and by the experience statement, and possibly by the personality of the candidates in part. When they get through they simply make the marks.

Q. Then the three Commissioners have before them the persons who are applicants for the place? A. Yes, sir.

Q. (Continuing) Of probation officer? A. Yes, sir.

Q. Now, in this examination that you are to hold for the probation officer of the Juvenile Court, will the Commissioners have the candidates before them personally, is that not a question which I should ask at this time? A. We have not outlined in any way the character of the examination yet and it has not been discussed. The date was simply fixed and we will meet Monday to outline the character of the examination. We have been asked, I have no objection to stating, we have been asked by influential members of the Humane Society to consult with Mr. Homer Folk regarding the character of the examination. That was an informal request that has not been considered, so that I cannot tell what the new examination will be, until we fix it.

Q. Well, now, did Mrs. Armstrong take this same examination Mr. Masters did? A. Mrs. Armstrong was in that same examination. There were three candidates in it.

BY CHAIRMAN PAGE:

Q. How many candidates took the examination at the time Mr. Masters did? A. There were three, with him; one woman, Mrs. Armstrong. So that we made two eligible lists. At first a requisition was made for a male probation officer and we certified the two. Then a requisition was made for a woman probation officer and we certified only the one. But it was the same examination and the same scale of marking.

BY CHAIRMAN FRANCIS:

Q. How many appeared for the examination altogether? A. Only three.

CHAIRMAN PAGE: The Commission stands adjourned subject to the call of the chairman.

Final Report

of the

Commission to Inquire Into Courts of Inferior

Criminal Jurisdiction in Cities of the

First Class

IN ASSEMBLY

April 4, 1910.

FINAL REPORT OF THE COMMISSION TO INQUIRE INTO THE COURTS OF INFERIOR CRIMINAL JURISDICTION IN CITIES OF THE FIRST CLASS.

To the Governor:

The Commission appointed, pursuant to chapter 211 of the Laws of 1908, to inquire into the manner in which justice is administered in the courts of inferior criminal jurisdiction in cities of the first class, herewith submits its final report.

On November 24, 1908, the Commission began its inquiry in the city of New York, and, under date of February 3, 1909, submitted a preliminary report, briefly setting forth the progress of its investigation into the condition of the courts of special sessions and magistrates' courts in that city. The Commission next pursued its investigations in the city of Buffalo, and, under date of March 20, 1909, submitted its final report in regard to the Buffalo courts, and thereafter resumed its work in the city of New York. On May 21 and 22, 1909, the Commission held hearings in the city of Rochester, and thereafter again continued its investigations in the city of New York, having heard many witnesses, taken in all over 5,000 pages of testimony, including exhibits, and having visited court houses and other institutions related to the work of these courts.

The Commission has pursued its labors upon the theory that it was charged with the duty of inquiring into the system, methods and procedure of these courts, rather than to investigate specific complaints against individual officials or employees. It has believed its duty to be to make recommendations as to substantive legislation, leaving to the proper authorities the prosecution, in the appropriate tribunals, of specific acts of wrongdoing.

CITY COURT OF BUFFALO.

The report on the administration of the courts in the city of Buffalo contained recommendations for a radical change in the system there prevailing and was accompanied by a proposed bill establishing the City Court of Buffalo. This bill became law, and is now chapter 570 of the Laws of 1909.

Under this statute, a court having both inferior civil and criminal jurisdiction was created and provision was made for a chief judge and five associate judges.

Three judges, whose terms would not expire, were continued in office, and a chief judge and two associate judges were required to be elected at the general election in November, 1909.

These officials were chosen at the last general election and the court has now been organized in accordance with the provisions of the statute establishing it.

So far as the Commission is able to judge, at present, there appears to be an earnest desire on the part of the judges of the new City Court of Buffalo to carry out the purposes and spirit of the enactment. The Commission is gratified to learn that, as a result of its inquiry and of the enactment in question, a detention home for children and suitable quarters for the various parts of the court, including the children's part, have been provided by the city of Buffalo. Among the other immediate reforms brought about through the establishment of the City Court of Buffalo may be mentioned the elimination of the police station " morning courts;" the discontinuance of the custom of confining children in police station cells; the separation of the trials of male and female prisoners; the establishment of a part of the court for the hearing of cases involving domestic relations, and the unification and extension of the work of probation among minor offenders. The larger benefits which the Commission hopes the city of Buffalo will derive from this act will, in its opinion, result even more from the correct principles upon which it believes the structure of the court to be based, and the system of administration provided for than from any direct inhibition or mandate as to matters of detail, contained in the enactment.

Police Court in Rochester.

In the city of Rochester there is one police judge and one court house for the hearing and trial of the cases of adults, and a room situated in another building for the hearing of children's cases.

The police court is well situated and well arranged. The clerical force, the probation officers and the attendants impressed the Commission most favorably as being intelligent and enthusiastic in their work and as taking an active, personal interest in the problems presented to a court of this jurisdiction.

There has been a commendable effort by means of a card index to perfect a useful system of identification, which, with the cooperation of the police officials, seems to be working effectively.

The police judge, who had followed the reports of the proceedings of the Commission in the city of New York, shortly before the visit of the Commission, had established a separate hearing for women. There is a complete separation not only in the detention of male and female defendants in the courthouse, but the judge hears the female defendants in a room on another floor from that where he sits in the hearings and trials of male defendants. This seems entirely practicable, owing to the comparatively small number of cases and small territorial jurisdiction of the court. While the experiment was too new for the Commission to express a final judgment, it nevertheless seemed to the Commission that there was every prospect that the plan would work out advantageously.

The police judge was of the opinion that the accommodations in the children's part were too limited, and it seemed to the Commission that provision for better accommodations would soon be necessary. This, however, is a subject with which the local authorities are able adequately to deal.

For the present, one police court seems ample for the city of Rochester; but provision should be made for the temporary appointment by the mayor for a period not to exceed thirty days of an attorney to perform the duties of the police judge in the event of his sickness or other disability, and to allow him a reasonable vacation. This work is now done by the municipal court judges, but they should not be taken from their regular duties for this purpose. With this exception, the Commission is of the opinion that no changes are necessary at this time.

Preliminary Report — New York City.

The preliminary report in regard to the courts in the city of
New York, submitted by the Commission to the Governor, briefly
called attention to some of the subjects under consideration and
recommended a plan to relieve, temporarily, the congested condition of the calendar of the court of special sessions of the first-
division.

On January 28, 1909, there were pending in that court 5,958
untried bail cases, and the court was about eleven months in
arrears in the trial of these cases.

As the result of the recommendation of the Commission, chapter 90 of Laws of 1909 was enacted. This act empowered
the mayor of the city of New York to designate two magistrates
to sit as justices of the court of special sessions in the first division until December 1, 1909, or until such earlier time as the
justices of the court certified to the mayor that only 300 bail
cases were remaining upon their calendar awaiting trial.

The act went into effect on March 17, 1909, and the mayor
promptly designated two magistrates in accordance therewith.

A second part of the court was organized, with the result that
in eight months (April to December, 1909) 14,947 cases were
disposed of in the two parts of the court and on December 1, 1909,
there were pending only about 525 untried bail cases.

Thus, at very slight expense to the city for additional clerical
help, the accumulation of a large number of untried bail cases
has been substantially ended, and if the legislation which the
Commission recommends is enacted there is every reason to believe
that misdemeanors can be promptly tried henceforth and that
long delays need not again occur.

The addition of a temporary second part of the court of special
sessions has also given to the Commission the opportunity of
deciding from experience whether such an addition is permanently necessary, and has enabled the Commission to reach more
intelligently its final conclusions.

The Courts of Inferior Criminal Jurisdiction.

It is desirable at the outset briefly to outline the relations to
each other of the courts of inferior criminal jurisdiction in the
city of New York.

The magistrates' court is the court of first instance and is held
by a city magistrate. To this court are brought persons charged

with the commission of (1) a felony, or (2) a misdemeanor, or (3) a violation of a law or ordinance not classified either as felony or misdemeanor. It is the duty of the magistrate to determine whether he shall hold to await the action of the grand jury a person charged with committing a felony, or hold for trial at the court of special sessions a person charged with committing a misdemeanor, while in respect of the third class of cases he has summary power and jurisdiction to determine guilt and to sentence accordingly.

Under the present law, there are two divisions of the magistrates' courts, each having its own organization, consisting of a board of city magistrates, with a president selected by the magistrates annually from their own number. The first division comprises the boroughs of Manhattan and The Bronx, and the second division, the boroughs of Brooklyn, Queens and Richmond.

The court of special sessions is separated into two similar territorial divisions.

The court of special sessions of the first division has two parts; one for the trial of misdemeanors committed by adults, and the other, known as the children's part, having jurisdiction of all offenses committed by children under the age of sixteen years, in the boroughs of Manhattan and The Bronx, except capital cases.

The jurisdiction of the court of special sessions of the second division is similar to that of the first division, except that there is a separate children's part only for the borough of Brooklyn, none having as yet been established for the boroughs of Queens and Richmond. In those boroughs offenses committed by children under the age of sixteen years are tried by the magistrates and hearing held separate and apart from the trial of adults.

In the year 1908 there were 175,371 arraignments in the magistrates' courts of Manhattan and The Bronx, being 37,324 in excess of 1907; while in the boroughs of Brooklyn, Queens and Richmond the total number of arraignments for 1908 was 60,185, being 7,388 more than in 1907.

These totals of arraignments do not, however, represent the number of different individuals, because in many instances the same persons have been arrested more than once, but up to the present time there has been no means of ascertaining how many different individuals have been arrested in the city of New York in any one year, and statistics in such regard cannot be accurately compiled until a comprehensive system of identification shall have been established. Nevertheless, even allowing for repeating offenders, the total number of persons arraigned in the city has undoubtedly been upwards of 200,000, and, in addition to these, many other persons have been brought into these courts by the service of summons, of which no record is kept. It has been estimated that the total number of summonses issued is upward of 100,000 annually, so that it is probable that somewhere in the neighborhood of 300,000 people are annually brought before the magistrates to answer to some charge or complaint made against them.

It thus becomes important to follow the procedure from the time of arrest until arraignment.

The Code of Criminal Procedure requires that a defendant, when arrested, must in all cases be taken before the magistrate without unnecessary delay, and that he shall not be subjected to any more restraint than is necessary for his arrest and detention (Code of Criminal Procedure, sections 165, 172). The Greater New York charter (section 338) specifically provides that " each member of the police force, under a penalty of ten dollars fine or dismissal from the force at the discretion of the police commissioner, shall, immediately upon an arrest, convey in person the offender before the nearest sitting magistrate, that he may be dealt with according to law. If the arrest is made during the hours that the magistrate does not regularly hold court, or if the magistrate is not holding court, such offender may be detained in a precinct or station-house thereof until the next regular public sitting of the magistrate and no longer, and shall then be conveyed without delay before the magistrate, to be dealt with according to law."

These plain provisions of the Greater New York charter enacted in pursuance of the general policy of the State as expressed in the Code of Criminal Procedure for the purpose of assuring a prompt hearing before the nearest sitting magistrate, have been repeatedly violated by the police, and from the testimony it appears that prisoners from time to time have been brought before a magistrate who is not " the nearest sitting magistrate." The practice is indefensible and has received the condemnation of the courts. (People ex rel. Gow v. Bingham, 57 Misc. 66.)

The intent of the charter provision was also to prevent the selection, by the prosecuting authorities, of the judicial officer before whom the defendant should be heard, and the protection thus assured by the charter should be vigorously safeguarded. By virtue of section 1844 of the Penal Law, it is a misdemeanor for a public officer, having arrested any person upon a criminal charge, willfully and wrongfully to delay to take such person before a magistrate having jurisdiction to take his examination, and therefore it should be the affirmative duty of the magistrate, in cases of delay, to ascertain the reason therefor, and where the magistrate is not " the nearest sitting magistrate," he should decline to hear the case and should order the defendant to be taken forthwith to " the nearest sitting magistrate."

It is, of course, to be remembered in this connection that the nearest sitting magistrate, within the meaning of this section of the charter, is not necessarily the magistrate sitting within the distance physically nearest to the place of arrest. The jurisdiction of the respective magistrates' courts must be arranged territorially, with a view to the situation and distribution of the police precincts, but there can be no question that " the nearest sitting magistrate " means that magistrate sitting at the courthouse to which are required to be brought all persons arrested for offenses committed within that territorial jurisdiction.

Before the prisoner is arraigned, he is usually detained in what is known as the detention pen.

The detention pens in the various courthouses are in charge of the police, and in many instances are in immediate proximity to the courtroom. In the construction of these courthouses, or in the adaptation for use as courthouses of buildings originally designed for other purposes, little thought seems to have been given either to appropriate accommodations or to the complete separation of male from female defendants.

Detention Pens; First Division.— In the First District Magistrates' Court, situated in the Criminal Courts building on Centre street, the detention pens are separated by a sheet iron division, with the women on one side and the men on the other. Police officers pass back and forth all the time, with more or less resultant disorder. In the Second or Jefferson Market Court, where the night court is held, the detention pens, to use the language of Magistrate House, " are in a horrible condition. There is a little bit of a lobby and two large pens. One side the women and the other side the men. In the women's detention pen, over in the corner of a little jog, is a toilet, but no door and no screen to shut it off. In order to pass these detention pens, you have to pass through a door that takes the prisoners back into the prison that is under the supervision of the Commissioner of Corrections, provided the prisoner is held for trial, is fined or is held for examination."

The Commission, upon the occasion of its several visits to the night court held at Jefferson Market, was shocked by the conditions resulting from these primitive and inadequate detention pens. Women were huddled together, young and old, first and hardened offenders, some innocent and subsequently discharged, and this women's pen immediately adjoins the men's pen similarly crowded. On several occasions there were more prisoners than these pens could accommodate, even with all the crowding, and the prisoners, men and women indifferently, stood in front of and beyond these pens. Some of the prisoners were engaged in loud talking, and the young and often the innocent were subjected to the indignity of being compelled to hear vile and blasphemous language.

Such a condition is disgraceful to a great, civilized community, and should no longer be tolerated. It must always be remembered in this connection that the person thus detained in the detention pen has not yet been arraigned before the magistrate and, under the law, is presumed to be innocent, and yet this detention is frequently an infinitely worse punishment than the small fine which is imposed for some minor offense.

To this and the other courts are brought large numbers of respectable persons, who are not charged with any offense involving moral turpitude, but merely with the breach of some regulative law or ordinance.

In the Third or Essex Market Court, the condition of the pens has been notoriously bad for years. In the Fourth or East Fifty-seventh Street Court there are two pens; one in which the women are detained, and, in the other immediately adjoining, the men. Owing to lack of facilities in this courtroom and in order to avoid noise and confusion as much as possible, benches are placed in the back of the room where these pens are situated. The police officers thus come into easy contact with the men and women prisoners, a condition which is most undesirable in the opportunity it affords for influencing such prisoners in the selection of lawyers or advising as to their conduct when arraigned.

In the Fifth District or Harlem Court the pens for the men and women are likewise adjoining. The Seventh or West Fifty-fourth Street Court is in somewhat better condition. The Sixth District or Bronx Court is temporary in character, awaiting the completion of the new courthouse now under construction at One Hundred and Sixty-first street and Third avenue. The Eighth or Westchester Court has as yet so very few prisoners that no complaints in respect thereof have been made.

Detention Pens; Second Division.— In the courts in the borough of Brooklyn the same conditions prevail, in the majority of instances, of inadequate accommodations and improper proximity of the pens for men to the pens for women and in some instances the conditions are not only reprehensible but absolutely intolerable.

These conditions are specially noticeable in the First District or Adams Street Court; the Second District or Butler Street Court; the Fourth District or Bedford Avenue Court; the Fifth District or Manhattan Avenue Court and the Tenth District or New Jersey Avenue Court.

The number of prisoners detained at any one time in the courts in Queens and Richmond is, in comparison with the other boroughs, so few that the Commission has not received any complaints in reference thereto.

Obviously, no provision can be made by statute to remedy these evils, except a directory requirement that the detention pens for men shall be separated as completely as practicable from the pens for women. The detention home for women, in connection with the women's night court, hereinafter recommended, will however, in itself, lessen to a great extent, the evils here indicated. The Commission, nevertheless, calls sharp attention to these conditions in order that, in the erection or adaptation of buildings for courthouses in the future, regard shall be had for the construction of proper detention pens; and the Commission brings this subject to the attention of the local authorities, so that these existing conditions may be remedied as soon as possible.

Court-rooms and Their Arrangement.— The next step in the progress of the prisoner is the arraignment before the magistrate.

Here the methods of the First and Second Divisions differ in several important particulars.

In the First Division the courtrooms are constructed on the following general plan: There is a magistrate's bench behind which sit the magistrate, the police clerk, police clerk's assistants, the stenographer and the interpreter. In front of the bench is a raised platform behind which is a rail. This platform has long been called, in the parlance of these courts, " the bridge." The complainant, who is in most instances a police officer, stands on " the bridge," close to the magistrate. The prisoner stands below the rail, or, as it is called, below " the bridge." The police clerk's assistants, who sit at one side of the magistrate, are preparing the complaints, and for that purpose necessarily engaged in conversation with the complainant and his witnesses. At the other side of the magistrate the police clerk is receiving money in payment of fines and making a record of such receipt.

Beyond " the bridge " is a space where prisoners about to be arraigned, and the policemen who have made the arrests, are ordinarily waiting in line until their cases come before the magistrate. Beyond this space is a railing or grating separating it from the general public.

The ordinary scene in the magistrates' court is one of confusion and utter lack of dignity, resulting from the noise of conversation between complainants, witnesses and court clerks, and this noise not infrequently interferes with the orderly conduct of the case under hearing before the magistrate.

While the hearing is going on, the complaining witness, in most instances a police officer, stands close to the bench, with his back to the defendant, often giving his statement or testimony in a voice so low that the defendant, when he is below " the bridge," cannot possibly hear him; the magistrate himself likewise frequently speaks in tones so subdued as to be inaudible to the prisoner, with the result that the policeman who is stationed on " the bridge " plays entirely too important a part, frequently conveying in laconic sentences to the prisoner the nature of the charge and the questions of the judge, and then conveying back to the judge the mumbled answers of the prisoner. On a number of occasions it was apparent to the Commission that the prisoner did not know what was going on, and that the hearing was one only in name. There being no witness chair, the whole proceeding lacked even the semblance of judicial procedure. Frequently, there are so many persons on and around the bridge that it is almost impossible for the prisoner to see the magistrate. The interior arrangement of these courtrooms thus briefly described, and this method of conducting hearings are disgraceful in an enlightened community and should be forthwith ended once and for all.

The rearrangement of these courtrooms so as to abolish "the bridge" and give the prisoner the same opportunity to hear and be heard as the witnesses against him, would involve a comparatively small expenditure and would bring about a substantial improvement in the method and manner of conducting hearings and examinations in the Magistrates' Courts.

The magistrates in many instances bring the prisoner to the bench from below "the bridge," thus indicating that the present arrangement of these courtrooms is not conducive to a full and fair hearing.

We are not unmindful of the fact that frequently persons are arraigned who are in such physical condition that they cannot be brought to the bench, and that they must stand at some distance from the magistrate, but in such cases the magistrate can readily arrange the hearing so that the defendant at least knows what is going on, if he is in the mental condition to understand. It has been urged that any procedure which would make for a more deliberate hearing would involve much time and cause much delay. This argument does not appeal to the Commission. These are practically courts of last resort in most instances, and the examination or trial of the defendant should be conducted in such manner, and surrounded with such safeguards as to assure a full, fair and deliberate hearing. While there is a congestion in some of these courts at the beginning of the day's calendar, the magistrate has plenty of time to dispose competently of all cases before him, without doing so with undue haste. The clerks framing the complaints should not be in the courtroom, but provision should be made for them in a separate room, so that the courtroom may be relieved of the noise and confusion incident upon the preparation of these papers, and also that these clerks may have a better opportunity to hear fully the statements of the persons concerned and, as a result, more carefully and competently to draw the complaints.

The attendants, posted throughout different parts of the room, are police officers, detailed to the magistrates' courts by the police commissioner. The Commission has no desire to include in a general criticism those officers who are courteous and respectful, but it is well known that many of these officers are discourteous, brusque and even impertinent to the general public having business of one kind or another in these courts.

In the Second Division, the courtrooms are laid out much more satisfactorily and more nearly in accordance with what the Commission regards as the proper arrangement.

GENERAL CONDITIONS OF THE COURTHOUSES; MAGISTRATES' COURTS.

In order that both the detention pens and the interior arrangement of the courts shall be altered or reconstructed to remedy the existing evils to which we have called attention, it is desirable to point out briefly the defects of some of the court houses.

The Commission fully realizes that these defects can only be remedied by the appropriation of adequate funds for that purpose. With many other necessary and contemplated improvements constantly under construction and in progress in the city of New York, the tendency has been to neglect or postpone the construction of proper courthouses for the Magistrates' Courts, Courts of Special Sessions and the Children's Courts. No better illustration of this tendency is to be found than the Essex Market Magistrate's Court.

For years this court has been situated in an old, dilapidated building, far too small to accommodate the persons there assembled and completely lacking every reasonable convenience. There is no place where the magistrate can comfortably hold a private examination, and no adequate room, outside of the courtroom, where the clerks can take complaints. The prisoners are brought up one flight of stairs from the detention pens and marched through the center of the courtroom in order to bring them before the magistrate. The ventilation or rather lack of ventilation is such as to be a constant menace to the health of the magistrates and employees assigned to the court.

For years attention has been constantly called to this condition; grand juries have investigated and made recommendations; but only very recently have these incessant complaints become effective. The city authorities have finally taken steps for the erection of a new courthouse in this district.

The Second District or Jefferson Market Court has already been referred to in connection with the detention pens, but in other respects this courtroom is unsuitable, because of the lack of accommodation, the magistrate's private room being about large enough to accommodate a desk, and the probation officers being required to use a room also used by the clerks for the filing of various papers and records. The constant passing of the elevated trains makes the noise insufferable at times, more especially in the summer, when the courtroom windows are open.

The magistrates have the use of the ground floor only of this building, while the upper part is utilized by one of the Municipal Court justices. The inadequacy of accommodation is emphasized because this court has been and is likely in future to be used for a night as well as a day court. If this building cannot be disposed of and another one obtained in a better location, it would be well for the city authorities to consider the advisability of using the whole building for the business of the Magistrates' Court, compelling the Municipal Court justice to use accommodations elsewhere provided.

In the Fourth or East Fifty-seventh Street Court, the toilet accommodations for the officials of the court are inadequate and inconvenient.

The First or Center Street Court, the Fifth or Harlem Court and the Seventh or West Side Court have much better accommodations, but here also there are certain defects which could probably be done away with by comparatively inexpensive alterations.

The new courthouse at One Hundred and Sixty-first street and Third avenue in The Bronx, now in the course of construction, is very badly situated, because of the noise from the surface and elevated railroads.

In the borough of Brooklyn the Commission found a similar lack of accommodations in a number of courthouses.

The First District Court is held in a building erected as a police station and at the present time occupied in part by a police precinct. The courtroom is in the back portion of the building and is very poorly ventilated. On the north side of the courtroom is an apartment-house; the south side abuts upon the rear of houses situated on Myrtle avenue, of which the second floors are on a level with the courtroom. In front of the easterly portion of the premises used as the clerk's office and magistrate's office is the elevated railroad; and on the westerly side is a blank wall. The foul air constantly comes up from the cells to the courtroom.

The Second District courtroom had apparently been used as a hall of some character and consists of one large room, with partitions for rooms occupied by the clerks and the magistrate. The cells attached to this court are very poorly ventilated and at times prisoners have escaped by reason of the cells being poorly secured. This building is all on one floor, the clerks' room and the magistrate's room being separated by a board partition from the courtroom; the toilet attached to the court is next to the clerk's office and is in a very unsanitary condition.

All prisoners arrested by the police of the 149th Precinct, located at 318 Adams street (same building as First District Court) and also by the police attached to the 150th Precinct located at 69 Fulton street, and the greater part of the prisoners arrested by the officers detailed to Police Headquarters in State street, are arraigned in the First District Court. The police of the 145th, 147th and 148th Precincts, which precincts are south of Atlantic avenue, bring their prisoners to the Second District Court. If there could be erected a suitable courthouse midway between the First and Second District Courts as at present located, say at Atlantic avenue, then the magistrates of the First and Second Districts could each hold sessions in such building, having two separate courtrooms.

The Third District Court, at the corner of Myrtle and Vanderbilt avenues, and the Sixth District Court, 495 Gates avenue, could also be consolidated in the same way. While the Third District courtroom is of itself properly equipped for the purposes of its use, yet by reason of the noise of the elevated road which passes the door and of the trolley on the side street it is almost impossible to conduct the examination of witnesses and this is particularly true in the warm weather when the windows are open. By sending the prisoners from the 157th Precinct to the First District Court it would not be inconvenient to have the precincts which now send their prisoners to the Third and Sixth District Courts, send them to the Sixth District Court and two magistrates could sit in one building.

The Fourth District Court is held in the three-story building 186 Bedford avenue, the first floor of which is occupied by the cells and clerk's room, the second floor by the courtroom and the third floor by the clerk's offices.

The Fifth District Court is held in a two story and basement brick building, corner of Manhattan avenue and Power street; the basement is used by the clerks for the taking of complaints, the next floor as the courtroom and the top floor for the clerk's offices and the magistrate's room. Neither of these buildings was originally erected for court purposes and they are situated about a mile apart.

If a central location, midway between these two courts, could be had and a courthouse erected having ample accommodation for two magistrates, the work of these courts would be expedited and the convenience of the public subserved.

The Seventh District Court, at 31 Snider ave., is properly equipped except that the present rooms are hardly sufficient to comfortably accommodate the clerks, magistrate and public, and as this court is situated in a section of the borough which is increasing rapidly in population, a larger courtroom will soon be needed.

The Eighth District Court, at West 8th street, Coney Island, is properly equipped.

The Ninth District Court, corner 23rd street and Fifth avenue, was formerly used as a public hall but is now well suited for use as a court.

The Tenth District Court, on New Jersey avenue is in a two-story building, the cellar of which is used for the reception of prisoners; the first floor is used as a courtroom and the second floor for clerk's offices. In order to reach the clerk's office it is necessary to ascend a lengthy stairway, to the great inconvenience of the public. While the courtroom itself answers the purpose, yet the location of the cells and clerks' rooms is a matter of just complaint.

COURTROOMS OF THE COURTS OF SPECIAL SESSIONS.

Adult Parts.— The present courtroom of the Court of Special Sessions of the First Division is situated in the Criminal Courts building and is well adapted for the uses of the court.

On the establishment of the second part of this court, to which reference will be more fully made hereinafter, it seems highly desirable that accommodations should be found in the same building. This will subserve convenience, save time and assist in centralizing the work of the clerk's office.

The present Criminal Courts building is very much crowded, but it would seem to be practicable for the local authorities to assign the rooms now occupied by the coroners to the Court of Special Sessions, finding some other place for the coroners' offices and courtroom.

In the Second Division the Court of Special Sessions is now held at the corner of Atlantic avenue and Clinton street. Here the court is excellently housed and the courthouse is in every way creditable to the city.

Children's Courts.— The Children's Court of the First Division is situated at Eleventh street and Third avenue, in the borough of Manhattan, and for a considerable time has been entirely too small and otherwise insufficient for the purposes of the court. An appropriation was recently made for the erection of a new court-house upon this site. In designing this building the introduction of several desirable new features is contemplated, among them a nursery for the smaller children and accommodations which will permit the mothers or other female relatives of the children to wait in a convenient place until their cases are reached.

In the construction of this Children's Court there is an excellent opportunity for the erection of a model court building for that purpose. In many of the jurisdictions throughout this country and abroad, the room in which the child's case is heard is small, and the usual features of the courtroom are eliminated. This is regarded by some experienced judges and students of the subject as the proper arrangement for the hearing of children's cases, so that each child's case can be heard by itself and privately without a curious audience, and in order also that the judge may come into a closer relation with the child, parental rather than judicial.

We recognize, however, that there are conditions and circumstances, in the administration of children's courts in the city of New York, which present problems that cannot necessarily be solved upon the same lines as in smaller jurisdictions.

Among the children brought to this court are many who are charged with serious offenses, such as breaking into cars, picking pockets, etc. A considerable proportion of these children cannot be dealt with successfully if the court and its proceedings impress them as too gentle and amiable. Besides, in very many instances, it is the effort of the court not merely to control the child but to impress responsibility upon the parent. Many of these parents are of foreign birth, who have recently immigrated to this country and who have much respect for dignified forms, and it is the opinion of experienced judges that their success in dealing with children's cases would be impaired if the formal surrounding of the courtroom were taken away. There should be no difficulty, however, in so constructing the courtroom that the child can come even physically closer to the judge than at present, and that the space in front of the judge's bench can be more conveniently arranged.

It seems clear also that after a child has been placed on probation, a closer personal relation can be aided by the judge hearing the child and conversing with it in a direct way in some room other than the court room, and where the interview may be private.

As the new courthouse for this Children's Court will presumably be in use for many years, we suggest to the judges the most careful consideration of every detail of its construction. Such a courthouse will no doubt be expected to be a model for many others throughout this country, and therefore there is imposed upon the present judges a highly responsible duty.

The Children's Court of the borough of Brooklyn at 102 Court street, seems adequate for the present, but in the event of the construction at a future date of a new Children's Court in that borough, the judges will be charged with a similar responsibility.

TERRITORIAL JURISDICTION AND REDISTRICTING OF MAGISTRATES' COURTS.

The present boundaries of the various Magistrates' Courts districts have not been changed for many years.

By virtue of the provisions of section 205 of the Greater New York charter, the Commissioners of the Sinking Fund have the authority, upon the application of the Board of City Magistrates, to designate additional places for the holding of Magistrates' Courts.

The legislative intent as to the principle governing the location and jurisdiction of these courts is aptly expressed in requiring that such courts shall be held at such places as may seem "most conducive to the public convenience," or, as stated in another section of the charter, referring to certain court districts (§ 1390), the districts shall be divided "in such manner as to make access to the courts convenient to the residents * * * and otherwise conserve public interest."

In the boroughs of Manhattan and The Bronx, it is apparent that there should be a readjustment of the territorial jurisdiction of these courts, based on convenience and ready access and also upon the location of the various police precincts.

In the borough of Brooklyn, there are two more day courts than in the borough of Manhattan, although the number of persons arraigned in that borough is only about a third of the number arraigned in the borough of Manhattan. Owing to the large territorial extent of the borough of Brooklyn more courts are needed than the number of cases seem to justify, but some of the courts should be consolidated, as hereinbefore pointed out.

In the borough of Queens, likewise by reason of its large area, four courts seem essential.

In the borough of Richmond, there are but two courts, which are sufficient for the amount of business there transacted. These courts, however, are far distant from certain parts of the borough and some arrangement should be made by which the present magistrates could sit from time to time in the Tottenville section of the borough.

The power to change the district territorial lines from time to time as necessity may arise should be conferred upon the Mayor, the Commissioner of Police and the Chief City Magistrate (reference to whom will be hereinafter made) of the division affected.

Realizing the many duties of the Mayor, authority should be given to him to designate, in his discretion, the President of the Board of Aldermen to perform this duty on his behalf. In the event of the passage of the legislation which we shall recommend the redistricting should take place promptly.

Duties and Assignments of Justices and Magistrates, Clerks and Employees, and Defects in Existing System.

Special Sessions.—The Court of Special Sessions has two divisions, as already described, each having jurisdiction of the trial of misdemeanors committed in the division within which it sits, and, in addition, having original jurisdiction in bastardy cases. Each has a part for the trial of adults and a separate part for the trial of children, except that in the Second Division there is a separate children's part only for the borough of Brooklyn.

In each division there are six justices, three of whom are assigned each month to sit in the court for the trial of adults and one in the children's part, the remaining two being unassigned. While the child has the right to demand a trial by three justices, such demand has never been made since the organization of these children's parts, and, in practice, a single justice presides in such parts.

The Court of Special Sessions of the Second Division sits three days each week in the borough of Brooklyn for the trial of misdemeanors and one day in each of the boroughs of Queens and Richmond.

In a sense, all the work of the court is judicial, but it is, perhaps, a more exact classification to divide the work into the judicial and the administrative.

The judicial work of the court consists in the hearing of cases and in the disposition of convicted persons.

The administrative side of the court has to do with the making up of calendars, the keeping of records and statistics, the supervision of the clerical force and the general overseeing of the conduct of the officers and employees of the court.

Under the present system in each division, no one justice is charged with this part of the work, which is so essential to the effective performance of the judicial duties of the court. There is in no sense any chief judge, either provided for by statute or selected by the members of the court. Under the system of rotation prevailing in the two divisions of this court, there are various months in the year, or parts of months, when a justice is sitting in the adult court or the children's court or when he is unassigned, and it is, of course, impossible for a justice sitting in one part of the court to supervise the condition of the calendars in the other, and as the justice presiding at the trials changes each month, there is no continuing presiding justice.

In the Court of Special Sessions of the First Division, the inquiry of the Commission showed utter lack of supervision of the clerk's office and led to an investigation which resulted in the clerk's retirement. That court was found to be far behind in its work. Up to 1907, the court had been abreast of its work and both bail and prison cases were tried with reasonable dispatch, but after that, partly because of the failure of the court to try bail cases in the summer months, partly because of the increase in the number of cases, and partly because of inadequate clerical force, there had accumulated a large number of untried bail cases. As the Commission stated in its preliminary report:

> " The long delays have resulted in many instances in a practical denial of justice either to the prosecution or to the defense; and in others, in a practical nullification of laws enacted for the peace and safety of the community. Witnesses have died, disappeared or removed; penalties imposed by statute upon conviction have not attached; and because of the immunity occasioned by delay, certain classes of misdemeanors have been repeated with impunity."

The delay in the trial of many of these cases could have been partly obviated by hearing bail cases in the summer months, but the failure so to do, together with the other causes referred to, resulted in long postponed trials, more especially of disorderly house, liquor tax and motor vehicle cases.

The manifest result was that the delays amounted to a continuing license, so that in the case, for instance, of disorderly house keepers, there was no abatement of the offense, because of the long postponed trials.

The Court should sit every day in the summer months (except Saturdays, Sundays and holidays) to dispose promptly of prison cases.

Magistrates' Courts.— In the first division there are eight day courts, one night court and sixteen magistrates.

In the borough of Brooklyn there are ten day courts and ten magistrates.

In the borough of Queens there are three day courts, and a fourth is nearing completion, and there are four magistrates.

In the borough of Richmond there are two day courts and two magistrates.

The Board of Magistrates in each division elects annually its presiding magistrate. The presiding magistrate thus has not a permanent tenure of his office nor a permanent responsibility, and his control over the clerks is greatly restricted. The assignment of the magistrates to the various courts is made by themselves, with no directing head.

In the Second Division of the Magistrates' Courts there have been unusual and unexplained delays in the trial of liquor tax and disorderly house cases, which classes of cases the magistrates of the First Division have usually disposed of promptly.

These results, both in the Courts of Special Sessions and in the Magistrates' Courts, have been due in some measure to a lack of adequate and authoritative supervision. Under a proper system, attention would have been promptly called to unwarrantable delays and to the lax methods and conduct of employees.

Removal of Cases from Court of Special Sessions.— Some of the delays, however, have not been due to any fault of the court, but to the dilatory tactics of defendants, who have availed themselves of the provisions of section 1409 of the Greater New York Charter to postpone motions for the removal of cases to the Court of General Sessions until the very last moment, and some remedy must be found to cover such instances.

A defendant desiring to remove a case to the Court of General Sessions or the Supreme Court, should be required to make application for the certificate of removal within ten days after the date that his case is first on for pleading.

Reforms Adopted During Inquiry.— It is gratifying to the Commission to observe that, as an immediate result, partly of its inquiry, and partly of temporary relief by legislation enacted upon its recommendation, these delays have in great measure ceased. Part I of the Court of Special Sessions of the First Division disposed of 3,767 cases during the months of June, July and August, 1909, and Part II disposed of 1,026 cases in June, 1909, adjourning during July and August to give the members of the court an opportunity for vacation.

In some other respects, changes have been effectuated or improvements made by these courts at the suggestion of the Commission or as the result of its inquiry, where the change or improvement seemed simple and obvious to the Commission.

Thus, it was found that much time was spent by the Court of Special Sessions of the First Division for the trial of adults in the hearing of reports in probation cases, when a single justice could receive these reports, thereby not only saving time for the trial of cases, but also serving the convenience of witnesses and giving a fuller opportunity for a careful hearing of these reports.

In the Magistrates' Courts of the First Division it appeared that with few exceptions the police clerks deposited the moneys collected by them with their own funds. This practice had gone on for years and it was not until after the Commission had examined these clerks that the magistrates made a rule requiring the clerks to keep their official accounts separate from their private accounts.

In the Magistrates' Courts of the Second Division, a number of the magistrates had paroled defendants held to await trial in the Court of Special Sessions, without any authority in law so to do. This questionable practice has, as we understand, been discontinued.

Other illustrations could be given, but enough has been shown to point out that the absence of central authority has led to lack of individual responsibility and, as a consequence, that little effort has been made to correct obvious errors or to improve lax methods.

Necessity for Centralized Responsibility.— In nearly all the higher courts, one judge, usually the chief, is charged with the general supervision of the clerk's office, and such, it is understood, is the practice in the Supreme Court of the United States, the Court of Appeals of this State and the various Appellate Divisions. The essential feature of the Chicago inferior court system, adopted by the Legislature of 1909 in the law recommended by this Commission establishing the City Court of Buffalo, is the fixing of responsibility for the administrative work of the court upon a chief judge.

This principle, we believe, should be applied to and adopted for the Court of Special Sessions and the Magistrates' Courts.

The chief judge should be charged with comprehensive administrative duties. He should prescribe the hour for the opening of the various parts of the court and for the attendance of the judges, clerks and other employees. He should establish and supervise a system for keeping the records of the court and should have authority to appoint the chief clerk and the chief probation officer.

All the judges of these courts, however, acting as a board, should select all of the clerks and other employees of the court, except the chief clerk and the chief probation officer. Thus, while the other judges would not be relieved of their just responsibility and each judge would be required to perform his judicial duties in accordance with his conscience and judgment, the chief judge would be the administrative head upon whom would rest the responsibility in the first instance for the conduct of the employees of the court, the condition of the calendars and the proper establishment and keeping of all records.

Assignment of Justices and Magistrates.— The chief justice of the Court of Special Sessions, in addition, should assign the justices to the various parts of the court.

The board of magistrates of each division should, by rule or regulation, assign the respective magistrates to the various courts in the division upon the principle of rotation, except, however, that the chief magistrate of the division should have authority to designate the magistrates to sit in the night courts and the courts of domestic relations.

The rotation should be genuine and the vicious so-called " Home Court " system prevailing in the borough of Brooklyn should be abolished. Under this system a magistrate sits two weeks out of each month in his so-called " Home Court," and we are of the opinion that this has led to evils among which may be

mentioned the constant adjournment of liquor tax and disorderly
house cases.

Subpœna Servers; Attendants and Other Employees.— The
Courts of Special Sessions at present employs its own subpœna
servers. In accordance with the suggestions already made, each of
the courts to be constituted as hereinafter recommended should
have one chief clerk and other necessary clerks, one chief probation
officer and other necessary probation officers, stenographers, interpreters, civilian attendants and such other employees as from
time to time may be deemed necessary.

Owing to the present inadequate number of subpœna servers
in the Court of Special Sessions of the First Division, a subpœna is rarely served personally, and in nearly all instances the
subpœenas are sent by mail. Under such a system, witnesses necessary for the prosecution of the People's case are frequently
overlooked or do not respond, and often through no fault of their
own in cases where the mail is delivered after the person sought
to be subpœnaed has left his home for the day.

The district attorney's office is equipped for this duty and
should perform it, thereby having full opportunity to prepare his
case properly and to subpœna such witnesses as he may think
necessary for that purpose.

The present subpœna servers in the Courts of Special Sessions
can either be retained for clerical work by arrangement with the
local authorities or transferred to the district attorney's office.

Police Officers Detailed to the Courts.— The police officers detailed to these courts should be withdrawn. There is no sound
argument for retaining them. The magistrates have only a
qualified control over men who necessarily remain under the
jurisdiction of the police commissioner. The assignment of these
men by the police commissioner and their withdrawal from time
to time have been the occasion for friction in the past and may be
at any time in the future, as so frequently occurs in cases of
divided jurisdiction.

It has been suggested by some of the magistrates that these
officers are necessary for the purpose of keeping order and to prevent or repress riotous or dangerous acts.

There seems to be no force in this suggestion, first, because
there are always police officers, necessarily in attendance at these
courts with their prisoners sufficient in number to protect against
any emergencies, and, second, because experience has shown that

uniformed civilian officers or attendants are entirely competent to do the work now done in these courts by these police attendants.

At the Court of General Sessions and at the criminal terms of the Supreme Court, civilian attendants are employed, even though the defendants there arraigned are indicted for the commission of grave crimes.

It is, moreover, the belief of the Commission that civilian attendants, under the control of the magistrates and removable at pleasure, will prove to be more considerate and courteous than the average police officer assigned to these courts, and that they will be fully as capable of performing the duties required of them.

There is no economy in keeping these detailed police officers in the Special Sessions Magistrates' Courts. We are informed by the police commissioner that the total number assigned to these courts is 189, of whom 8 are lieutenants, each receiving a salary of $2,250 per annum, 12 sergeants at $1,500 per annum, 167 patrolmen at $1,400 per annum, and 1 patrolman at $1,250 per annum, making a total of $271,050 which the city is spending for the pay of these men.

No doubt civilian attendants can be obtained at a salary less than that now paid to police officer attendants and with a lesser number of such civilian attendants than the present number of detailed police officers, it is not unlikely that the city would save $75,000 to $100,000 per annum, by the proposed change, while the police department would regain for full duty the services of this large number of men.

The Police Commissioner, however, should, from time to time, assign to the Magistrates' Courts such number of officers as the magistrates may certify to be necessary, for the sole purpose of serving warrants, and while such officers are thus assigned they should be under the jurisdiction and immediate direction of the magistrates and subject only to their orders when engaged in the business of the court.

Jurisdiction Recommended for Special Sessions.

The Courts of Special Sessions were established for the purpose of relieving the courts of superior criminal jurisdiction of the trial of misdemeanors, and to enable persons charged with the commission of such offenses to have a speedy trial.

Some suggestions have been made that the Court of Special Sessions should be abolished and that there should be a return to the system prevailing prior to 1895 of a single court of magistrates with the assignment from time to time of three members thereof to act as justices of the Court of Special Sessions. These suggestions have not impressed the Commission favorably, and while such a plan might be workable in a smaller community, the Commission believes that it would be unsuccessful in dealing with the situation in the city of New York.

Parts for the Trial of Adults.— It has also been urged that in the event of the continuance of the Court of Special Sessions separate from the Magistrates' Courts, the magistrates should be empowered to hear and determine certain classes of misdemeanors which are now tried by the Court of Special Sessions. Some of the magistrates have presented the view that the magistrates should have power to dispose of cases of misdemeanor where the defendant pleads guilty and should also have power of final disposition in the trial of minor offenses classified as misdemeanors.

The Commission has made thorough inquiry to determine the merits of these suggestions and has concluded that the jurisdiction of the magistrates should not be enlarged except in two specific instances to which reference will presently be made. In most cases of misdemeanor, the defendant may be sentenced to a penitentiary for a term of one year and in addition there may be imposed upon him a fine of five hundred dollars, in default of which he must serve one day for each dollar unpaid, thus aggregating really a sentence of two years, four and one-half months. It is vital to the proper administration of justice that the trial of a case which may lead to so serious a result should be carefully safeguarded, so as to assure a calm and just judgment. The experience of those who have been and now are justices of the Court of Special Sessions is warrant for the statement that a discussion between three judges, both upon the law and the facts and as to the punishment, if any, to be administered in case of guilt, is of great value, and frequently results in a conclusion which represents a proper accommodation of views originally widely divergent. In considering this subject it must always be remembered that the fundamental principle of American criminal jurisprudence is trial by jury and any departure therefrom must not only be constitutional, but must be of a character which will assure to the People and to the defendant not only a speedy but a fair trial, unaffected by passion, prejudice or clamor.

It not infrequently occurs that the public is greatly aroused in regard to certain classes of offenses. A person charged with a violation of law, is entitled to a fair hearing and has the right to be released on reasonable bail. Yet instances have occurred where magistrates, responsive to public clamor and regardless of the particular case before them, have imposed excessive bail for which there was no justification. If the power were confided in such instance and at that time to a single judicial officer both to hear and determine, the defendant might not have the protection to which he is entitled. Too much care cannot be taken to prevent hasty or unjust action, and while in the city of New York, because of its large, varied and complex population and the great number of charges of misdemeanor, trial by jury is impracticable and Courts of Special Sessions, with complete jurisdiction over misdemeanors, are necessities, yet by reason of these same complex conditions, the authority to try misdemeanors generally should be restricted to a court of three justices and not extended to a single justice or magistrate.

In addition to its jurisdiction in cases of misdemeanors, the Court of Special Sessions has original jurisdiction in bastardy cases.

In these cases there is usually a sharp conflict in the testimony and the task of determining the truth is very difficult. It would be unwise to disturb the present jurisdiction of the Court of Special Sessions in this regard. Rules should be made, however, aimed to conserve public decency, so far as is not inconsistent with the constitutional safeguard as to a public trial. Many curious spectators attend at the court and means should be taken to exclude them.

There are, however, minor misdemeanors which can now be summarily tried by the magistrates.

Thus, under existing law, a violation of the Sanitary Code constitutes a misdemeanor. Some of these violations, such as the adulteration of milk and food, are serious in character and have been and should be tried in the Court of Special Sessions, but other violations can readily be disposed of by the magistrates.

Pursuant to section 1265 of the Greater New York Charter, full authority is now vested in the Department of Health to have cases tried by the magistrates and not by the Court of Special Sessions. In fact, the case must proceed before the magistrate unless the Department of Health applies, before the trial is commenced, for the removal of the case to the Court of Special Sessions.

The Commission is of the opinion that this very important power which may be at times essential to the welfare of the people and the city, should not be taken from the Department of Health nor in any manner impaired. Nevertheless, by conference between the officials of the Department of Health and representatives of the Court of Special Sessions and Magistrates' Courts, it should at all times be easy to determine what classes of cases should be triable by the magistrates and not by the Court of Special Sessions.

In the case, however, of violation of the motor vehicle law, first offense, where the defendant pleads guilty, the magistrate should be empowered to impose the punishment.

The testimony before the Commission is that in many of these cases persons charged with these violations are anxious to plead guilty before the magistrate and have their cases promptly disposed of.

It often happens that the charge for violating the speed limit of motor vehicles is not accompanied by any suggestion that the vehicle was traveling at a dangerous rate of speed, and the person charged is ready and anxious to have his case promptly disposed of. This not infrequently occurs with non-residents to whom it is a hardship to be compelled to return for trial at the Court of Special Sessions. The acceptance of pleas of guilty in such cases by the magistrates would eliminate many cases in the Court of Special Sessions, which consume time and which could be adequately dealt with by the magistrates.

The objection made to this suggestion is that there would be great difficulty in ascertaining whether the person was a first offender. This objection can be overcome by the enactment by the Legislature of a satisfactory law upon this subject, providing, among other things, that the license card of the driver should show by indorsement the number of convictions for violation of the statute. If no such law is enacted, there need be no difficulty in having as competent a system of identification as now exists in the information bureau of the district attorney's office. In that bureau a blotter or index is kept containing the names of persons convicted of violation of the Motor Vehicle Law. All the information on this subject can be transmitted to the magistrates, and each Magistrate's Court can likewise keep a record which through the office of the chief clerk can be transmitted daily to the various courts throughout the city, and thus a check kept in regard to convictions for violation of this law.

The magistrates should also be empowered to impose punishment upon a plea of guilty to the charge of cruelty to animals. The Commission, in making this recommendation, has the fullest appreciation of the gravity of this offense, but it appears from the testimony that in a very large number of cases the Court of Special Sessions has found the alleged cruelty of a character so slight as to warrant only a suspension of sentence or a very small fine. For many years the American Society for the Prevention of Cruelty to Animals was the only society of that character in the city of New York, but since the advent in 1906 of the New York City Humane Society which is also engaged in prosecutions of this character, the total of arrests has increased appreciably. From the testimony adduced before the Commission, it would appear that the cases where pleas of guilty are interposed can be adequately and promptly disposed of by the magistrates, who, in most instances, can if they desire examine the animal within a very short time of the commission of the offense. Such disposition will eliminate from the calendar of the Court of Special Sessions a considerable number of cases in which the result would be no different than if more promptly disposed of in the Magistrates' Courts.

Children's Courts. Prior to September 1, 1902, children under the age of 16 were arraigned in or brought to the Magistrates' Courts. In 1902, the Legislature conferred upon the Court of Special Sessions of the First Division the power to try all cases affecting children under 16 years of age, except capital cases.

In 1903, similar jurisdiction was conferred upon the Court of Special Sessions of the Second Division for the borough of Brooklyn.

In the year ending December 31, 1908, there were brought to the Children's Court of the First Division 11,409 children and to the Children's Court in the borough of Brooklyn, 4,475 children. These children may be divided, broadly, into two classes, (1) those charged with the violation of some ordinance or law or with being ungovernable and (2) those who are the victims of improper guardianship.

During the short time that these courts have been in existence in the city of New York, great progress has been made in the study of the problems affecting the dependent and delinquent child and in the development of children's courts throughout the country. The problems, however, which are presented in the city of New York are vastly more difficult than those presented in any other jurisdiction, for in some other parts of the country where much has been said and written about children's courts, the number of children brought before the judge in a year is less than the number brought before the two children's courts in the city of New York in a fortnight. Besides, in other jurisdictions, there is not the difficulty of so varied a population, with parents most of whom do not understand the English language and who are not yet fully familiar with American customs and requirements. Here, more than anywhere else in the country, the population is constantly shifting, and the effort to deal with the child is frequently made additionally embarrassing by the removal from the neighborhood of the family of which the child is a member. Therefore, although profiting by experience in other jurisdictions, the problems of the children's courts in New York must be approached with careful regard to difficulties peculiarly their own.

The Commission has been urged to follow the precedent of certain other jurisdictions and to recommend the establishment of a court in the nature of a court of chancery to which the child should be brought by civil process. The constitutional and legal difficulties involved in an attempt to confer such jurisdiction, except in the Supreme Court where it now resides, would not warrant such an experiment.

The Commission has also been urged to recommend the establishment of a children's court separate and apart from the Court of Special Sessions.

It has been argued that the judge of the Children's Court should devote all his time to that work and that a limited number of judges, selected for a completely separate court, would more efficiently carry on this important work.

The Commission is in entire sympathy with the proposition that the Children's Court requires something more than brief or temporary sittings of a judge.

The judge sitting at the Children's Court should so far as practicable follow the case of a child from the beginning until its final disposition. Under the present system, the justices in the First Division sit for a term of one month only twice each year and in the Second Division for a term of two months only once in each year, unless by voluntary arrangement they exchange their assignments. This is a radical defect which needs remedying; for the Commission is of the opinion that it is vital to the successful administration of this work that the justice before whom the child is originally brought shall follow the course of that child through all the stages, which end either in permitting the child finally to go at large or in committing the child to a reformatory institution. The justice before whom the child originally comes is familiar with the details of the case, has presumably caused to be investigated every fact or circumstance throwing light upon the child's conduct, history and surroundings, has formed his own estimate of the child and his theory of what can be done with it, and he should follow that case in every judicial detail to completion.

Our observation has shown us that there are certain of the justices of the two divisions of this court who are peculiarly adapted for the work of Children's Courts who have the patience and enthusiasm which are so necessary to successful accomplishment, and who would be glad to devote themselves for long periods of time to this particular branch of work.

On the other hand, other justices, fully as capable in other directions, are not by temperament fitted to deal so well with the children.

More than this, a justice passing on the cases of children should fully acquaint himself with the character and conditions of the institutions to which he must commit these children. He must be so fully informed that he knows exactly what he is doing in each case. He must keep himself in touch with the general work and discussions engaged in by all interested in this subject. To do all this will require time beyond that of the hours during which the court is in session. To attain this equipment, a justice must be permitted to sit in the Children's Court for a reasonably long period of assignment.

It is not necessary, however, to establish a separate court to assure the assignment to this work of equipped judges for substantial periods of time. It is impossible in the selection of the judge to determine beforehand whether he will be successful in handling children, and if a separate children's court were established, there would be no way of removing a judge who might prove to be temperamentally unfit, although in every respect an upright and conscientious man. Provision must also be made for the contingencies of vacation, sickness or other disability, and the probabilities are that if a separate children's court were established five judges would be required for the greater city. It is much better for the city to avail itself of the present force of judges, with such additions as the Commission will recommend, for out of this number there can be assigned to this work those justices peculiarly fitted for it. There should be a directory provision that in the assignment of a justice to sit at the children's court, consideration be had to the fitness of the justice and the permanency of the assignment, and the intention of the Legislature should be made clear that so far as practicable the justice assigned to the children's court should devote his sole attention to that work.

The Commission has also been urged to codify the laws relating to children.

Such a codification whenever attempted should be State wide, but the Commission at this time cannot see any necessity for such codification. The statutes affecting children have been construed to such an extent that few appeals or arguments on writs of habeas corpus are presented to the courts, and the fundamental and substantial legal questions involved are well settled.

It may be that the various provisions found in the Penal Law, the Code of Criminal Procedure and other statutes might be more conveniently arranged in one codification, but the courts and judges dealing with the subject matter in the first instance soon become specialists familiar with these statutes.

Children's courts are as yet so new in our jurisprudence that the Commission believes it to be safer that the development of the law governing their administration be along careful and steady lines of gradual improvement based upon the experience of actual administration in the various Juvenile Courts throughout the state, than that there be adopted at this time any departure, experimental in character, which involves in the main the application of theories not yet fully tried out. Children under sixteen should, however, be relieved, where possible, of the stigma of conviction for crime.

The Legislature last year enacted chapter 478 of the Laws of 1909, amending section 2186 of the Penal Law, and, with the same purpose in view, upon the recommendation of this Commission, incorporated section 92 in the law establishing the City Court of Buffalo.

The statute first mentioned makes it mandatory, when a child is found guilty of any act or omission which, if committed by an adult, would be a crime (except where punishable by death or life imprisonment), that the child shall not be deemed guilty of any crime, but of " juvenile delinquency " only.

In the opinion of the Commission, the term " juvenile delinquency " is too comprehensive and if applied in all cases, as provided in the statute, would defeat the very purpose for which it is intended.

To illustrate, a judge might find it necessary to hold a child guilty of a violation of some minor ordinance or law. Thus a child might be found guilty of playing ball in the streets, playing " shinney," indulging in some boyish prank or striking another child in a childish quarrel. Under the statute referred to, the judge, if he finds a child guilty, must find him guilty, not of a violation of the ordinance, nor of the particular infraction, but of " juvenile delinquency," and thus the child would receive a designation which would likewise be applied to a child who had been found guilty of breaking into a store or of picking a pocket or of some other more or less serious offense. It has seemed to the Commission that the safer plan is to give to the judge the largest measure of discretion.

With that purpose in view, it was provided in the Buffalo City Court Act, to which reference has been made, that whenever a child is charged with an offense which, if committed by an adult, would be a misdemeanor or a felony,

> " The judge sitting in the Children's Court shall as far as is consistent with the interest of the child and of the State consider the child not as upon trial for the commission of a crime but as a child in need of the care and protection of the State: to that end he may, if the child or either parent or any guardian or custodian of such child shall so request, before proceeding with the trial of the child for the offense charged, or at any stage of the trial and before conviction, suspend the trial and inquire into all the facts and surrounding circumstances of the case, and if the judge shall so find, he may in his discretion in lieu of proceeding with the trial, adjudge the child to be in need of the care and protection of the State and thereupon he shall deal with such child in all respects in the manner provided in section 486 of the penal law in the case of a child not having proper guardianship."

This provision was drawn, having in mind the question of treating the child, not as a criminal, but rather as needing the protection of the State, or, in the language of the Court of Appeals in the Knowack case (158 N. Y. 482), as coming within the class " where the State intervenes to care for and protect the homeless and destitute child."

In explaining its recommendation, the Commission, in its report to the Governor, stated:

> " By virtue of this provision it is intended that at any time before or during the trial of a child the judge, at the request of the child, its parents or guardian, may suspend the trial and inquire into the facts and surrounding circumstances of the case and, in lieu of proceeding with the trial, adjudge the child to be in need of the care and protection of the State and thereupon deal with the child as provided in the case of a child not having proper guardianship.
>
> " Under this method where the judge is of the opinion that such a course is consistent, both with the interest of the child and of the State, he may relieve the child of conviction for crime and treat the child rather as an unfortunate around whom the State throws its protecting arm.
>
> " Having adjudged the child in need of the State's protection, the judge, in his discretion, may then place him on probation, commit him to the detention hom, or to a charitable or reformatory institution. Thus existing procedure is added to but not disturbed and we believe that any judge assigned to the work of the Children's Court will take such course in these respects as he may consider proper both in the interest of the child and the community in which it lives."

After extended discussion and deliberation, the Commission is of the opinion that the principles involved in both of the statutes under consideration can be readily and consistently combined, so that the Children's Court or judge shall have all the power conferred under the provisions of the Buffalo Act, except that if the child be adjudged guilty of a crime which, if committed by an adult, would be a felony, then the child shall not be adjudged guilty of a crime but of " juvenile delinquency."

In this manner the judge in any case is at liberty to do what he thinks best, provided, however, that if he concludes that the child must be convicted of what would be felony in the case of an

adult, he shall be adjudged guilty only of " juvenile delinquency,"
while, if the judge is constrained to find the child guilty of a
minor infraction, he can so adjudge without being compelled to
adjudge the child guilty of " juvenile delinquency."

Having thus considered the jurisdiction of the Court of Special
Sessions, it becomes necessary to determine whether the present
system of two divisions should be continued.

Necessity for Single Court of Special Sessions.

We took occasion in our preliminary report to call attention
to the lack of uniformity in the interpretation of the law and in
the administrative methods of the Courts of Special Sessions of
the respective divisions.

In prosecutions for selling liquor without a liquor tax certificate, the Court of Special Sessions of the Second Division (some
justices dissenting) held that, unless the person who has trafficked
in liquor can be shown to be the proprietor, he is not guilty of a
violation of law. The Court of Special Sessions of the First
Division has properly held to the contrary. Thus, the extraordinary situation arose that defendants were being sent to jail by
the Court of Special Sessions of the First Division, where a misdemeanor was committed in the boroughs of Manhattan and The
Bronx, while other defendants, who had committed precisely the
same character of offense in the borough of Brooklyn, Queens or
Richmond, were escaping, upon a question of law, the conse-
quences of their acts and were being acquitted by the Court of
Special Sessions of the Second Division.

On the other hand, the testimony shows that where a conviction was had in the same class of cases, to wit, the traffic in liquor
without a liquor tax certificate, in the Second Division the justices pursued a policy of refusing to substitute a brief imprisonment in default of payment of the statutory fine, while in the
First Division the contrary practice prevailed, thus releasing some
of these convicted persons after a very short period of imprisonment. Certain justices of the Court of Special Sessions of the Second Division have held, where a defendant charged with selling
liquor in violation of law testified that he knew the person to whom
the liquor was sold to be a police officer, that such sale is not a violation of law, but is made under duress and without intent to commit a crime, and is, therefore, not a crime. The contrary view
of the law is held, and, as we believe, properly, by the Court of
Special Sessions of the First Division.

In the First Division, the testimony of an officer that the liquor he tasted was beer or whiskey, is sufficient for a *prima facie* case, while in the Second Division, some magistrates have required chemical analysis and the testimony of experts.

The practice and procedure in the two divisions vary greatly, as do the methods of conducting calendar practice, keeping records and applying the probation system.

The Court of Special Sessions of the First Division has police probation officers, while that of the Second Division has not.

In the Children's Court of the First Division, there are no official probation officers, while in the Second Division there are official probation officers representing the respective religious faiths.

These courts, having the same jurisdiction in different sections of the same city, should administer the law in such manner as to prevent the mere accident of residence making a difference in result. It seems too obvious for argument that a man should not be acquitted in one borough for an offense of which he would have been convicted in another, or *vice versa*.

These conditions and this lack of uniformity have led the Commission to the conclusion that there should be one Court of Special Sessions for the entire city, with a sufficient number of justices and such clerical and other force as may be necessary to perform its important work.

As a part of this plan for uniformity, the jurisdiction of children's cases in the boroughs of Queens and Richmond should be transferred from the magistrates to the Court of Special Sessions.

In the borough of Queens, the population is rapidly increasing and last year the children's cases exceeded by about 100 the total number of the previous year. The justices of the Second Division and the superintendent of the Brooklyn Society for the Prevention of Cruelty to Children have assured the Commission that there will be no practical difficulty in handling this work, and the children of these two boroughs should be subject to the same treatment, methods and jurisdiction as the children of the other boroughs.

COMPOSITION OF PROPOSED COURT OF SPECIAL SESSIONS.

To carry out the views hereinbefore expressed, it will be necessary that there should be, in all, fifteen justices of the Court of Special Sessions, seven of whom should be residents of the territory now known as the First Division, seven of the territory now known as the Second Division, and one from any part of the city, irrespective of residential qualification. Three justices would thus be added to the existing number. The mayor should have authority to designate any one of the present justices or any one of the three additional justices to be the chief justice.

The assignment of the justices to sit in various parts of the greater city, irrespective of residence, must necessarily develop a more comprehensive view and tend to a better understanding of the conditions existing commonly throughout the city as well as those peculiar to respective localities. In the assignment of the justices, however, it should be required that in the court for the trial of adult misdemeanants there should always sit one justice who is a resident of the section of the city in which the court is held.

With fifteen justices, it should be possible to dispose promptly and efficiently of the cases coming to this court. There would always be a part for the trial of adults accused of misdemeanors committed in the borough of Manhattan or The Bronx; similarly, an adult part for the boroughs of Brooklyn, Queens, and Richmond; a children's court for Manhattan and The Bronx; and a children's court for Brooklyn. For this work eight justices would be needed. There would remain seven justices (of whom one would be the chief justice), three of whom would be available to hold a second part for the trial of adults in the borough of Manhattan, when the business of the court required, and one to take pleas in the borough of Brooklyn while the part for the trial of adults was sitting in the borough of Queens or Richmond, or *vice versa*. There would be in reserve a sufficient number of justices to attend to the hearing of children's cases in the boroughs of Queens and Richmond, and to dispose of such other work as might be assigned therein, and there would be enough unoccupied time to allow for reasonable vacations as well as for illness, disability or other emergency.

As much time can be saved, more especially in what is now known as the Second Division, if one justice is empowered to take pleas, that power should be clearly conferred.

In addition to the chief clerk, there should be five clerks of parts, three for the adult courts and two for the children's courts.

The court should be empowered to appoint such clerical force, stenographers, interpreters, attendants, messengers and other employees as may be necessary for the proper conduct of its business.

COMPOSITION OF MAGISTRATE'S COURTS; CHANGES PROPOSED.

The Commission is of the opinion that it will not be practicable to have one Board of Magistrates for the greater city. The large number of separate courts renders it necessary to retain the existing divisions in order to provide for efficient supervision.

Therefore, there should be, as now, the Magistrates' Courts of the First and Second Divisions, the former to be comprised of those courts situated in the boroughs of Manhattan and The Bronx and the latter of those in the boroughs of Brooklyn, Queens and Richmond. In each division there should be a chief city magistrate, designated by the mayor.

There are now 16 magistrates in each of the two divisions and, in the opinion of the Commission, it will be necessary to add only one magistrate to each division.

In the Second Division at least 10 of the magistrates should be residents of the borough of Brooklyn, at least four of the borough of Queens and at least two of the borough of Richmond, thus leaving the mayor free to appoint one magistrate from any part of the territory comprised in the Second Division.

In order that the magistrates may become acquainted with the work of the courts throughout the greater city, the magistrates of both divisions should meet together at least twice in each year.

By means of these conventions, it is hoped that the magistrates may agree on uniform rules of practice and procedure, so far as practicable, and may also interchange views leading to results advantageous to the administration of justice in these courts. There may be details of practice and procedure peculiarly applicable to various localities, but, generally speaking, the same a uniform system as to essentials should be ultimately established.

Each chief city magistrate should have the power to appoint at will a chief clerk, who, subject to his direction, should have supervision of the clerical force and should be secretary of the Board of Magistrates. All other clerks, stenographers, interpreters and attendants should be appointed by a majority of the magistrates.

THE SUMMONS IN THE MAGISTRATES' COURT.

The evidence shows that a very large number of papers called summonses are issued each year by the various magistrates. No records are kept of the summonses and therefore the total can only be estimated. It is not an exaggeration to put this estimate at well over one hundred thousand.

The summons as employed is a very useful means of settling controversies which might otherwise lead to a warrant with consequent serious hardship or injustice. The magistrate in this regard has a very useful function to perform and is frequently the means of composing petty disputes, of bringing quarreling relatives or neighbors together and effectuating amicable adjustments of their grievances. In cases of more serious import, the magistrate, after inquiry, may determine that a warrant should not issue, and thus save the person complained against from what might otherwise have been a grave wrong.

On the other hand, it is supposed that the summons is sometimes used by those imposing upon the court, for the purpose of extorting money settlements in cases where there are only civil remedies. Doubt as to the legality of the summons has been expressed and there should be statutory authority for its issuance. A record should be kept of the summonses issued.

SUMMONS IN LIEU OF ARREST FOR MINOR OFFENSES.

In 1908, in Manhattan and The Bronx, 32,322 persons were arraigned for violations of corporation ordinances, 6,724 for violations of the Sanitary Code, and 3,709 for violations of the Motor Vehicle Law. In the Second Division, 6,378 were arraigned for violations of corporation ordinances, 975 for violations of the Sanitary Code, and 933 for violations of the Motor Vehicle Law; total 51,041.

Many of the persons so arraigned could have been easily identified and in many of these instances the violation of a regulative ordinance or statute was not willful, nor did it involve moral turpitude. The arrest of a citizen under such circumstances frequently leads to unnecessary hardship and humiliation, and, at the same time, deprives the city of the services of a police officer whose time is thus occupied in conveying the prisoner to the station house and thence to the court, if open, or otherwise, to the court the following day.

In England and in many of the Continental countries, such arrests are rarely made and only in cases involving either peculiar circumstances or where the person charged with a violation is unable satisfactorily to identify himself.

Drivers in charge of trucks and delivery wagons of all kinds carrying perishable or other goods, who violate some traffic regulation, are frequently delayed, to the great inconvenience and possibly the financial loss of the business concern shipping or receiving the goods. Where the violation of the Motor Vehicle Law is a violation of the speed limit without any attending circumstances of danger or nuisance, such arrests work unnecessary inconvenience in many instances where the violation is no fault of the persons in the vehicle other than the driver.

Householders or janitors whose residence is ordinarily well known and fixed, are similarly subjected to arrest for the violation of some regulative ordinance. These arrests swell the total of arrests in the city of New York to an enormous figure and the city has suffered from a reputation unjustly attributed because of this undue number or arrests. The subject demands remedy if possible.

The Commission has devised a plan which is the result of its own labors and of conference with the police commissioner and his assistants. It is much more difficult to initiate a workable plan here than in countries like France or Germany, where there is a complete system of police registration and supervision. We would be glad to recommend an extensive change but we deem it advisable to be conservative in an initial departure of this kind.

We believe that if the plan recommended by the Commission is adopted, it will be a substantial forward step and that persons resident in or frequently coming to the city of New York will, by their own conduct, bring the plan into public favor.

In devising any plan it must be remembered that some features must be made mandatory. This is because the police officials will not exercise discretion vested in them by statute, the subordinate officers, fearing that if they err in the exercise of discretion they will be subjected to disciplinary punishment by their superiors.

The Legislature has, in numerous instances, given a fair measure of discretion to the police, which, if properly exercised, would prevent unnecessary annoyance, but such authority has not been availed of.

To illustrate, subdivision 3, section 554 of the Code of Criminal Procedure provides that if a person is charged with the violation of a corporation ordinance, conviction whereof would render him liable to imprisonment for thirty days or less, then the captain, sergeant (lieutenant) or acting sergeant (lieutenant) of police has authority to parole the prisoner on his promise to appear on the following day before the proper magistrate.

Inquiry of the police officials elicited the response that none of them could ever recall an instance where this very desirable authority had ever been exercised by any captain or other officer in charge of a precinct. They frankly stated that none of these subordinate officers would take the chance of paroling a prisoner, for fear that, if he did not appear at court, they would be reprimanded or punished.

In view of the foregoing, the Commission recommends that, within a reasonable period after the taking effect of the act, the police commissioner shall prescribe a card or token of identification which may be obtained free of charge by any person who applies to the police department and is satisfactorily identified.

In the event that the holder of such card or token violates a corporation ordinance or violates the speed provisions of the Motor Vehicle Law, the officer shall be prohibited from arresting him if he produces his identification card.

In lieu of arrest the officer shall issue to him a summons, setting forth the date, hour and court when and where he shall appear. The summons shall be returnable at the Magistrate's Court in the precinct nearest to the place where the arrest was made, at the opening of the court on the morning following the arrest, unless otherwise provided by unanimous rule adopted by the chief city magistrate of the division and the police commissioner. The chief city magistrate and the police commissioner can by conference and consultation determine whether summonses for persons charged with these violations, or any of them, shall be returnable at the Night Court (if in the First Division) or on the following day or the day after. Thus appropriate rules can be made for the convenient distribution of the business of the courts, with due regard to the practical questions and difficulties of police administration. If it should appear that it is desirable to have these summonses returnable at the Night Court, the rules may so provide. On the other hand, the disposition of the platoons on duty may be such that the following day or the second day may be the more convenient method. Due regard can also be had for the convenience of the citizen who might be able more readily to attend at one time than the other. A sane and sensible administration of this provision will undoubtedly result in great benefit, both to the persons who may be affected thereby and the administration of the police department.

The faithful service of these notices by the police can be readily safeguarded by providing the police officer on patrol with a proper book of numbered blanks and corresponding stubs upon which he shall make entry, a report of which shall be made by him to his superior officer who shall transmit a list or copy of the summonses thus served to the various courts at which they are returnable.

In order, however, to insure obedience to these summonses, provision should be made for severe punishment in the event of failure to appear in accordance with the terms thereof.

Doubtless, it will be necessary to except from the provisions of this act, cases of persons who are not in a condition to take care of themselves, or are engaged in conduct in the streets tending to a breach of the peace.

The present system of issuing licenses in the city of New York is inadequate and confused. The result is that there is no practicable method of identifying by the number of the license many of those who are engaged in business in public thoroughfares, such as peddlers, certain classes of hackmen, hucksters, etc. Likewise, under the present Motor Vehicle Law, there is no adequate means of identifying a chauffeur or other person driving a motor car, by reason of the fact that there is no sufficient check upon the use or transfer, temporarily at least, of a license obtained from the Secretary of State.

In many other instances there is no power in law to compel a person to take out a license.

While the details of the card of identification are to be left to the police commissioner, the problem seems easy of solution. The police department will probably require that the card of identification shall contain a photograph of the person entitled to the same, and there should be no difficulty in applying this regulation to violations of the Motor Vehicle Law as to speed, where no danger to any person or property has occurred. We are informed by the police commissioner that one of the large taxicab companies has already arranged to have its chauffeurs photographed, and this plan will no doubt be followed by other individuals and companies conducting the business of carrying passengers or goods on the public thoroughfares.

It appears that upon some of the railroads where passes are issued pursuant to law to police officials, the requirement is that the official have a small photograph, which is made a part of a small pass book. It is well known that those desiring commutation books on the Swiss and other railways must have a photograph for purposes of identification. Thus to have an identification card will involve no humiliation, because the photograph is carried by the person himself and is his means of identification for a privilege; that is to say, to be spared the annoyance and humiliation, of arrest, and to be served with a summons instead. Under the system proposed, it seems to the Commission that persons constantly traveling the public thoroughfares in vehicles of one kind or another, proprietors of shipping establishments, department stores, express companies, truck and van drivers, and others similarly occupied, will be glad to take advantage of this opportunity for the avoidance of arrest of themselves or their employees.

A system of summonsing is in practical effect at present in regard to violations of the Sanitary Code, whereby the magistrates issue in blank large numbers of summonses to the health squad of the police force and the police officers fill in the names and serve these summonses instead of making arrests.

It has also occurred to the Commission that there may be many instances of persons who are temporarily sojourning in the city, or of residents, who may not obtain such cards. and yet who can be easily identified. The Commission believes that the police commissioner should be empowered to make such rules and regulations from time to time and issue such orders to the police force as he may deem wise, for the avoidance of arrest of persons charged with violating ordinances or the Motor Vehicle Law who can be satisfactorily identified even though they have not an identification card.

If this innovation works successfully, succeeding legislatures can enlarge the scope of the experiment. If faithfully carried out, there is every reason to believe that the number of arrests in the greater city will be decreased by many thousands.

DOMESTIC RELATIONS COURTS.

The testimony is that there are many cases brought to the attention of the magistrates where wives claim that their husbands do not support them. These cases require the most patient and careful investigation, and cannot be quickly disposed of, because if the claim of the complainant be sustained, it involves the making of an order against the husband to support the wife or his commitment to the work-house.

Many times these unfortunate women must sit for hours in the magistrates' court until other business is disposed of, because in the daily routine the magistrate first hears those cases which constitute "the watch;" that is to say, the prisoners arrested during the night preceding, and then the bail cases returnable before him, many of which require extended and careful examination. It is after this business is disposed of that the magistrate calls for those who desire to see him, and among these are nearly always some unfortunate women left penniless by their husbands.

The magistrate may deem it wise to issue a warrant or a summons against the husband returnable at a future day, and when the husband is brought into court upon the warrant or summons another magistrate in the course of rotation may be sitting. The wife must repeat her story to the new magistrate and he may decide to place the defendant on probation upon his promise to pay the wife a certain amount. When complaint for failure to comply with the magistrate's order or direction is to be made, the wife frequently must return to the court and perhaps finds still another magistrate, who, to satisfy himself, may desire to hear the whole story over again.

Many of the magistrates consider their work in this regard as of the highest importance, for they feel that they have an opportunity of not merely saving the wife from distress, but of uniting and preserving the family, and with hardly an exception they strongly favor the establishment of a separate part of the court in which all the work relating to this subject matter can be concentrated. In this view they are strongly supported by various charitable organizations, who have given the subject matter close study and inquiry.

It frequently happens that the unfortunate woman must take with her to court one or more young children, because there is no one with whom she can leave them while absent from her home. One of the reasons which animated the establishment of Children's Courts was to keep young children away from the environment of the criminal courts. With a central domestic relations part or court, the decent woman who has her child or her children with her, who has committed no crime but is merely poor and unfortunate, will find herself in a court where it is hoped there will be a patient and consistent effort to do justice. The magistrates have said that it is very difficult for them to give the time they should like in the ordinary grist of the Magistrates' Court to this important work, and that they would welcome the opportunity of dealing with the subject in a specialized way.

The only objection which is made to such a separate part is that the women will, in some instances, have a considerable distance to go.

There is very little force in this objection, because in those meritorious cases where the complaint against the husband is sustained, and the husband pays pursuant to the magistrate's order, the wife must at present go to the office of the Department of Charities in each borough, which frequently involves a long trip. The office for Manhattan and the Bronx is in East Twenty-sixth street, and for the borough of Brooklyn, is in Schermerhorn street.

Against this single objection are many advantages. A magistrate can be assigned to this part who may be specially fitted for this class of work, and in any event magistrates will, no doubt, be assigned to this part for a reasonable period of time. The clerks and other court employees will, presumably, be permanently assigned to such part during good conduct, and they will become familiar with the persons and the cases.

We recommend that a branch office of the Superintendent of Outdoor Poor of the Department of Charities be established in the building in which is located the Domestic Relations Court, or adjoining or convenient thereto, so that it may work in complete harmony with the court and for the convenience of the parties concerned. The various philanthropic societies, institutions and organizations which are interested in these cases, will have an opportunity of concentrating their investigators or other employees in a single place in each borough, and thereby they will be enabled to co-operate effectively with the courts.

In this court should also be tried the cases now brought in the Court of General Sessions to compel the support of aged and infirm parents by their children.

NIGHT COURTS.

The night court was established pursuant to the provisions of chapter 598 of the Laws of 1907. The purpose of the enactment was to put a stop to the evil known as the station-house bond. It was claimed that certain of the police and certain bondsmen were in league, so that by constant arrests of prostitutes these women were compelled to get bail in order to be released until the following morning, and for that bail to pay heavily to the professional bondsmen.

The testimony before the Commission is somewhat conflicting as to the results of the night court. Apparently the business of the professional bondsman in this regard has been in great measure impaired. But unfortunately other evils have sprung up, for there always seems to be some new scheme or device invented to meet every effort of the law maker to stop or repress such evils. From the testimony before the Commission it would seem that the modern method is for certain of these unfortunate women of the streets to have a working arrangement with certain houses of assignation, called hotels, whereby, upon the imposition of a fine upon conviction, the woman, if without money, sends a messenger to some one in authority in one of these hotels and receives from that source the means whereby to pay the fine. In return it is manifest that she must work out her debt by bringing men to the resort.

While this and other evils no doubt continue, nevertheless the night court has been of much service. One direction in which it has been highly useful is the opportunity of many persons who have been arrested for minor offenses to have a prompt hearing, and, even though convicted, to be punished in such a manner that they may be released in time to go to their business or work the following day without running the chances of discharge from employment. Many persons are arrested for intoxication who, after a few hours, are fit to go home. The previous police commissioner issued an order, without authority so far as we can ascertain and contrary to statute, limiting the cases to be tried in the night court. We think that there are probably very few cases, where the accusation is one of felony, which should be undertaken at the night court, but there are many cases of charges of misdemeanor where the magistrate should examine the case as soon as possible if the defendant so demands and the police commissioner should have no authority to regulate what prisoners should be brought to the night court.

On many nights there is a very large number of prisoners brought to this court. The cases are disposed of sometimes at the rate of a case per minute. Obviously appropriate attention cannot be given under such circumstances.

The Commission personally observed a striking illustration of the injustice which may be done by failure to inquire thoroughly into all the circumstances and fully to hear the prisoner. The failure to do so in the case of a defendant charged with violating a minor corporation ordinance resulted in the imposition of a fine of two dollars or the alternative of two days' imprisonment. Upon investigation the Commission ascertained that the defendant was not guilty of any violation but was fully within his rights, having received a lawful permit to do the very act which was charged against him as being a violation of law. Seven other persons had been unjustly convicted earlier in the evening upon precisely the same charge and were imprisoned for non-payment of the fine, and had it not been for the Commission's investigation all of these defendants would have been compelled to pay a sum of money large to them, or would have been imprisoned until the following midday. How many had been compelled unlawfully to pay a fine, could not be ascertained. Such instances naturally have an evil influence, for the person improperly convicted feels that he has been the victim of injustice and that the courts do not extend to him the protection to which he is entitled. It has frequently been stated, and correctly, that failure to accord to a defendant, and more especially to those of foreign birth, a fair hearing breeds discontent, dissatisfaction and in many instances defiance of the law.

The treatment of the cases connected with prostitution will be more fully discussed hereinafter, but it is sufficient at this point to say that this subject requires much more careful attention than it has thus far received. The mingling of women with men, more especially when so many women are arraigned at the night court, is unwise and has a demoralizing tendency. The character of work imposed upon the magistrates when women are arraigned at night differs very greatly from their work in the cases of men.

Further, a person arrested at half past 3 or a quarter of 4 in the afternoon, has no opportunity to be heard until 9 o'clock at the earliest and the result is that when the court opens at 9 o'clock at night, there are not infrequently upwards of 100 people waiting to be heard.

Two Night Courts Necessary.— We have concluded that there should be two night courts in the First Division; one devoted entirely to the cases of women and one devoted entirely to the cases of men.

Our view is to leave the matter of the location of these courts to the magistrates, but it seems to us that the present night court at Jefferson Market would be well situated for the cases of women, while the East Fifty-seventh Street Court would be for the present centrally located for the cases of men. These courts should open at 7 o'clock in the evening instead of 9 as now, and close no earlier than 3 in the morning.

By opening these courts earlier, persons arrested after half past 3, during the afternoon, can be heard at a reasonable hour and by distribution over this longer period there will not be such a congestion as we have on several occasions noticed in the night court. Vagrants and persons who are found habitually intoxicated can be handled with much greater discrimination if at night the court has more time, while those who are unjustly charged or who have committed some trivial offense may be more speedily heard.

The night courts can also be made more useful for the purpose of giving bail. It seems, by reason of the provisions of section 550 of the Code of Criminal Procedure, as amended by chapter 411 of Laws of 1909, that where a defendant is held to appear for examination, bail for such appearance may be taken only by the magistrate who issued the warrant or before whom the same is returnable, except in cases where either magistrate is incapacitated or absent from the jurisdiction.

If, therefore, a magistrate during the session of the court in the day time has fixed bail for examination before him, the defendant cannot be enlarged on bail, although he is able to furnish the bail at night, unless he can find the magistrate who has originally fixed the bail, or unless the magistrate sitting at the night court was the one before whom the warrant was returnable. If this provision of the Code is properly amended, then the magistrate sitting at either of the night courts can take bail and thus save much inconvenience and occasional hardship.

While each magistrate is required to take bail except where there is specific statutory restriction, yet the magistrates are entitled to be relieved wherever practicable of this duty at night, and at the same time the person desiring to give bail should be so situated that he may apply therefor as a matter of right and without any sense of favor or embarrassment involved in applying to a magistrate after the day courts have closed. The amendment of the law in this respect will add one more element of usefulness to the work of these courts.

Night Court for Women.— The establishment of a night court for women only will undoubtedly limit the number of doubtful male characters who are seen from time to time among the spectators at the night court. It will give an opportunity for concentration of effort in relation to cases of women and will enable those philanthropically inclined more effectively to give their assistance to the prisoners as well as to the magistrates and probation officers.

In connection with a night court for women, there should be established under the jurisdiction of the Department of Correction detention rooms in or convenient to the court, for defendants waiting to be heard and also for those who are held for examination or trial.

It should be the duty of the officials in charge to separate, so far as practicable, the older and more hardened offenders from the younger and less hardened. Thus a young girl or woman charged with petit larceny should not be compelled to come into close association with a prostitute or vagrant.

The attention of the Commission has been called to several instances where women charged with abduction for immoral purposes were detained in the same cell with the young girls whom they were charged with abducting.

The conditions which result in indiscriminately mingling prisoners in the detention pens and district prisons are intolerable.

THE CUMULATIVE SENTENCE LAW.

Section 707 et seq. of the Charter.—If a person convicted upon a charge of vagrancy, is a prostitute between the ages of sixteen and twenty-one, she may be committed to certain reformatory institutions. All other persons convicted upon a charge of vagrancy, including persons convicted as prostitutes and not committed to a reformatory, are committed in the boroughs of Manhattan and the Bronx, to the workhouse on Blackwell's Island, in the borough of Brooklyn to the penitentiaary of that borough and in the other boroughs to a county jail for the term of six months.

Upon a charge of public intoxication or disorderly conduct, tending to a breach of the peace, the court or magistrate may (1) impose a fine not exceeding $10 or (2) commit the person so convicted in the boroughs of Manhattan and the Bronx to the workhouse, in the borough of Brooklyn to the penitentiary of that county and in the other boroughs of the city to a county jail or to the workhouse or to the penitentiary to be detained for the term of six months, or (3) require any person convicted of disorderly conduct to give surety for his good behavior for a period of time to be recited in the commitment of not more than six months.

In cases of public intoxication and disorderly conduct, the term of the commitment is automatically determined pursuant to the provisions of the statute by the number of times that the person has been previously committed under the so-called Cumulative Sentence Law, which is familiarly called the Cumulative Sentence Law, and an order of discharge is accordingly made by the Commissioner of Correction without further consent or intervention by the magistrates. Upon the first offense the term is five days; upon the second, twenty days, and upon succeeding offenses an increased number of days, until the maximum term of six months.

In case, however, of a person committed upon conviction for vagrancy, no order for the discharge of such person before the period fixed by the warrant of commitment, can be made without the written consent endorsed upon such order of the court or magistrate by which or whom such vagrant was committed.

A careful record should be kept by the magistrates of each and every case in which they consent to the discharge of a prisoner and the reasons for such discharge should be briefly set forth and filed in the clerk's office.

The law was passed in 1895 as the result of extended discussion as to the best method of dealing with these classes of recidivists. It is said that prior to that time commitments for vagrancy, public intoxication and disorderly conduct were made in haphazard fashion, without sufficient regard to the previous record of the prisoner.

The difficulties of identification at the time of arraignment and conviction of the prisoner were realized and the system above described was devised. The Legislature did its part, but the administrative authorities have failed to do theirs. Since 1905, the statute has made it mandatory that the Bertillon system shall be installed at the workhouse. Our information is that the sum of $4,500 was requested by the Department of Correction in its annual estimate for the budget of 1907, to establish the Bertillon system, and that this request was granted by the Board of Estimate, but that the Department has not utilized the funds for this purpose. The result is that the clear command of the Legislature has been disregarded and that identification at the workhouse is entirely one of memory, dependent upon the recognition of some of the veteran matrons and keepers. As a consequence, the Cumulative Sentence law has not had a fair trial.

The testimony adduced before the Commission shows that under the existing system many mistakes and cases of injustice have occurred. It is asserted that persons have been released earlier than they should have been had they been properly identified, and it is believed that as the result there has been an impression among many of this class of offenders that from time to time favor and improper influence have prevailed.

Under the Cumulative Sentence law it is provided that if a person has not been convicted for the period of two years he should be treated as a first offender. This is a wise provision calculated to encourage and reward efforts at reform. Strangely enough, this provision of law has been interpreted by the administrative authorities to mean that at the end of two years the person's previous record should be wiped out, even though during that two years he or she may have been frequently convicted. Thus instances came to the attention of the Commission where, notwithstanding that habitual drunkards and vagrants were frequently sent to the workhouse, yet at the end of two years, upon a new conviction, they were required to serve only the term imposed on first offenders.

This condition clearly calls for remedy. It should be the affirmative duty of the chief magistrate of the respective divisions to ascertain from time to time in what manner the statute is applied, and, if not properly applied by the administrative authorities, that fact should be called to the attention of the Mayor.

Until an efficient system of identification can be put in practical operation in each magistrate's court, it will be necessary to continue the cumulative sentence in relation to certain offenses.

This brings us now to a consideration of the classes of offenses referred to in section 707 *et seq.* of the charter.

Vagrancy.— Cases of vagrancy (Code of Criminal Procedure section 887) may be divided broadly into the following classes:

1. Habitual vagrant.

2. The person who lives wholly or in part on the earnings of prostitution.

3. The prostitute who has no lawful employment whereby to maintain herself.

4. The person not giving a good account of himself and the criminal convicted more than once, found loitering in public places.

5. The temporary unfortunate who is out of work and unable to provide for himself.

(1) The habitual vagrant is a constant menace to and a drain upon society. He is a parasite whom the State must support at the expense of the taxation, in one form or another, of the industrious and self-supporting.

Many persons of this class treat the City of New York as a haven where they can find comfortable housing during the winter months and gain release in the early spring or summer, so as to enable them to enjoy the benefits of the pleasant weather throughout the country, only to return again in the late fall or winter.

These cases in many instances have been disposed of by some magistrates without careful consideration, and it is not infrequent for magistrates to give to the vagrant exactly the term of imprisonment which the vagrant himself requests. Thus a vagrant states to a magistrate that he is out of work and desires to be committed for a certain period of time and the magistrate accommodatingly complies with his request. In such instances the magistrate looks solely at the vagrant's point of view and considers that if this unfortunate or delinquent wishes to be housed and fed for a certain period of time, no less nor no longer period of commitment should be imposed upon him.

The city, however, has a very large interest in these cases and carries a heavy burden for the support of such persons. The Legislature has been urged by those who have given this important subject careful study to establish farms throughout the State where such men and women shall be compelled to work and in that manner contribute to their own support. Until such legislation shall have been enacted, there can only be a makeshift treatment in a great city like New York of this very important problem.

But the magistrates themselves can do much toward decreasing the return of these recurring offenders. If magistrates will commit in such manner, wherever practicable, as to make these offenders serve during the pleasant months of the year, it will doubtless be found that they will seek other refuges than the City of New York. To commit such persons during the winter months, letting them go in the spring or summer, is equivalent to an invitation to return. If genuine vagrants realize that they are not to be thus gently dealt with, such information will soon be spread abroad in the peculiar way in which such news travels among these men. If to a more careful administration of this branch of work is added an effective system of identification at the work-house, the evil will be at least to some extent diminished.

(2) The person who lives wholly or in part upon the earnings of prostitution, or who in any public place solicits for immoral purposes, is of an unspeakably vile character. Section 887 of the Code of Criminal Procedure defines as a vagrant (subdivision 9),

" Every male person who lives wholly or in part on the earnings of prostitution, or who in any public place solicits for immoral purposes. A male person who lives with or is habitually in the company of a prostitute, and has no visible means of support, shall be deemed to be living on the earnings of prostitution."

A construction has been placed on this statute by which it has been regarded as necessary to show that the person accused has not visible means of support. It seems clear that the legislative intent was to create a presumption and thus to point out that a person who lives with or is habitually in the company of a prostitute, and has no visible means of support, is living wholly or in part on the earnings of prostitution, unless by proof adduced by him he can show that such is not the fact.

We are of the opinion that this section can be clarified so as to accomplish the purpose intended by changing the word " deemed " in the statute to " presumed," the word " presumed " having a well defined legal signification. As hitherto construed, the second sentence of the statute has been regarded as the definition of the offense, when it was intended merely as a legal presumption, and we are of the opinion that the difficulty will be overcome by the suggested change.

At present, the maximum punishment for this offense is only six months, which, for the first offense, can be reduced to five days, with the consent of the magistrate, under the operation of the Cumulative Sentence Law.

The Commission is of the opinion that this subdivision should be taken out of section 887 of the Code of Criminal Procedure and that the offense should be made a misdemeanor.

(3) The subject of the prostitute will be considered hereinafter.

(4) Cases arising under this classification call for no comment.

(5) In the cases of persons who are not persistent vagrants, but who are temporarily out of employment and unable to take care of themselves, the workhouse commitment is a harsh and unsuitable remedy. Such persons, however, may apply for admission to the almshouse which they can leave whenever they please. Greater care should be taken in these cases to explain to an unfortunate but worthy person that the effort to be admitted to the almshouse should be first exhausted before he is committed to the workhouse. This, however, is a matter of administration which depends upon good judgment and co-operation between the magistrates and the heads of departments dealing with these subjects, and cannot be automatically regulated by statute.

Public Intoxication.— The Commission learned, both from the testimony before it and from its visit to the workhouse, and conversations with the officials in charge, that there were many cases of persons who were habitual drunkards, and, indeed, not a few cases of those who have practically lived at the workhouse, or in the almshouse or other institutions, for periods of ten to twenty years, being released only long enough to become again intoxicated and to be again committed.

This subject like that of vagrancy cannot be adequately dealt with until institutions are established and systems applied which will have for their purpose the cure of drunkenness, wherever possible, and, in any event, the doing of useful work by the inmates. A bill to accomplish this result is now pending in the legislature.

The workhouse, penitentiary or county jails are not kept for such purposes nor can they ever be so kept. The commitments to a workhouse or jail for short periods of time result in little good, and the prisoner in many cases is discharged only to return soon again. Cases of this character present very difficult problems to the magistrates, and they are unable to deal with them effectively because there are not any proper institutions to which to commit such offenders.

The Cumulative Sentence Law can be made more effective if persons convicted of public intoxication can be properly identified, and it should be required that records and identification should be made and kept of all those confined in the workhouse, whether committed under the Cumulative Sentence Law or otherwise.

There are cases where the magistrate, from information furnished to him, believes that the commitment to the workhouse, under the Cumulative Sentence Law, would not be a satisfactory disposition of the case, while at the same time the imposition of a fine would not be an adequate deterrent. He may be of the opinion that the defendant should be committed for a period longer or shorter, as the case may be, than he would be detained under a Cumulative Sentence law commitment. The Commission is, therefore, of the opinion that the fullest discretion should be conferred upon the magistrates and that they should have power, in these cases, to fine or to sentence under the Cumulative Sentence law or to sentence for a definite term.

Prostitution.—No subject of greater difficulty is presented to the police authorities, the magistrates, courts and departments of Charities and Corrections than that of prostitution.

Women of this class are arrested upon various charges, such as vagrancy, soliciting for purposes of prostitution, disorderly conduct, violation of the Tenement House Law, etc.

It is practically impossible to obtain accurate statistics on this subject because some are convicted as vagrants under the Code of Criminal Procedure, some of disorderly conduct under subdivision 2 of section 1458 of the Consolidation Act and some under other provisions of law. The magistrates differ widely as to the disposition of such cases. It is a problem so old and so difficult that there is of necessity a conflict of opinion as to how such cases should be disposed of. At present, some magistrates pursue a practically consistent course of sending these women to the workhouse. Others quite as consistently impose fines, and others discharge, while nearly all place on probation some cases which suggest in their opinion possibilities of reform. The magistrates realize that each of these dispositions has serious defects and leads to resultant evils of one kind or another, and in justice to them it may be said that the Commission fully appreciates the difficulty and the gravity of the problem.

If a young woman is committed to the workhouse or county jail, she is thrown into association with older and more hardened offenders. Often she returns from imprisonment to find that what little possessions she had have been stolen or have disappeared. Her incarceration has done her no good, for if it be her first imprisonment she is detained but five days. She has no opportunity to learn a useful occupation, and she returns, perforce, to her previous method of living. If she is fined, she must in some manner earn the money thus lost by the fine, and she earns it in the same way as before and, possibly, also by thievery.

On the other hand, if she is discharged, she becomes defiant and plies her occupation the more flagrantly upon the public thoroughfare. The cumulative sentence as applied to prostitutes works most inequitably. Thus, instances have come to the attention of the Commission where a prostitute has been fined many times and yet when she is committed to the workhouse, if that be her first commitment, she can be detained only five days, while on the other hand another woman who has been convicted, perhaps for the first or second time, may be punished to an equal or greater extent than the constant offender. This condition has largely arisen because of the almost complete lack of any system of identification at the magistrates' courts. Unless the magistrate is satisfied from the testimony that the prostitute has previously been convicted, he has no means of ascertaining her previous record and through no fault of his own, frequently imposes a punishment which is unjust as compared with the punishment which he might have inflicted upon some other woman at the same sitting of the court where the information furnished him has been more or less complete.

It is also stated that through lack of identification at the workhouse, women there confined have exchanged the passes given to them upon release, so that some have been permitted to go at large prior to the conclusion of their sentence.

The difference of views of the magistrates as to the disposition of cases of this character leads to other results. If a magistrate has the reputation of sending these women to the workhouse, the public streets are much less patrolled by them than if the magistrate has the reputation of fining or discharging. Some of the magistrates who commit to the workhouse fear that the severity of the punishment leads to greater opportunity for oppression by police officers, because such a woman will more readily accede to extortion where she fears that she may be imprisoned. We have no desire to stigmatize the police force for the offenses of individual members, but in dealing with this problem it must be remembered that there are on record not a few instances of police officers who have disgraced their uniform by extorting money from these unfortunates who have been convicted of that offense. It is apparent that some step must be taken to deal more adequately and intelligently with this problem, and although the Commission realizes that no law which can be devised at this time will solve the problem, nevertheless steps can be taken which may at least to some extent diminish the attendant evils.

It seems clear that the cumulative sentence has proven of no service in dealing with the problem and the Commission is therefore of the opinion that it should not be applied to cases of this character.

We believe that the first step in the combating of this problem is an accurate and ready means of identification.

By the establishment of the night court for women, it will be possible to install at that court an efficient system of identification.

In the event of a conviction for any offense connected with prostitution, the magistrate would not find himself imposing punishment blindly or upon unsatisfactory or doubtful identification. Therefore the Commission recommends that after conviction and before disposition of the prisoner, the magistrate shall direct that the identification of the convicted person be taken by the finger print system and that there be presented to him the record, if any, of such convicted person.

Testimony has been adduced before the Commission (see test. Katherine Bement Davis, Superintendent of Bedford Reformatory and Dr. Frederic Bierhoff), showing the prevalence of contagious and infectious venereal diseases, thus making these women the means of spreading these dread afflictions.

We hold the view that a court has the authority to take into consideration the physical condition of any prisoner and that, where such condition is of a character calculated to spread contagion or infection, the court can deal with the case accordingly.

This is not a novel view, for it is now provided in section 887, subdivision 3, of the Code of Criminal Procedure, that " a person who has contracted an infectious or other disease, in the practice of drunkenness or debauchery, requiring charitable aid to restore him to health," is a vagrant. See also section 1, chapter 11 of Laws of 1833.

Physical Examination.— We deem it wise, therefore, to recommend that in every case where a woman is convicted of an offense connected with prostitution, such woman must be examined by a woman physician detailed for that purpose by the Board of Health and such physician shall certify to the magistrate the results of her examination. We recommend, where such certificate shows that the woman has a venereal disease, that the magistrate shall be required to commit her for an indeterminate sentence of not to exceed one year. A transcript of this certificate should accompany the commitment to the officers of the institution to which the woman is committed and these officers should be empowered to discharge the woman at any time between the minimum and maximum periods of the indeterminate sentence, upon the certificate of a physician connected with such institution that the woman is cured.

Thus under the plan proposed, the magistrate when he is called upon to make disposition of the case will have before him, first, all the facts and surrounding circumstances connected with the particular offense charged; secondly, the identification and record of the woman, and, thirdly, the fact as to whether the woman is a menace to the community because of her affliction with disease. With all these data before him he will be enabled to act intelligently.

The power above referred to should be in addition to and not exclusive of the power to commit to reformatory institutions which have authority to detain inmates for more than one year.

The magistrate should have the fullest power to deal with each case upon its merits, placing on probation if he thinks wise, or taking such other steps as he may deem proper, with the limitation, however, that he must commit to an institution in a case of disease as above described.

We are aware that there is at present a lack of proper institutions to which women of this character can be committed and receive adequate medical attention, but for the time being by segregation in such cases, where necessary, in existing institutions to which commitments may be made much can be accomplished. We have hestitated to go beyond this suggestion because we belivee that the best results are attained by gradual steps.

known the fact that they have been arraigned in a police court. The warden in charge of the district prisons testified that there were certain rules regulating the amount of charges of these messengers and that in certain of the prisons there were messenger boxes by means of which an American District messenger boy could be called. The examination of the Commission disclosed that in a number of these prisons there were no American District Telegraph messenger boxes, and that there was no notice of any kind whereby the prisoner could be informed of his opportunity, at reasonable cost, to communicate with his friends.

If a prisoner has no funds, he can only succeed in reaching his family or friends by the good offices of one of these messengers, who, to use his own descriptive language, stated that in such cases, " If the party looked good to him, he would take a chance " on delivering the message.

As a result of the Commission's inquiry, the warden in charge of the district prisons has caused to be placed in each district prison a notice in several languages, informing the prisoners of their right to send for a messenger and setting forth the rates of service.

There is no assurance, however, that these notices come to the attention of many of the prisoners.

Any person arrested, whether having funds or not, should have the fullest opportunity to notify his family or friends and this opportunity should be accorded to him from the time he is brought to the police station. We recommend, therefore, that it shall be the duty of the lieutenant or other officer in charge at the police station to inform the prisoner that he may have an opportunity to communicate with his friends, and the officer in charge should be required to telephone free of charge to three numbers given to him by the prisoner, in the effort to reach his friends.

If the prisoner is detained in a district prison, the keeper or other person in charge should similarly inform the prisoner and similarly telephone without cost to three numbers and at the option of the prisoner give him a two cent stamped envelope free of charge or at cost an envelope with necessary postage for a special delivery letter. It should be required that there should be posted conspicuously in each place of detention, whether police station or district prison, a notice in various languages that the prisoner has the opportunity of notifying his family or his friends by telephoning in the manner stated, and in each place of detention no person shall be permitted to charge for telegraph messenger service more than the customary rate for a similar service charged by any telegraph messenger company, and the same shall apply to the charges for telephone service where it has not been possible to communicate with the persons desired by calling up three telephone numbers.

It should be the duty of the magistrate to inform a defendant committed by him of his rights and privileges thus accorded by statute, and, if the person does not understand English, to cause the information to be fully and clearly conveyed to him. It is hoped in this way that a fair opportunity will be given to persons under arrest to communicate with their friends.

The matter is one concerning which the magistrates seem to have little information, but we regard it as highly important for protection against abuse of ignorant or unfortunate persons. The subject should be one of constant supervision by the heads of the Police and Correction Departments.

PROBATION.

In the past few years the theory and practical application of probation have greatly progressed. Instead of the alternative of immediate suspension of sentence or of commitment to a penal institution, the Legislature and the courts have appreciated the wisdom of giving to a defendant, under proper circumstances and surroundings, an opportunity to redeem himself and, by proving his worthiness to the satisfaction of the court, to be released in due time on a susupended sentence.

We know of no more marked step forward in the administration of criminal jurisprudence than the probation system.

Court of Special Sessions, Adult Part. — In the adult part of the Court of Special Sessions in both divisions, the justices have given this matter much consideration and have accomplished a great deal. The civilian officers, male and female, in both divisions, impressed the Commission favorably and evidently had a competent grasp of their work as well as the enthusiasm necessary for success.

In addition to the civilian officers, in the First Division, there were four police officers, assigned by the police commissioner, as probation officers to the justices of the court. Of these four, one has done no probation work at all, another very little, while the remaining two have apparently been conscientious in their investigation work, but under the orders of the Court they are not probation officers, but investigators only, who gather information and data under the direction of the male civilian probation officer. In addition to these, in the First Division a representative of the Society of St. Vincent de Paul has served as a probation officer without pay from the city.

In the Court of Special Sessions of the Second Division the probation work is done entirely by one male and one female probation officer.

It is manifest that the amount of work which the male probation officer in the First Division is required to perform is physically beyond the limit of one man. If that work is to be thorough and efficient, the court and the probation system must be provided with an adequate corps of civilian officers.

Children's Courts.— From about September, 1902, when the Children's Part of the Court of Special Sessions of the First Division was opened, until March, 1908, the superintendent of the New York Society for the Prevention of Cruelty to Children was the chief probation officer of that court. Since his resignation in March, 1908, as such probation officer, there has not been any probation officer in this Children's Court.

It is true that various philanthropic organizations have assigned to the court representatives for the purpose of doing the best they can with children allowed to go on parole, but these persons are merely volunteers, who do not represent in any manner the court or its justices. What they do is done in aid of the cause but without official standing. The justices of the Court of Special Sessions have proceeded upon the theory of placing the child either on parole or on probation with its parents, when in many instances it is the parent who is at fault and who is manifestly an unfit person to be in any sense a probation officer.

In the law creating the Children's Court in the First Division, there was no requirement as to the appointment of any particular number of persons to serve as probation officers, but there has always been the fullest authority under the provisions of section 11-a of the Code of Criminal Procedure to appoint probation officers, and the legislative mandate is clear that it is the policy of the State that " When practicable, any child under the age of sixteen years, placed on probation, shall be placed with a probation officer of the same religious faith as the child's parents " (Code of Crim. Pro. § 483).

This mandate must no longer be disregarded. It is not for the justices to determine whether it shall be obeyed. The most important field of probation is with the children. Its office is preventive. It is an agency for making good citizens at the time when the prospect is most encouraging. It demands the most sympathetic and thoughtful consideration from the judicial officers who have this great privilege of dealing with the young. Provision, therefore, should be made requiring the justices of the Court of Special Sessions to appoint probation officers for the Children's Court and in selecting them to have in mind the long settled policy of the State expressed in section 483 of the Code of Criminal Procedure above referred to.

The statute creating the Children's Court for the borough of Brooklyn (Laws of 1903, chapter 150) provided that " The justice (children's part) shall have authority to appoint or designate not more than three discreet persons of good character to serve as probation officers during the pleasure of the court." Pursuant thereto, three probation officers have been appointed, representing, respectively, the Protestant, Catholic and Jewish faiths. These officers as yet do not receive salaries, but are paid by private philanthropic or charitable associations.

So far as we can ascertain there is the greatest harmony existing between the court, its probation officers, the Brooklyn Society for the Prevention of Cruelty to Children, and the various philanthropic organizations representing different faiths, who follow with keen interest the affairs of this court.

In view of the needs of the Court of Special Sessions as proposed to be established, we are of the opinion that a chief probation officer and at least twelve additional probation officers will be required for the new court.

The chief probation officer should have general supervision of all of the probation officers, subject in turn to the supervision of the chief justice, doing such probation work as his supervisory duties permit. The twelve probation officers should be distributed as follows: For the adult court in Manhattan and the Bronx, four; for the adult court for the other boroughs, two; for each of the two children's courts now existing, three.

It is not our intention to provide in the proposed law for the salaries of these officers, but we call the attention of the local administrative authorities to the importance of the work and the desirability of making it of an attractive and permanent char-

3

acter and for that reason of giving those who engage in it at least living salaries.

Magistrates' Courts, First Division.— In the first division each magistrate has a police officer who is assigned to the individual magistrate and follows him in his rotation and is not assigned when the magistrate is off duty. The police probation officer is required to report at the First District Court in Center street, each day, for the purpose of the police department's records, but when the magistrate is not on duty the probation officer is practically without supervision.

These officers, apparently, are appointed under the authority of section 11-a of the Code of Criminal Procedure. Such appointment, while lawful, seems nevertheless to have been in clear defiance of the legislative intent, as indicated by section 707 of the Greater New York charter, which provides:

> " The board of city magistrates of each division of the city of New York shall have authority to appoint such number of discreet persons of good character, either men or women, to serve as probation officers, as said boards may deem necessary, to serve during the pleasure of the court of board of magistrates appointing them. The board of city magistrates of each division of the city of New York shall assign the probation officers appointed by it to the various city magistrates' courts in its division and each probation officer shall act only as an officer of the city magistrates' courts to which he is assigned. * * * If two or more probation officers are attached to any city magistrates' court, the board of magistrates shall designate the officer under whose charge each person on probation shall be placed."

From the foregoing it is apparent that the Legislature intended that the appointment of probation officers should be by the board and that these officers were to be assigned to the various city magistrates' courts, and not as personal officers or attaches of the magistrates.

The account which many of these probation officers gave of themselves was highly discreditable. There were a few who apparently were earnest and faithful in their work, but the remainder evidenced neither the capacity, industry nor disposition necessary for this important work. The supervision by the magistrates has been ineffective and inadequate. These officers have been required to meet twice each week at the West Fifty-fourth Street Court and on one of these evenings the women probation officers have been present. The magistrates have rarely attended.

Women of all ages, who were on probation for various kinds of offenses, including drunkenness, disorderly conduct and offenses connected with prostitution, have been required to report at night — in other words, at the very worst time for them. The attempted justification for this system of reporting is that the probation officers might become acquainted with the name and especially with the features of probationers, so that they might be informed sufficiently to advise magistrates as to the previous record of prisoners, in the event of their being arraigned at a future time.

The reason advanced for the meetings at the West Fifty-fourth street court is obviously at variance with the fundamental idea of probation and it is plain that no good purpose is served by the holding of these meetings.

Some of the police probation officers frequently and others occasionally failed to attend. There apparently was no attempt by the magistrates to punish such remissness or in any manner to discipline these men. The blame for this system is almost wholly with the magistrates.

Another difficulty in the assignment of police officers for probation work is illustrated by the friction which has heretofore arisen, under a previous administration, between the police commissioner and certain magistrates. If a magistrate is dependent upon the police commissioner for the assignment of a police officer, there is no assurance of permanency in the work, for the police commissioner is at liberty to withdraw the officer at any time and for any or no reason.

The magistrate is frequently confronted with grave problems in certain classes of cases. If the husband who has failed to support his wife or who has become intoxicated is sentenced to imprisonment, nothing is gained. The wife becomes an object of public or private charity and the husband returns from his incarceration usually worse than he was before. In the case of youths, imprisonment frequently results in further degradation and degeneration, instead of improvement or reform. The young girl who has taken her first false step is more likely injured than helped by commitment to a penal institution.

On the other hand, a person supervised by an intelligent, capable and sympathetic probation officer has at least the opportunity of saving himself for a decent career. The probation officer can bring the husband and wife together, assist in preserving the home, watch the young man or woman sufficiently to prevent them from returning to evil associates, and, in brief, render invaluable service not only to the persons themselves but to society at large. No probation system, however, can be fully effective unless the probation officers are subject to the watchful eye of the court and unless the court insists, so far as practicable, upon personal information, and unless the probationer realizes, if discharged, that such discharge comes from the court, and not from the probation officer. In very many instances in the first division the magistrates discharge merely upon the recommendation of the probation officer, and do not have brought before them the probationer himself. This, we believe, is both an unwise and unsound method, and it is our view that when the probationer is to be discharged he should be brought before the magistrate and should be made to realize the reasons and the conditions of his discharge. Magistrates have contended that this is difficult because of the system of rotation and because such discharges frequently occur while they are off duty. This, we think, is a trifling objection, which can be easily disposed of by appropriate arrangement.

These and other defects of the system can be cured and in any event improved by orderly methods, supervised by competent authority. Each chief city magistrate should have the authority to appoint at pleasure a chief probation officer. Each board of magistrates should have authority to appoint a sufficient number of probation officers for the needs of this important branch of the work of the Magistrates' Courts. In our opinion there will be needed in the First Division at least ten male officers and ten female officers, and in the Second Division the same number of civilian male officers and female officers as are now employed. The statute should prohibit the appointment or retention of police probation officers and these men should be returned to the police department.

Period of Probation.— The Court of Special Sessions should have power to place adult defendants upon probation for two years, and the Children's Court should have power to extend probation over a period of three years, and within such limit should have jurisdiction over the child after it has reached the age of sixteen.

The magistrates should have power to place a person on probation for one year. These recommendations are made in view of the fact that there is some question now as to whether the Court of Special Sessions has power to place on probation for more than one year and the magistrates for more than six months and the Children's Courts after the child has reached the age of sixteen.

Method of Appointment of Probation Officers.— The probation officers hold a place of trust second only to that of the justice or magistrate, and they stand in a peculiarly confidential relation to the court, and should be selected with the greatest possible care.

The chief probation officer should be appointed without examination by the chief justice or the chief city magistrate of each division, as the case may be. All other probation officers should be appointed in like manner by the Court of Special Sessions or by the respective boards of magistrates, as the case may be, and not by the individual justices or magistrates.

In order that the fullest responsibility shall be imposed upon the justices and magistrates, and a full measure of watchfulness attained, the chief probation officer and all other probation officers should be removable at will by the chief justice or chief city magistrate or by a majority of the justices or magistrates of the respective courts, as the case may be.

BAIL.

As heretofore indicated, section 550 of the Code of Criminal Procedure should be amended so as to authorize a magistrate sitting at a night court in the borough of Manhattan to admit to bail.

The chief city magistrate of the Second Division should designate a magistrate resident in any of the other boroughs, to take bail from the time of the closing of the courts until two o'clock the following morning. Such designation should not be exclusive of the power of any other magistrate to take bail, but should be for the purpose of enabling the public to know that a particular magistrate may be conveniently applied to for that purpose.

Under the present system a defendant cannot give cash bail at the Magistrates' Court, but if he desires to give such bail he must deposit the cash with the chamberlain. This is frequently impracticable, more especially if the defendant be arraigned late in the day. Provision should be made whereby defendants may deposit cash bail with the clerk of the Magistrates' Court, who shall be required to make report and return of the same, in accordance with such rules as may be prescribed by the city chamberlain.

COMPLAINTS AGAINST ATTORNEYS.

Much complaint is heard from time to time of the conduct of a certain class of lawyers, who, it is said, impose on the poor and ignorant who come to the courts of Special Sessions and the Magistrates' Courts. Every person has the constitutional right to be defended by counsel, and in many cases counsel is needed. There is no statute which can be devised to regulate automatically the conduct of attorneys of this kind. To each of these courts are detailed officers whose duty it is to serve warrants issued by the magistrates, and it has been supposed that an alliance has existed between some of these officers and some of the attorneys, of the kind mentioned. It is exceedingly difficult to obtain competent proof upon the subject.

Only recently the Board of Magistrates of the First Division has caused to be posted in the Magistrates' Courts notices in different languages, informing persons that there is no need of employing counsel upon an application for the issue of a summons. This may be of some service but the whole subject is a difficult one and should have the constant vigilance of the magistrates.

As a necessary record the name and address of counsel appearing in any case should be endorsed on the papers. The chief city magistrates will be in a peculiarly advantageous position to investigate information or complaint as to the unprofessional conduct of attorneys and measures should be taken to devise means for protecting the ignorant •from deception and imposition by the unscrupulous.

We are of the opinion that it is impossible to prescribe a remedy by statutory enactment but that the improvement in the situation must come from constant supervision and appropriate regulation, from time to time, as experience may suggest and that these results can be attained under the system of centralized responsibility which we have recommended.

DEPUTY ASSISTANT DISTRICT-ATTORNEYS.

The assignment of a deputy assistant district-attorney to each Magistrate's Court can also be of great service in protecting the rights of defendants as well as of the people.

If there were a realization of the fact that it is the duty of the district-attorney to move for the dismissal of a case where he believes that such course is right, and in the interest of justice, many persons would be discharged in the Magistrates' Courts who are now held because the magistrate hesitates to assume the responsibility of discharge. A deputy assistant district-attorney would also be of great service in examining complaints drawn by court clerks and, generally, in making a proper investigation of cases brought before the magistrates. A competent administration of this work would also result in protecting many defendants against imposition by attorneys of the kind to which we have already referred, and if it becomes known that the district-attorney is seeking, not for convictions, but for just results, the poor or ignorant will soon find that there will be no need of employing counsel in minor and petty cases.

It may be remarked in this connection, however, that the Commission does not look with favor upon the designation of a representative of the district-attorney's office at the Children's Court, for in line with modern development the hearing in the cases of children is not to be deemed as a prosecution for crime, and the judges are much better able to do this important work, if permitted to bring out the facts in their own way. While this report has been in preparation, the present district-attorney of the county of New York has applied to the local authorities for an appropriation sufficient to enable him to appoint and designate deputy assistants to the various Magistrates' Courts, thus carrying out a policy which the Commission favors.

We do not recommend that the attendance at the Magistrates' Courts by a deputy assistant be made mandatory, for the reason that in some of the courts in the greater city the number of cases presented might not justify such mandatory requirement.

The appropriation of sufficient funds for this purpose is within the power of the local authorities, and if such appropriation be made and the work of deputy assistant district-attorneys prove successful, a mandatory provision can at any time hereafter be incorporated in the statute relating to these courts.

INSTITUTIONS TO WHICH COMMITMENTS ARE MADE.

The Commission visited various institutions, including the penitentiary, the workhouse, certain of the city hospitals and the New York City Reformatory for Misdemeanants situated at Hart's Island.

The workhouse is entirely inadequate for its purposes and the accommodations are shockingly insufficient. Upon the occasion of the visit of the Commission, the workhouse was so crowded that as many as eight men were in one cell.

The workhouse authorities are making efforts to utilize the labor of the inmates and to teach them some useful occupation, but they are unable to accomplish anything of value in cases of short commitment.

At the time of the visit of the Commission to Hart's Island, the institutions there were likewise wholly inadequate. Former Commissioner of Correction Barry obtained from the city authorities a substantial appropriation, which when applied will undoubtedly improve conditions.

This institution is one of the very greatest importance in correctional and reformatory work in a class of cases coming from the Magistrates and Special Sessions Courts.

By an amendment to the Greater New York charter (§ 698), passed in 1904, " The New York City Reformatory for Misdemeanants " was required to be established. Up to that time the curious anomaly had existed that there was no reformatory to which to send males, between the ages of 16 and 30 years, convicted of misdemeanors, although there had long been reformatories to which could be committed males between these ages convicted of felony. Thus, to illustrate, in the case of a youth of sixteen who had stolen any sum up to $25, the Courts of Special Sessions had no option, if the case was not one for suspension or probation, except to send such a boy to the city prison or the penitentiary, while a youth of the same age, who was convicted of grand larceny or graver offenses, could be sent to a reformatory where he would have an opportunity of learning a useful trade.

The purpose of establishing " The New York City Reformatory for Misdemeanants " was to reform these young men convicted of lesser offenses and also to give them an opportunity to obtain some education and, if possible, to learn a useful trade.

Such an institution deserves well of the city of New York and the money necessary to develop it to a proper state of efficiency would be well expended.

The Commission from its investigation was astounded to learn in how many cases these youths were illiterate and unacquainted with and untrained in any useful occupation. Obviously, if such youths are taught to read and write and obtain a reasonable equipment in mathematics as well as a knowledge of some trade, they will be much better fitted to earn a living and will cease to be a burden on the taxpayer.

This institution is under the jurisdiction of the Department of Correction as to its administrative features and of a board of parole which passes upon applications for discharge. This board consists of a representative of the Court of Special Sessions and of the Board of Magistrates in each division, the Commissioner of Correction, and four citizens appointed by the mayor. The board has manifested an earnest interest in the work and has done much for the institution.

VISITING OF INSTITUTIONS BY JUSTICES AND MAGISTRATES.

The Commission was surprised to learn that justices and magistrates, with some exceptions, rarely if ever visited the institutions to which they have authority to commit.

It seems plain that they would have a much better understanding of the disposition to be made in cases if they knew the condition of the institution to which they were making commitments and, in addition, their visits would have a valuable effect upon the institutions themselves. Thus, the activity of the members of the board of parole of the New York City Reformatory for Misdemeanants, contributed in no little degree to obtaining for that institution a substantial appropriation for its betterment. Had the magistrates examined into the reasons for the inadequate identification at the workhouse and the failure to install the Bertillon system, they could have called it sharply to the attention of the city authorities.

The same comment may be made in regard to the conditions of the detention pens and the messenger service in the district prisons. There is no reason why many of the observations made by the Commission should not have been made by the justices and magistrates. Indeed, there should be a complete spirit of co-operation between the magistrates, the police department, the department of correction and the various reformatory and other institutions which receive commitments. Only in this way can there be comprehensive and intelligent administration.

In view, however, of the failure to carry out in practice this point of view, the Commission recommends that each justice and magistrate be required to visit at least once in each year those institutions in the city of New York to which he is empowered to make commitments and that he visit such institutions outside of the city from time. to time as he may be directed by the chief justice or the chief city magistrate, as the case may be.

The justices and magistrates should be required to report in writing to the chief justice or chief city magistrate, as the case may be, the observations made by them upon their visits, and such recommendations as they may deem proper.

TENURE AND SALARIES OF JUSTICES, MAGISTRATES, CLERKS AND OTHER EMPLOYEES.

Terms of Office and Removal.— The terms of the justices and magistrates should be ten years as now, and all the clerks of the courts five years.

It was urged by the police clerks that their term of office should be during good behavior, but it must be remembered that upon their efficiency depends much of the success of the administration of these courts, and the magistrates should not be unduly hampered in regard to their appointment.

It may very well be that it would be impossible to sustain the removal of a clerk " for cause," and yet he might not possess those qualities which entitle him to reappointment. The magistrates have reappointed in many instances clerks who have served faithfully and the tenure of five years is a fair term.

Justices and magistrates should be removable by the Appellate Division for cause.

The chief clerk of the Court of Special Sessions should be removable for cause by a majority of the justices or by the Appellate Division.

Similarly, the chief clerk of each of the Board of Magistrates should be removable for cause by a majority of the magistrates or by the Appellate Division.

The clerks of the various parts of the Court of Special Sessions and of the various Magistrates' Courts, should be removable for cause by a majority of the justices and magistrates, as the case may be, or by the Appellate Division.

All other employees (except probation officers, removable at will) should be removable as now provided by section 1,407 of the Greater New York charter, after an opportunity to make an explanation.

In addition to the chief clerks of these courts, the clerks of the various parts of the Court of Special Sessions, the clerks of the various Magistrates' Courts and the chief probation officers, should be exempt from civil service examination and appointed at will.

The chief justice and the chief magistrates should have power to suspend any clerk or other employee for a period not to exceed thirty days.

Salaries of Justices and Magistrates.— The salary of the justices of the Court of Special Sessions of the First Division is $9,000 per annum and of the Second Division $6,000 per annum.

The salary of the magistrates resident in the First Division is $7,000 per annum; of the magistrates in the borough of Brooklyn, $6,000 per annum; and of the magistrates in the boroughs of Queens and Richmond, $5,000 per annum. It will be noted that the justices of the Court of Special Sessions of the Second Division receive the same salary as the magistrates resident in the borough of Brooklyn.

The Commission does not feel at liberty to recommend an increase in salaries by mandatory legislation. It would seem but just, however, that with the creation of a single Court of Special Sessions, all of the justices should receive the same salaries, and we think the local authorities should equalize the salaries at $9,000 per annum.

The chief justice of the Court of Special Sessions should receive a salary of $10,000 per annum; the chief magistrate of the First Division, $8,000 per annum, and of the Second Division, $7,000 per annum.

Salaries of Clerks.— The clerk of the Court of Special Sessions receives $5,000 per annum, the deputy clerk $4,500 per annum, and the clerk of the Children's Court, $3,000 per annum. In the Second Division, the clerk of the court receives $3,000 per annum and the clerk of the Children's Court $3,000 per annum.

The police clerks receive $2,500 per annum, and the police clerks' assistants $2,000 per annum, and the latter, under the existing statute, cannot receive more than that amount.

The Commission was impressed by the argument made on behalf of the police clerks that the salary of $2,500, more especially when compared with the salary of $3,000 accorded to these clerks some years ago and the salaries of clerks of other courts, is inadequate. These clerks must be on duty practically every day in the year and their vacations are limited. If the recommendations of the Commission are adopted, additional responsibility will be cast upon them, such as the taking of cash bail and the preparation of more elaborate and complete records and statistics.

The Commission cannot see any good reason why the police clerks' assistants should be prohibited from receiving more than $2,000 per annum.

Salaries of Interpreters.— In addition to the inquiries of this Commission, the Commissioner of Immigration, appointed by the Governor, made an exhaustive investigation into the qualifications of interpreters and found that, in many instances, these men lacked the special knowledge which is necessary in order competently to perform their duties. (Report of the Commission of Immigration. Transmitted to the Legislature April 5, 1909, pp. 55–61.)

A very large number of persons coming to these courts are unable to speak the English language and the various dialects of some languages are especially difficult. Some of the interpreters are men of excellent education and well equipped, while others are seriously lacking in an acquaintance with the various languages and dialects which are so frequently heard in these courts.

It is obvious that the magistrate is seriously hampered and that injustice may be done where there is not a correct interpretation of the statements of persons speaking in foreign tongues.

As the Commission of Immigration stated:

" The insufficiency of the present staff of interpreters seems to be due largely to two causes — the low salaries paid and the perfunctory methods of the Civil Service Commission in choosing men."

The interpreters are frequently employed to assist in clerical work, and thus a large part of the interpreter's time is diverted from the duties for which he is appointed.

In the Second Division, notwithstanding a great increase in the foreign population of Brooklyn and Queens, no corresponding increase has been made in the number of official interpreters, and, thus, in many instances interpreters are required to cover two or more courts.

It is not remarkable that there should be difficulty in obtaining competent men, in view of the inadequate salary of $1,500 per annum paid to interpreters. These men naturally look for promotion to clerkships or other interpreters' positions paying larger salaries, and frequently when they become highly useful they leave the service.

Under the circumstances it seems to the Commission that the salaries of competent interpreters should be equivalent at least to the salaries of the police clerks' assistants, and the Commission commends this subject to the careful consideration of the local authorities.

The Commission is of the opinion that great improvement can be made by the Municipal Civil Service Commission in the examinations for interpreters, so as to obtain practical results. It is especially important that interpreters should be qualified in the various dialects. A man may be well versed in the classic phraseology of some foreign tongue and yet be utterly unable to make himself understood in the dialect spoken by the person appearing before the court.

It is also manifestly absurd to appoint from the Civil Service Commission a person who is qualified, for instance, in Italian, when an interpreter in Yiddish is needed, or *vice versa*.

It seems to us that with the appointment of the chief justice and of the chief city magistrates there will be a closer watchfulness and more concentrated responsibility in regard to the selection and assignment of interpreters.

Salaries of Stenographers.— These courts require a high degree of efficiency on the part of stenographers. The evidence is quickly given and frequently in broken language, and as a result accurate work can be performed only by those possessing a high degree of skill. The stenographers receive $2,000 per annum, with very little opportunity of making fees from transcripts.

The adequacy of the compensation of these men might well be examined into by the local authorities, for, as in the case of interpreters, when they become highly proficient in the peculiarly difficult work of the Magistrates' Courts, they leave for more lucrative employment.

Salaries of the Other Employees.— The salaries of all officers and employees of these courts other than those of the justices should be fixed by the local authorities. We therefore call the attention of the local authorities to the necessity and the wisdom of fixing the salaries of all of these employees at an amount sufficient to attract honest and capable men to this very important public service.

DISPOSITION OF FINES.

Heretofore the relation between the clerks to whom fines are paid and the city has been in the nature of debtor and creditor, the clerk being required to make returns on or before the 5th day of each month of the sums paid to him during the previous month, and many of the clerks having deposited these funds in their private accounts.

This practice has led to evil results and should be completely discontinued. This was the practice of the clerk of the Court of Special Sessions of the First Division and of many of the clerks of the Magistrates' Courts, until the Commission's inquiry directed sharp attention to the subject. Hereafter, the funds received by the clerks should be regarded as public moneys from the moment of their receipt and they should be deposited in such depositaries as may be directed by the local fiscal authorities and in accordance with such rules and regulations as to the keeping of accounts and the making of returns as may be prescribed by such authorities.

Where defendants after commitment pay fines to the Department of Correction, that department should be required to furnish to the clerks of these courts an exact statement of the fines thus received.

FINES PAYABLE TO VARIOUS SOCIETIES.

By virtue of various statutes passed from time to time, the fines paid by defendants to the Courts of Special Sessions and Magistrates' Courts in certain instances go, in whole or in part, to certain societies, such as the New York Society for the Prevention of Cruelty to Children, the American Society for the Prevention of Cruelty to Animals, the New York Humane Society, and the Medical, Dental, Pharmacy, Pedic and Veterinary Societies and the Association of State Nurses.

The disposition of these moneys in this manner can no longer be justified, for all such sums are paid in satisfaction of a violation of law and belong initially to the people. They should be paid into the city treasury and become city moneys. The city authorities, in making their appropriations to various of these societies, may take such course as they deem best and as the law may permit, but the specific fine should not be earmarked as belonging to any society or association of a private of even a quasi-public character.

PROVISION FOR ADDITIONAL JUSTICES AND MAGISTRATES, ADDITIONAL PARTS AND TEMPORARY APPOINTMENTS.

It should be within the power of the local authorities from time to time to provide for the appointment of additional justices and magistrates, when needed, without application to the Legislature. The Commission, therefore, recommends that whenever a majority of the justices of the Court of Special Sessions or a majority of the respective Boards of Magistrates may certify to the Board of Estimate that there is need of additional justices or magistrates, as the case may be, the Board of Aldermen, upon recommendation of the Board of Estimate, may, by ordinance approved by the mayor, provide for such increase. In this connection, the local authorities should be fully empowered to provide such additional accommodations as may be necessary from time to time.

In the administration of these courts, the chief justice and the respective chief city magistrates, or a majority of the justices and a majority of the magistrates should have full authority (with the concurrence of the local fiscal authorities wherever funds are needed), to establish additional parts of these courts.

Thus, if it should be deemed desirable to establish a night court in Brooklyn, the chief city magistrate or a majority of the magistrates of the Second Division should have the power so to do without any further enactment of the State Legislature, and similarly, in regard to the establishment of any other parts which may be deemed necessary or desirable.

In order to provide against the contingencies of physical or mental disability, the mayor should be empowered to appoint a temporary city magistrate for a period of not to exceed thirty days, upon the certificate of either of the chief city magistrates that, owing to such disability of any magistrate or magistrates, the public business of these courts requires the appointment temporarily of a person in the place of the magistrate or magistrates thus disabled. Upon similar certificates, the mayor should have authority, at the end of each thirty days, to renew such appointment from time to time for a period not exceeding thirty days.

Where a magistrate has faithfully served and is overtaken by illness, it seems unjust and harsh to require his removal unless it is apparent that he cannot serve again. At the same time the business of these courts is liable to fall behind, and an undue burden is thus placed upon the remaining magistrates, which can be relieved by the appropriate exercise by the mayor of the power to make temporary appointments.

JUSTICES AND MAGISTRATES HOLDING OFFICE AS EXECUTIVE MEMBERS OF PARTY ORGANIZATIONS.

The Commission regards it as inconsistent with the duties of the office for a justice of the Court of Special Sessions or a magistrate to hold the position of executive member of any party organization, or, as it is familiarly known, the position of "district leader."

It is not any answer to the impropriety involved to state that a judge holding a district leadership may nevertheless be upright and impartial in the discharge of his duties. For these courts and judges to be efficient, there must be no belief in any quarter that political influence can be successfully brought to bear in judicial administration. The impression created upon many of those who come or who are brought into these courts, can only be unfavorably affected if the judge is actively in charge of political affairs. In addition, the duties of the "district leader" are onerous and occupy much time which must entrench upon that which a judge should give to the duties of his office. There are few instances of justices or magistrates holding district leadership and the great body of these judicial officers are united in the opinion that a justice or magistrate should not be a district leader.

JUSTICES AND MAGISTRATES SHOULD BE APPOINTED AND NOT ELECTED.

From the plan outlined by the Commission it will appear that the purpose is to have a Court of Special Sessions whose jurisdiction shall not depend upon the residences of the justices. Similarly, in respect of the Magistrates' Courts in the two divisions, it is clear that several of the features now in existence and those herein recommended look to a broad, comprehensive plan by which these respective divisions can be considered as a unit, rather than as being separated into subdivisions bounded by the territorial limits of each Magistrates' Court.

The plan for night courts for men and for women, for a domestic relations' court, for a comprehensive system of probation, of records and identification, for adequate supervision exercised by and responsibility imposed upon a chief magistrate, a chief clerk and a chief probation officer, would utterly fail if the Magistrates' Courts were treated as district courts of the locality. The Commission has been urged to favor the election of magistrates, but, irrespective of any arguments which may be advanced in favor of the election or appointment of these judicial officers, the Commission recommends the appointment of these officers as a necessary part of the general plan herein outlined.

The Court of Appeals, in the case of People v. Dooley, 171 N. Y. 74, considered the question of jurisdiction of magistrates elected from districts.

Judge Werner writing the opinion of the court said:

" But since some of our brethren think we ought to decide the question whether it was constitutional to elect magistrates by districts, we may add that we fully concur in the opinion of Judge Cullen upon that question."

Chief Judge Cullen, after stating that he inclined to the belief that the principle underlies our form of government that all public officers must be elected by constituencies, coextensive with their jurisdiction, unless express provision is made to the contrary, said:

" I think that the Legislature might create in cities district criminal courts as well as district civil courts with justices to be elected by the electors of the districts, but in such case the courts must be really district courts; that is to say, courts held for the districts, and the jurisdiction of whose magistrate is in some way limited to, or at least connected with, the districts, of which there is not a trace in the present case."

Not only is the Commission practically unanimous in believing that these justices and magistrates should be appointed and not elected but the effect of the decision of the Court of Appeals is, in its opinion, conclusive upon the question.

INFERIOR CRIMINAL COURTS ACT FOR THE CITY OF NEW YORK.

The statutes affecting the administration of these courts are scattered about in various codifications and enactments. The charter of the city of New York contains many of the provisions applicable to these courts, and also many penal provisions which have no place in that instrument.

While sections of the Penal Law and of the Code of Criminal Procedure of general application throughout the State should be omitted, all the provisions peculiarly applicable to the administration of the Court of Special Sessions and of the Magistrates' Courts in the greater city should be comprised within one statute, so that ready reference may be had thereto and amendments thereof conveniently made.

With this purpose in view, the Commission has been drafting such a proposed law in which will be incorporated those provisions of existing law which the Commission believe should be retained, and to which will be added the various changes or additions here recommended.

SUMMARY OF RECOMMENDATIONS.

The principal recommendations herein made by the Commission may be summarized as follows:

Court of Special Sessions.— 1. A Court of Special Sessions for the city of New York, having in the first instance exclusive jurisdiction in all cases of misdemeanor except (a) charges of libel, (b) pleas of guilty for violation of Motor Vehicle Law, first offense, and (c) pleas of guilty for violation of the laws relating to the prevention of cruelty to animals.

2. The court to consist of a chief justice, designated by the mayor, and fourteen associate justices, seven of whom shall be residents of the territory comprised within the boroughs of Manhattan and the Bronx, and seven of the territory comprised within the boroughs of Brooklyn, Queens and Richmond.

3. The present justices to be continued in office and the additional justices to be appointed by the mayor within ninety days of the taking effect of the act.

4. The chief justice to have full power to assign the justices, and in the assignment to the Children's Court the controlling features to be permanency of assignment and fitness for this particular work.

5. The transfer from the court to the district attorney of the duty of serving subpoenas.

6. The appointment of civilian probation officers and civilian attendants and the elimination of police probation officers and police attendants; the chief justice to appoint the chief probation officer.

7. The installation, under the jurisdiction of the chief justice, of a complete system of records, and the requirement that the chief justice shall report to the mayor annually.

8. All applications for removal of the trial of cases from the Court of Special Sessions to the Supreme Court or the Court of General Sessions, to be made within ten days after the case is first on for pleading.

9. Children's Courts to be extended so as to comprehend Children's Courts in the boroughs of Queens and Richmond, transferring that jurisdiction from the magistrates to the Court of Special Sessions.

10. Power in the Children's Court to suspend a trial at any time and adjudge the child in need of the care and protection of the State, and, in any event, not to permit the conviction of a child for an act which, if committed by an adult would be felony, but to require that the conviction in such case shall be of juvenile delinquency.

11. The mandatory appointment by the justices of probation officers for the Children's Courts, so that, so far as practicable, children shall be placed on probation with persons of like religious faith.

12. Extension of the period of probation, (a) for children to three years, and within that limit to apply to children after they have reached the age of sixteen; and (b) for adults to two years.

Magistrates Courts. 13. The magistrates to have, in addition to their present jurisdiction, authority to impose sentence in cases where defendants plead guilty to violations of the Motor Vehicle Law, first offense, and to violations of statutes for the prevention of cruelty to animals.

14. A Board of Magistrates for the First and for the Second Divisions, the former comprising the boroughs of Manhattan and The Bronx, and the latter the boroughs of Brooklyn, Queens and Richmond.

15. In the First Division, a chief city magistrate and sixteen city magistrates, all seventeen residents of the boroughs of Manhattan or The Bronx.

16. In the Second Division, a chief city magistrate, selected from any part in said division, and ten magistrates resident of the borough of Brooklyn, four of the borough of Queens and two of the borough of Richmond.

17. The redistricting of the various Magistrates' Court districts in the two divisions on or before September 1, 1910 by the mayor (or the president of the board of aldermen upon the

designation of the mayor), the chief city magistrate of the division and the police commissioner.

18. Each chief city magistrate to have authority in his division to assign the magistrates to the courts for domestic relations and to the night courts, but, otherwise, the Boards of Magistrates to make assignments on the principle of rotation.

19. The establishment in the First Division of a night court for men and a night court for women, each of which shall open at seven o'clock in the evening and remain open until three o'clock in the morning. The establishment of a detention place convenient to the night court for women where persons may be detained both before and after being heard and where the young and less hardened shall be segregated as far as practicable from the older and more hardened offenders.

20. The establishment in the First Division and in the borough of Brooklyn of a central court of domestic relations.

21. The appointment by each chief city magistrate of a chief clerk and a chief probation officer.

22. The appointment of a clerk for each Magistrates' Court, and all other probation officers, clerks, stenographers, interpreters, attendants and other employees, by a majority of the magistrates of the respective divisions.

23. The appointment of civilian probation officers and civilian attendants, instead of police probation officers and police attendants.

24. The establishment of a system of records and statistics.

25. The abolition of the cumulative sentence in cases where women are convicted of offenses connected with prostitution, and the compulsory installation of the finger print system of identification in connection with the night court and other courts at which women charged with these offenses are arraigned.

26. Compulsory medical examination of all women convicted of prostitution and indeterminate sentence where defendant thus convicted is suffering from venereal disease, for a minimum period to be fixed by the magistrate and a maximum period not to exceed one year except in those cases where he commits to an institution having authority to receive inmates for detention for a period of more than one year.

27. Probation in cases where the magistrate has summary jurisdiction to be for a period of not to exceed one year.

28. The summons to be legalized and a record to be kept of the issuance thereof.

29. In lieu of arrest for violation of the Motor Vehicle Law or for breach of ordinances, except in cases where persons are unable to take care of themselves, or are charged with conduct tending to a breach of the peace, the service of a summons if the person has a card or other token of identification. The Police Commissioner to prescribe a card or token of identification for such purpose and to make rules and regulations from time to time for the service, by police officers, of the summonses above referred to.

30. Provision for the complaint clerks in a room separate from the courtroom and reference to the local authorities of the conditions of the court houses, detention pens and arrangement of the courtrooms so to abolish " the bridge " and enable the defendant in all cases to have the same opportunity to be heard as the complainant.

31. Provision whereby persons detained in police stations or district prisons may promptly notify relatives or friends by letter or telephone.

General Provisions.— 32. Salary and compensation of all officers and employees except justices and magistrates to be fixed by the local authorities.

33. Power to be conferred upon the local authorities to provide for additional justices and magistrates from time to time as necessity may require.

34. No justice or magistrate to be the executive member of any political organization.

35. All justices and magistrates to visit institutions to which they have the power to commit persons, (a) once in each year if situated in the city of New York; (b) other institutions whenever required by the Chief Justice or the Chief City Magistrate as the case may be.

36. All fines now payable in whole or in part to private societies to be paid to the city.

CONCLUSION.

It has been the effort of the Commission to present in condensed form the result of personal observations and of the examination of many witnesses. Details of great interest have, of necessity, been omitted for purposes of brevity and conclusions expressed in a paragraph have been arrived at only after extended discussion and consultation.

In the observations which the Commission has made it has been impossible to refer to the work of particular justices or magistrates. With the view of ascertaining its quality and effectiveness the Commission has necessarily considered the work as a whole.

It is interesting to note that many of the defects pointed out have not been due to lack of statutory provisions, but to failure to observe them; for existing laws show that the legislature has considered almost every subject herein referred to.

We have called attention, however, to what we regard as essential recommendations looking to the betterment of the procedure which begins with arrest and ends with the discharge or the commitment of the prisoner. There are many details of a technical character which must be embodied in any proposed legislation, but reference to which in this report is not deemed necessary. We have pursued our investigations and arrived at our conclusions with an appreciation of the fact that laws alone cannot compel intelligent and conscientious administration. Over and above all in importance is the judge himself,— upon whom depends, in greatest measure, the careful and wise disposition of these thousands of cases dealing with people and subjects which touch the city's life at every point.

Trite as the expression may be, we may well repeat that the humble, the defenseless and the ignorant, gain their impressions of American institutions in large degree from these judges and courts, and to them these are the courts of last resort. Whether they shall be convinced that justice is patient and even handed, rests almost entirely upon the treatment they receive from these courts and judges. It is not enough to discharge mechanically though conscientiously the daily duty, but the judge should contribute his share to the study and the solution of the many complexities of city life in regard to which he has, perhaps, greater opportunities of observation than any other public officer. There should be a spirit of co-operation, a desire to undertake the solution of some of these problems, and we are confident that if this spirit generally animated these judicial officers, they would find a greater tendency on the part of the public to accord to them the respect and confidence which their important and dignified offices and duties should command. It is the hope of the Commission that its recommendations if enacted into law, will be of service to these courts and to the administration of justice. The rest depends upon the judges themselves.

Bills embodying our recommendations will be promptly submitted.

Respectfully submitted,

Dated, New York, April 4, 1910.

ALFRED R. PAGE, *Chairman,*
THOMAS F. GRADY,
JAMES A. FRANCIS,
CHARLES F. MURPHY,
ALFRED E. SMITH,
BRONSON WINTHROP,
JOHN ALAN HAMILTON,

Commission.

Criminal Justice in America

AN ARNO PRESS COLLECTION

Administration of Justice in the United States. 1910

Barnes, Harry Elmer. A History of the Penal, Reformatory and Correctional Institutions of the State of New Jersey. 1918

Capital Punishment: Nineteenth-Century Arguments. 1974

Chicago Community Trust. Reports Comprising the Survey of the Cook County Jail. [1923]

Connecticut General Assembly. Minutes of the Testimony Taken Before John Q. Wilson, Joseph Eaton, and Morris Woodruff, Committee from the General Assembly, to Inquire Into the Condition of Connecticut State Prison. 1834

Criminal Courts in New York State. 1909/1910

Finley, James B[radley]. Memorials of Prison Life. 1855

Georgia General Assembly. Proceedings of the Joint Committee Appointed to Investigate the Condition of the Georgia Penitentiary. 1870

Glueck, Sheldon, editor. Probation and Criminal Justice. 1933

Goldman, Mayer C[larence]. The Public Defender. 1917

Howe, S[amuel] G[ridley]. An Essay on Separate and Congregate Systems of Prison Discipline. 1846

Kohn, Aaron, editor. The Kohn Report: Crime and Politics in Chicago. 1953

Lawes, Lewis E. Twenty Thousand Years in Sing Sing. 1932

Los Angeles Police Department (Chief August Vollmer). Law Enforcement in Los Angeles: Los Angeles Police Department Annual Report, 1924. New Introduction by Joseph G. Woods. 1924

Maine Joint Special Committee. **Report of the Joint Special Committee on Investigation of the Affairs of the Maine State Prison.** 1874

Massachusetts, Commonwealth of. **Report of the Special Commission on Investigation of the Judicial System.** 1936

Moley, Raymond. **Our Criminal Courts.** 1930

Morse, Wayne L. and Ronald H. Beattie. **Survey of the Administration of Criminal Justice in Oregon.** 1932

National Conference on Bail and Criminal Justice. **Proceedings of May 27-29, 1964 and Interim Report, May 1964-April 1965.** 1965

New York. Kings County, Grand Jury. **A Presentment Concerning the Enforcement by the Police Department of the City of New York of the Laws Against Gambling by the Grand Jury for the Additional Extraordinary Special and Trial Term.** 1942

New York State. **Proceedings of the Governor's Conference on Crime, the Criminal and Society.** 1935

New York State. **Report of the Crime Commission, 1928.** 1928

New York State Committee on State Prisons. **Investigation of the New York State Prisons.** 1883

New York State Crime Commission. **Crime and the Community.** 1930

New York State Supreme Court, Apellate Division. **The Investigation of the Magistrates' Courts in the First Judicial Department.** 1932

O'Sullivan, John L. **Report in Favor of the Abolition of the Punishment of Death by Law, Made to the Legislature of the State of New York.** 1841

Pennsylvania Parole Commission. **The Report of the Pennsylvania State Parole Commission to the Legislature.** 1927. Two volumes in one.

Pennsylvania Special Grand Jury. **Investigation of Vice, Crime and Law Enforcement.** 1939

Reform of the Criminal Law and Procedure. 1911

Reporter of the Post. **Selections from the Court Reports Originally Published in the Boston Morning Post, From 1834-1837.** 1837

Shalloo, J. P., editor. **Crime in the United States.** 1941

Smith, Bruce. **Rural Crime Control.** 1933

Smith, Ralph Lee. **The Tarnished Badge.** 1965

Society for the Prevention of Pauperism. **Report on the Penitentiary System in the United States.** 1822

South Carolina General Assembly. **Report of Joint Committee Created Under Joint Resolution 662 of 1937 to Investigate Law Enforcement.** 1937

Sutherland, Edwin H. and Thorsten Sellin, editors. **Prisons of Tomorrow.** 1931

Texas Penitentiary Investigating Committee. **A Record of Evidence and Statements Before the Penitentiary Investigating Committee.** [1913]

Train, Arthur. **Courts and Criminals.** 1926

Train, Arthur. **The Prisoner at the Bar.** 1906

United States Department of Justice. **Attorney General's Survey of Release Procedures.** Volume II: Probation. 1939

United States Department of Justice. **Attorney General's Survey of Release Procedures.** Volume IV: Parole. 1939

United States. House of Representatives. Committee on the District of Columbia. **Investigation of the Metropolitan Police Department.** 1941

Waite, John Barker. **Criminal Law in Action.** 1934

Warner, Sam Bass. **Crime and Criminal Statistics in Boston.** 1934

Warner, Sam Bass and Henry B. Cabot. **Judges and Law Reform.** 1936

Wiretapping in New York City. 1916